The Spanish-American Homeland

CREATING THE NORTH AMERICAN LANDSCAPE

Gregory Conniff
Bonnie Loyd
David Schuyler
Consulting Editors

George F. Thompson
Project Editor

Four Centuries in
New Mexico's Río Arriba

WITHDRAWN

The
Spanish-American
Homeland

ALVAR W. CARLSON

The Johns Hopkins University Press   Baltimore and London

© 1990 The Johns Hopkins University Press
All rights reserved
Printed in the United States of America

The Johns Hopkins University Press, 701 West 40th Street, Baltimore, Maryland 21211
The Johns Hopkins Press Ltd., London

The paper used in this book meets the minimum requirements of American National
Standard for Information Sciences—Permanence of Paper for Printed Library Materials,
ANSI Z39.48-1984.

Library of Congress Cataloging-in-Publication Data
Carlson, Alvar W., 1937–
    The Spanish-American homeland: four centuries in New Mexico's Río Arriba /
Alvar W. Carlson.
        p.   cm.—(Creating the North American landscape)
    Includes bibliographical references.
    ISBN 0-8018-3990-4 (alk. paper)
    1. Río Arriba County (N.M.)—Historical geography. 2. Río Arriba County
(N.M.)—History. I. Title. II. Series.
    F802.R4C37   1990   90-4345 CIP
    987.9′52—dc20

For Lynne, Eden, and Kurt,

with love and appreciation

Their families have lived here for centuries;

their roots are in the land;

their hearts and souls are there.

The tie is really mystical.

Father Benedict Cuesta, ca. 1973
Arroyo Hondo, N.M.

Contents

PART FOUR **Clinging to the Homeland**

Preface

Nearly four centuries ago, Spaniards began to settle the upper Río Grande Valley of northern New Mexico known as the Río Arriba. In 1598, don Juan de Oñate led a small group of colonists from Zacatecas, Mexico, to a site north of present-day Española along the Río Grande, where they established a settlement. More settlements followed along the Río Grande and its tributaries, and effective colonization was under way, a movement temporarily interrupted in 1680 by the Pueblo Indian Revolt. Eventually, the upper Río Grande watershed became one of the most distinctive historic cultural regions in the United States. Although they expanded their sphere of settlement somewhat beyond the Río Arriba, Spanish Americans have recognized this rural area as their true homeland. Many have migrated from the area, but despite extended controversies over land and an increasing awareness of the region's unfavorable economic conditions, most have remained with relatives and friends in the numerous villages. Even today, this region has some of the most densely populated rural settlements in the United States.

The establishment of either an ethnic homeland or a cultural region depends upon a people's ability to acquire, use, and retain land. Governmental land policies—of Spain, Mexico, and the United States—were crucial in this evolutionary process in northern New Mexico. Spanish Americans derived their subsistence from the land of the Río Arriba. However, by the twentieth century subsistence agriculture and rural overpopulation were increasingly at odds with the engulfing and more dynamic Anglo-American economic system. Through time, rural economic poverty in the region intensified in comparison to other areas of the country, and the homeland was isolated not only by language and culture but by economics as well. Massive out-migration would have alleviated the problem, but the people's social and settlement systems, their adaptations to seasonal labor, and in particular their attachment to this land provided forms of security and a sense of belonging and place. Consequently, the Spanish Americans maximized in their own way the use of the land resources and, when combined with local customs, developed a distinctive human ecology and folk culture. Despite increasing depopulation of the Spanish-American villages in recent years, coupled with the growing influx of Anglo Americans who frequently replace them, the Río Arriba is still thought of by the remaining Spanish Americans, and even by those who have out-migrated, as their homeland.

This analysis of the development and survival of the Spanish Americans' historic homeland and of the spatial behavior of its people within a semiarid environment is based upon more than two decades of research and fieldwork in the region. Spanish Americans have revealed a gritty determination and self-reliance in the face of seemingly impossible odds. Recent literature on the upper Río Grande Valley tends to blame the U.S. government for the subculture's economic plight. Scholars have relentlessly stressed the adversarial role played by Anglo Americans and the U.S. government toward Spanish Americans. In particular, they have focused on the lingering issue of whether the Spanish and Mexican land-grant claims were adjudicated fairly by American officials, and frequently the authors advocate that these claims be reexamined and undergo further litigation.

The U.S. government has been roundly criticized not only for unfair treatment in the adjudication of the nineteenth-century land-grant claims (many of which were rejected) but also for continuing policies that hinder rural economic development by Spanish Americans within the region. This viewpoint is evident in the ongoing controversy over the U.S. Forest Service's livestock grazing permit program, discussed in Chapter 7. As a result, a picture is presented continuously of Spanish Americans having been cheated and manipulated by unscrupulous Anglo Americans (Yankees), always contributing to the impoverishment of the former and to the benefit of the latter. This arrangement, it is argued, has led to anti-Anglo-American feelings in the region, highlighted eventually by the confrontation and ensuing violence in the 1960s between the Alianza Federal de Mercedes and personnel of the Forest Service and law enforcement agencies. For instance, Charles L. Briggs and John R. Van Ness, anthropologists and members of the Center for Land Grant Studies in Santa Fe, emphasize this mistreatment in their recent book, *Land, Water, and Culture: New Perspectives on Hispanic Land Grants*. They claim that "a large body of evidence suggests . . . that both the United States government and a host of individuals who came to the Southwest from the eastern states systematically violated the rights of individuals and communities to hold and use land and water that they had legally acquired through grants from Spain and Mexico. These violations left a legacy of bitterness that has not diminished in the ensuing decades."[1]

Despite the allusions of perpetual victimization, Spanish Americans have not been evicted in large numbers from their settlements in the region. Indeed, if they had been, no subculture would exist there today. Instead, and in comparison to the out-migration from other areas of rural America, Spanish Americans in large numbers have remained in the region despite controversies and hardships. Thus, by adding a revisionist perspective that depends upon the methodology of a geographer who is detached from any political or other cause and the literature of many disciplines, including that published by geographers that has been largely heretofore ignored, this analysis will provide readers with a fuller appreciation of the enduring Spanish Americans and their fascinating, but waning, cultural region, as exemplified in case studies of four villages. My conclusions undoubtedly tend to temper the harsh criticism of Anglo Americans. Further understanding of the Río Arriba can be achieved only by allowing new and dissenting viewpoints to be published. Tolerance for all viewpoints may stimulate even greater discussion of the situation found in the Río Arriba by advancing it from a regional and parochial topic to one of interest to scholars nationally.[2] And to show spatial organization and instill a geographic feeling for the region, many maps as well as aerial and ground photographs illustrate the text.

Acknowledgments

My appreciation is extended here to the countless Spanish-American villagers who talked to me during my fieldwork. I would be remiss if I did not express my gratitude to the National Science Foundation for a research grant in 1980 to do fieldwork in the Río Arriba and conduct library research at the National Archives in Washington, D.C., and Suitland, Maryland. In addition, the Bowling Green State University Faculty Research Committee granted me a sabbatical leave in 1982 and provided financial assistance in 1981 and 1984 to do fieldwork in the Río Arriba. The interpretation and presentation of the varied data remain my responsibility alone.

I must thank certain individuals for providing me with that special encouragement I needed to complete this project. Cotton Mather, my mentor and now professor emeritus of the University of Minnesota, introduced me in 1960 to the possibilities of doing research in the upper Río Grande Valley. Subsequently, I did my master's thesis on Colorado's San Luis Valley and my doctoral dissertation on the Río Arriba. I will always cherish the memories of our travels in the region and his remarkable ability to observe and interpret aspects of the cultural landscape. My family allowed me many opportunities to do fieldwork. We often traveled together in the region and still enjoy it immensely. Eden's first playmates were Spanish American. Kurt has not forgotten the adventures we had locating *moradas*. Lynne and I maintain that Spanish-American cuisine is the best and head for particular restaurants during each visit. My father, an immigrant, never really understood my academic pursuits but he never discouraged them, for which I will always remember him.

Thank yous are extended here to those scholars who reviewed the manuscript and made constructive and much appreciated comments and suggestions. They include geographers Daniel Arreola of Texas A&M University and Charles Gritzner of South Dakota State University; historians John G. Clark of the University of Kansas and David Schuyler of Franklin and Marshall University; and sociologist Clark S. Knowlton of the University of Utah. George Thompson of the Johns Hopkins University Press recommended insightful changes in the organization of the text.

Lastly, I must acknowledge the talented job of copyediting done by Mary Hill of Eugene, Oregon, and the excellent skills of Marie Derkis, the Department of Geography's secretary at Bowling Green State University, who typed the entire manuscript.

PART ONE

Settlement in the Río Arriba, 1598–1949

Spanish and Mexican Land Grants

E arly migrating peoples onto frontiers had to consider the accessibility, availability, and potential of unclaimed and unsettled land. After a number of reconnaissance expeditions between 1536 and 1591 into New Mexico from bases in northern Mexico, don Juan de Oñate, heir to a silver-mining fortune, and his colony settled in 1598 in the upper Río Grande Valley, at the confluence of the Río Chama and the Río Grande, near present-day Española.[1] The earlier forays undoubtedly had provided New Spain's officials in Mexico, interested largely in securing the territory to the north for religious and political reasons, with information about the Pueblo Indians, the sedentary inhabitants of the northern Río Grande Valley, and their survival skills within a semiarid environment.[2]

Oñate's colonization scheme, which was personally financed and contracted, was the first to be approved officially by the viceroyalty of New Spain. It was, for the era, carefully planned, and the caravan of more than a hundred colonists, four hundred soldiers, and several Franciscan friars was equipped with more than sixty wagons of supplies and livestock. On the trek northward from Zacatecas, Mexico, Oñate, who had been made governor, chose not to venture far from the Río Grande Valley, a long rift valley that has a north-south orientation. The location of his colony, San Gabriel, at the confluence of the two rivers upon the site of a partially abandoned Indian pueblo (village) and adjacent to the existing San Juan pueblo indicates that he realized his colonists could depend at least for subsistence upon the nearby Pueblos' irrigated agriculture.[3] Oñate was also aware of the Pueblos' docile and acquiescent attitude toward newcomers. His colonists, and recruits who came later, were assigned small tracts of dispossessed irrigable land and they used the surrounding uplands for pasturage.

After experiencing various hardships and realizing their limitations for gaining wealth, dissatisfied settlers began to defect from the colony. Missionary considerations kept government officials, however, from abandoning the region then and later. According to geographer Carl O. Sauer, "New Mexico gave little promise of material returns to Crown or individuals, nor did it have the strategic importance of Florida or California. There remained the responsibility of the Spanish Crown as Christian Kings to extend the true faith to all their realm, an obligation acknowledged since the time of Queen Isabella. The Council of the Indies decided that New Mexico should be maintained as a Christian mission."[4] Oñate was recalled in 1608 to Mexico City, where he faced charges of abuse of authority as well as misconduct against the Pueblos. Allegations filed against him included claims of collecting excessive tributes, plundering several pueblos, and killing Indians indiscriminately. He was banished forever from New Mexico.[5]

Oñate's successor as governor, don Pedro de Peralta, implemented plans in 1610 that moved most of the remaining colonists approximately twenty-one miles south, to a site along the Río Santa Fe. This location was not near an existing Indian pueblo; following Spanish law, which prohibited settling on Indian land in use, it was located on the site of an abandoned pueblo. It also fulfilled Spanish planning and environmental precepts for the founding of a town: it was an elevated site (approximately 7,000 feet) and in a healthy location (no fog) with available fresh water and good accessibility.[6] It was also a strategic meeting place for the Pueblos and Plains Indians. From this governmental and religious center and *presidio* (military garrison) known as Villa Real de Santa Fé, Spanish officials proceeded to colonize the upper Río Grande Valley, concentrating their initial efforts in the watershed between Albuquerque and Taos (established in 1706 and 1617, respectively) or the area known as the Río Arriba, found today in Río Arriba, Sandoval, Santa Fe, and Taos counties (Figure 1). The Río Abajo (downriver) was the valley to the south of Albuquerque that included lengthy stretches of desert, especially the Jornada del Muerto (journey of death). A region is a mental construct; that is, its boundaries are inexact and depend upon certain criteria that provide a sense of homogeneity. In this case, the Río Arriba is a recognizable region with a distinct physiography of many small microbasins containing perennial streams and was for the most part settled earlier and differently from the Río Abajo, resulting in ongoing controversy.

Because of the intensity of colonization, the Río Arriba became the early core of Spanish settlement in New Mexico. After Spain's rule was

ended in 1821, the region became the source of Spanish settlers who
migrated largely into neighboring valleys. Mexico essentially continued
Spain's settlement policies and strategies until its expulsion in 1846 by
the United States, which found most of New Mexico's Spanish-speaking
people still residing in the Río Arriba. They became known as Spanish
Americans, a term still preferred by many who compose the largest share
of the rural population of the four counties, making up nearly 12 percent
of New Mexico's land area.[7] (Los Alamos County, created in 1949 from
Sandoval County, is the location of atomic research laboratories and has
no rural Spanish Americans.) It is often necessary to include data, especially those from the government censuses that are available only by
county, for the entire four counties to represent the Río Arriba.

Like other European countries colonizing the New World, Spain
implemented land policies that enabled its colonists to obtain land, thus

FIGURE 1

allowing them a means for survival and at the same time providing a
sense of permanency. Accounts of Spanish land use in the Río Arriba
during the 1600s are sketchy, but there is some evidence that the colonial
government rewarded a few of its officials and military officers by giving
them the privilege of using large areas of land, mostly between Albuquerque and Española, which took on the characteristics of *estancias* (livestock ranches).[8] Quasi-farming settlements developed here and there
composed primarily of militiamen who possessed smaller parcels. From
the Spanish custom of dividing conquered land, a cavalryman or an officer received a *caballería,* approximately 106 acres, while a foot soldier
was given a *peonía,* one-fifth of a *caballería.* Often, these militiamen also
received house sites, *solares,* in Santa Fe.[9]

The Spanish colonists produced few agricultural surpluses and basic
necessities because supply caravans occasionally brought provisions from
outposts in northern Mexico, and then, too, Spanish officials had introduced the *encomienda* system.[10] As used in New Mexico, this system
gave the recipients, *encomenderos,* who were mainly military officers, the
right to extract labor for both private and governmental purposes from
indigenous peoples, namely the Pueblos. In return for their labor, *encomenderos* were to pay the Indians and assist them in defending their
pueblos against marauding tribes, especially the Apaches and Navajos.
Against the advice of the Franciscan friars, who had witnessed abuses
and exploitation of the Pueblos, the colonial government supported the
encomienda system, claiming it had facilitated Christian conversion of the
Indians and the *encomenderos* with Pueblo assistance had provided protection for the supply caravans.[11] Approximately thirty-five *encomiendas*
were bestowed in New Mexico, largely in the Río Arriba, where most of
the Indian pueblos were located.[12] They were designated to remain in
effect for three generations.

In addition to providing labor, the Pueblos paid the colonial government tributes of foodstuffs and materials, some of which were reallocated
among colonists and used to pay soldiers. Disenchantment among New
Mexico's approximately sixteen thousand Indians (mostly Pueblos) had
been growing for several decades, largely in response to the collection of
tributes, acts of brutality, and repression of their religions.[13] When combined with raids by hostile Indians, pestilence, and food shortages, the
situation for the Pueblos grew worse. Sauer summarizes the situation:

> New Mexico, a remote and unprofitable appendage of New Spain, had small
> attention and support from the Viceroyalty and the Council of the Indies. Its
> governors were poorly paid; the soldiers were supported by being assigned
> pueblos which were in turn obligated to pay the beneficiary a prescribed trib-
> ute, payable yearly by each household. The tribute, mainly maize, beans, and
> cotton mantas, exacted in the same amount whether the season was good or

poor, increasingly reduced the pueblos to a state of want. Officials added to their income by stocking cattle ranches that intruded on Pueblo lands, the livestock damaging Indian fields. Indians were forced to work in salines, the salt sold to mines in the south. The Spanish prospered little; the Pueblos suffered more loss of food and freedom. The distant authorities regretted the state of affairs but took little action.[14]

Conspiracies to rebel finally culminated in the Pueblo Revolt of 1680, which led to the bloody expulsion of New Mexico's entire twenty-five hundred Spanish settlers.[15]

After taking refuge for more than a decade at El Paso del Norte, a few survivors, along with newly recruited colonists and militiamen, seventy families, and more than a dozen friars, joined don Diego de Vargas's government-sanctioned reconquest of New Mexico in 1692.[16] This time, the Spanish government was not only concerned about its missionary commitment but also wanted to thwart possible French intrusion into New Mexico.[17] Furthermore, it sought new sources of minerals, especially quicksilver, for use in blending metallic ores.[18]

Santa Fe was chosen again for the establishment of the colonial government and to be the military stronghold for protecting both the Spanish settlers and the Pueblos, who were not brought to full submission until 1697. More colonists arrived in the Río Arriba, increasing the number to more than one thousand by 1700.[19] Although Vargas's request for an *encomienda* was recommended, it never became operational because of continuous delays in its approval by officials in Mexico City. Not surprisingly, little enthusiasm existed for reestablishing the *encomienda* system because of fears of renewing antagonisms. Rather, Spanish officials had to reassess their ideas about how to survive in the Río Arriba.

Agrarian planning, based primarily upon the environmental realities of the Río Grande watershed, became an integral part of the new colonization scheme. In an area dominated by rough terrain and high elevations, aridity was just one of several limitations to be considered. Despite the basin's low annual precipitation (ten inches at its center in Española), the adjacent high Sangre de Cristo Mountains to the east and the San Juan and Jémez mountains to the west receive more than twenty inches of precipitation per year. Consequently, the Río Arriba has the greatest surface runoff in New Mexico, which gives rise to a number of short but perennial streams that are tributaries of the Río Grande (Figure 2). Spring meltwater and to a lesser extent precipitation from intense summer thunderstorms create most of this runoff, but maximum evaporation also occurs in summer. In addition, elevations of 5,000 to 8,000 feet make for a relatively short growing season in much of the watershed, which means supplies of irrigation water must be both adequate and timely for crops.[20] Spaniards did not boast about New Mexico's physical environment. Their

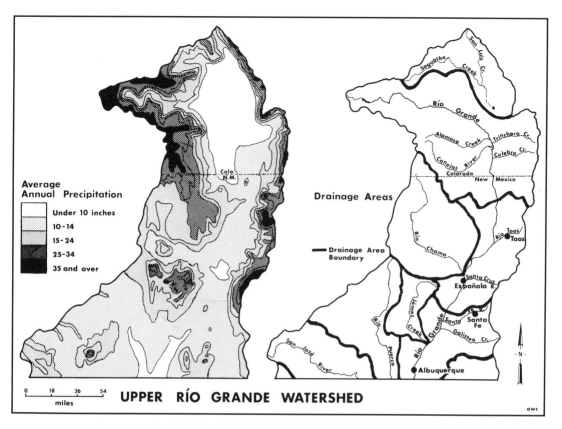

Average Annual Precipitation

Under 10 inches
10-14
15-24
25-34
35 and over

Drainage Areas

Drainage Area Boundary

UPPER RÍO GRANDE WATERSHED

0 18 36 54
miles

FIGURE 2

Source: Redrawn from maps published by the U.S. Department of Agriculture, Soil Conservation Service, Region 8, Albuquerque, 1936 (National Archives, Washington, D.C.).

perceptions are revealed by Sauer, who found that "the friars told little and the officials even less of the nature of the country. It had hotter summers and colder winters than Old Mexico. Winter was bitterly cold in the high country. There were years when the summer rains failed and there was great suffering. At times drought lasted for several years. . . . New Mexico impressed the Spaniards mainly as a semi-arid land."[21] The colonists, some of whom had come from Spain via Mexico, may have been undisturbed by the region's physical environment because it was similar to that of both Spain and northern Mexico.[22]

Spanish officials, knowledgeable about the region's physical limitations, implemented settlement plans allowed by laws that provided for land grants, *mercedes,* to both private individuals and communities. Private grants were given mostly to prominent people, especially former military personnel or their descendants who had provided services to the government or were owed salary. Aside from Spain's political and religious rationale for settling the frontier, its private grants were intended to foster and maintain a livestock industry. Because they included primarily pasturage with low grazing or carrying capacities, these grants had to be large, involving thousands of acres, in order to sustain sizable numbers of livestock. Their owners became part of the region's small aristocracy.[23]

Although the large land grants have been emphasized in historical research, smaller parcels were given shortly after the reconquest to less influential individuals who sought to earn a livelihood by grazing small numbers of cattle or sheep. They were (in approximate acreages) the *sitio de ganado mayor* for cattle, measuring one square league, or forty-three hundred acres; *sitio de ganado menor* for sheep, nineteen hundred acres; *criadero de ganado major* for cattle, eleven hundred acres; and *criadero de ganado menor* for sheep, five hundred acres.[24] Furthermore, Spanish officials donated even smaller parcels of cropland to families to satisfy their immediate needs. Their sizes were based upon the planting of a few *fanegas, cuartillas, arrobas,* or *almuds* of specified grains, usually corn, wheat, and beans. The *fanega*, the largest unit of 2.6 bushels, was used most often, resulting in New Spain in the *fanega de sembradura*, the amount of ground, depending upon local conditions and kind of seed, needed to sow the seed (figured as high as nearly nine acres), and the *fanega de tierra*, a plot of ground of about three acres, which became the more standard measure. Variations of these measurements produced smaller land units, the smallest being the *almud de tierra*, usually about half an acre.[25] These land units replaced the earlier *peonías* and *caballerías*.

The Río Arriba had throughout the 1700s few economic attractions that created an overwhelming demand for land. It experienced slow population growth, but there were yet poor and mostly landless people in Mexico as well as in the Río Arriba who wanted land. By implementing the government plan of giving community land grants to groups of people, Spanish settlement was to be extended throughout the Río Arriba because of the groups' greater ability to protect themselves in the mountain valleys farther from Santa Fe. Each settler received a tract of irrigable bottomland, an integral part of the community grant, and the rest of the grant was to be used communally by all of the grantees. This layout is discussed in Chapter 2. These grants, with their larger agricultural communities, more nearly fulfilled the government's strategy of establishing effective political control with an assumed defensive bulwark than did the sparsely populated private grants. They also differentiated the settlement pattern of the Río Arriba from that of the Río Abajo; the Río Arriba allowed a denser population of small farmers because of its more numerous valleys or microbasins with irrigable bottomland on floodplains.

Both private and community land grants had to be approved by the proper government officials, as all unassigned land was presumed to be vacant and included in the royal domain, *tierras realengas y baldías,* according to the Spanish laws and instructions for settlement, the *Recopilación de leyes de los reynos de las Indias,* codified in 1681.[26] To begin the process, an individual or a group of settlers filed a petition, *expediente,* which indicated that the parcel of land had been looked over and was vacant and thought to be suitable for settlement and that no third parties, adjacent landowners, or Indians were to be injured. Additional information, such as the names of the heads of households, their needs, and the intended use of the land as well as a sketch map, *diseño,* was to accompany the petition. Occasionally, the petitioner would remind officials that a relative had served in the reconquest or that he was of the right ancestry, making him an *escudero,* a gentleman related to a prominent family.

The written petition was normally filed with the local *alcalde* (mayor and justice of the peace), who forwarded it with his comments to the governor in Santa Fe. It could also be filed directly with the governor. There were six *alcaldes* who had jurisdiction over local administrative areas, *alcaldías,* that were wholly or partially within the Río Arriba.[27] Because the *alcaldes* were very knowledgeable about local environmental conditions and settlement patterns, the governor relied heavily upon their inspections of the proposed grants and recommendations. For instance, an *alcalde,* with several witnesses, could assure the governor that the land was vacant, *baldíos,* no Indians or third parties would be affected adversely, and there would be no subsequent disputes over landownership. The governor, in some cases, would also request more information, such as the number of animals to be grazed, and would occasionally stipulate certain requirements for settlement, especially in the cases of community grants. For example, he could require that a church be built or located not too far away and that there be at least springs for sources of water or sites where storage dams could be built, but no dam could deprive other residents or livestock of water. These and similar decisions made by government officials contributed to what have become known as the region's "customary laws."[28]

In addition, other laws and provisions applicable to land grants indicate the important role that the government played in controlling and managing settlement within the Río Arriba. No land speculators were to receive land and there was to be no absentee ownership. All grantees were to be landless and they were to possess the means for the continuous occupation and use of their grants, except for "accidents of war." Consequently, the settlers had to be able to defend themselves, and their defensive capabilities were reviewed. Grantees were to use their land within a specified time, usually three months, and the construction of

dwellings had to be completed within four years. Tracts of land within a
community grant were not to be sold or transferred for normally ten
years. No grants were to be given to the Catholic Church and no grantee
was to sell or transfer land to any ecclesiastical person or monastery.
Grantees were prohibited from receiving two grants or tracts of land
within more than one grant. A grantee could request, however, a larger
grant to expand his operations or another parcel with water resources if
his land did not support him and his family adequately. Abandonment
would be cause for forfeiture of a grant.[29]

Upon his approval, the governor would order the appropriate *alcalde,*
who had previously helped to determine the grant's boundaries, to take
the petitioner or petitioners to the land grant. By using the metes-and-
bounds cadastral system of selecting salient landscape features such as
large rocks and trees, mountain ridges, or streams, he would outline the
exterior limits and mark the corner points. In the case of a community
grant, he would divide the irrigable bottomland into small tracts for the
grantees to draw by lot. Upon the collection of a small payment, each
landowner received a *hijuela,* a deed. An *alcalde* occasionally would not
give titles until he had been assured that the grantees had in fact occupied
and used the land continuously.[30] A documentary record, consisting of a
copy of the approved petition and map, of the grant's transfer was to be
filed with all government records in Santa Fe. Spanish authorities had
procedures established, therefore, for an orderly alienation of their public
domain and for planned settlement in the Río Arriba. It can be assumed
that they denied few petitions for grants because they actually supervised
and even negotiated conditions that would assure successful, permanent
settlement.

In 1821 the Republic of Mexico gained its independence from Spain
by the Treaty of Cordova, and it acquired what is today the American
Southwest, including New Mexico. Mexican officials continued the Spanish policies of awarding land grants in order to put much of New Mexico's remaining public domain into the possession of Spanish-speaking
settlers at a time when American expansion west of the Mississippi River
was becoming evident.[31] The largest Mexican grants were to be located,
however, east of the Río Arriba, where suitable land was available largely
in the Mora and upper Canadian and Pecos river valleys and Indian
threats had been lessened. Several included land in Colorado, including
the Río Arriba's Tierra Amarilla and Sangre de Cristo grants. Mexican
colonization laws limited the size of a private grant to eleven square
leagues (approximately 48,000 acres).[32]

After Gen. Stephen W. Kearny took Santa Fe in 1846 during the Mexican War and Mexico conceded the American Southwest to the United
States, the two governments agreed in 1848 to the Treaty of Guadalupe

Hidalgo. The treaty assured existing landowners of their continued property rights if they were found to be legitimate under Spanish and Mexican laws.[33] In order to implement its own land policies to allow further settlement, the U.S. government had to determine what land was in the public domain. Accurate land records would not only accommodate alienating land for new settlement but would also provide the basis for establishing a tax system to generate revenues for county and territorial governments. (New Mexico, organized as a territory in 1851, had been divided into counties. Arizona was separated from New Mexico in 1863.) The American legal system, therefore, was left the difficult task of determining the validity of land claims, particularly grants that included vague boundaries and a paucity of documentation.

This process began with the establishment in 1854 of the General Land Office in Santa Fe. Headed by the surveyor-general for the Territory of New Mexico, it informed territorial residents in both English and Spanish that if they owned land they were to file claims to substantiate their proof of legitimate ownership. It was imperative for the Spanish Americans as individuals or communities to file claims that would help them to retain their presence in the Río Arriba and prevent their dislocation or resettlement. This action involved complying with the legal procedures established by the U.S. government rather than those established earlier by the Spanish and Mexican governments. Consequently, the surveyor-general's major responsibility became eventually the review of these claims, especially those involving land grants.[34] Once approved by him, the land-grant claims were sent to the secretary of the interior for forwarding to Congress, where they were to be confirmed before patents (quitclaims) could be issued to the many claimants.

The confirmation and the ultimate patent each required a formal survey to determine the grant's acreage and precise boundaries. These requirements created problems and delays because the Spanish and Mexican metes-and-bounds cadastral system had used descriptions based on impermanent and questionable features of the landscape. An example is the description for the Rancho de Nuestra Señora de la Luz (Bishop Lamy) Grant: "On the north, by the road leading from Santa Fe to Pecos, the lands of Lorenzo Marquez, deceased, and El Cerro del Divisidera; on the east, by the Cañoncito de Los Apaches, including the water of said cañon, on the south, by the road leading from Galisteo, which is called La Cañada Colorado, to where the Bridle Path de Los Soldados crosses it, and on the west by the Bridle Path de Los Soldados, and the Cerro Colorado including said Cerro, together with the rights of water of the said Cañon de 'Los Apaches.' "[35]

Determining the validity of New Mexico's land grants became a slow and confusing process and consequently dissatisfaction grew among gov-

ernment officials and claimants. The Civil War had also delayed the confirmation of several land-grant claims. Claims grew larger and larger and
conflicted with the original grant petitions. By 1890, millions of acres
languished in pending litigation. All the confirmed and alleged land-grant
claims amounted to nearly half of New Mexico's acreage. Adolf Bandelier charged in 1886 that "the old land grants cover a vast portion of
New Mexico, and are, through their immobility, an almost insurmount-
able obstacle to the growth of the Territory."[36] Unconfirmed claims made
buying real estate a risky endeavor and retarded growth and progress.
George W. Julian, the last surveyor-general, complained, too, in 1889
that "immigration is thus kept out by the belief that no government land
can be found. Investments in permanent improvements are discouraged,
and industry and thrift paralyzed."[37]

Growing demands to accelerate the process of determining legitimate
land titles and to eliminate alleged abuses and greed led Congress to
establish in 1891 the nonpartisan Court of Private Land Claims. Comprised of five judges, its mandate was to adjudicate land-grant claims in
New Mexico, Colorado, and Arizona.[38] Congress stipulated in its legislation that all claims be filed within two years and that appeals could be
made quickly to the U.S. Supreme Court.

The Court of Private Land Claims processed the bulk of New Mexico's land-grant claims before being dissolved in 1904. It adjudicated
ninety-one of the one hundred rejected claims and fifty-seven of the
seventy-six patented grants involving land in the Río Arriba.[39] Four-fifths
of the rejected claims were allegedly Spanish land grants and the others
were Mexican and more recent in origin. Eleven Mexican land-grant
claims were patented in comparison with sixty-five patented claims dating
to the Spanish colonial government. Some claimants did not, however,
receive patents until years later and even after the Territory of New Mexico had become a state in 1912 (Figure 3 and Appendix A). An average
of eleven years passed from confirmation to the time claimants actually
received their patents. This delay was attributable largely to problems
with determining the official surveys.

Land-grant claims were usually rejected for one of four reasons: (1)
claimants lacked documentary evidence that the alleged grant had been
bestowed by Spain or Mexico; (2) the grant had not been occupied continuously; (3) improper authorities of either the Spanish or Mexican government had bestowed the grant; or (4) the grant had been found to be
partially or even totally within another grant, sometimes already confirmed, or within a Pueblo Indian grant (discussed in Chapter 3).[40]

Under both the surveyor-generals and the Court of Private Land
Claims, claimants had the burden of proving ownership of their grants
by filing *testimonios,* affidavits or depositions. Admittedly, this created

legal and consequently financial problems for those who lacked the required documents. There is no doubt that chicanery took place. Anglo-American lawyers actively solicited claimants to represent their cases and probably encouraged some of them to file for excessive acreages, while others were enlisted willingly by claimants to research their cases and present documentary evidence. Either way was often costly for poor, non-English-speaking Spanish Americans who did not realize the total impact of the litigation until they had to pay for their legal services, frequently by losing portions of their pasturage, especially the communal lands of community grants. For instance, the Juan José Lobato Grant was patented in 1902 for 205,616 acres, but half of its communal land was transferred to the claimants' lawyer.[41] The Santa Fe Ring, a group of mostly Anglo-American lawyers, is accused of having acquired considerable acreage through these means.[42]

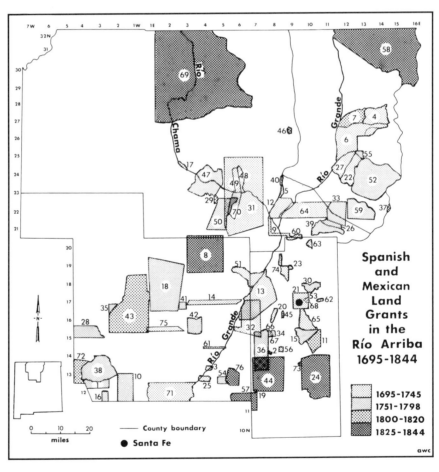

FIGURE 3

Spanish Americans hired these lawyers, several fluent in Spanish, because they were not knowledgeable about the American legal system and there were very few Spanish-American lawyers—about half a dozen represented Spanish Americans, but they were not all above reproach. Allegations persist that the Anglo-American lawyers, sometimes in conjunction with surveyor-generals, manipulated cases to dispossess Spanish-American claimants of their grants. For instance, Thomas B. Catron, the acknowledged leader of the Santa Fe Ring, acquired some 2 million acres of grant land in New Mexico. Victor Westphall, a historian, claims that Catron was involved in the adjudication of more than sixty of New Mexico's land-grant claims.[43] Although Catron had purchased some of this land at an undeniably low cost, questions about his practices and

1-Agua Salada (Luis Jaramillo)
2-Alamitos (Juan Salas)
3-Angostura
4-Antoine Leroux
5-Antonio de Abeytia
6-Antonio Martínez (Lucero de Godoi)
7-Arroyo Hondo
8-Baca Location No. 1 (Luis María Cabeza de Baca)
9-Bartolome Sanchez
10-Bernabe Montaño
11-Bishop John Lamy (Rancho de Nuestra Señora del la Luz)
12-Black Mesa (Medina)
13-Caja del Río
14-Cañada de Cochití
15-Cañada de los Alamos
16-Cañada de los Alamos
17-Cañon de Chama
18-Cañon de San Diego
19-Cañon del Agua
20-Cieneguilla (Francisco de Anaya Almazan)
21-City of Santa Fe
22-Cristoval de la Serna
23-Cuyamungue
24-E. W. Eaton (Domingo Fernandez)

25-Felipe Gutierrez (Bernallilo)
26-Francisco Montes Vigil
27-Gijosa
28-Ignasio Chávez (Chaca Mesa)
29-Juan Bautista Valdez
30-Juan de Gabaldón
31-Juan José Lobato
32-La Majada
33-Las Trampas
34-Los Cerrillos
35-Miguel and Santiago Montoya
36-Mesita de Juana Lopez
37-Mora
38-Nuestra Señora de la Luz de Las Lagunitas (Antonio Baca)
39-Nuestra Señora del Rosario San Fernando y Santiago
40-Ojo Caliente
41-Ojo de San José
42-Ojo del Borrego
43-Ojo del Espíritu Santo
44-Ortiz Mine
45-Pacheco
46-Petaca
47-Piedra Lumbre
48-Plaza Blanca
49-Plaza Colorado

50-Polvadera
51-Ramón Vigil
52-Rancho del Río Grande
53-Salvador Gonzáles (Cañada Ancha)
54-San Antonio de las Huertas
55-San Fernando de Taos
56-San Marcos Pueblo
57-San Pedro
58-Sangre de Cristo
59-Santa Barbara
60-Santa Cruz
61-Santa Rosa de Cubero
62-Santiago Ramirez
63-Santo Domingo de Cundiyó
64-Sebastian Martínez
65-Sebastian de Vargas
66-Sitio de Juana Lopez
67-Sitio de Los Cerrillos
68-Talaya Hill
69-Tierra Amarilla
70-Town of Abiquiú
71-Town of Alameda
72-Town of Cebolleta
73-Town of Galisteo
74-Town of Jacona
75-Town of San Isidro
76-Town of Tejon
(see Appendix A)

ethics linger. Despite the allegations, he received strong support from the Spanish Americans when he became one of New Mexico's foremost elected officials.[44]

Many land-grant claimants blamed their lack of documentary evidence upon both the alleged neglect and misuse of archival files at the governmental depository in Santa Fe by American territorial officials in the late 1860s and a fire in 1870. This accusation was made despite the abundance of other early records, such as those concerning numerous lawsuits filed by both Spanish and Mexican settlers, who used their legal systems quite extensively.[45] Claimants used much oral testimony and accounts of genealogy to establish proof of continuous settlement on their grants. No tax records existed that would have helped to prove continuous occupation because the Spanish and Mexican governments taxed according to what the land produced rather than upon sizes and types of land. Furthermore, documents that approved petitions occasionally mentioned that no taxes were to be collected for a specified number of years.[46] Even if record-keeping practices were poor in colonial New Mexico, an unmanageable number of grants had not been bestowed between 1695 and 1846. In fact, in the case of the Río Arriba, where most grant activity took place in New Mexico, the total number of 176 claims would have amounted to approximately one grant being awarded each year. This certainly did not create a burden of records, especially of such importance. In addition, some claimants argued that verbal contracts were a part of Spanish land customs and therefore were legal in the conveyance of grants.[47] These contracts emphasized possession and supposedly replaced aspects of de jure settlement on frontiers.

Nearly 20 percent of the land-grant claims were rejected because the original petitions were approved by government officials who were not vested with the proper authority. During Spanish colonization, only the governor could approve land grants after the *alcaldes,* serving as intermediaries, had assured him that certain requirements had been met and the grant's boundaries had been understood by the grantees. Several claimants maintained that an *alcalde* had approved their grants. Because the *alcalde* was supposed to have been very knowledgeable about Spanish law, it is not known why he would have approved grants, except for expediency, but then there was no reason for haste. These claimants may have had spurious documents or presented evidence that implicated an *alcalde* without knowing that he lacked the authority to approve grants.

Under Mexican rule, until 1828 all land grants had to be approved by officials in Mexico City. Thereafter, the Territorial Deputation in Santa Fe, headed by the governor, was empowered to approve grants, but again the governor had the final authority. Mexico instituted another type of grant whereby an *empresario,* or promoter, could contract with the gov-

ernment to settle approximately two hundred families as a colony. This
contract had to be approved in Mexico City, but no such colony grant
was approved for the Río Arriba. Most were to be founded in Texas.[48]

Several land-grant claims dating to the Mexican era were likewise
rejected because of their alleged improper approval by unauthorized officials, especially the *ayuntamiento* (town council). Concern emerged also
over grants that exceeded the Mexican stipulation of eleven square
leagues, of which only one league could be irrigable land.[49] Again, these
discrepancies were for the most part not the fault of the U.S. government, which according to the Treaty of Guadalupe Hidalgo was to honor
Spanish and Mexican laws.

One of the baffling revelations of the adjudication proceedings was the
fairly large number of land-grant claims that were partially, and even
totally, within other claims. Both Spain and Mexico had insisted that no
third parties were to be injured when grants were approved. In particular, one of five rejected claims involved land wholly or partially within
the City of Santa Fe Grant, finally patented for 17,361 acres in 1901.
Admittedly, there was considerable confusion over this grant. Some sort
of grant was given in 1715 to the inhabitants of Santa Fe, but it could
not be determined whether it was a municipal grant, which would have
been for four square leagues (*fundo legal*).[50] Congress more or less recre-
ated the grant in 1900, after the U.S. Supreme Court ruled against the
plaintiff (City of Santa Fe), reversing the affirmative decision rendered
earlier by the Court of Private Land Claims. Nevertheless, it is highly
improbable that officials would have approved grants that would have
conflicted with the city. Another one-fifth of the rejected claims involved
land in Santa Fe County which was already within confirmed grants.[51]
Again, officials certainly would have had to be aware of the landownership pattern in such close proximity to Santa Fe. In several cases, however, grants were found to overlap and they were patented (Figure 3).

Five rejected land-grant claims were filed by non-Indian settlers residing within Pueblo Indian grants, which was prohibited by Spanish law. In
several other cases, different parties claimed the same grant. One example
is the Sierra Mosca claim in Santa Fe County, where two groups filed for
the same estimated 155,200 acres but a government survey in 1879 put
it at 33,250 acres. Both claims were rejected in 1900.[52] Although the
claimants maintained the grant had been bestowed by Mexico as late as
1846, neither party could substantiate its validity.

In addition to the total rejection of land-grant claims, most of the criticism against the U.S. government centered on the outcome of claims
which involved the losses of communal lands within community grants.
From the outset, these lands had been recognized by the American legal
system as integral parts of this type of grant. Of the Río Arriba's seventy-

six patented grants, nineteen were approved by the surveyor-generals and confirmed by Congress. Several of them were community grants, including the huge Sangre de Cristo Grant (998,781 acres) and the Town of Cebolleta Grant (199,568 acres), but also the smaller Las Trampas Grant (28,132 acres) and Antoine Leroux Grant (56,428 acres). The Court of Private Land Claims continued the policy of confirming community grants, although it quickly reduced the acreages of many claims before their approval. For instance, claimants frequently argued that they and their forebears had used a grant's surrounding lands over the years largely as pasturage for their livestock. They therefore claimed these lands to be part of their grants. This de facto use, however, did not constitute ownership under the provisions of either Spanish or Mexican land policies. If it had, both governments in time would have had a very difficult task determining where new grants could have been laid out within the region's existing ownership and land-use patterns. No provisions existed in these policies that allowed residents or owners of land grants to enlarge the sizes of their grants by merely using the royal or public domain.

No evidence exists that the surveyor-generals and the Court of Private Land Claims had biases against community land grants simply because communally held land was nontraditional in U.S. land policies. Instead, the U.S. government was concerned principally with either the private or community land-grant claims' validity, legality, and integrity. To add to the confusion, a number of private grants had become, in essence, community grants when the original petitioners and their heirs allowed additional settlers to reside on them. For instance, the Cristoval de la Serna Grant was given to an individual in 1715, but it had more than three hundred residents by the 1870s.[53]

In a dramatic reversal of earlier policy, the U.S. Supreme Court ruled in May 1897 in *U.S. v. Julian Sandoval* that

> unallotted lands within the exterior boundaries of a grant made on condition that a settlement should be formed and that the tract should be in common to all settlers who joined in the formation of a town thereon were, by the laws of Spain and Mexico, subject to the disposition of the government, and neither the settlers nor the town have any right to such lands in New Mexico which the court of private land claims . . . can confirm as a claim which the United States are "bound to recognize and confirm by virtue of the treaties of cession of said country by Mexico to the United States."[54]

Based on a review of appropriate Spanish and Mexican laws, this ruling meant that the Court of Private Land Claims was to reject the claimed communal (unalloted) acreages included in all pending land-grant claims because they were never given to the grantees in fee simple or perpetuity. This case was based upon the San Miguel de Bado claim for 315,300 acres in neighboring San Miguel County, where more than fifty settlers had been given a grant in 1794. The claim was reduced and patented for 5,024 acres, the land owned by the individual settlers.

Of the fifty-seven land-grant claims confirmed by the Court of Private Land Claims and eventually patented in the Río Arriba, forty-four had their acreages reduced (a total of 1,856,900 acres or over 60 percent of the 2,968,000 claimed acres), mostly after 1897.[55] The average size of 52,000 acres was reduced to 19,500 acres. The rejected acreages were largely communal lands. Some of these claims appear to have been nothing more than attempts to create larger land grants. An example is the claim that became the Salvador Gonzáles (Cañada Ancha) Grant. The grant had been given to Gonzáles in 1742 after he requested land suitable for a cornfield near Santa Fe to support his family, but claimants filed a claim with a sketch map covering 25,000 acres.[56] It was confirmed in 1897 and ultimately patented in 1917 as a land grant of 201 acres, probably only because the claimants had insisted that their claim be adjudicated. The court generously set the final acreage to include that land suitable for cultivation because there was no mention in the original petition of any livestock or need for pasturage. On the other hand, a similar claim led to the confirmation of a large land grant. In this case, in 1728 an Albuquerque resident received cropland sufficient to plant 10 *fanegas* of wheat and 2 *fanegas* of corn—at the most a total of approximately 100 acres—and pasturage for a few livestock. The claim was for a community grant of 104,554 acres, which was eventually patented in 1901 for 19,113 acres as the Cañada de Cochití Grant.[57]

Of the Río Arriba's ninety-one land-grant claims totally rejected by the Court of Private Land Claims, most were adjudicated after 1897 and were not for large acreages, indicating claims for community grants. In fact, 60 percent of all the region's rejected claims were less than 10,000 acres each, hardly large enough to be sufficient for a village, considering the region's physical environment (Appendix B). Patented community grants confirmed before 1897, excluding the exceptionally large Sangre de Cristo, Mora, and Town of Cebolleta grants, averaged about 25,000 acres. These rejected claims indicate also that the U.S. government did not favor the approval of small over large grants.

An analysis of the region's land-grant claims must include the fact that the U.S. government accommodated the claimants of the rejected claims and squatters who preempted small landholdings on its frontiers by allowing them to continue to reside on their parcels. Squatters were given ownership of their land largely under the homestead acts (discussed in Chapter 4). Those who had possessed tracts of irrigable land within the rejected community land-grant claims for more than twenty years were protected by provisions of the Court of Private Land Claims Act. For example, residents on the rejected Río Tesuque claim in Santa Fe County maintained that their grant, an estimated 7,300 acres, had been bestowed to one person in 1747 but had by 1871 more than fifty residents.[58] They were allowed here, and in other cases, to receive titles to their individual parcels.

Misunderstandings were bound to occur. For example, the large Tierra Amarilla Grant, patented as a private grant in 1881 for 594,516 acres, may have been intended by the Mexican government to be a community grant, but the petitioner appears initially to have requested a private grant.[59] Mexican officials may have made land available for a community grant, although the names and the number of settlers were not listed, unlike in the petitions for other community grants. Also, the *alcalde* did not divide the cropland according to the terms of a community grant or provide a list of recipients, the required minimum being ten or more families or no less than twelve adult persons who must settle the grant within two years.[60] No evidence was presented that this took place. On the other hand, the Tierra Amarilla Grant far exceeds the Mexican law of no more than 11 square leagues that could be given to one individual.

Land-grant claims were also rejected, for instance, in Arizona and California. California's Board of Land Commissioners, established in 1851, adjudicated 813 claims, of which 604 were confirmed, 190 rejected, and 19 withdrawn, a 75 percent approval rate. These claims involved over 12 million acres, but fewer than 9 million acres were patented, approximately the same amount of acreage that was patented in smaller New Mexico.[61] They were adjudicated and confirmed in haste and some may have been fraudulent.[62] On the whole, there was less confusion surrounding California's claims because they were more recent and documents with surveys were available for verification.[63] Historian Andrew F. Rolle points out that "it was during the Mexican regime . . . that most of the 'Spanish land grants' were made; after the establishment of the Mexican Republic more liberal policies caused the number of land-grant applications to increase rapidly."[64] In contrast, more than 40 percent of the 176 land-grant claims in the Río Arriba dated back to the colonial period before 1750. The Court of Private Land Claims adjudicated seventeen land-grant claims, amounting to 838,000 acres, in Arizona, but only eight claims were confirmed for 116,000 acres.[65] No serious controversy has lingered in California or Arizona over the outcome of the claims.

The seventy-six patented grants involving land in the Río Arriba added up to 4,501,080 acres, out of claims which amounted to 9,043,000 acres—more than the region's 8,879,000 acres. By excluding the patented land that extended outside of the region and the western half of Río Arriba County and the adjoining northwestern corner of Sandoval County, which were not subjected to land-grant claims, approximately

half the Río Grande's watershed ended up in patented land grants. In
particular, these grants included nearly all of the region's best irrigable
bottomland outside of the Pueblo Indian grants (discussed in Chapter 3).
Elsewhere in New Mexico, a total of forty-five grants was patented for a
total of 5,063,883 acres.[66] Approximately 12 percent of New Mexico's
78 million acres became patented land grants.

Although Spanish and Mexican laws and procedures were explicit in
laying out land grants, their implementation left many questions for legal
interpretations to be made by the U.S. government. Myra Ellen Jenkins,
New Mexico's former archivist, pointed out, too, that Spain and Mexico
had established an ordered "system in which the governor made individual farming or grazing grants to Spaniards, as well as settlement grants,
according to a clearly defined procedure, [which] marked the land tenure
system up through the period of Mexican sovereignty until the United
States occupied New Mexico in 1846."[67] New questions continue to arise
to the present day and they will undoubtedly fuel controversy over the
status of the region's land grants. For instance, some of the private grants
may have been given as usufructuary grants with stipulations that they be
used only for the grazing of livestock and only during the grantee's life-
time, thus precluding them from having agricultural settlements.[68]

Ongoing criticism and condemnation of the U.S. government also continue to highlight much of the literature on the region, especially in
regard to the losses of communal lands that are used to explain many of
the region's economic problems.[69] Historian William deBuys claims that
"the real culprit in land grant crime was the U.S. government, whose
slowness in settling grant claims created a situation in which corruption
and dishonesty were inevitable and whose failure to effect a just transition between Spanish and American codes of law made possible the widespread abuse of the property rights of Hispanos."[70] Sociologist Clark S.
Knowlton maintains that "if the Spanish-American rural population had
managed to retain ownership of the common lands of their community
land grants, the region might have maintained a large rural Spanish-
American population supported by communal and individual development of the natural resources."[71]

Unfortunately, responsibility for the rejected land-grant claims in the
Río Arriba must also rest upon the Spanish and Mexican officials who
did not enforce colonization laws and procedures, which later came
under legal scrutiny after the Treaty of Guadalupe Hidalgo, and upon the
claimants. As historian Marc Simmons has pointed out, this frontier colony was distant from the Spanish headquarters in Mexico City, but it
was not isolated from its responsibility to administer governmental policies.[72] The argument that the Spanish and Mexican settlers' mere use of
land constituted ownership must be tempered by the realization that the

Pueblo Indians had previously used the expanses of the Río Arriba, assuredly for different purposes. Critics of the U.S. government's actions must justify the Spanish and Mexican colonists' taking land from these indigenous peoples without a treaty that left provisions to be interpreted later. They do not attribute much, if any, neglect to either the Spanish or the Mexican government or condemn the claimants, who knowingly and obviously exaggerated their claims with or without the assistance of unscrupulous lawyers, compounding the confusion. Attempts at chicanery, greed, duplicity, fraud, forgery, and the like must be considered, but in a realistic manner: these human weaknesses were not to be found only with Anglo Americans.[73]

Controversy over the outcome of the land-grant claims will continue and the purpose here is not to absolve the U.S. government of all alleged wrongdoings. It is important to remember, moreover, that there was no widespread physical displacement or eviction of Spanish Americans from these claims and many other landholdings. Rather, the Río Arriba had become the self-identified homeland of these people, who revealed their tenacity in retaining land through lengthy adjudication. In addition, this process designated the remaining public domain, which became available not only for further settlement by Spanish Americans but also by Anglo Americans.

Community Land Grants, Long-Lots, and Irrigation

2

S panish and Mexican community land grants reveal the environmental perceptions and strategies employed by Spanish and Mexican officials in the establishment of settlements in a semiarid region with limited resources for agriculture. To adjust to these limitations, settlers were assigned individual tracts of bottomland, *joya,* which in most cases had an elongated shape, resulting in strips, or long-lots, with a length to width ratio of at least 3 to 1 (Figure 4). This layout assured all settlers access to irrigation and proper drainage, accommodated population growth, and facilitated close-knit social organizations.[1] Long-lots ultimately became the basis for the development and retention of much of the Spanish-American subculture.

Spanish officials moved quickly after the reconquest to impose effective occupation upon the Río Arriba. An *alcalde,* with the approval of Governor don Diego de Vargas, laid out in 1695 small tracts of land for forty-four families on the region's first community grant (Santa Cruz Grant) in the Santa Cruz Valley east of present-day Española. To accomplish this, Pueblos, who had relocated there in two small settlements after the Pueblo Revolt, were removed from their irrigated parcels.[2] Here, and in later cases, settlers were expected to practice farming and pastoralism in order to establish self-sufficient communities that would be willing and able to defend themselves. Community land grants were bestowed upon groups of a minimum of ten families or twelve adults, but more people were usually involved in the initial settling of a community. Occasionally, a *poblador principal* fulfilled the role of land developer by promising officials to recruit the required number (and more) of settlers, *pobladores,* in

FIGURE 4

Long-lots are found between Ranchos de Taos and Talpa on the Cristoval de la Serna Grant (Taos County), which was bestowed in 1715 and patented in 1903 for 22,233 acres. Elevation: approximately 7,040 ft.

Source: USDA, ASCS, Salt Lake City, DXG-4CC-143, 10 November 1962.

exchange for additional land.[3] By bestowing community grants, the
Mexican government continued to accommodate the region's growing
native-born population by giving needy people land and at the same
time ensuring greater control of its northern frontier. An analysis of the
seventy-six patented land grants shows that approximately one-third were
settled initially by communities that in time grew larger because of additional in-migration and steady rates of natural increase among their residents.[4]

Locating sizable areas of arable bottomland and sources of irrigation
water were major determinants in the site selection of a community
grant. Bottomland situated on perennial streams was scarce and found
largely on elongated, alluvial floodplains along the Río Grande from
Albuquerque to north of Española, along the Río Chama, and in the
foothills of the surrounding mountains (Figure 5). Bottomland represented but a small fraction of the total grant. The adjacent meadows,
vegas, and surrounding uplands were designated as communal pastures,
dehesas, for livestock. Additional communal pasturage was to be found
on those grants with mountains, *montes,* covered by forests of piñon,
juniper, and ponderosa pine, which could be used also as sources for
fuel, building materials, and game.

Upon the approval of a community grant, the petitioners gathered at
the floodplain where an *alcalde* supervised, before three witnesses, the
assignments of bottomland. Each tract, *suerte,* started customarily at the
break between the floodplain and the uplands where the major irrigation
ditch would be built. It then ran at right angles across the breadth of the
floodplain to the river, allowing each to be irrigated by gravitational flow
and to have proper drainage because of its riverine frontage.

Each *suerte* was laid out by *varas* (one *vara* equals approximately
thirty-three inches). Unless specified otherwise, *varas* were used to indicate only the parcel's width, not length, leaving *suertes* without definite
measurements.[5] The widths ranged generally from 50 to 300 *varas,*
depending upon the *alcalde*'s assessment of the situation. Most were
between 100 and 150 *varas* and were often laid out by a premeasured
rope, *cordel,* which consisted usually of 50 *varas.* Sizes of *suertes*
depended largely on the extent of the floodplain and the number of settlers, but factors such as marital status, family size, and ability to cultivate land were also taken into consideration. Double lots would be given
to a *poblador principal.* It was common to assign additional *varas* to settlers who were to live where the floodplain narrowed because of stream
meandering and toward the ends of the valley. These wider parcels rarely
resembled long-lots, as in the case of the narrower, smaller assignments.
Most *suertes* amounted to 10 to 20 acres and all were to be fenced after
their boundaries had been marked by mounds of stone. Nondesignated

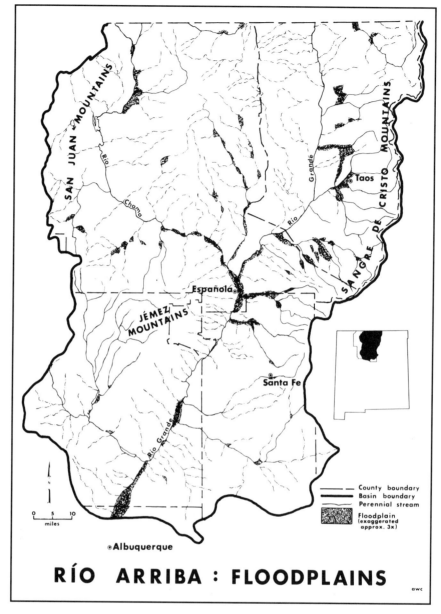

RÍO ARRIBA : FLOODPLAINS

FIGURE 5

Source: Aerial photography from the Río Grande Project, 1935, in the National Archives,
Washington, D.C., and from the USDA, ASCS, Salt Lake City, 1962–63 as well as U.S.
Geological Survey maps and fieldwork.

bottomland was left for future assignments during the growth of a community. In the meantime, it was used as an unfenced commons, *ejido,* where the settlers were allowed to graze livestock and to gather for community and recreational functions (Figure 6).[6]

In approving the Las Trampas Grant of 28,132 acres in 1751, Governor don Tomás Velez Cachupin found that Santa Fe's population had

> increased to a great extent, many of whom are yet of a youthful age, consequently there is not land or water sufficient for their support, neither have they any other occupation or trades or means of traffic excepting agriculture and the raising of stock, and whereas in the King's domains which are unoccupied there are lands which up to this time are uncultivated and which will yield comforts to those who cultivate them and where such persons as shall be named in this town who have no occupation or employment can settle upon and cultivate such lands as shall be assigned to them, from which the further benefit will result that the hostile Indians will not travel over them, and will serve as a barrier against their entrance to despoil the interior settlements. . . . I hereby assign and distribute said site in the manner and to the persons following:
>
> To Juan de Arguello one hundred and eighty *varas* of wheat growing land, with corresponding water, pastures and watering places, entrances and exits, without injury to third parties. . . .
>
> Luis de Leyva is placed on an equality with the others in lands and measurements. . . .
>
> . . . I grant . . . two thousand one hundred and sixty *varas* of arable lands all of which are wheat growing and under irrigation in the cañon and streams of the Trampas River which runs from East to West, for themselves, their children, successors . . . to have, cultivate, and reap the benefits of its fruits, crops and other profits without injury to third parties, and considering that this quantity of wheat growing land will not be sufficient on account of the increase of their families and as in the cañon or place where they are to settle, from East to West there are no other lands under irrigation that they can use, and whereas there are two cañons called De Los Alamos and Ojo Sarco south of the Trampas River which although not susceptible of irrigation, are most fertile, and of good quality, I also grant them to the above mentioned persons, to be equally divided between them in the same manner as the two thousand one hundred and sixty *varas.* . . . And on condition that they shall not sell, transfer or convey or in other manner dispose of all or a portion of said lands until the expiration of the four years provided by law, and not even then to Ecclesiastics, convents, colleges or other communities.[7]

Correspondence between Governor Fernando de la Concha and *alcalde* Manuel García de la Mora in 1793 provides further insights into the procedures used in the settling of a community grant (Ojo Caliente Grant). The governor informed the *alcalde* that he was to place the parties in royal possession of the land grant . . . and will thereafter make up the papers in such form as will forever accredit them to be legal holders of the land by virtue of the grant aforesaid, setting forth therein the boundaries which correspond on every side, not forgetting the circumstances that the watering-places on the Ojo Caliente River being common between themselves and the balance of the neighborhood of the district of Río Arriba, with the condition that the latter do not injure them in their fields. When the above papers are concluded upon stamped paper, as is required in various royal mandates, the same will be forwarded to me for me to attach my approval thereto, and to be filed among the archives of this government, making a copy thereof upon the same stamped paper for delivery to the parties interested, to the end that the same may serve them as evidence and security in all time.

The *alcalde* replied that he had

proceeded to the said place, Ojo Caliente . . . to assemble together all the fifty-three citizens who were to take the possession into which I am directed to place them, and they being collected, I proceeded to the mouth of the Cañada de los Comanches . . . and in the presence of three witnesses . . . proceeded to deliver one hundred and fifty *varas* of land to each of these fifty-three citizens, and the fifty-three families having entered upon the land granted them . . . from the Cañada de los Comanches to the tower of José Baca, deceased, with a small difference just below, its boundaries being on the north the said Cañada de los Comanches, on the south a landmark which I ordered to be constructed of stone and mortar, with a holy cross made of cedar placed in the center, just below the said tower of José Baca; on the east the foot of the hill, and on the west the foot of the other hills on the opposite side of the river, the pastures and watering-places of the said Ojo Caliente River remaining for the benefit of these parties and of the people of the Río Arriba, under the binding obligation upon the residents . . . not to damage with their stock the former, in their fields, and there remained below the measured land a narrow slip and two arroyos not measured, owing to their worthlessness, for cultivation, and which were left for common entrances and exits . . . each individual walked over the land assigned to him, and they jumped and leaped about and plucked up weeds with their hands, and expressed their thanks.[8]

Because of the limited number of floodplains scattered within the rough terrain, small communities became a part of the region's discontinuous pattern of settlement, which was vulnerable to Indian raids. Spanish officials believed not only that communities would provide the militia to thwart attacks in their locales, but also that the inhabitants should live close together within the communities for even greater mutual protection. Governor Pedro Fermin de Mendinueta complained in the 1760s that settlers were not living within walled *plazas* but on their *suertes*.[9] To facilitate the construction of a *plaza*, settlers were provided occasionally with house sites, *solares,* that were laid out around a rectangular or square

FIGURE 6

A commons, ejido, *is still evident near San Luis, Colorado, on the Sangre de Cristo* Grant, *which is located partially in the Río Arriba. Bestowed in 1843 as a private grant, it soon became a community grant in the 1850s when the original petitioners began to sell the irrigable bottomland to additional settlers, many from the Río Arriba. Elevation: approximately 7,900 ft.*

Source: *USDA, ASCS, Salt Lake City, CWS-1DD-137, 28 July 1963.*

plot of ground. This *plaza,* located above the floodplain, was to be enclosed by continuous-walled houses (*cordilleras*) abutting each other so that they created a fortress and a livestock corral.[10] Garden plots were designated nearby in addition to the *suertes,* which could be more distant from the *plaza.* These garden plots had specific measurements, such as

FIGURE 7

Cerro, located 32 miles north of Taos and not on a land grant, was settled in the 1850s by families from Taos and nearby Questa. Elevation: approximately 7,600 ft.

Source: USDA, ASCS, Salt Lake City, DXG-4CC-209, 210, 10 November 1962.

those of twelve *varas* by seventy-five *varas* found on the Don Fernando de Taos Grant, where a *plaza* was laid out in 1796.[11]

Following the establishment of several U.S. military forts in New Mexico, marauding Indians (Comanches, Jicarilla Apaches, Navajos, and Utes) were increasingly subjugated, resulting in most Spanish Americans building their farmsteads adjacent to their fields, largely for convenience.[12] By building them on the break between the floodplain and the upland, they were located above floodstage and consumed none of their *suerte*'s irrigable cropland. The main irrigation ditch, *acequia madre* (mother ditch), was also close at hand for domestic use. Consequently, the farmsteads formed line villages, *rancherías,* where the roads usually were laid out above the houses. Landowners normally planted fruit trees on the upper coarse and stony alluvial soils found in their backyards. They converted the fertile and heavier bottomland soils into plots of chiles, beans, corn, and other crops, including fodder.

This settlement pattern developed throughout the Río Arriba as well as on land outside the community land grants (Figure 7).[13] Squatters used it and, in particular, it was used on private grants that

> eventually became community property through the breaking up of the great estates of the dons and impoverishment of their children and grandchildren among whom the grants were parceled out, the subdivisions sometimes being disposed of, bit by bit, to raise money, until in certain cases the descendants of the original servants or peons have now become themselves the landowners. The many long, narrow strips of small acreage found under some of the New Mexico community ditches are strongly suggestive of this long-continued subdividing process.[14]

Long-lot farms, *ranchos,* often became smaller and narrower through inheritance because of the custom of dividing the scarce irrigable land equally between heirs rather than practicing primogeniture. Consequently, the farms were subdivided lengthwise, intensifying the long-lot pattern. The extent of partitioning was reduced somewhat by the out-migration of excess populations from the Río Arriba's communities to nearby valleys beginning toward the mid-1850s. Meanwhile, internal migrations after the 1850s onto land acquired within the Pueblos' grants (Chapter 3) and homesteads (Chapter 4) further alleviated the pressure for land, especially during the confusion over the adjudication of the land-grant claims.

Long-lots developed in the Río Arriba apparently as a result of local assessments of physical conditions. They represent a practical and equitable method of partitioning irrigable land. Antecedents of these riverine farms are not to be found in Spain, which did have communal grazing lands.[15] Although the Spanish officials in Santa Fe had limited contact with French traders and military men in the 1700s, there is no indication that the French influenced them to develop a long-lot system after that found in French Canada and America.[16] Beginning in the 1630s, French officials laid out riverine long-lots within seigneuries (land grants) bestowed in Canada's St. Lawrence River Valley. These long-lots fronted rivers to allow settlers accessibility to fishing and transportation.[17] Later, French communities as Kaskaskia, Illinois (1703), Vincennes, Indiana (ca. 1717–1735), and Ste. Genevieve, Missouri (1730s–1740s) and in Louisiana were all founded on the long-lot system. French long-lots were much larger than those found in the Río Arriba mostly because they were laid out in arpents (1 arpent equals 192 feet). After acquiring the French territory by the Treaty of Paris in 1763, the Spaniards continued the French system of alienating land for new settlements, including the laying out of long-lots, in the middle and lower Mississippi River basin.[18] Several of the Río Arriba's community grants, including the Las Trampas Grant in 1751, predate Spanish control of the French possessions.

Spaniards used the long-lot survey even earlier in the granting of land in 1731 to settlers at San Antonio, Texas. According to geographer Terry Jordan, an official reported that "he had 'allotted to each one of said sixteen families one *suerte*,' measuring one 'hundred and five *varas* wide . . . and in length the distance from San Pedro Creek to the San Antonio River.' "[19] The Spaniards are credited with developing this land system in Texas.[20] Although the Pueblos at Spanish contact were in the process of building irrigation networks as the result of a prolonged drought in the late 1500s, they had no field pattern resembling riverine long-lots.[21] The Spaniards appear to have developed their own long-lot system as one method for establishing effective occupation of their frontiers in Texas and New Mexico. They had, however, no special term for long-lots.[22]

Because irrigation water had long been an invaluable resource in southern Spain, Spanish authorities had formulated numerous laws and policies on water rights that were extended to New Spain by being condensed and included in the *Recopilación de leyes de los reynos de los Indias*.[23] For instance, one law stipulated that communities or townsites "should be in fertile areas with an abundance of fruits and fields, of good land to plant and harvest, of grasslands to grow livestock, of mountains and forests for wood and building materials for homes and edifices, and of good and plentiful water supply for drinking and irrigation."[24]

Land grants in Spain were given with irrigation rights (*tierra en regadizo*) or without them (*tierra en secano*), thereby regulating who could use large quantities of surface water. Unless specified, water from rivers could be withdrawn only in small amounts and then for domestic use. Likewise in New Spain, recipients of a land grant that included or fronted a stream had the implied right to take water, unless stated otherwise, only for domestic purposes. Irrigation rights, therefore, had to be designated by the proper authorities. Exceptions were watering holes (*aguajes*), which livestock could use without dispute, and all subsurface water, wells, and springs.[25]

Michael C. Meyer and Robert E. Clark, authorities on water rights and water historiography, maintain that Spanish and Mexican land grants facing or including streams did not carry riperian water rights, where water could be taken for irrigation, unless such rights were clearly stated in the documentation accompanying the approval of a grant.[26] Meyer concluded that "the grant of a piece of land fronting on a river entitled the owner, without additional authorization, to use the water for domestic purposes, but for nothing else. The water was still royal patrimony to be disposed of at the discretion of the Crown or its designated authorities. The only automatic alienation of water with a land grant was for water that originated on the piece of land."[27]

An examination of the documents concerning the Río Arriba's patented grants shows that designations of irrigation rights appear to be both quite explicit and vague. For instance, an *alcalde* appears to have conveyed in 1806 irrigation rights to the recipients of the Cañon de Chama Grant when he "proceeded personally to visit and examine the spot (*río*) called the Chama River Cañon . . . as well as the land itself . . . the places for taking out the heads of irrigating canals and the pastures and watering places . . . there are about two leagues, somewhat more or less, cultivable land and the town being placed in the centre, the thirty-one families applying for it may be accommodated and land enough remain for the increase they may have in the way of children and sons in law (*hijos y llernos*) . . . and the heads of *acequias* along the length of the planting land there are five or six of them."[28] Likewise, irrigation rights are rather explicit in the case of the Las Trampas Grant. On the other hand, whether irrigation rights were included in the granting of the Ojo Caliente Grant is not as clear.

Although uncertainty regarding specified irrigation rights may exist in the documentation of some of the Río Arriba's land grants, it would seem that the Spanish and Mexican officials would have wanted the settlers, at least in the case of the community grants, to have had sufficient water to maintain stable, productive settlements. Grantees without designated irrigation rights could petition the governor and acquire them in the form of a grant or gift (*merced de agua*).[29] Where irrigation rights were not given explicitly with a grant, settlers obviously assumed them, believing that their *suertes* were meant to be irrigated. Private grants that developed into community grants more than likely did not have the proper irrigation rights, but residents were not deterred from developing irrigation systems where possible.[30]

Additional uncertainty, which could be the potential for more legal controversy in the region, centers on whether all of the *suertes* on community grants carry irrigation rights.[31] Only *suertes* designated as *tierras de labor* actually had irrigation rights. These tracts were assigned in the Río Arriba, which indicates that some differentiation was in place.[32] For instance, only one-third of the *suertes* on the Cañon de Chama Grant had designated irrigation rights.[33] Meyer claims that "in those cases in which *suertes* were awarded without mention of water, the case for implied rights is very weak unless there is independent indication in the documentation that the land in question is intended to be irrigated. On occasion, part of the *suerte* is designated as a *huerta,* or family garden. The *huerta* . . . was an irrigated plot and therefore carried water rights. The remaining portion of the *suerte* could not be irrigated unless the water right was extended in some way."[34]

Irrigation systems ensured the survival of the Río Arriba's riverine communities. Upon locating the proper site for diverting a perennial stream at an elevation above the community, frequently a mile or two away, settlers would begin construction of the *acequia madre* to divert water and have it flow by gravitation toward the community below. This diversion point was occasionally found on land that was not included in the community grant, but if the community had irrigation rights, Spanish law allowed for the transfer of water across the public domain and even across private property, if necessary, to reach the desired destination.[35] Settlers who were located downstream and possessed irrigation rights were not to have their supply diminished or denied by an upstream community. Access to irrigation water was to be extended to the land of all new settlers of a community.[36] If a community were confronted with deriving its irrigation water from an intermittent stream, the settlers often solved their problem by building upstream a crude log and earthen dam (*presa*) that formed a reservoir to collect spring meltwater and early summer rainfall. Care had to be taken in all cases, however, in diverting and damning water so as not to cause a detriment to a third party, including the Pueblos.

Communities were characterized by networks of canals and ditches. The larger canals were often found along the Río Grande and the lower Río Chama, which had sufficient flows of water that allowed for considerable diversions upstream without affecting drastically the level for downstream communities. Canals, too, were used to divert and manage water from the large and sometimes roaring flows and where the larger farms on the lower and wider floodplains needed greater quantities of water. Ditches, smaller than canals, were found in the higher elevations, where they diverted water from smaller streams bounded by narrow floodplains and rough topography.

Considerable communal manpower and cooperation were needed in

FIGURE 8

A flume made from a hollowed-out log carries irrigation water across a small canyon in Taos County, December 1941.

Source: National Archives, Washington, D.C. A similar flume is still in use near Las Trampas, Taos County.

each community to establish an irrigation network. Arduous labor was expended on the construction of the canals and main ditches and to a lesser extent on the smaller secondary or lateral ditches, *sangrías,* that carried water to the individual fields. Wooden scrapers pulled by oxen were used to dig the initial trough and the landowners completed the canal or ditch by hand digging with wooden spades and tools, sometimes taking years to complete and perfect a network.[37] Dirt removed by the construction was used to build embankments, enabling the canals and ditches to contain larger flows of irrigation water. As expected, some water was lost to seepage.

Canals and especially ditches were built in a somewhat winding fashion to avoid the removal of large trees and other obstacles, but with the ultimate aim of allowing water to flow by gravity. In fact, these irrigation networks were accomplished by employing trial-and-error techniques rather than by using survey instruments. Flumes (*cañoas*) made of hollowed logs carried water across gullies and small canyons and over ditches and canals that belonged to other communities (Figure 8).[38] Landowners installed a series of wooden headgates along the *acequia madre* and *sangrías* to control the eventual diversion of water onto their fields. Upon opening a headgate, the water flowed into a landowner's shallow ditches from where it would spread over a field or onto small plots enclosed by embankments. By using this method, a landowner could irrigate approximately 5 to 6 acres a day, approximately half his irrigable land. A landowner in the 1850s irrigated and cultivated an average of 10 acres.[39]

Each community's landowners formed a cooperative association, *acequia* (the term is used also for a ditch), to ensure not only the proper construction of a network but also the required maintenance of the irrigation network and an equitable distribution of the water. This association elected a ditch boss or overseer (*mayordomo*), who was given considerable authority, dating back to traditions in Spain.[40] He determined the irrigator's (*parciantes*) equitable shares (*piones*) of water and the days and hours that the water could be used. Assignments were given to landowners detailing the amount of labor (*fatiga*) expected from them for new construction and upkeep, such as reinforcing the embankments and cleaning the ditches of sediment and debris.[41] Labor was contributed proportionately, depending upon the amount of one's irrigable land, regardless if it were cultivated or not.[42] In times of drought, often in late summer, the *mayordomo* had to ration irrigation water, which brought tense times and disputes that he, aided occasionally by a mediating priest, was expected to resolve.[43]

Because the *acequia madre* was considered to be communal property, it was often used for purposes other than irrigation. Farmers allowed their roaming and even stray livestock to drink from it and households used it for washing clothes, bathing, and, to a lesser extent, the disposal of kitchen waste. To keep impurities out of irrigation water and flowing water in general, New Mexico passed legislation in the late 1880s that provided for fines to be assessed against anyone convicted of depositing filth in irrigation networks and rivers.[44] Consequently, the *mayordomo* became involved in more disputes in his attempts to prevent pollution of his community's irrigation water.

New Mexico also enacted after 1880 legislation that provided for the election of water commissioners where enlarged irrigation districts were established, involving mostly communities that derived water from the same source. The commissioners were given by 1900 increased power over the remaining *mayordomos* in an attempt to standardize statewide irrigation procedures and to prevent legal controversies and lawsuits.[45] *Mayordomos* are still found, however, in some communities where they have retained considerable influence and responsibilities.[46]

Colonization and population growth were accommodated by the development of riverine long-lots in a region characterized by scarcities of irrigation water and irrigable bottomland. This land system provided residents not only with the most advantageous utilization of resources but also with an egalitarian way of life in which they shared the disadvantages of the physical environment. Spanish Americans clung tenaciously to their irrigated long-lots on the patented community and quasi-private grants as well as on the unpatented claims. Private ownership of the long-lots was important in keeping Spanish Americans in the region's communities, whose sizes and raison d'être could be determined by the extent of their irrigation networks.[47]

3 The Pueblo Indian Grants

During Spanish rule, non-Indians were supposed to remain separate from the Río Arriba's Pueblo Indians. However, much of the Pueblos' irrigable bottomland within their land grants, established by Spanish officials, came into the possession of Spanish Americans.[1] Some of the densest Spanish-American settlement is located today on this land, including several of the region's largest towns, Española (Santa Clara Pueblo Grant), Taos (Taos Pueblo Grant), and Peñasco (Picurís Pueblo Grant). This situation is largely ignored in the literature by those who emphasize the loss of land by Spanish Americans as a result of the adjudication of the Spanish and Mexican land-grant claims. The availability of Pueblo land to sustain additional Spanish-American settlement was a major factor in the region's ability to accommodate this growing population during the 1800s and in explaining its current presence in the Río Arriba.

Upon Spanish contact, approximately 10,000 Pueblos were located in the Río Arriba, residing in sixteen agrarian, riverine, centralized villages (pueblos) comprised often of adjoining flat-roofed, multiterraced apartment dwellings built of adobe made from the local sandy clay (Figure 9).[2] Oñate found them living "house by house, and having quadrate plazas; they do not have streets, but live in pueblos of many plazas and quarters, going from one to another by narrow alleys, the houses of two or three stories, some of four to seven."[3] These pueblos were located on upland so as not to consume valuable irrigable bottomland, and they ranged in population from several hundred to two thousand, the average size being four hundred to six hundred people.[4] Each pueblo was for the most part

FIGURE 9

Some Taos Pueblo Indians still use the above adobe structure (pueblo) for their homes. It was built prior to Spanish colonization when the Pueblos moved from their semisubterranean pithouses to larger surface communities as they developed more sophisticated architecture.

Source: Author, August 1971.

an autonomous, self-contained entity separated by considerable distances from the others because of the scattered floodplains.

Other small villages had been abandoned in favor of moving to the larger, successful pueblos, and some of their residents dispersed outside the region. Overall, the Río Arriba's Pueblo population was declining prior to Spanish contact, particularly because of increased intertribal hostilities and natural problems such as drought. It has been estimated that a dozen or more pueblos were abandoned in the 1500s.[5]

In contrast to California's Indians, who lived in scattered habitations, Spanish officials and missionaries did not need to round up the sedentary Pueblos and put them into villages (*reducciones*) or large mission compounds in order to achieve greater political and religious control over them and at the same time open land for colonization. Pueblos constituted one of the highest population densities in America.

Pueblo men cultivated gardens and small fields on the region's best bottomland, depending upon summer rainfall and practicing floodwater irrigation, which also brought silt deposits and nutrients to their fields annually. Networks of ditches were under development to assure timely supplies of irrigation water.[6] Besides consuming maize, squash, and beans, planted together for symbiotic reasons, the Pueblos supplemented their diet with wild plants and animals. Tobacco and cotton were also grown and turkeys were raised, but only for their feathers.[7] When Pueblos produced small surpluses of maize, used largely for flour, and cotton blankets, they bartered them mostly for meat, mainly buffalo, from the Plains Indians.[8] Moreover, the Pueblos did not have private ownership of real property. Although their irrigation systems and land were used on an individual basis, they were held communally.[9] Spaniards introduced them not only to the concept of private ownership of land but also to the practice of extensive land use in the form of pasturage for grazing livestock.

From the outset, Spain declared it would provide guardianship for the Pueblos and respect their rights to land adjacent to the pueblos. (Oñate's settlement of San Gabriel near the San Juan pueblo in 1598 was itself in violation of Spanish law.)[10] Before the Pueblo Revolt in 1680, no Pueblo cropland was to be included within the land assigned to an *encomendero,* who was usually engaged in livestock ranching. Non-Indian settlers were required to remain between 500 to 600 *varas* from a pueblo. Eventually grants, mostly of four square leagues, or approximately 17,500 acres, were designated reportedly in 1689 by Governor Domingo Jironzo Petroz de Cruzate just prior to the reconquest for fifteen of the pueblos (Appendix C).[11] The Sandia Pueblos claim they did not receive their grant until 1748. These grants were to be owned by corporate communities, not by individuals who could alienate land on their own.

A number of proclamations and royal decrees (*cédulas*), based on the laws of the Indies, were made after the reconquest to keep the colonizers and Pueblos apart and to protect Indian lands from encroachment.[12] Specifically, Governor Francisco Cuervo y Valdez proclaimed in the early 1700s that Spaniards were not to reside within Indian pueblos or go into them without permits. Spaniards already living within pueblos were to move out and Pueblos were to have their dwellings located within a village and not move from one pueblo to another.[13] Spanish settlers were banned in 1718 from using land surrounding the San Juan pueblo and a similar order was issued in the 1730s to protect the lands of the Taos Pueblos.[14] In 1781, Spain prohibited the selling, leasing, renting, and disposing of land by Indians to non-Indians without its consent.[15] Other decrees prohibited cattle ranches, *estancias,* from being located within 1½ leagues of an Indian pueblo, and non-Indian cattle were not to trespass and damage Indian irrigation systems and crops or graze their designated lands.[16] Even local officials issued their own proclamations to protect the Pueblos' welfare. The *alcalde* don Ygnacio María Sanchez Vergara proclaimed in 1813 that "animals should be kept out of the farms of the Indians under all circumstances. And if the Indians should suffer serious damage, severe penalties will be imposed on transgressors, whose excuses

will avail them nothing."[17] It was feared that the Pueblos were losing the
irrigable bottomland that sustained their livelihoods. Furthermore, these
actions limited the Pueblos to specified places so the remaining land
could be claimed by non-Indian settlers.[18]

Before the Pueblo Indian grants were confirmed in 1858 by the U.S.
government, there was considerable debate over the extent of the square
league and how it was employed, because two land leagues were used in
New Spain.[19] The *legua legal* (13,780 feet, 5,000 *varas*, or 2.6 miles) was
employed in judicial or official matters and the *legua comun* (18,282 feet
or 3.5 miles) was used traditionally by travelers. It was determined in this
case that the *legua legal* was meant to be used. There was confusion too
over whether these leagues were to be measured from the last houses on
the periphery of a pueblo or from its cemetery or chapel.[20] For instance,
the Taos pueblo governor testified in 1856 that their "lands extended one
league to each of the cardinal points, measured from the cross in the centre of the burial ground."[21] The leagues were ruled eventually to extend
outward from the center of a pueblo. Documentary evidence showing
that grants were actually given to all of the Pueblos was lacking, but the
unquestionable fact that the pueblos had been inhabited continuously led
to recommendations for confirmation. Patents were not issued until 1864
except for Santa Ana pueblo, which received its patent in 1883 (Figure
10, Appendix C).

Despite the decrees that prohibited Indians from selling or alienating
their lands, Pueblos started in the 1700s to trade parcels of bottomland
for Spanish livestock and goods. Spanish settlers found this method of
land acquisition to be more expedient than if they were to petition the
government for land. The rate of exchange increased in the next century,
indicating the Pueblos' greater acceptance of the concept of private ownership of land.[22] Frequently, these parcels included idle or abandoned
fields of proven fertility that required little expenditure of energy in preparing them for crops. A considerable amount of land had been abandoned near the pueblos as their populations declined in the 1700s and
early 1800s, resulting from out-migration and in particular a smallpox
epidemic in the 1780s. For example, the Pojoaque Pueblos nearly became
extinct as the remaining dozen or so residents moved to other pueblos,
especially Nambé.[23] The Pecos Pueblo Grant was totally abandoned in
the 1830s. Once having a population in the hundreds, the number of
Pecos Pueblos dwindled, largely because of smallpox and Comanche
raids, to approximately twenty residents. Historian John L. Kessell claims
that they could not have survived much longer. "Just as well. The Hispanos wanted their lands so much that they had threatened in the previous decade to remove them bodily and scatter them among the other
pueblos. Now they were too few to cope."[24] The residual Pecos Pueblos

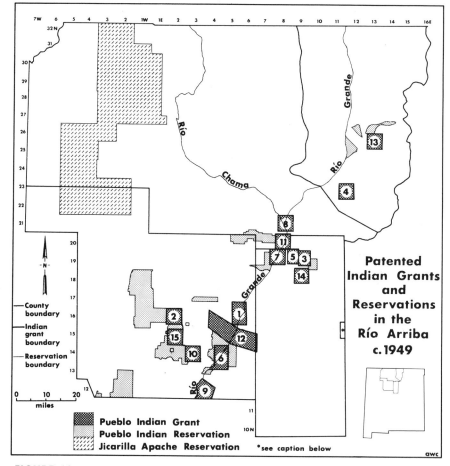

FIGURE 10

*(1) Cochití, (2) Jémez, (3) Nambé, (4) Picurís, (5) Pojoaque, (6) San Felipe, (7) San
Ildefonso, (8) San Juan, (9) Sandía, (10) Santa Ana, (11) Santa Clara, (12) Santo
Domingo, (13) Taos, (14) Tesuque, and (15) Zía. The asterisk indicates the
location of the Pecos Pueblo Grant, which was patented in 1864 for 18,763 acres,
located partially in neighboring San Miguel County. The grant was acquired by
non-Indians and eventually all Indian titles were extinguished. In time, additional
lands were acquired by different Pueblo tribes between 1902 and 1942 as
reservations. The Jicarilla Apache Reservation was established in 1887 and
enlarged, especially in 1908, by executive orders. It had 742,315 acres in 1975.*
Source: *Bureau of Land Management, Santa Fe.*

migrated to the Jémez Pueblo Grant.[25] Their abandoned grant (18,763
acres) was squatted upon or sold in small, affordable parcels to
non-Indians.[26]

Some Pueblos encouraged non-Indians to settle near their villages to
provide a common defense against Indian raids as well as to build and

maintain joint irrigation systems. Spaniards were allegedly invited in the 1700s to settle within both the Taos and Cochití Pueblo grants to help thwart Comanche, Navajo, and Ute raids.[27] Later, Governor Fernando de Chacón reportedly allowed more than sixty non-Indians to settle on the Taos Pueblo Grant in 1796. They ended up farming sizable portions of the irrigable bottomland. When the Taos Pueblos petitioned the Spanish government in 1815 for confirmation of their grant, an investigation revealed that approximately one-fifteenth of their land was occupied by non-Indians. Some of the two hundred non-Indian residents argued that they had both purchased the land and been asked to locate near the five hundred Indians to provide protection against the Comanches. The Taos Pueblos now wanted them expelled and rejected an offer to take livestock in exchange.[28] They tried as late as 1919 to have the non-Indians ejected forcibly, but the latter requested military troops to put down what turned out to be a bloodless uprising.[29] John Dixon, an Indian judge, explains what happened in the case of the Cochití Pueblos: "When the Navajos came here to fight and steal because they were hungry, my people took in Mexicans to help protect them. The Mexicans say, 'Let me have one little room for my wife and family.' Then, 'Compadre, could you not let me have a little lot for a little house?' 'All right, Compadre, you build a little house.' All the Mexicans, they just came in that way—did not buy. Then he would move, and sell his land to some other Mexican."[30]

Local *alcaldes* were often called upon to seek settlements or compromises in those cases where the Pueblos wanted to remove non-Indian settlers from their irrigable lands. This was, however, often complicated by the small number of Spaniards, mostly males, who intermarried with Pueblos and subsequently obtained ownership of land within their spouse's grants. In general, Spanish Americans ignored governmental proclamations and decrees and the local officials did not enforce or simply ignored them. By 1821, non-Indians outnumbered Indians on most Pueblo Indian grants.[31] The rate of encroachment was to accelerate during the eras of the Mexican and American governments.

Spanish Americans acquired in the latter half of the 1800s sizable areas of unused irrigable land within the sparsely populated Pueblo Indian grants, apparently without much objection from the Indians. They had all along acquired strips of land in *varas* and imposed long-lots extending from uplands to a river (Figure 11).[32] Large areas of bottomland had to be available for long-lot farms to cross the floodplain without disrupting the irregularly shaped and randomly arranged Indian fields (Figure 12). Indeed, Spanish Americans acquired entire floodplains on the Picurís Pueblo Grant. Nearly all of these acquisitions were obtained without written deeds.

Unclaimed irrigable bottomland elsewhere in the Río Arriba had

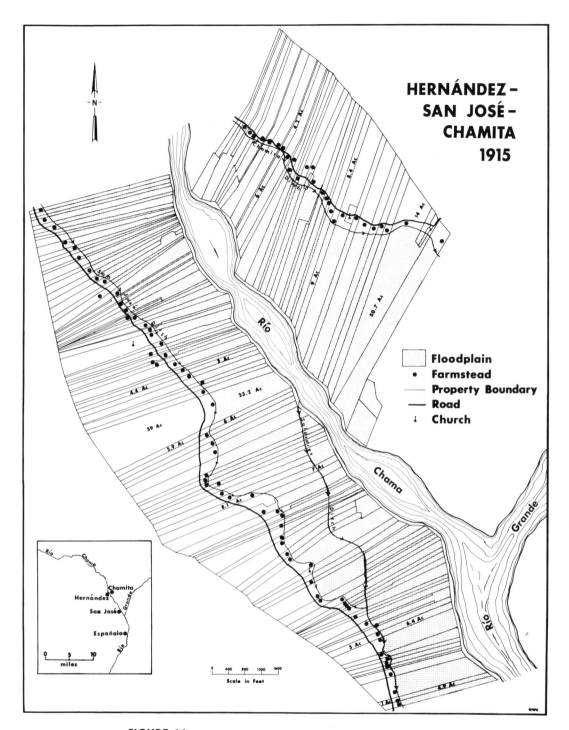

FIGURE 11

Hernández, San José, and Chamita are Spanish-American communities located on the San Juan Pueblo Grant. Francis Joy of the General Land Office surveyed the non-Indian claims, which included bottomland and upland.

Source: F. E. Joy Survey Records, United Pueblo Agency, Albuquerque.

become practically unavailable by the time the Anglo Americans started to arrive in the 1850s. Anglo Americans began to compete with Spanish Americans for land by purchasing and homesteading parcels not only in the Río Arriba but also in the surrounding areas that could have served as outlets for the growing land-hungry Spanish-American population, which doubled between 1840 and 1880, reaching 35,000. Out-migration, which could have alleviated the situation, was slow into the 1900s. Consequently, the intensified need for irrigable cropland was satisfied largely by movement onto the Pueblo Indian grants, which served as safety valves in accommodating Spanish Americans. Most of the fifteen Pueblo Indian grants whose total Indian population in 1890 numbered only 3,500 had witnessed the growth of sizable non-Indian communities.[33] Spanish Americans continued their acquisitions of Pueblo lands into the early 1900s. Finally, growing concern about the welfare of the remaining Pueblos and their loss of land to non-Indians along with the U.S. government's desire to ascertain boundaries and ownership of all private property in the Territory of New Mexico began to focus attention upon the thousands of non-Indian landholdings within the Pueblo Indian grants.

By this time, considerable debate had evolved around the Pueblos' legal status. Whereas Spanish law had prohibited the Pueblos from alienating their land, several New Mexico territorial court decisions (*U.S.* v. *Lucero* in 1869, *U.S.* v. *Santistevan* and *U.S.* v. *Joseph* in 1874) ruled that the Pueblos were able to alienate their land according to Mexican law, which had declared them to be citizens under the Mexican Declaration of Independence.[34] In 1877, the U.S. Supreme Court in *U.S.* v. *Joseph* upheld these decisions. It ruled also that the Trade and Intercourse Act of 1834, subjecting non-Indian squatters and settlers on Indian land to a monetary penalty, was not applicable to the Pueblos, despite the passage in 1851 of the Indian Trade and Intercourse Act, which had extended this penalty specifically to claims involving Indian lands in the territories of New Mexico and Utah. In the *U.S.* v. *Joseph* case, a non-Indian had settled on 10 acres in the Taos Pueblo Grant, and the United States, on behalf of the Taos Pueblos, wanted to penalize the person for trespassing. The U.S. Supreme Court concluded that the self-governed Pueblos were responsible, civilized agriculturalists and Christians who did not need federal protection. The Court's chief justice argued that they were "as intelligent as most nations or people deprived of means or facilities for education. . . . In short, they are a peaceable, industrious, intelligent, honest, and virtuous people. They are Indians only in feature, complexion, and a few of their habits; in all other respects superior to all but a few of the civilized Indian tribes of the country."[35]

No American law therefore specifically prohibited non-Indian settlement on the Pueblos' grants until the decision rendered in *U.S.* v. *Felipe Sandoval* in 1913, after New Mexico had gained statehood. In this case, the U.S. Supreme Court reversed its earlier opinion in *U.S.* v. *Joseph* and ruled that the Pueblos, like other Indians, came under the constitutional guardianship and protection of Congress. It maintained that "the people of the Pueblos, although sedentary rather than nomadic in their inclinations and disposed to peace and industry, are nevertheless Indians in race, customs, and domestic government, always living in separate and isolated communities, adhering to primitive modes of life, largely influenced by superstition and fetishism and chiefly governed according to the crude customs inherited from their ancestors. They are essentially a simple, uninformed, and inferior people."[36] The Pueblos, as wards now of the federal government, could no longer alienate land without federal approval, as under Spanish law and the Intercourse Acts of 1834 and 1851. On the other hand, Spanish Americans could no longer count on encroachment upon Pueblo Indian grants to acquire farmland.

Following *U.S.* v. *Sandoval*, which also allowed for the Pueblos to reclaim their alienated lands, the U.S. government initiated efforts to determine the extent and validity of the approximately three thousand non-Indian claims. Non-Indian claimants who could not substantiate the legality of their possessions would have their land returned to the Pueblos. Most non-Indians were naturally upset over their uncertainty in proving ownership. Controversy and confusion reigned again after the adjudication of the Spanish and Mexican land-grant claims.

The Office of Indian Affairs had arranged earlier, beginning in 1913, for surveyor Francis Joy and his associates from the General Land Office to determine and mark the boundaries of the Pueblo Indian grants as well as the claims of non-Indians. Their field-checked plats revealed the considerable extent of the private land claims. John Collier, later commissioner of Indian Affairs, reported that

> the year 1922 found the following situation: First, many of the pueblos were in distress and two were destitute because of their illegal losses of farmlands. All the water that had flowed through the ancient ditches of Tesuque had been taken by whites. San Ildefonso with about 150 inhabitants retained the use of fewer than 250 irrigated acres; Santa Clara retained fewer than 375 acres for a population of over 300. San Juan had lost the use of 3,500 of its 4,000 irrigated acres. Taos had lost over three thousand acres of its usable land.[37]

New Mexico's Senator Holm Bursum introduced in 1922 a bill in the U.S. Congress to confirm all non-Indian claims within the Pueblo Indian grants. When his bill was defeated, it was replaced by the Pueblo Lands Board Bill, which passed Congress in 1924. This legislation established a hearing board for the purpose of adjudicating all the non-Indian claims.[38]

The Pueblo Lands Board began hearings to quiet title to the private

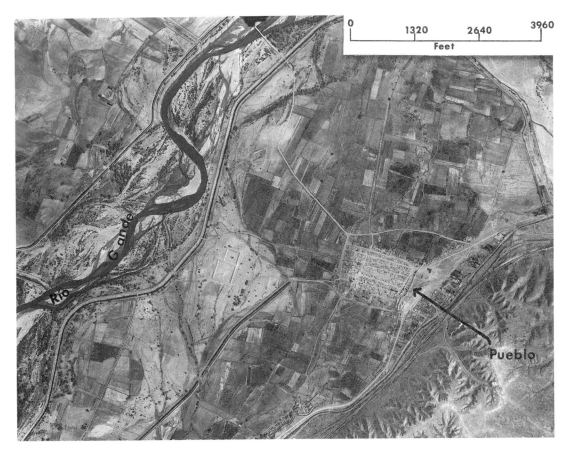

FIGURE 12

The field patterns surrounding the Santo Domingo Indian pueblo are in sharp contrast to the Spanish-American long-lots.

Source: USDA, ASCS, Salt Lake City, DFD-1DD-106, 4 May 1963.

land claims. All non-Indians had to demonstrate ownership by proving continuous possession for at least twenty years, or payment of taxes since January 1902, or possession of documents showing proof of acquisition. Most lacked any written evidence and instead filed affidavits to prove ownership and boundaries. An examination of these affidavits reveals that many of them claimed their ancestors had purchased the land and that they had merely inherited or bought the land later, usually from relatives. In the case of 524 private land claims on the San Juan Pueblo Grant, largely in the communities of Chamita and Los Ranchitos, nearly 53 percent of the parcels had been allegedly purchased, 13 percent involved combined parcels that had been both purchased from Pueblos and inherited from relatives, and the remaining 34 percent had been inherited.

Although most of the parcels were settled in the period of the 1840s and 1850s, the San Juan Pueblos allegedly sold land as late as 1914.[39] However, in the cases of 209 private land claims on the Taos Pueblo Grant, largely in the community of El Prado, 53 percent had been allegedly inherited, 39 percent purchased, and 8 percent resulted from a combination of inheritance and purchase. Although non-Indians had acquired some of these land parcels in the 1820s, many were acquired between the 1840s and 1870s. Purchased parcels were paid for largely in kind with

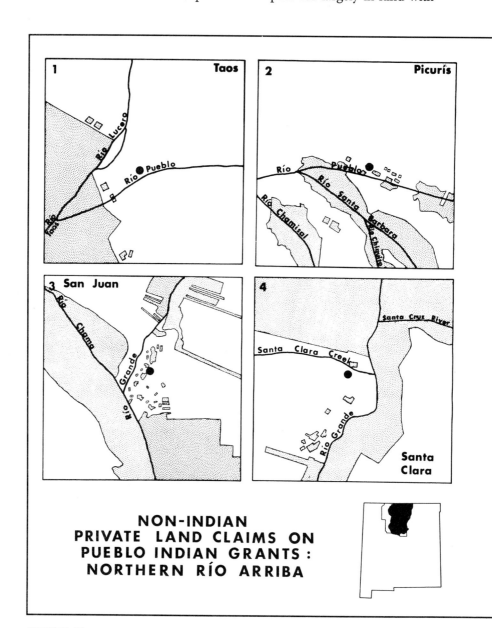

NON-INDIAN PRIVATE LAND CLAIMS ON PUEBLO INDIAN GRANTS: NORTHERN RÍO ARRIBA

FIGURE 13

livestock or commonly with items such as furniture, clothes, and hides.[40]

Many Spanish-American claimants had in reality squatted on the Pueblos' grants and claimed the "right to possession and occupance" of unused cropland, *tierra sobrante,* which they argued was sufficient for ownership under Spanish and Mexican customs. Others claimed they were unaware of being located within a Pueblo Indian grant because of the approximate boundaries laid out by the metes-and-bounds survey. The grants had been, however, surveyed in the 1850s prior to their con-

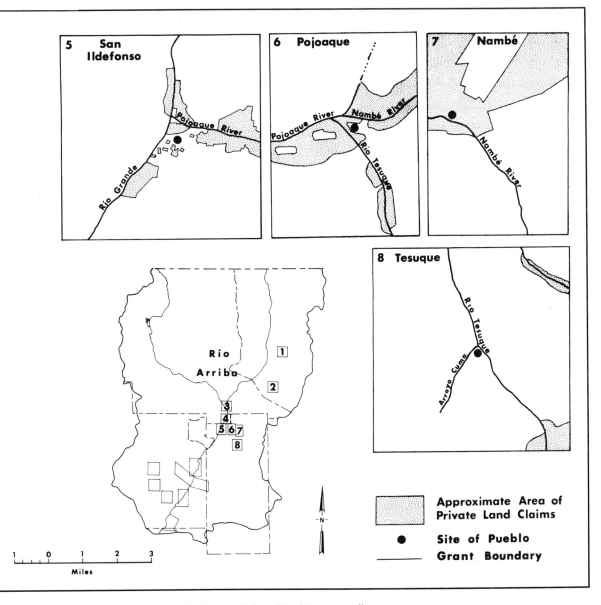

Source: United Pueblo Agency, Office of Real Property, Albuquerque.

firmation. Some contended too that the Pueblos had "donated" land to them or to their forebears. An interesting argument was also advanced that the small Pueblo populations on many of the grants could not utilize all the irrigable cropland and water, so why displace an active and stabilized farming population. In addition, of the 327 non-Indian claimants on the San Juan Pueblo Grant, for instance, more than 70 percent of them were forty years or more of age (27 percent were in their forties, 22 percent in their fifties, 17 percent in their sixties, 4 percent in their seventies, 1 percent in their eighties). A claimant's average age was forty-seven years. Many of those who were in their sixties were widows.[41] In regard to 235 non-Indian claimants in the community of El Prado on the Taos Pueblo Grant, the average age was forty-six years. Here too, 67 percent of them were forty years or more of age (29 percent in their forties, 17 percent in their fifties, 14 percent in their sixties, 6 percent in their seventies, 1 percent in their eighties).[42] If evicted, there would be no place to relocate this population made up largely of aging heads of households.

Approximately three thousand land claims, with an estimated total value of $10 to 12 million, were filed by non-Indians, but more than two-thirds of them were for land in the eight northern Pueblo Indian grants (Nambé, Picurís, Pojoaque, San Ildefonso, San Juan, Santa Clara, Taos, and Tesuque) (Figure 13).[43] These claims affected an estimated ten thousand Spanish Americans, nearly one-fourth of the Spanish-American population in the Río Arriba north of Santa Fe in the 1920s. The small Pueblo populations, totaling about nineteen hundred on these grants, contested only a fraction of the land claims.[44] Ironically, too, the Pueblo Lands Board generously overlooked the precise requirements needed by the Spanish Americans to prove their claims. Generally, only some proof of continuous occupancy was sufficient for them to receive titles to their land parcels. By 1932, when the land claims were largely resolved, 80 percent of the land lost to the non-Indians was located within the eight northern Pueblo Indian grants, which had rich bottomland and reliable sources of irrigation water. The populations on the southern Pueblo Indian grants (Cochití, Jémez, San Felipe, Sandía, Santa Ana, Santo Domingo, and Zía) remained generally larger and as a result used continuously more of their irrigable lands. They were located on the whole farther from Spanish-American communities.[45]

The land lost by the Pueblos of the eight northern grants amounted to approximately 18,200 acres, ranging from 250 acres on the Tesuque Pueblo Grant to 4,300 acres on the Santa Clara Pueblo Grant, but averaging 2,200 acres per grant (Appendix C).[46] Because most of this land was irrigable, water rights were assumed to have been transferred with the approval of the non-Indian claims. The remaining nonirrigable land was used primarily as farmsteads. Of the 340 claims, which averaged 8.6

acres and amounted to 2,900 acres on the Taos Pueblo Grant, only 200 acres were nonirrigable. Likewise, there were 725 non-Indian claims of an average size of 8.3 acres or nearly 6,000 acres on the San Juan Pueblo Grant, of which 2,700 acres were nonirrigable. The San Juan Pueblos retained only one-fourth of their irrigable land.[47]

Limited funds were appropriated by the U.S. Congress to compensate both Pueblos and non-Indians for their losses of land as determined by the Pueblo Lands Board (Appendix C). The Pueblo Lands Relief Act (1933) provided additional funds to compensate the Pueblos for title extinguishment. Several of the Pueblo tribes began to acquire, even before 1924, adjacent lands with the assistance of the U.S. government. During and shortly after the Pueblo Lands Board hearings, the northern Pueblos were able to reclaim nine hundred acres of the non-Indian claims by relinquishment as well as purchase. All of these acquisitions consisted primarily of nonirrigable land that was suitable only for pasturage.

Fewer than one-quarter of the residents on six of the eight northern Pueblo Indian grants/reservations in 1980 were Pueblos (Appendix D). On the other hand, more than 70 percent of the total resident population on the region's southern Pueblo Indian grants/reservations was Pueblo. These Pueblos for various reasons have been able to acquire considerable amounts of additional available acreage. In contrast, the northern Pueblo grants are engulfed by more densely populated areas and the Carson and Santa Fe national forests, established in the early 1900s. In any case, no appreciable amounts of irrigable cropland were added to any of the original Pueblo Indian grants. For example, in cases where compensatory funds were used by the fifteen Pueblo tribes to purchase a total of 47,000 acres, only 2,869 acres were irrigable.[48] Both the northern and southern Pueblos utilize their grants today mostly for grazing livestock.[49] Their remaining irrigated and fallow cropland is used largely for hay and pasture. Gardens are found on small irrigated parcels, and cash crops, other than hay, are practically nonexistent. The interspersion of Spanish-American landholdings prevents the Pueblos from consolidating irrigable cropland on their grants and also makes it difficult to implement land-use programs.

Although the Pueblo Lands Board resolved many of the controversial land claims filed by the Spanish Americans, questions have persisted over the extent of the water rights held by the Pueblos. A history of disputes between the Pueblos and non-Indian settlers dates back to the colonial period. These disputes involve Indian water rights both on and off their grants. For example, the Taos Pueblos challenged in the 1820s the nearby non-Indian farmers of Arroyo Seco, who had diverted water from Lucero Creek.[50] Inadequate water supplies have been a problem in the 1900s for a number of the Pueblos.[51] They have filed in recent years several lawsuits regarding the water rights that were to have been commensurate with the bestowing of their grants.[52] In essence, the unresolved question remains whether the Spanish, Mexican, or U.S. government could limit, quantify, transfer, or deny an aboriginal right of a people.[53] This question has been the basis of contention in other cases filed by Indians across the country.[54] Because of ever-increasing demands for water, any legal review of the non-Indian sources and uses of water could certainly add another dimension to the Río Arriba's history of controversy. In the meantime, many Spanish Americans will continue to reside within the Pueblo Indian grants, where the availability of irrigable bottomland was important in anchoring them in the region.

U.S. Land Policies and Homesteading

D uring the adjudication of the Spanish and Mexican land-grant claims and the confirmation of the Pueblo Indian grants, the U.S. government implemented its land policies in the Territory of New Mexico. As the extent of the public domain became known, many of the Río Arriba's Spanish Americans filed for homesteads, but they found competition from Anglo Americans who had learned about New Mexico through media reports and stories about its healthy climate and availability of land.

Congressional legislation between 1842 and 1853 provided for donations of 160 acres as an inducement for settling the public domain, especially in the West. It required recipients to be in the militia. The U.S. surveyor-general, established by Congress in 1854, in the General Land Office in Santa Fe was to handle the applications for donations, which were limited to white males of twenty-one years of age or over who were citizens of the United States or naturalized or had lived in the territory before 1853. Land units of 160 acres for a single person and 320 acres for a married couple could be patented after two years of residence and evidence of cultivation, or they could be purchased for $1.25 an acre.[1] Claimants of Mexican and Spanish land grants could not apply. The donation system was terminated in 1883 without alienating any appreciable amount of land within the Río Arriba.[2] It had, however, laid the groundwork for establishing the delivery system to be used in alienating land under the Homestead Act of 1862.

This act provided, too, for a head of a household, a widow-widower, or a single person, male or female, who was at least twenty-one years of age and a citizen regardless of race or color, to file an entry and pay a small filing fee for up to 160 acres for his or her exclusive use. The applicant had to build a residence, improve an unspecified amount of land for agriculture, and remain continuously on the claim for a minimum of five years in order to receive a patent for a nominal land office fee. Homesteaders could not sell their claims until they had received titles and could not alienate any part of the claim to churches, schools, or railroads. If homesteaders abandoned or relinquished their claims willfully, they were forbidden to make second entries.[3] They could speed up the acquisition of their claims by commutation, which allowed them, after a period of not less than six months and amended to fourteen months in 1891, to pay the U.S. government $1.25 per acre upon establishing proof of residence and cultivation of any amount of land.[4] Beginning in 1872 and amended in 1879, legislation enabled a homesteader who had a patented homestead to obtain an additional homestead, usually adjacent land.

More legislation followed the Homestead Act. The Timber Culture Act and the Desert Land Act were passed in 1873 and 1877, respectively.[5] Both acts, however, were insignificant in alienating land from the Río Arriba's public domain. Only nine Spanish Americans filed timber culture entries, totaling 1,425 acres, but only two received patents, for a total of 305 acres. Anglo Americans claimed sixty-seven parcels, totaling 10,096 acres, but none of the entries was patented. And in the case of desert land homesteads, nineteen Spanish Americans claimed 3,401 acres, of which 800 acres were patented by five of them. Anglo Americans numbering one hundred forty claimed 25,933 acres, but only fourteen received patents, for a total of 2,517 acres (Appendixes E, F). Less than 21,000 acres in New Mexico were disposed of under the Timber Culture Act before it was terminated in 1891, but the desert land homesteads were available until the 1920s, largely sought by commutation. The Public Lands Commission had recommended as early as 1879 that larger parcels be made available for free entry in areas that were suitable only for pasturage or dry farming. John Wesley Powell, director of the U.S. Geological Survey, recommended to Congress in the same year that land units of at least 2,560 acres be made available from the public domain where it was feasible only to graze livestock, but also with the requirement that each parcel include an unspecified amount of irrigable land for forage crops. Actually, his recommendation followed the earlier Spanish and Mexican land policies in that the land units should be laid out by metes-and-bounds survey rather than by the rectangular township and range (grid) survey in order to coincide with topographic features and the availability of irrigation water. Furthermore, he advocated that the farmsteads be clustered and the pastures be held in common, not fenced.[6]

It was not until 1909, however, that the Enlarged Homestead Act was enacted, allowing a claimant a maximum of 320 acres of nonirrigable land. It required that a certain amount of the larger homestead be cultivated within specified years. Government policies, therefore, encouraged dry farming, which required deep plowing and covering the field's entire surface with fine soil in order to limit evaporation. The Three-Year Homestead Act followed in 1911 and allowed patents in only three years and absences of up to five months per year.[7] With demands for even larger units, legislation produced in 1916 the Stock-Raising Homestead Act, the last of the homestead acts, which allowed 640 acres of nonirrigable land for a homesteader who lived on the acreage for only three years and used it for pasture. Cultivation was not required and commutation was prohibited.[8]

Each type of homestead was made available in the Río Arriba as more land was designated in the public domain. Applications for homesteads were completed in the General Land Office in Santa Fe, where records were kept on each entry until it was patented. Because counties had been laid out and the American cadastral system of townships, ranges, and sections had been superimposed on the landscape, American officials introduced a land system that made land easily accountable and taxable.

Meanwhile, despite concerns that the territory had some hostile Indians, New Mexico's amenities were extolled in the national and regional media by the territory's Bureau of Immigration (established in 1880), railroad companies, and private land developers.[9] Travel accounts by Zebulon Pike in 1806, Josiah Gregg in his *Commerce of the Prairies* of 1844, and others who traveled the Santa Fe Trail praised New Mexico's climate.[10] Merchants, trappers, and travelers continued after 1850 to promote the amenities of this portion of the "Great American Desert" and its long-time Indian and Spanish residents, who were allegedly free of various diseases, particularly pleurisy, asthma, rheumatism, tuberculosis (consumption), and malaria (ague).[11] After the Civil War, health-seekers, on the advice from their doctors, sought cures for their physical disorders by traveling to the sunny, high, and dry areas of the West, including northern New Mexico.[12] Mineral and thermal springs enhanced the therapeutic value of New Mexico. Railroads either built or contributed to the establishment of health resorts or spas at some of these sites. Notably, the Atchinson, Topeka, and Santa Fe Railway opened the famous Montezuma Resort in 1879 at a hot springs near Las Vegas immediately to the east of the Río Arriba. The Denver and Río Grande Railway brought healthseekers after 1885 to a similar resort at Ojo Caliente in the Río Arriba. After arriving by railroad in Albuquerque, healthseekers could use a stage line to travel to Jémez Hot Springs, another of the Río Arriba's health spas, established in 1902. In fact, Santa Fe, without these springs, had become recognized also as a health center.[13]

JNO. W. BOST, *T. F. JENKINS.*
Ex-Surveyor General of California.

NEW MEXICO LAND GRANTS,

FOR SALE BY

BOST & JENKINS, AGENTS,

No. 331 Montgomery Street, Stevenson Building, Room 18,

SAN FRANCISCO, CAL.

Have on hand large quantities of *agricultural, grazing, coal, timber* and *mineral* lands, in tracts to suit, situate on and near contemplated railroads in New Mexico.

These lands cannot be surpassed on the American continent for grazing purposes, being covered with the black-head grama grass, so celebrated for its nutritious qualities, and being well watered with large, pure running streams, renders large quantities susceptible of irrigation for agricultural purposes.

The large and profitable returns for the capitalist or stock-raiser are apparent at this time for an investment in these lands. We offer these lands for the nominal sum of from twenty-five to fifty Cents per acre, according to location, quality and quantity.

There are now being built three railroads, all of which are approaching this Territory. Two of them will undoubtedly be completed as far as Santa Fé within two years.

New Mexico is conceded to be the finest SHEEP country in the United States, and this is the last chance to buy LARGE quantities of land in a body cheap.

We have an agent in the City of Santa Fé who will be ready at all times to wait upon our customers.

Titles, Spanish and Mexican grants, confirmed by U. S. Congress. For further particulars call upon the undersigned.

We have also large tracts of improved and unimproved lands in all parts of the State of California.

BOST & JENKINS.

REFERENCES:

MESSRS. CHRISTY & WISE, San Francisco; HON. J. P. JONES, Nevada; ELIAS BREVOORT, Santa Fe, N. M.; WIGGINGTON, BLAIR & CO., Merced, Cal.

FIGURE 14

Similar advertisements appeared in various types of literature during New Mexico's territorial years.

Source: Brevoort, *New Mexico, Her Natural Resources and Attractions* (see chap. 4, n. 9), 176.

Railroad and land companies pointed out in particular that livestock could thrive on the alleged abundant pastures during the yearlong mild climate, reducing their losses, and that irrigable land was available for cultivation (Figure 14). Charles P. Clever, an attorney representing railroad interests in the territory, provided in 1868 an example of these claims: "In New Mexico, the range is so extensive the flocks can spread out, and can move over different pasturage every successive day. No shelter is needed in the winter time. . . . Of course, what is said of the facility and cheapness of raising sheep and goats, will equally apply to the raising of horses and cattle."[14]

Much of the promotion was designed to give the territory the favorable recognition needed to attract Anglo-American settlers. An underlying belief had emerged that the only way New Mexico could develop its resources to the fullest extent and gain statehood was to encourage Anglo Americans to move there. Elias Brevoort, a land promoter, advocated this view in 1874: "The population of New Mexico hitherto has not, unfortunately, been of the progressive kind. The Spanish and Mexican race, of whom until recently ten tenths, and at this time nine tenths of the population is composed, has caused the country to progress scarcely a move in the march of material improvement and wealth beyond what it was in the days of the Spanish vice-royalty in Mexico to which it was once subject."[15] New Mexico's population growth between 1850 and 1880 was slow in comparison to that of most other western states and territories, indicating little in-migration of Anglo Americans. Although its population nearly doubled from 61,500 in 1850 to 119,600 in 1880, this increase was based largely upon a long-time resident population with a high birth rate. The territory had considerably fewer people in 1880 than neighboring Colorado or Utah, or even distant Oregon and California.[16] Thousands of Anglo-American homesteaders, however, were to answer the call of the promoters and developers.

In analyzing homesteading in the Río Arriba by both Anglo Americans and Spanish Americans, data were gathered from Bureau of Land Management plat books on each type of homestead for the four counties (305 townships).[17] All patented and unpatented entries were recorded for the period of the 1860s through the 1940s. They were then checked in the tract books, located in the National Archives, to determine the applicants' surnames. A total of 9,231 entries were processed: 4,610 patented homesteads (1,190,586 acres, or nearly 52 townships) and 4,621 unpatented homesteads (1,320,599 acres, approximately 57 townships), including desert land and timber culture entries but excluding cash entries (Figures 15, 16).

Spanish-American applicants (those with Spanish surnames) received more than half (2,595, 56 percent) of all the patented homesteads, or

516,659 acres, whereas the Anglo Americans (those with non-Spanish surnames) acquired more patented acreage (673,927 acres). On the other hand, Anglo Americans had a higher noncompliance rate as they filed for approximately two-thirds (2,926 entries, 63 percent) of the 4,621 nonpatented entries and unpatented acreage (881,428 acres, 67 percent). The

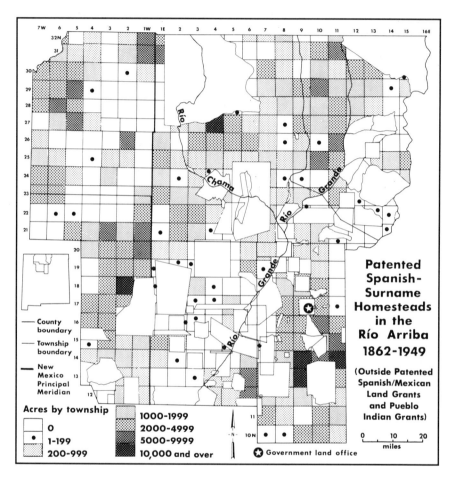

FIGURE 15

Patented Spanish-surname (Spanish-American) homesteads were located throughout the Río Arriba. This is partially because many Spanish-American homesteaders were settled on land within the alleged Spanish and Mexican grants and on preempted land and chose to receive patents for these lands under the homestead laws. Homesteads that were found to be located in two or more townships were mapped only in one township, the one with most of the particular homestead's acreage. Of the 2,595 patents received by Spanish-American homesteaders, 10 percent (260) went to women, many being widows.

Source: Bureau of Land Management, Santa Fe, and National Archives, Suitland, Maryland.

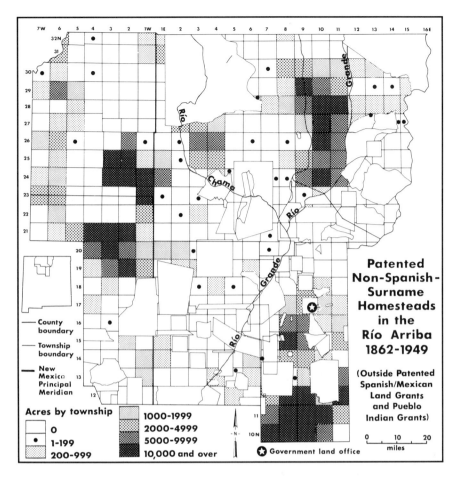

FIGURE 16

*Patented non-Spanish-surname (Anglo-American) homesteads were more
concentrated in particular locales within the Río Arriba than in the case of the
patented Spanish-surname (Spanish-American) homesteads. Of the 2,015 patents
received by Anglo-American homesteaders, 12 percent (238) went to women.*
Source: Bureau of Land Management, Santa Fe, and National Archives, Suitland, Maryland.

Spanish-American patented homesteads averaged 199 acres in contrast
with the Anglo-American average of 335 acres. Anglo Americans
acquired more of the larger patented homesteads, enlarged homesteads,
and stock-raising homesteads than the Spanish-American applicants.
Twice the number of late-arriving Anglo Americans (870) received patents on the large stock-raising homesteads in comparison with the 439
Spanish-American recipients (Appendixes E, F).

Previously settled parcels of land in the Río Arriba could be claimed as
small holding claims (SHCs) under the Pre-emption Act of 1841 and later

as private land claims (PLCs) under the Court of Private Land Claims Act of 1891. The Private Land Claims Act enabled Spanish-American claimants who had possessed land for more than twenty years prior to the official survey of a township to receive a free patent of up to 160 acres. If desired, settlers on preempted land could include that land in their applications for homesteads. Many Spanish-American landholders, however, filed PLCs or SHCs rather than choosing to apply for homesteads or to pursue claims to alleged Spanish or Mexican land grants. For example, in the case of the rejected Vallecito land-grant claim, thirteen Spanish-American claimants were given titles to their small landholdings as homesteads.[18] The same occurred in regard to the settlements on the rejected Town of El Rito land-grant claim. Here, the U.S. government honored the ownership of the small individual tracts by allowing them to be restored to public entry and then providing perfected titles to the claimants.[19] Consequently, these maneuvers contributed to a sizable number of rather small Spanish-American homesteads, thereby lowering the average size of patented Spanish-surname homesteads (Appendix E).

Although some of these homesteads turned out later to be within the boundaries of national forests established in the Río Arriba, the U.S. government allowed them to remain. In addition, settlers were allowed to apply for homesteads within designated areas of the national forests when they were reopened for public entry, but this policy was terminated by 1930. Homesteads were found even within the patented Juan José Lobato Grant. When finally patented in 1902 for 205,616 acres, it was discovered there were thirteen Spanish-American homesteads, amounting to 1,857 acres, located within its boundaries. The homesteaders had settled their land units prior to the filing of the land-grant claim. When the grant's plaintiffs wanted the homesteaders removed, the case was brought before the Court of Private Land Claims, which ruled that the plaintiffs had waited too long to initiate their protest.[20] Again, the U.S. government did not evict Spanish Americans from their landholdings.

Dating back to 1820, public land had been made available in the states and territories for outright purchase or cash entries. Many of the cash entries averaging 160 acres in the Río Arriba involved land in the vicinity of Stanley in southern Santa Fe County, where the settlers were Anglo-American dry farmers largely from western Texas and Oklahoma. They built substantial farmsteads and planted grains, mainly wheat, oats, barley, and sorghum.[21] Many had gone to the Río Arriba with not only financial and material resources but also with experience in commercial agriculture. Most of these cash entries were abandoned or sold, however, by the end of World War II and incorporated into livestock ranches.

There is no doubt that the patented Spanish and Mexican land grants, particularly the community grants, and the Pueblo Indian grants had incorporated the vast majority of the Río Arriba's irrigable bottomland. Squatters outside these land grants also claimed their small irrigable tracts under the Pre-emption Act. On the whole, therefore, the land left for homesteading was found largely on scattered uplands and plateaus, where the possibilities for irrigation were limited because of the lack of surface water. Unlike many parts of the West, railroad companies received no extensive land grants from the public domain in the Río Arriba.

In analyzing local situations at Alire and Cebolla in Río Arriba County, homesteaders sought out first the land in the Río Nutrias and Río Cebolla valleys and then on the fairly level, open uplands. Both Spanish-American and Anglo-American homesteaders settled in these communities, but it was the Spanish Americans who selected first, beginning in the late 1800s, the bottomland along the Río Nutrias as they applied for homesteads or claimed preempted parcels. As natives, they knew the local conditions and not surprisingly claimed what they perceived to be the best land, especially that with a possibility for irrigation. Anglo Americans started in about 1914 to homestead in these two communities, but most arrived in the 1920s and 1930s. Nearly all of them originated from the communities of Panhandle, Perryton, Borger, and Sudan in the Texas Panhandle. Having arrived later, they received larger homesteads, especially the enlarged and stock-raising homesteads, than those acquired by the earlier Spanish-American homesteaders.

In the case of Carson in western Taos County, however, the non-Spanish-surname (Anglo-American) homesteaders settled first the level land on the high plateau and were followed by Spanish-surname (Spanish-American) homesteaders. Most of the fewer than ten Anglo-American families who had started to homestead here in about 1910 originated in Virginia. Several of them had gone to Colorado to be with other Mormons, but they were attracted instead to New Mexico because of the availability of land, which they looked at at least once before they filed homestead entries, some being desert land entries. Having cleared the sagebrush, they quickly sowed crested wheat grass to establish pastures and started to raise pinto beans and corn as commercial crops to sell in Santa Fe and Albuquerque. By damming a large nearby arroyo to hold surface runoff, the Anglo Americans were able to irrigate some of their acreage, especially that with pinto beans. The Spanish-American homesteaders in this case were for the most part the latecomers and claimed the higher elevations of the township where irrigation was more impractical than in the immediate proximity of Carson. When the reservoir's bottom cracked in the drought of 1936 and it was no longer capable of holding water, Carson's residents started to leave and others left later to get jobs associated with the outbreak of World War II.[22] This home-steaded area was gradually abandoned, a process that was underway in other areas that were homesteaded in the Río Arriba, other parts of New Mexico, and the rest of the country. The vignette here of Carson illustrates the fact that Anglo Americans found, too, that the Río Arriba presented a difficult challenge for economic survival.

Because Anglo-American homesteaders arrived later in many locales, they were left the unclaimed land. Consequently, there appeared to be a tendency for the Spanish Americans and the Anglo Americans to settle deliberately apart from each other. Spanish-Americans homesteaders were confronted with something they had not encountered previously—dispersed farmsteads on comparatively large, individually owned land units that were for the most part suitable only for dry farming.[23] This was in sharp contrast to living in communities that had resulted from the development of contiguous, riverine long-lots. On the other hand, the Anglo-American homesteader was accustomed to the isolated farmstead on a large land unit, for he "was primarily a dry farmer, not an irrigationist; he was a seeker after a cash crop, not mere subsistence."[24]

Much of the homesteading in the Río Arriba took place between 1910 and 1929, after the Spanish and Mexican land-grant claims had been adjudicated and New Mexico had become a state. During these two decades, Spanish Americans acquired patents on 1,595 homesteads, 61 percent of their total. Meanwhile, Anglo Americans obtained 1,481 (74 percent) of their patented homesteads, including three-fifths of their total patented acreage under the Stock-Raising Homestead Act. This flurry of homesteading coincided, however, with the relinquishment of many homesteads. Approximately 70 percent of the unpatented acreage for both the Spanish Americans (301,055 acres) and the Anglo Americans (622,037 acres) was recorded in these two decades (Appendixes E, F). Homesteading in the Río Arriba reflected what was happening in much of New Mexico and the Southwest, one of the last parts of the country to attract homesteaders. Of the 1,493,000 homesteads patented nationally between 1868 and 1935, one-fourth of them were settled between 1910 and 1919, after the enactment of the Enlarged Homestead Act and the Stock-Raising Homestead Act.[25]

By World War II, homesteading was no longer important in alienating land from the Río Arriba's public domain. With the enactment of the Taylor Grazing Act in 1934, the remaining public grasslands, including many unpatented homesteads, were organized into grazing districts where permits were required to prevent overgrazing. This policy curtailed homesteading, much like the fencing of homesteads had curtailed the open range. After the war, land opened to homesteading was placed under the jurisdiction of the newly established Bureau of Land Management, which consolidated the functions of the General Land Office and the Grazing Service.

Allegations that some Anglo Americans had arranged bogus or spurious entries by having their ranchhands or dummy entrymen file claims in order to obtain additional land are probably true. Furthermore, some allegedly used illegal commutation practices to increase the sizes of their landholdings and for land speculation. These practices, however, may not have been limited only to Anglo Americans. If impropriety existed, it occurred not only in the Río Arriba but evidently in all frontier areas where there was homesteading.[26] To investigate the extent of fraudulent behavior in the Río Arriba is beyond the scope of this study. It is known, however, that Spanish Americans made nearly 4,300 homestead entries and received patents for 60 percent of them—what they did with their homesteads is another matter.

Moreover, U.S. land policies had accommodated the agricultural intentions of many Spanish-American and Anglo-American homesteaders in the Río Arriba. The Spanish Americans were from the region's small, densely populated communities whereas the Anglo Americans represented an intrusion by outsiders who undoubtedly instilled the same feeling among the native-born residents that the Pueblos must have had when the Spaniards used their policies to organize and settle the region. Similarly, Anglo-American land policies, many like those of the Spaniards, were thrust upon the Río Arriba. Spanish-American villagers took advantage of the U.S. land policies despite the fact that in order to do so, they had to adapt to a dispersed settlement pattern that necessitated their residing on relatively large land units, mostly without irrigable acreage and separated from nearby neighbors.[27] This was accomplished by their understanding of the legal procedures, dispelling any notion that the Spanish Americans were a passive people. Whether Spanish American or Anglo American, homesteaders everywhere, as historian Paul W. Gates acknowledged, were left generally the less desirable portions of the public domain.[28] This was especially true in the Río Arriba, where homesteading was the final means in a long process by which Spanish Americans were able to obtain land under governmental policies and to reinforce their rural presence.

PART TWO

A History of Economic Survival

A Region of Self-sufficiency, 1600–1930

5

Although Spanish Americans had taken the opportunities to acquire land under various governmental policies and from the Pueblo Indians by questionable encroachment, their land units were used largely for subsistence agriculture, which long characterized the Río Arriba and persisted into the Depression of the 1930s. Much of the rest of the country during the late 1800s and early 1900s was developing commercial agricultural practices on larger and larger farms. Spanish Americans found themselves unable to compete in this type of economic development and remained comparatively backward. Most fashioned and adjusted their customs and livelihoods to enable themselves to remain in the Río Arriba. Others out-migrated to surrounding areas, which served temporarily as safety valves and alleviated somewhat the region's problems due largely to the shortages of irrigable land and an increasing rate of population growth.

These migrations, which had begun in earnest in the 1820s, led to the establishment of Spanish-American agricultural communities along the eastern flank of the Sangre de Cristo Mountains, particularly in the upper Mora River Valley and on the eastern plains, especially where the Mexican government bestowed a number of outlying land grants during the 1830s and 1840s. The settlers originated largely in the Las Trampas–Chamisal–Santa Bárbara area on the western flank of the Sangre de Cristo Mountains and the Alcalde–Velarde–Embudo area along the Río Grande. In addition, San Luis, Chama, San Francisco, and several other communities were founded during the early 1850s in the nearby San Luis Valley of Colorado by families who had migrated from the Taos–Arroyo

Seco–Arroyo Hondo, Chamita–San Juan, and Ojo Caliente–El Rito areas. Other small Spanish-American villages, such as Conejos, were founded at the same time on the western side of the San Luis Valley by settlers mainly from the lower Río Chama Valley. More settlers from the Río Arriba settled in the San Luis Valley in the 1860s. Meanwhile, the Río Chama Valley became the source of further out-migration by Spanish Americans who, in this case, moved to the San Juan River Valley in northwestern New Mexico and southwestern Colorado. They were either poor or landless or both, and in some cases they were probably indebted peons who wanted to escape from their financial obligations.[1] In his in-depth analysis of the region's population, geographer Richard Nostrand found that by 1900 the Río Arriba, which had an estimated 40,000 Spanish Americans, had been the major source of Spanish Americans living in Colorado.[2]

Despite the fact that Spanish Americans had in the meantime acquired patented homesteads, most continued to live on small land units found within both the rejected and patented Spanish and Mexican land grants and the Pueblo Indian grants. Like Anglo Americans, many Spanish Americans who had acquired homesteads relinquished or abandoned them, at which time they were returned to the public domain, many end-ing up in the region's newly established national forests. Other Spanish Americans sold their patented homesteads to neighboring cattlemen or to dry-land farmers because they themselves were unfamiliar with dry farming techniques and lacked the capital for the required investments. But Anglo Americans also experienced problems with dry farming, in-cluding those Texans and Oklahomans who settled, for instance, in the early 1920s near Cuba in the upper Río Puerco watershed. In this case, "three or four years were sufficient to prove to many of the settlers that dry farming would not succeed on these semi-arid plains, and a majority soon went back to tenant farming or to the oil fields which they had left. The remaining settlers, most of whom had some experience in stockkeep-ing, switched over to cattle raising."[3] Extensive Anglo-American home-steading in eastern and southern New Mexico had closed off the safety or escape valves for Spanish Americans who may have wanted to re-locate. Even then, these areas were suited primarily for dry farming. Located immediately to the west of the Río Arriba were the large Navajo and Jicarilla Apache Indian reservations, established in 1868 and 1887, respectively. Spanish Americans had, therefore, become stymied in acquir-ing suitable land while economic intimidation and domination were beginning to engulf them.

Partible inheritance had become by the late 1800s another solution for the Spanish Americans to cope with the growing shortage of especially irrigable land within the Río Arriba. It is not known for sure when partible inheritance, the parents' custom of bequeathing land equally to all children, became a common practice in the Río Arriba. Historian Lynn Perrigo maintains that the Mexican government enacted legislation that made primogeniture illegal and instituted the practice of dividing equally the deceased parents' cropland among all the children.[4] This implies that primogeniture may have been practiced earlier under Spanish colonial rule. Anthropologist Nancie González suggests that the enactment of the Mexican law was coincidental with the Río Arriba's increased population pressures on irrigable farmlands. This contention is supported by economic historians Gary Libecap and George Alter, who maintain that population pressure appeared in the mid-1800s.[5] Many Spanish Americans, succumbing to this pressure, sought irrigable plots within the Pueblo Indian grants. Other researchers argue that equal inheritance of land was found during the Spanish colonial period. If so, it appears that it was not used extensively because of the availability of land in the public domain. It is true that antecedents for this practice were present in southern Spain, especially in the provinces of Castilla La Nueva and Andalucía, sources of much of the immigration to New Spain.[6]

Inheritance practices in colonial New Mexico became actually a matter of custom and convenience rather than civil law primarily because probate courts and lawyers were not readily available either to execute or enforce laws until the introduction of the American legal system. If a will had been left, the local *alcalde* would normally divide the property as stated. Even during the territorial years, custom prevailed when Spanish Americans continued to honor verbal agreements, frequently to avoid the cost of written wills. Generally, these verbal agreements were not contested in the disposition of the estates. After the land had been subdivided, it was common for the new owners not to receive deeds and the new parcels were not recorded with a governmental agency. If there were deeds, they were usually kept by the owners and not recorded either.[7]

Parents, on occasion, divided their land prior to their deaths because they wanted their children to have land "to enjoy." Sons could, therefore, receive land upon marriage to support their families and daughters as part of their dowries. Not every village and not all farmers adhered to the practice of equal descent among children. For example, only sons inherited land in Cundiyó.[8] In other cases, the oldest son and especially the children who remained the longest with their parents received larger parcels than their siblings.

Partible inheritance was applied mostly to the division of irrigable land. Therefore, long-lots were divided lengthwise so that each parcel retained a similar shape, extending from an irrigation ditch to the river. After one generation, a long-lot of 100 *varas* theoretically could have become four or five individual land units if siblings did not sell out to one another upon inheriting their shares. There is no doubt that this custom intensified the ribbon-shaped pattern of land units and led to more densely populated communities.[9] Some heirs did sell, but many did not either because they could not acquire irrigable land elsewhere or for emotional and personal reasons. Many heirs also preferred to remain within their own villages because there were very few economic opportunities in the region. Like other peasantries, the Spanish Americans' possession of land provided them with a sense of security, giving them assurances that they could eke out a living. These conveyances of land allowed, too, for relatively low or no capital entry into agriculture and the continued dependence upon land. On the other hand, it thwarted the expansion of farms, out-migration of youth, and accumulation of wealth.

This type of inheritance combined with the settlers' acquisitions of acreages here and there produced many small and fragmented farm units. For instance, in 1928, the cultivated portions of nearly one thousand parcels ranged in size from 0.1 acre to 24.5 acres in two Spanish-American communities located within the San Juan and Taos Pueblo Indian grants. Half the farmers owned only one parcel, averaging 7.9 acres, of which 2.3 acres were in alfalfa, 3.4 acres were in cultivated crops, and the remaining 2.2 acres were arid and used for the farmsteads. One-fourth of the landowners owned two parcels and the other quarter owned between three and six parcels.[10] It must be remembered that many of these parcels had not gone through generations of subdivision as they had been acquired largely in the late 1800s. If they had, the parcels would have been much smaller and the farms even more fragmented.

Partible inheritance was used to divide not only land but also other realty and material possessions listed in a person's written or oral *hijuela*, inventory, which was intended to be a will for distributing property and had been witnessed. This extension of egalitarianism led to the division of a deceased person's orchard trees, corrals, and houses.[11] For instance, a woman in northern Santa Fe County inherited in 1883 two parcels of land (one measured 12 *varas*, 9 inches in La Joya and the other measured 9 *varas* in Agua Fría), several *vigas*, ceiling beams, in one room of a house, and fifty-five posts of a corral.[12] Heirs frequently divided houses by *vigas* and on occasion would build interior walls to make several separate units. Elderly Spanish Americans used the *hijuela* into the mid-1900s, mostly to avoid legal expenses.

From the outset of Spanish colonization, Spanish settlers in the Río Arriba were immersed in subsistence agriculture. Even then, production was meager because of internal conditions and the lack of markets. Governor Chacón described in 1803 the situation:

> Agriculture in said Province does not appear in the best state owing to a lack
> of know-how. Nevertheless, the most common grains are sown, like wheat,

corn and barley, and all kind of vegetables in limited quantity, there being no practical way to export them to the provinces because of the great distances intervening between all of them. As a result the majority of its inhabitants are little dedicated to farming, in particular the Spaniards and *castas* who content themselves with sowing and cultivating only what is necessary for their sustenance. [Living] by luck through the scarce years, like the current one, they experience great need which is met by resort to wild plants, roots, milk, beef and mutton. . . .

Although the Province possesses sufficient oxen for farming, what is most in abundance is sheep. Without counting what is consumed locally, there is exported to [Nueva] Vizcaya and the lesser [frontier] presidios from one year to the next from twenty-five to twenty-six thousand head of sheep. Of swine there exists no great number because the natives of this country are more accustomed to the use of fat from beef than from hogs, and there is no one dedicated to the manufacture of soap. The raising of horses and mules is little encouraged because of the continual raids by the enemy [Indians]. But annually more than 600 animals of each kind are brought in from the Sonora and Vizcaya, not counting the herds of mustangs (*mesteñada*), which the citizenry are in the habit of hunting whenever they go out on the frontier.[13]

Similar observations of the region's submarginal economic conditions were made periodically by other Spaniards and Anglo Americans alike.[14]

Advances in agricultural technology lagged in the Río Arriba, where Spanish Americans continued to use only simple, familiar, and affordable methods and equipment on their small acreages, restricting their agricultural production. Initially, some colonists on the community grants were provided limited assistance in the form of tools, seed, and livestock from Mexican sources in order to entice them and make them independent of the Pueblos. Although horses were sent to aid New Mexican settlers as late as 1780, much of this support was discontinued by the mid-1700s because of the cost.[15] Beginning in the 1760s, Spain's interests were diverted to California and Louisiana, leaving the New Mexicans totally dependent upon themselves. When Zebulon Pike passed through the Río Arriba in 1807, he found the New Mexicans were "a century behind us in the art of cultivation . . . I have seen them frequently breaking up whole fields with a hoe."[16] Wooden hoes, shovels, and plows persisted in use into the 1900s on the small irrigable tracts, which for the most part were tilled every year without crop rotation, leading to their decreased fertility. Except for a milch cow or two, many landowners did not own draft animals that could have pulled plows or barnyard animals that could have produced manure for fertilizing the fields. Meanwhile, wheat was cut by scythes, threshed by treading animals, and ground by waterwheels. Diets depended largely upon the hand cultivation and harvests of chile peppers, beans (*frijoles*), onions, corn to make tortillas (flat cakes) and *atole* (porridge), wheat for bread, and orchard fruits (especially peaches and plums). These foodstuffs were supplemented by cheese made from cow or goat milk, and mutton, salted beef, and sometimes buffalo jerky (*charqui*) obtained largely by trade.[17]

Mechanization made little headway in this old agricultural region as the small subsistence farms allowed for no accumulation of capital needed to expand agriculture by the introduction of new and efficient machinery. Improved farm technology, too, was geared toward production on large-scale farms, not long-lots, whose expansion was limited by a locale's physical environment. Less than 2 percent of New Mexico's total value of machinery was found in the 1880s in Santa Fe, Taos, and Río Arriba counties. In fact, these three counties had only 13 percent of the territory's total value of farmland, houses, and improvements. Río Arriba County had the lowest value of all counties. What is also revealing in 1900 about Río Arriba agriculture is that 40 percent of the reported farms were less than 10 acres.[18]

Spanish colonists had introduced livestock, which were quickly sought by nomadic Indians (Apaches, Comanches, Navajos, and Utes) to supplement or sustain their new life-styles. This is particularly true of the horse, which was adopted, for instance, by the Comanches and Utes, who established equestrian life-styles and their own ranges.[19] Numerous accounts reveal that Indian raids claimed many sheep, which were stolen and driven off or slaughtered on the range. Comanches alone stole three hundred head of livestock, mostly sheep, and killed many more in one raid near Albuquerque in 1774. Within one three-month period in the late 1700s, Indians reportedly took several thousand head of livestock from the Río Arriba. These losses contributed to sheep becoming so scarce that occasionally governmental decrees were issued to prohibit the province's sheep and wool from being exported.[20]

Indian hostilities can be attributed also to the Spanish policy of protecting the Pueblos from their adversaries, the Plains Indians, and Spanish decrees (*bandos*) prohibiting or limiting trade and contact between them. By the 1740s, raids had started to replace trade. The Spanish civilian militia, later with the assistance of Pueblo auxiliaries, expended considerable time and effort in making punitive expeditions and defending against these raids, leaving their fields sometimes unattended for days. Frequently, crops were destroyed or stolen and cultivable land was left idle. Fray Juan Agustín de Morfi reported in 1782 that land had been left fallow near both Taos and Albuquerque because of the lack of draft animals and Indian terror.[21] The Peñasco Valley in southern Taos County was frequently raided, resulting in periodic abandonment for years. Approximately three thousand Comanches swept in 1760 through the Taos Valley, attacking both the Taos Pueblos and Spanish settlers, capturing fifty Spanish women and children and destroying property.[22] After several attempts, the Comanches finally agreed in 1786 to a peace plan, assuring New Mexico's Spanish settlers that they would no longer inflict injury and damage upon them. Both parties honored this peace, which also allied them against the remaining marauding Indians, who continued their attacks into the 1830s and 1840s.[23]

When the U.S. government took control of New Mexico, it found that the Mexicans, after their separation from Spain in 1821, had expended little military effort against raiding Indians. In fact, Mexico had simply informed the province's residents that they were to defend themselves and would lose their land if they left it for a lengthy period of time. In contrast, the U.S. military spent millions of dollars from the late 1840s through the 1860s to subdue the raiding Indians (Figure 17). Even then, there were in the 1850s occasional land abandonment and idle fields in the Taos Valley and the lower Río Chama Valley, for example. Because many of these raids were for many years along the region's periphery, they in essence tended to keep the Spanish settlers in the Río Arriba.

Spain did not emphasize the development of commercial agriculture in the Río Arriba. The feudalistic *encomiendas* and even the community land grants were not intended to produce surpluses that would have promoted strong economic development.[24] Both the Spanish and Mexican officials ranked political and strategic considerations above economic development. They perceived New Mexico as merely a buffer against an advancing American frontier. Moreover, neither the Río Arriba's nor New Mexico's population was large enough to provide thriving farm markets. The territory's non-Indian population of only 3,000 in 1750 and 19,000 in 1800 had increased by 1850 to more than 60,000, but they were largely agricultural residents. Although the territory's population had increased to 92,000 by 1870 and to 195,000 by 1900 with the influx of homesteaders, the only urban markets were Albuquerque, founded in 1706, and Santa Fe, which had in 1900 a total population of approximately 12,000.[25] No sizable middle class had developed that possessed disposable income to buy large amounts of regional farm products. Historian David J. Weber agrees that the lack of economic development was because "New Mexico was also afflicted by the same problem that affected Spain and all of her colonies—inexperience in business and lack of a strong middle class."[26]

Largely in collaboration with the Mexican merchants of Chihuahua, Spain openly discouraged trade for its colonists in the Río Arriba. Its restrictions had stultifying effects on economic growth. For example, New Mexicans were disallowed, starting in the 1760s, external markets for their small quantities of *punche,* a poor-grade tobacco. Proclamations also discouraged or prohibited trade with the Indians, such as in 1712, when settlers were banned from contacting them to trade goods, and in

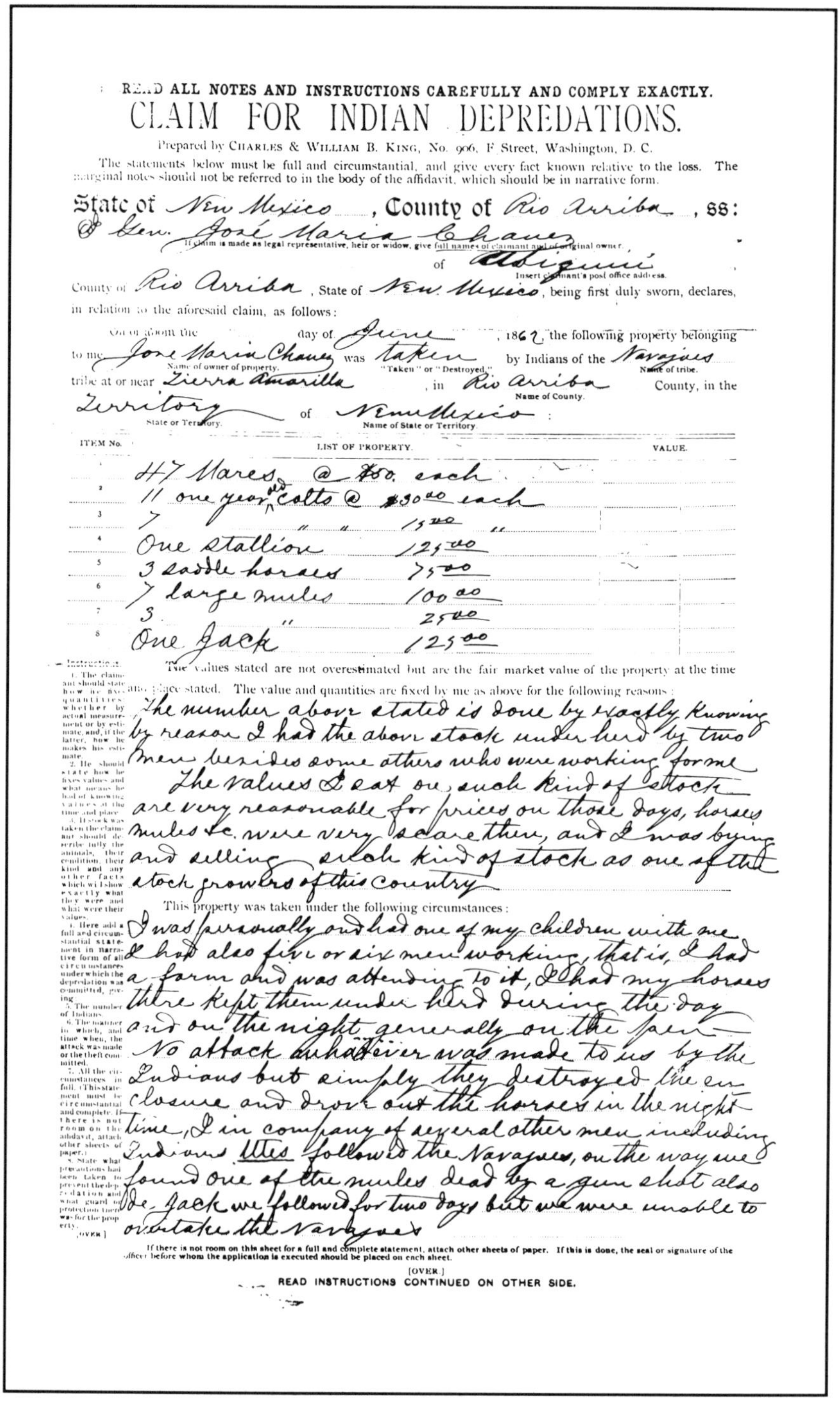

READ ALL NOTES AND INSTRUCTIONS CAREFULLY AND COMPLY EXACTLY.

CLAIM FOR INDIAN DEPREDATIONS.

Prepared by CHARLES & WILLIAM B. KING, No. 906, F Street, Washington, D. C.

The statements below must be full and circumstantial, and give every fact known relative to the loss. The marginal notes should not be referred to in the body of the affidavit, which should be in narrative form.

State of New Mexico, County of Rio Arriba, ss:

I Gen. José Maria Chaves
(If claim is made as legal representative, heir or widow, give full names of claimant and of original owner.)
of Abiquiu
(Insert claimant's post office address.)
County of Rio Arriba, State of New Mexico, being first duly sworn, declares, in relation to the aforesaid claim, as follows:

On or about the day of June, 1862 the following property belonging to me Jose Maria Chaves (Name of owner of property.) was taken ("Taken" or "Destroyed.") by Indians of the Navajoes (Name of tribe.) tribe at or near Tierra Amarilla, in Rio Arriba (Name of County.) County, in the Territory (State or Territory.) of New Mexico (Name of State or Territory.):

ITEM No.	LIST OF PROPERTY.	VALUE.
1	47 Mares @ $50. each	
2	11 one year old colts @ $30.00 each	
3	7 " " 15.00 "	
4	One stallion 125.00	
5	3 saddle horses 75.00	
6	7 large mules 100.00	
7	3 " 25.00	
8	One Jack 125.00	

Instructions.

1. The claimant should state how he fixes quantities: whether by actual measurement or by estimate, and, if the latter, how he makes his estimate.
2. He should state how he fixes values and what means he had of knowing values at the time and place.
3. If stock was taken the claimant should describe fully the animals, their condition, their kind and any other facts which will show exactly what they were and what were their values.
4. Here add a full and circumstantial statement in narrative form of all circumstances under which the depredation was committed, giving:
5. The number of Indians.
6. The manner in which, and time when, the attack was made or the theft committed.
7. All the circumstances in full. (This statement must be circumstantial and complete. If there is not room on the affidavit, attach other sheets of paper.)
8. State what precautions had been taken to prevent the depredation and what guard or protection there was for the property.

[OVER.]

The values stated are not overestimated but are the fair market value of the property at the time and place stated. The value and quantities are fixed by me as above for the following reasons:

The number above stated is done by exactly knowing by reason I had the above stock under herd by two men besides some others who were working for me.
The values I sat on such kind of stock are very reasonable for prices on those days, horses mules &c. were very scare then, and I was buying and selling such kind of stock as one of the stock growers of this country.

This property was taken under the following circumstances:

I was personally and had one of my children with me. I had also five or six men working, that is, I had a farm and was attending to it, I had my horses there kept them under herd during the day and on the night generally on the pen. No attack whatever was made to us by the Indians but simply they destroyed the enclosure and drove out the horses in the night time, I in company of several other men including Indians Utes followed the Navajoes, on the way we found one of the mules dead by a gun shot also de Jack we followed for two days but we were unable to overtake the Navajoes.

If there is not room on this sheet for a full and complete statement, attach other sheets of paper. If this is done, the seal or signature of the officer before whom the application is executed should be placed on each sheet.

[OVER.]

READ INSTRUCTIONS CONTINUED ON OTHER SIDE.

FIGURE 17

Many landowners in the Río Arriba filed claims for their losses resulting from Indian depredations.

Source: Albert B. Fall Collection, Huntington Library, San Marino, California.

the mid-1700s, when a decree forbade the trading of horses or mules to the Indians.[27] Furthermore, Spanish settlers were forbidden, beginning in 1723, to trade with Louisiana's French traders, who had started to pursue, with their government's support, trade with Indians in Texas. Despite the ongoing violence on the plains to the east of the Río Arriba, limited contraband trade, largely French goods exchanged for Mexican silver, was carried on between Louisiana and Santa Fe. Spain continued to reject French overtures, and much of this trade ended before France ceded Louisiana to Spain in 1763.[28]

Meanwhile, fairs, *rescates,* had developed before 1750 and continued for many years at Taos and Abiquiú, where Indians, especially Comanches and Utes, came to barter their buffalo, elk, and deer hides, chamois, meat, and captives (for use in Mexican mining camps) in exchange largely for regionally-produced corn flour, woven cotton, and wool blankets. These items were supplied mostly by the Pueblos. Spanish settlers had actually little to offer in this barter economy (*cambalache*) except livestock, especially small numbers of horses, trinkets, wild piñon nuts, and *punche.*[29]

Taos had also become in the early 1800s a focal point for the fur trade in the southern Rocky Mountains, but both the trapping and the trading were dominated by a few Anglo Americans along with several French traders, some of whom had illegal trade connections outside of New Mexico. Several French traders were arrested, as late as 1817, for entering New Mexico, where their acquired furs and other items were confiscated. Interestingly enough, the Spaniards and Mexicans showed no appreciable interest in becoming involved in this trade. As Weber has concluded, "there is, perhaps, good reason for attributing Spanish disinterest in the fur trade to ignorance. Even in 1831, during the heyday of Anglo trapping in the Southwest, Antonio Barreiro, a New Mexican, criticized Mexico's failure to utilize its fur resources 'from which great benefits might be derived if the country were more enlightened.' But causation is usually a complex matter; lack of wisdom does not sufficiently explain Spain's failure to develop an important commerce in furs."[30]

Mining within the Río Arriba provided virtually no opportunities for Spanish Americans to establish agricultural markets or for employment. Although early accounts indicated the presence of different mineral resources, Fray Gerónimo de Zárate Salmerón claimed in the 1620s that "the Spaniards that are there are too poor in capital to work the deposits, and are of less spirit: enemies to work of any sort."[31] An 1827 census report pointed out that mines were not being worked because of the "absence of capable men."[32] Gold was mined largely in the Ortiz Mountains south of Santa Fe, and some copper, silver, and coal were also mined elsewhere in the region during the 1800s. The few mines that were

FIGURE 18

*The Taos Valley was referred to as the "breadbasket" of the Río Arriba. This flour
mill was built in the late 1800s at Cañoncito, Taos County.* Photo: *December
1941.*

Source: National Archives, Washington, D.C.

opened were in most cases abandoned quickly because of the lack of
good ores and Indian raids.

In addition, only small numbers of American troops were stationed at
New Mexico's military posts, which could have served as markets for
agricultural products. Of the territory's twenty-two U.S. military posts,
only three were located in the Río Arriba: Fort Lowell (1866–1869), near
Tierra Amarilla; Fort Fernando de Taos or Cantonment Burgwin (1852–
1860), near Taos; and Santa Fe's Fort Marcy (1846–1894).[33] As in the
earlier case, when Santa Fe's *presidio* was under Spanish and Mexican
rule, Fort Marcy, in particular, provided limited opportunities for a small
number of nearby Spanish-American farmers to sell fruit, meat, cheese,
wheat flour, whisky, grain, native grass hay, and wood (Figure 18). A
few of the region's Spanish-American farmers sold similar items to Fort
Union (1851–1891), located east of the Sangre de Cristo Mountains in
adjacent Mora County near Watrous. But Fort Union, like the other posts

in New Mexico, was supplied largely by its surrounding farmers and ranchers.

Aside from the internal problems of establishing economic opportunities, the distance from Santa Fe to northern Mexico's largest mining and distribution center, Chihuahua, other mining centers such as Durango, Zacatecas, and Querétero, Mexico City, and later California precluded transporting bulky, low-value, perishable farm products. At the outset of colonization, Franciscans operated mission-supply caravans (*cuadrillas de carros*) that traveled from Mexico City to several northern destinations, including the Río Arriba.[34] Dispatched every three years during the 1600s and accompanied by a small military force, a wagon train would take about three or four months to cover the difficult trip of more than twelve hundred miles from Mexico City to isolated Santa Fe. The wagons were

> of heavy construction, each capable of carrying two tons of cargo and, when fully laden, requiring a team of eight mules. . . . Certain other specifications suggest the rugged nature of the long, unimproved road. . . . Each group of eight wagons was required to carry sixteen spare axles, 150 extra spokes, twenty-four reserve tires, five hundred pounds of lubricating tallow, twenty-four pounds of cord for repairing the cover and cargo wrappings, and an assortment of nails, bolts, washers, harping pins, cleats, linch pins, and ribs. Among the required tools for each trip were hammers, sledges, adzes, axes, picks, and crowbars.[35]

Private contractors also began to operate caravans to supply the *presidios* and missions in northern New Spain.

These caravans were replaced gradually after the reconquest by commercial caravans (*conductas*), which involved a few of New Mexico's merchants and ranchers. Several of them originated in the Río Arriba and had the fairs in Chihuahua and northern Mexican mining communities as their destinations. The round trip took up to five months, and the caravans increasingly depended upon pack horses and burros and less upon ox- or mule-drawn carts (*carretas*).[36] To prevent Indian raids, small escorts of Spanish soldiers would occasionally join the caravans, which, in addition to sheep and Indian slaves for mine labor, carried antelope skins, buffalo robes, piñon nuts, woolen blankets (made by the Pueblos), chile, salt, and jerked meat. These goods were exchanged for comparatively costly items such as cloth, shoes, sugar, tools, ammunition, mules, horses, and some gold and silver specie and bullion.[37]

Mexico quickly liberalized the trade constraints that Spain had imposed upon New Mexico. Its policies led in the 1820s to the rapid development of the Santa Fe Trail trade, which was initiated by Anglo Americans. This trade between Kansas City, Missouri, and Santa Fe, a distance of approximately eight hundred miles, was developed despite the

Mexican government's imposition of high import tariffs and at first no provisions by either government to provide military protection. Josiah Gregg, a trader, estimated that on average about 150 men were employed annually in the caravans that operated between 1822 and 1843. Only 50 men were reportedly employed in the caravans of 1823 and 1829 and a high of 350 men in the caravan of 1843. In addition, the number of proprietors peaked at 90 in 1825 and dropped to 30 in 1843, of which the majority were New Mexicans.[38] Historians Connor and Skaggs contend that Gregg's "figures are considerably lower than the actual number, perhaps half too low."[39] If so, this would put the total number of drovers, teamsters, and proprietors during the period of 1822 to 1843 at not much more than probably 700 in the best years, but averaging about 350 men in the other years. Probably not all of these men were from New Mexico or the Río Arriba.

At first, buffalo rugs, beaver pelts, wool, mules, and horses (mostly from Mexico and California) to be used as pack and draft animals, and some silver and gold specie and bullion, were sent from Santa Fe to Missouri. Freighters quickly realized, however, that the Plains Indians could stampede and steal the mules and horses. Consequently, Missourians turned to the South as a source of their draft mules, and slower ox-drawn wagons gradually replaced the pack-animal trains on the Santa Fe Trail. Oxen could also pull very heavy loads.[40] American traders sent westward largely dry goods, hardware, and other manufactured items. Because of the shortage of cash in New Mexico and the abundance of gold and silver specie and bullion in northern Mexico, traders realized as early as 1824 that their profits could be maximized by taking a large share of their merchandise beyond Santa Fe southward down the Camino Real to the Mexican cities, especially Chihuahua. Connors and Skaggs found that "businessmen from Missouri obviously and understandably preferred to consummate sales in cash, which in northern Mexico meant gold dust, silver bullion, or intrinsic coins."[41]

Chihuahua, therefore, became by the early 1830s the ultimate destination for many of the traders. According to Gregg's data, more than 40 percent of the Santa Fe Trail's merchandise in terms of value after 1824 ended up in Chihuahua. By 1840, this figure was greater than 50 percent.[42] When President Antonio López de Santa Anna placed in 1843 an embargo on this trade, it virtually halted much of the Santa Fe Trail trade before the Mexican War (1846–1848). A limited amount of trade continued until 1860 between Missouri and New Mexico, but it was plagued by Indian raids and low profits. Eventually, the railroad put an end to all trade moving over trails.

Aside from the employment of several hundred men as traders and teamsters and the limited economic ripples that the trade had upon the immediate environs of Santa Fe, the rest of the Río Arriba experienced little, if any, economic growth as a result of the Santa Fe Trail trade. A small number of Spanish Americans may have been able to move into an emerging middle class.[43] Again, however, very few of the Río Arriba's subsistence farmers could penetrate this trade network, but many of them had been made aware of Anglo-American merchandise, capitalism, and economic domination.[44] This breakthrough had gone far in removing the region from cultural isolation.

But the region still had few economic opportunities as exemplified by the fact that no railroad entered New Mexico until 1879. Even then, Santa Fe, once the region's commercial hub, had no connection to a railroad until a freight spur of the Atchinson, Topeka and Santa Fe Railway linked it later to the main route that passed instead through Albuquerque. Connor and Skaggs claim that "by the time the railroad finally approached the community of Santa Fe, corporate officials had concluded that the sleepy town of six-thousand souls was hardly worth their attention or their firm's investment."[45] It is true that the regional Denver and Río Grande Railway entered Santa Fe in 1886, but overall the city had become relatively unimportant in the emergence of a new and different economic network. Then, too, the Río Arriba's crude internal transportation system of rough trails and cart roads did not foster economic development.[46]

Meanwhile, livestock, especially sheep, had long been able to overcome many of the Río Arriba's difficulties associated with distance and isolation because of their ability to transport themselves on the hoof long distances to markets. From the early 1700s, droves of sheep (*carneradas*), often totaling between twenty to twenty-five thousand per year, were trailed to the mining areas in northern Mexico. Contrary to other bans, New Mexico's colonial government openly encouraged sheep production, which became the province's leading industry by 1750. Although the sheep, *churros,* were small degenerates of Spain's common sheep, they provided tasty meat and long, coarse wool suitable for hand spinning and weaving. They were prolific and especially capable of withstanding long drives and arid conditions. Their importance in the livelihoods of the Río Arriba's residents is reflected in the New Mexico governors' occasional bans or limits placed upon their exportation in order to prevent the depletion of breeding stock and to satisfy domestic needs.[47] These Mexican markets for sheep ended with the Mexican War. But before the Mexican era was over, trade had been opened between Santa Fe and Los Angeles by using the Old Spanish Trail. Woolen blankets and beaver pelts were exchanged in Los Angeles for mules and horses, which were driven to New Mexico, and some entered into the Santa Fe Trail trade.[48] Sheep were, however, insignificant in this trade.

New Mexico's sheep industry grew dramatically after the United States acquired the Southwest and after the California gold rush created a demand for meat. Partially in response to the new demands, the territory's number of sheep doubled in the 1850s, but most of this growth took place outside the Río Arriba. An analysis of government ledgers that recorded external sheep sales indicates this trade was monopolized by a small number of individuals, a few Spanish-American *ricos* and later several Anglo-American merchants.[49] They employed local men as drovers and often continued the Spanish *partido* system, which had been a widespread practice in New Mexico since the early 1700s. Under this system, Spanish-American herders, many very poor and landless, contracted with large sheepmen to raise sheep in exchange for a share of the lambs and the possibility of creating or enlarging their own flocks. "These sheep were put out on shares to *partidarios*. A *partidario* received a flock, or *partida* . . . consisting mostly of ewes and a few breeding rams. [His] . . . contract with a *rico* essentially required him to return between ten and twenty per cent of each year's increment in sheep and the same amount in wool. Twenty per cent was the general rule. In addition, the original number of sheep had to be repaid to the owner, normally after five years."[50]

Because of Indian raids, disease, and winter storms, *partidarios* commonly lost part of their flocks. Consequently, many of them, especially those who had also pledged their labor to cover default, were placed in perpetual indebtedness to *ricos,* creating in essence a system of peonage. Although a few of the *partidarios* may have resided within the community land grants, it is doubtful that many grant settlers would have allowed their neighbors to have very large *partidas* because of the grants' limited pasturage. Consequently, most *partidarios* grazed their flocks by placing them on the open range or the public domain. As pointed out in Chapter 1, the Spanish colonial government was aware of what land constituted the public domain and what land was privately owned. It ordered as early as 1736, therefore, the termination of herders' encroachment of the open range and the destruction of their temporary structures, corrals, and other improvements.[51] Despite these efforts, *partidarios* often continued to move their flocks from the region's pastures that were already becoming overgrazed to more distant, open, and better pastures, especially on the plains east of the Sangre de Cristo Mountains.

Unlike what was alleged in the adjudication of the land-grant claims and non-Indian private claims within the Pueblo Indian grants when claimants lacked documentation, the *partidarios* and *ricos* were keenly aware of the importance of keeping documents and their rights to resort to the legal system to redress grievances. Historian John Baxter found in his analysis of the *partido* system that "many such contracts survive in writing, an indication of the importance attached to them in an era when paper, ink, and writing skills were rare."[52] He concludes that there were so many disputes between the two parties that their cases resulted in "endless litigation," which "filled New Mexico's court dockets for the next two hundred years."[53] Obviously, the Spanish Americans were not as naive about legal procedures and systems as alleged later in the afore-mentioned land-grant adjudication proceedings.

The Río Arriba's *rancheros* would sell on occasion some of their sheep to the *ricos*, but at low prices because of the lack of competitive markets. These sheep as well as those raised under the *partido* system made up considerable portions of the annual drives to Mexico and later to California. In 1883, Kit Carson was one of the drovers on the Old Spanish Trail, which started at Abiquiú and passed through Colorado and Utah on to Los Angeles and even to Sacramento. An American trader, Francis X. Aubry, and three Spanish-American *ricos*, Judge A. J. Otero, José Francisco Chávez, and Francisco Perea, alone had fifty-five herdsmen drive forty thousand sheep to California in the next year.[54] New Mexico's growing number of sheep used in this trade, however, originated in areas outside the Río Arriba. California's markets declined in the 1860s after the outbreak of the Civil War, when Confederate sympathizers controlled the sheep trails, and competition from within the state and other states lowered prices and offered better breeds. New Mexico's sheep were soon driven to other western states, but these drives ended with the closing of the open range by the fencing of homesteads, states passing preventive disease laws, and shrinking markets. Eventually, the railroads, too, made the long drives obsolete.[55]

Spanish officials early on as well as Americans later took note of problems with New Mexico's livestock industry. Because the territory was long isolated from the sheep-rearing areas of New England and the Middle West, which had better breeds, and because of poor breeding practices locally, the *churros* had become entrenched as the mainstay of the livestock industry. As Baxter pointed out, any sizable investment to upgrade these sheep would have been risky because of unfavorable environmental conditions such as severe drought and winter storms as well as Indian raids and diseases. In fact, Spanish governor de Chacón called in 1802 for a reduction in the prevalence of livestock diseases.[56] Furthermore, *partidarios* surely had no incentives to upgrade their contracted sheep. Consequently, William W. H. Davis wrote in 1856 that "no branch of industry in New Mexico has been more neglected than that of agriculture . . . It has been pursued merely as the means of living, and no effort has been made to add science to culture in the introduction of an improved mode of husbandry."[57] Anglo Americans later upgraded the territory's sheep industry by cross breeding the *churros* with larger sheep, especially the French merino, to produce heavier carcasses and better fleeces.

Efforts by New Mexicans to raise other marketable livestock, especially horses, were not pursued largely because they were prized bounty in Indian raids and because of a lack of markets. Interestingly enough, Pedro Bautista Pino, New Mexico's delegate to Spain's Cortes (legislature), recommended in 1810 that New Mexicans domesticate the buffalo and have its dried meat marketed in the Caribbean and its wool made into cloth.[58] His advice was ignored.

Most Spanish Americans preferred sheep to cattle because they could be herded and protected easier than the more far-ranging cattle; required less fodder in the winter, as five sheep can be sustained for every one cow (an important factor considering the small land units); and provided meat as well as wool for blankets and clothing. Anglo Americans tended, on the other hand, to prefer cattle, resulting in New Mexico's number of cattle being increased substantially at the expense of sheep during the late 1800s and early 1900s.[59] In attempts to expand their livestock operations in the face of diminished ranges because of homesteading, Spanish Americans placed more livestock on nearby pastures. They sometimes burned the foothills in the spring to promote the growth of grass and to improve the carrying capacities, ranging on average from 40 to 60 acres per cow yearlong. Upland pastures, in many cases, had even lower carrying capacities, with averages up to 80 to 100 acres per cow yearlong. Evidence of overstocking and overgrazing was apparent by the 1880s, when gullying and erosion became commonplace.[60] Droughts became omnipresent. Unlike what the promotional literature described, E. H. Ruffner, an army engineer, observed in 1876 that "there is no grass except during the few weeks succeeding an unusually protracted rainy season. Cattle learn to eat anything that is green, and the sight of the goat eating the thorny stems of the tall cactus is no more striking to the stranger than to see the gaunt ox feeding on the running pine and the dwarf cedar. Sheep and cattle are driven from this region to the 'Conejos Country' [southern Colorado], full sixty miles, to pasture and to winter."[61]

Neither the Spanish-American War nor World War I had any significant impact upon boosting the Río Arriba's agricultural economy. Carloads of apples, largely from the Española Valley, and wild piñon nuts were shipped in the 1920s by rail to different destinations in the United States.[62] Hay was sold occasionally to local ranching operations, and fresh vegetables and fruits were sold seasonally by vendors in Albuquerque and Santa Fe. Road improvements led to a greater exchange of farm products. Chile peppers, fruit, and woolen blankets were taken by wagons to Colorado's San Luis Valley, (just north of the New Mexico border), where they were exchanged for beans and potatoes. Standard barter based upon the "value of a peso" given to different items derived from the land (*peso de la tierra*) remained as the region's internal monetary system.[63] Livestock continued to produce the largest amount of external revenue for the region's farmers.

With the growing importance placed nationally upon a cash economy, most of the Spanish-American landowners, and even some Pueblo Indians, had little to offer except themselves as unskilled laborers. Although Spanish Americans had been employed by the region's *ricos,* many started in the late 1800s to seek seasonal wage labor. First, they became members of railroad construction gangs and sawmill crews that cut railroad ties and poles used in trestles and mining props. Others turned to seasonal farm labor in the San Luis Valley, where Anglo Americans had established specialty crop farms.

In the early 1900s, Río Arriba's Spanish-American males traveled farther to work in the mines of Utah, Colorado, and Arizona, logging and sheep camps throughout the western mountain ranges, and sugar beet fields of Colorado's South Platte Valley. Instead of World War I having an impact upon the region's agricultural economy, it created rather a national shortage of cheap seasonal labor, which was filled partially by the Spanish Americans, who were recruited by western mining and agricultural processing companies but who also faced increasing competition from Mexicans.[64] Some found employment locally in Madrid's coal mines (Santa Fe County) and in those near Gallup in western New Mexico. By the late 1920s, two-thirds of the Spanish-American male heads of households had left the Río Arriba for seasonal work and as many as 85 percent had left some villages. In most cases, each worked for four to seven months to earn only $300 to $500 after deductions for room and board. Some of the families supplemented their incomes by traveling and being employed together in the San Luis Valley's potato harvests.[65] The seasonal laborers normally returned before Christmas to spend the mild winters on their small landholdings. Only a small number worked in winter and those who did were employed as members of railroad snow crews. Overall, many Spanish-American farm operators came to rely upon seasonal off-farm employment and left much of the farming, after the spring plowing, to their families. Although a considerable number of Spanish Americans relocated permanently near Colorado's coal mines and beetfields and a smaller number, for example, in more distant locations such as near the steel mills of Detroit, permanent out-migration was limited (Figure 19).[66] For most Spanish Americans, seasonal migration for wages had become what historian Sarah Deutsch has defined as a "study for survival" and a "solution to the problem of increasing population density."[67]

General mercantile stores, saloons, and other commercial businesses, established and operated mostly by Anglo Americans, did not get their

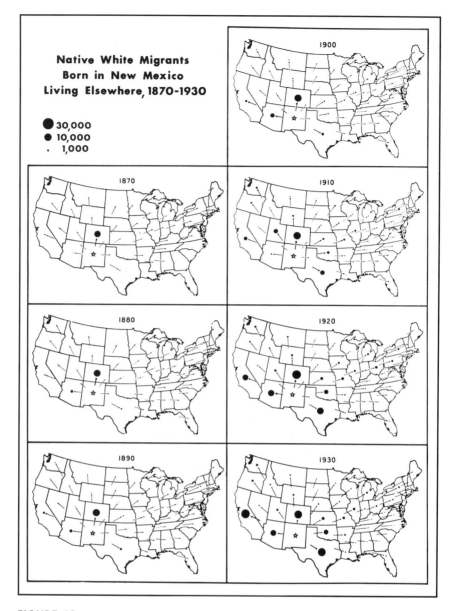

FIGURE 19

Until 1900, Colorado was the major destination for white persons born in New Mexico, including Spanish Americans from the Río Arriba. After 1900, New Mexicans moved to other neighboring states and to California in increasing numbers. Many were Anglo Americans from the dry-farming areas of eastern and southern New Mexico. By 1930, the outward flow was mostly urban bound.

Source: National Archives, USDA, Bureau of Agricultural Economics, Record Group 83, Series 183, 1934, Washington, D.C.

real impetus in the Río Arriba until Spanish Americans became seasonal laborers who returned to spend their earnings, largely by paying off the credit extended to their families during their absences. Out of approximately two hundred commercial businesses in the 1880s in Bernalillo and nearby Albuquerque, only ten of the proprietors had Spanish surnames.[68] As capitalism and credit mounted in the region, barter declined in importance.

Although the Spanish Americans attempted to lift themselves above subsistence livelihoods, indicating a discontent with their situations, many Anglo Americans considered them to be lackadaisical and disinterested in self-improvement, consequently making the Río Arriba an area of inertia and contributing to its regionalism.[69] Spanish Americans, who were often called Mexicans and locally, mestizos, *lobos,* and coyotes (mixed bloods), were supposedly content with "just making a living" and did not put great emphasis upon monetary gains and material wealth. Governor Chacón complained as early as 1802 that "most New Mexicans avoided physical labor whenever possible, planting only enough to sustain themselves from one year to the next."[70] To them, the future seemed not to be as important as the present and they avoided a spirit of economic competition in their family-oriented villages. Anglo Americans contended, therefore, that Spanish-American agricultural production lagged because of the lack of motivation. H. T. Wilson wrote in 1880 that "the average Mexican greaser, or half-breed, is slow, generally lazy, quite ignorant, very superstitious, and non-progressive; and as they can live upon less than any other nationality, they have little ambition to accumulate property or wealth."[71] Their communities remained stagnant and tolerated, if not protected, seemingly strange customs such as those of the Penitentes (discussed in Chapter 8). Charles F. Lummis in his book *The Land of Poco Tiempo* portrayed the residents as "Mexicans; in-bred and isolation-shrunken descendants of the Castilian worldfinders; living almost as much against the house as in it; ignorant as slaves, and more courteous than kings; poor as Lazarus, and more hospitable than Croesus; Catholics from A to Izzard, except when they take occasion to be Penitentes."[72] In contrast, Anglo-American attitudes were generally favorable toward the "picturesque," "industrious," and "artistic" Pueblo Indians, who became known for their pottery and handicrafts.

Ricos, or *gente de razón,* referred to themselves largely as Spaniards. New Mexico's governors and small aristocracy during Spanish colonization were largely Spaniards. Direct contact with Spain was kept alive by New Mexico sending a representative regularly to the Spanish Cortes until 1810. Mexico attempted in 1828–29 to expel those few who had been born in Spain (*peninsulares* or *europeos*) from the colony by passage

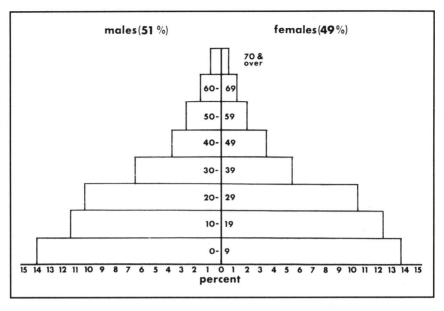

FIGURE 20

*Sex-age pyramid of the Río Arriba's (Río Arriba, Santa Anna, Santa Fe, and Taos
counties) white (Spanish-American) population in 1850.*

Source: Superintendent of the U.S. Census, *The Seventh Census of the United States: 1850*
(Washington, D.C.: Robert Armstrong, 1853), xxxvi, 988–89, 993, 996.

of an expulsion law.[73] Through bribery, they were for the most part
allowed to remain. Most of New Mexico's colonists between 1693 and
1821 were born in Mexico, some being mestizos. In fact, Mexico represented in 1850 two-thirds of New Mexico's foreign-born population
(2,150), but only 4 percent of the territory's total population was born
outside the United States. Approximately one-fourth of the foreign-born
population was born in Germany and Ireland—only eight persons had
been born in Spain.[74] Natural increase, therefore, was the major factor
for the growth of the territory's Spanish-American population. More than
50 percent of the Río Arriba's white (Spanish-American) population in
1850 (estimated 30,000) was under twenty years of age, making for a
youthful population that would soon enter the reproductive stage of life
(Figure 20).[75] Unfortunately, New Mexico lacked the parallel growth in
its economy that would have absorbed the Río Arriba's growing surplus
rural population.

When the Spanish Americans learned about the advantages of a wage
economy, their land took on a new dimension. Small farms and rural villages had become places characterized by residences that provided stabil-

ity for the seasonal laborers' families who did not have to move from
place to place for employment. Thus, the Río Arriba had become early a
region of considerable part-time farming and a source of seasonal laborers, an indication of significant underemployment. Established by Spain as
communities for political, strategic, and missionary, and not economic,
objectives, the region's Spanish Americans were now confronted with
Anglo-American economic motives and assessments. Critics of Spanish
colonization have pointed out that Spain often left its colonies without
strong economic bases.[76] Consequently, the transition into the American
economic system would be difficult. Moreover, the symptoms of impoverishment had been long present in this region, which was to become identified in the twentieth century as having intense, chronic rural poverty.

6 A Region of Poverty, 1930–1990

Based upon a long history of subsistence agriculture, the Río Arriba had emerged by the 1930s as a distinct and poor socioeconomic region within New Mexico and the western United States. For the most part, it was identified by its dominant rural Spanish-American population, preponderance of small land units in overpopulated microbasins, low farm incomes, and continued dependence upon distant and off-farm employment. Those characteristics, which described the region in the 1930s, continue to be dominant criteria today for delineating an area where a high percentage of rural Spanish Americans have clung tenaciously to their land. The Spanish Americans' self-reliant practices, however, have led to endemic rural poverty and dependency upon government assistance programs. Unfortunately, this economic situation has been a factor in the Spanish Americans' resentment toward the U.S. government and Anglo Americans.

Native-born Spanish Americans constitute the dominant rural population in the Río Arriba and contribute to New Mexico's highest percentage of Spanish-surname population of all states. Since World War I, the term Spanish American has largely replaced Mexican, partially because the people, as self-referents, made it known that they wanted recognition of their Spanish origin and heritage. Many Anglo Americans liked the term, too, because they believed it reflected patriotism for America when many Spanish-American males served in the U.S. armed forces during both world wars.[1] Although they have had little, if any, association with Spain, Spanish Americans have been proud of their perceived origin or ancestry, descendancy from the Spanish *conquistadores*, and long history of settlement. Anthropologist John J. Bodine, when studying Spanish Americans in Taos, found in 1968 that "one rather small victory the bearers of Hispanic culture have achieved is to insist on the term 'Spanish American.' They point out rather vehemently that they are the pure and direct descendants of the Spanish *Conquistadores*. They are Spanish, not Mexican. Use of the term 'Mexican' is definitely derogatory in Taos. Significantly the Indians insist on calling them just that, although not too openly anymore."[2]

Even one of New Mexico's former governors, Tony Anaya, quickly traced his heritage to Spain on the national television program "Today" during the rededication of the Statue of Liberty on 4 July 1986. Spanish-American restauranteurs offer menus featuring "Spanish American," "Native New Mexican," or "Northern New Mexican" cuisine, which they distinguish from Mexican food by emphasizing, for instance, the common use of green chile, the *sopaipilla,* a fritter that is eaten with honey, blue-corn tortillas, and *carne adovada* (heavy chunks of pork marinated in red chile). Spanish Americans are also reminded daily of their heritage by the region's toponyms, which are of Spanish-Christian origin. These place-names sanctified the landscapes, providing the colonists with a sense of security on an isolated frontier.[3] The use of names and terms from the Pueblos' languages was avoided, in sharp contrast to other European colonists, who tended to Indianize the landscape with the terminology of local Indian tribes.

To differentiate the Spanish-origin populations, the Bureau of the Census developed in 1980 the identifier "other Spanish," which excluded peoples of Mexican, Puerto Rican, and Cuban origins. "Other Spanish" populations included persons from Spain, Central and South America, and Spanish Americans. Because there are few persons in the Río Arriba from these other areas, the region's data on "other Spanish" pertain to the Spanish Americans. But Spanish Americans want an identifier in the 1990 census that will identify specifically those persons "who can trace their roots to Spain and the first Spanish explorers."[4] Linguists claim that the Spanish spoken into the 1900s in the Río Arriba was similar to that used in sixteenth-century Spain.[5] Some Spanish Americans still point out how their Spanish differs from that used in Mexico and how their customs differ from those found in New Mexico's "Mexicanized" lower Río Grande Valley. For instance, Hispanos living in the lower Río Grande Valley celebrate in Mesilla with fiestas the Mexican holidays Cinco de Mayo, which acknowledges Mexico's military victory over the French invasion instigated by Napoleon III at Puebla, Mexico, in 1862, and Diez y Seis de Septiembre, which commemorates Mexico's independence day. In contrast, many aspects of the Río Arriba's folklore, drama, ballads, and superstitions were used in or relate directly to Spain, including cre-

FIGURE 21

The drama "Los Moros y Cristianos," which commemorates the Spanish reconquest of Spain from the Moors, is held at La Fiesta de Señor Santiago in Chimayó, Santa Fe County. Two dozen horsemen perform the reenacted battles in which the Christians defeat the Islamic Moors after 700 years of rule. During the drama, a song, "La Santa Espina," from Spain's province of Catalonia is played and the script is written in a Spanish dialect.
Source: Author, July 1980.

dence in the spell of the *mal de ojo* (evil eye), which possessed harmful power, and witchcraft practiced by a village's suspected *bruja* (practitioner) (Figure 21). In addition, Santa Fe's annual fiesta celebrates the Spanish reconquest and the role played by La Conquistadora, a statue of the Virgin Mary that accompanied the soldiers and settlers.[6]

By remaining on their small land units, the rural Spanish Americans have continued to constitute a relatively large component of the region's total population. Except for Santa Fe County, with its city of Santa Fe, Río Arriba, Sandoval, and Taos counties had in 1930 wholly rural populations. The farm and rural nonfarm populations each accounted for approximately 40 percent of the region's total population (66,000) (Appendix G).[7] There is no doubt that the Río Arriba had become a distinct "refuge" during the Depression of the 1930s, when opportunities in seasonal employment had declined sharply and thousands of workers had to stay home. Consequently, the region reported in 1935 more than thirty-one hundred more farms than in 1925 and experienced a 30 percent increase in its pent-up population because of low out-migration and high rates of natural increase (Appendixes G and H).[8]

Since the outbreak of World War II, thousands of Spanish Americans have left the Río Arriba, yet the region has continued to have a relatively high, stable, native-born, rural Spanish-American population. In 1957, one in five households had "seven or more members, and 44 percent had five or more members. Only 22 per cent of all U.S. households had five or more members in the same year."[9] Anthropologist Margaret Mead claimed that the Spanish Americans had long wanted many children because upon old age they would then have some of them yet at home or nearby to provide assistance.[10] This attitude is commonly held by peasants in traditional societies, which are maintained by an established community system of welfare. In 1960, the region's Spanish Americans numbered nearly three-fifths of the region's population of 100,000, with less than one percent of them having been foreign born, especially in Mexico, placing the region's counties among the lowest percentages in the state.[11] Seventy percent of Río Arriba and Taos counties' Spanish-American populations resided in rural communities on small land units, which were taking on increasingly nonfarm characteristics. In fact, the rural nonfarm population had increased in 1970 to nearly three-fifths of the Río Arriba's total population (115,000) (Appendix G).

Another change in the demographic characteristics of the region's population has resulted from net migration. For instance, in-migration between 1975 and 1980 produced a net gain of 6,200 people, overwhelmingly Anglo Americans, but a net loss of 1,400 Spanish Americans. While Santa Fe and Sandoval counties had excess numbers of Anglo-American in-migrants because of urban Santa Fe and the northern suburbs of Albuquerque, respectively, rural Río Arriba and Taos counties had negative net migration, which was heavily Spanish American and greatest in the fifteen to nineteen and twenty to twenty-four year-old age groups.[12] Incessant Anglo-American in-migration had reduced by 1980 the Spanish-American population to approximately two-fifths of the Río Arriba's population (160,000). Spanish Americans constitute now a large minority population, but they continue to be in the majority in rural Río Arriba and Taos counties, where they comprise nearly 60 percent of the population, and in certain rural communities of Sandoval and Santa Fe counties. Nostrand found that the Río Arriba has still the highest percentages of Spanish Americans within census tracts for New Mexico and Colorado.[13] Spanish-American rural communities established outside the Río Arriba have been largely abandoned or Anglo Americans have supplanted or surpassed the decreasing numbers of Spanish Americans.

Historically, Spanish Americans have stayed in the Río Arriba because of strong family and kinship bonds, which resulted often from intermarriage. In many cases, they were united by a loose *compadrazgo* (godparenthood) or coparentage system where the godparents (*padrinos*) lived nearby and took care of the children in times of the loss or absence of the parents.[14] Clans or extended families shared and bartered foodstuffs and handicrafts. Later, local store operators provided credit, which further encouraged a sense of security. Villages were, therefore, havens for the many poor Spanish Americans who depended upon mutual assistance and a certain community spirit or feeling (*campanilismo*), homogeneity, and loyalty. Anthropologist Carolyn Zeleny concluded in 1944 that "the people were rooted deep in a fundamentally communal mode of existence, which gave little premium to individual enterprise, in which the good of the family or the village was the object of endeavor and where competition as we know it did not exist."[15]

They lived, too, by accepting *fatalismo,* a belief that nature will take its course rather than that they have control of their situation or destiny, and *misericordia,* a realization of misery.[16] *Médicas, parteras* (midwives), and *curanderas,* women specializing in medicinal herbs (*remedios*) and poultices, were found in many villages where malnutrition and high rates of infant mortality were common problems.[17] The region's infant mortality rate was, as late as 1940, nearly twice the national average and the highest in the United States.[18] Villagers depended also upon a local *político, patrón,* or *don,* usually a relatively large landowner, to represent them in external affairs. The Catholic Church provided social and recreational activities, including religious *fiestas,* many with antecedents in Spain, and celebrations that honored a village's patron saint, marriages, and baptisms.[19] These events further promoted communal solidarity.

Spanish Americans' deficiencies in gaining formal educations and fluency in English were also deterrents to out-migration. A formal educational structure for Spanish Americans had lagged in New Mexico in comparison with other areas in the United States. It is true that the Catholic Church provided, during the Spanish and Mexican eras, very limited religious education, but only for a few youths. No public schools were in existence in the Río Arriba when the U.S. government acquired New Mexico. Eighty-five percent of the region's white (Spanish-American) adults could neither read nor write in 1850. Seventeen public schools, with an enrollment of 220 students, had been established by 1860 in the territory, but New Mexico's educational situation was in sharp contrast to that found, for instance, in the Utah Territory, where there were already 173 public schools and nearly 5,500 students enrolled. The establishment of an extensive public school system was delayed in New Mexico because of the controversy over secular versus sectarian control.[20] Although compulsory school attendance was made law in 1891, public schools were notably absent from many of the Río Arriba's villages until the early 1900s. For instance, when New Mexico obtained statehood in 1912, several school districts in Río Arriba County alone had no schools. There was no public high school in the county until World War I. Moreover, most of the county's established schools met for only one-third of the school year. Students were frequently kept at home to do farm work or household chores, in many cases for their mothers because their fathers were off doing seasonal work.[21]

Consequently, educational achievements for the Río Arriba's youth were far below the national norms, and illiteracy rates were abnormally high until World War II. One-third of the region's population of ten years of age and over was illiterate in 1910 and nearly one-fifth of this age group was illiterate in 1930.[22] Spanish Americans had a particularly high dropout rate after the fourth grade. In fact, more than one-fourth of the adult rural population in both Río Arriba and Taos counties had in 1950 no schooling beyond four years.[23] By the mid-1960s, 70 percent of the region's farmers, especially those in Río Arriba and Taos counties, had not completed more than eight years of schooling and only 11 percent had completed high school.[24] Río Arriba, Sandoval, and Taos counties, with low tax bases and high numbers of children, were consistently ranked at the bottom (Santa Fe County was near the bottom) in school expenditures per pupil at the outbreak of World War II.[25] Anglo Americans have long been criticized for neglecting public education in this Spanish-speaking area of the state, even though Spanish Americans have comprised the local school boards, which found, too, that the region's poor economic situation did not provide the necessary revenues to permit opportunities for high-quality education and the incentives to remain in school.[26]

Small landholdings have long characterized agriculture in the Río Arriba and they need to be analyzed to understand further the region's path to endemic rural poverty. More than 40 percent of New Mexico's farms of under ten acres and one-third of those under 50 acres were found in 1925 in the Río Arriba (Appendix H). During the Depression of the 1930s, when the region's number of farms peaked at 8,845, three-fourths of them averaged only 12 acres. Census data for 1945 and 1954 indicate similar figures but fewer farms. The region had still by 1964 approximately one-fifth of the state's farms and more than 40 percent of the state's farms of under ten acres. Farms of under 10 acres averaged only 5 acres upon which per capita income was to be derived from approximately 1 acre or less.

Numerous reports exist that point out the severity of the problem in regard to the Spanish Americans' small landholdings. In the case of ten villages that had 630 families in the mid 1930s, each landholding family had an average of 6.6 acres, with the range between 3 and 8 acres.

Nearly 15 percent of the families were landless.[27] New Mexico's Engineer's Office found in the 1960s in the case of Córdova, located on the patented Spanish community Nuestra Señora del Rosario San Fernando y Santiago Grant, that of the approximately 100 tracts that encompassed the nearly 158 irrigated acres, only fourteen tracts were more than 2 acres. No landowner had more than 7 acres.[28] This situation was found on a grant of 14,787 acres, consisting mostly of upland and rough terrain with low carrying capacity that would have allowed only a few livestock per landowner. At the same time, some individually owned strips on the patented Cristoval de la Serna Grant of 22,233 acres measured only 30 to 40 *varas* in width.[29] Sociologist John Burma reported in 1954 he had found tracts in the region that included only one-tenth to one-eighth of an acre of irrigated land.[30]

Approximately 20 percent of all farms in the Río Arriba in 1982 were under 10 acres. They averaged 4.5 acres each, and two of three that had irrigated land had an average of only 3.9 irrigated acres. More than 30 percent of the farms were between 10 and 50 acres, averaging 23.3 acres. In these cases, four-fifths of them had irrigated land with an average of only 13.7 acres.[31] Comparable figures are found in the 1987 agricultural census data: 22 percent of the 2,136 farms were under 10 acres and 31 percent were between 10 and 49 acres.[32] Obviously, over the years many small landholdings never met the Bureau of the Census's requirements of minimum acreage and sales to be listed as farms.[33]

The region's Spanish Americans have lost or sold most of the common lands on their patented community grants. A considerable amount of this land was lost in the 1930s because of the nonpayment of taxes. Heirs refused to pay or could not afford to pay taxes. Communal portions of land grants were assessed communally. Consequently, residents who could not pay their share and those who refused to pay taxes in principle on the communal portion created a problem of tax delinquency for all the land grant's residents. Residents of some land grants were in arrears for thousands of dollars. For instance, the Jacona Grant was lost in 1909 for delinquent taxes. Although it was repurchased by some of its heirs, they, too, faced tax delinquency in 1929.[34] Many Spanish Americans worked seasonally and were accordingly less interested in farming.

Lawyers for the Spanish Americans had started in the late 1800s during the adjudication of the land-grant claims to oppose the taxability of Spanish and Mexican land grants by arguing that the Treaty of Guadalupe Hidalgo exempted them in perpetuity from any real property and land taxes. Their case rested on the argument that land grants, especially the unallocated communal lands, were held in usufruct, not in fee simple, and by the sovereign government which bestowed them.[35] Therefore, only products of value could be taxed. The lawyers did not make it clear whether their argument applied only to the original settlers or grantees and their descendants, however, or included the many other residents who came to live on the community grants over the years and in some cases turned private grants into de facto community grants. Although Spanish and Mexican colonization procedures were quite explicit in laying out land grants, they had left a very complex question for legal interpretation by Anglo Americans.

New Mexico's legislature in 1891 and again in 1917 allowed land grant trustees and heirs to sell the communal portions of community land grants, implying that these lands were held in fee simple. Courts also ruled that the communal lands were not held by usufructory right but in fee simple and therefore could be both taxed and sold.[36] In lingering challenges, a federal court reaffirmed in 1939 an earlier court decision that Spanish and Mexican land grants held either privately or communally could be taxed and that in cases of tax delinquency it was legal for the State Tax Commission to foreclose after three years and sell the land grant for the accumulated taxes.[37] Spanish Americans were undoubtedly confronted with a different tax system under the Anglo Americans, but each government has its own system of taxation. Even the Spaniards imposed their tax system upon the Pueblos. Then too, interestingly enough, Spanish Americans substantiated many of their private land claims on the Pueblo Indian grants by using tax records.

Heirs and other residents with the concurrence of land grant trustees sold in the 1930s their land grants or portions thereof to stockmen, both Anglo American and Spanish American, and to the federal government. Federal legislation had provided the necessary authority to the government to purchase the lands of thousands of Americans who were in financial trouble during the Depression.[38] Many were located in marginal agricultural areas. The end result was the purchasing of nearly 11 million acres nationwide. More than 80 percent of this acreage was placed under the administration of the U.S. Forest Service, but only a very small percentage of it was located in the Río Arriba or even in New Mexico. Nevertheless, the federal government purchased portions or all of the communal lands of a fairly large number of the Río Arriba's large and small patented Spanish and Mexican land grants, including those on the Sebastian Martínez Grant; Town of San Isidro Grant; Juan José Lobato Grant; Ojo del Espíritu Santo Grant; Caja del Río Grant; Juan de Gabaldón Grant; Bernabe Montaño Grant; Polvadera Grant; Ojo del Borrego Grant; and Ojo de San José Grant (Appendix A). There was, however, no buyout of the occupants' privately owned irrigated acreages. The federal government also bought land from banks that had foreclosed on individual landowners, including Anglo-American homesteaders.

Government agencies had an underlying belief that they could better manage the resources of these purchased lands for the greater benefit of the region's residents because of past overstocking and general mismanagement. The majority of the acreages were placed largely in the 1930s in Soil Conservation Service land utilization projects for analyses on how best to use them within their ecological parameters. Advisory boards, consisting of Spanish Americans, were established and public hearings were held to discuss types of management. Commercial developments were disallowed and most of the acreages continued to be used for livestock grazing, but at reduced levels. Eventually, these acreages ended up largely under the Forest Service, which imposed grazing regulations (discussed in Chapter 7) to achieve equitable grazing privileges, prevent overgrazing and erosion, and stabilize the livestock operations. One of its intentions was to give the small livestock operators an opportunity for improving their economic situation on better managed land.[39] Although there is resentment today against the Forest Service because of its regulations, not all Spanish Americans opposed at the outset the imposition of controlled grazing. For instance, residents of the Ojo del Borrego and Ojo de San José grants realized that their land units of 16,080 and 4,340 acres, respectively, were too small. It was advantageous, therefore, for them to use the public domain under grazing permits where their livestock could gain weight rather than on unregulated, overgrazed communal lands.[40]

Sentiments have been expressed that the Spanish Americans' loss of communal grant lands for delinquent taxes was not only unfair but that Spanish Americans were also singled out during these unfortunate times. Many similar incidents occurred, however, throughout the country where landowners, including thousands of Anglo Americans who lived in New Mexico, lost their real property and land for noncompliance.

In acquiring land by the methods discussed in previous chapters, which allowed for low capital entry into agriculture, Spanish-American landholders owned their small land units without debts. Only 8 percent of the Río Arriba's farmers reported in the 1920s farm mortgages, the state's lowest rate. In contrast, nearly 60 percent of the Anglo-American farmers on New Mexico's Staked Plains (Llano Estacado) reported farm mortgages, indicating attempts to expand and mechanize their operations.[41] Spanish Americans have had few reasons to mortgage their irrigable tracts, and they could not as individuals, in the cases of community land grants, mortgage communally owned lands. Many lacked also legal titles and detailed abstracts with property descriptions, which created difficulties in obtaining loans from commercial banks or other lending institutions. This situation was especially the case within patented land grants where no surveys were made of the individual landholdings.

Thousands of tracts had not yet been assessed in 1970 for county taxes because there was no official record of their existence. For instance, in a 1969 reappraisal project, nearly 10,000 small parcels of land were placed on the tax ledgers in Taos County alone.[42] These parcels lacked marketable titles and abstracts because they had been inherited or acquired without recorded transactions, largely by oral agreements.[43] Many were probably the result of partible inheritance prior to World War II. The extent of partible inheritance, however, declined significantly after World War II because of permanent out-migration. Furthermore, agricultural economist Marlowe Taylor found in 1957 that "division and subdivision of farmland through inheritance has progressed to the point beyond which further division, in some instances, is almost a physical impossibility."[44]

Spanish Americans did not record these conveyances of ownership because of legal and probate costs, apprehension in regard to increased taxes, inadequate descriptions that would have required professional and costly surveys, and fear that ownership of land or additional land would make them ineligible for welfare benefits or at least have them reduced.[45] This situation contributed actually to their ability to keep much of their irrigated acreage from the hands of Anglo Americans, who did not want to purchase nontitled land.[46]

With the expansion of agriculture in New Mexico, disparities increased between the agricultural production and incomes of the Río Arriba and other regions. Farms in the Río Arriba ranked after World War II at the bottom in agricultural sales. In 1945, more than 70 percent of them produced less than $1,000 in farm products. Taos County had average farm sales of less than $600.[47] Decades later, in 1964, the region's counties were again extremely low in average value ($3,020) of all farm products sold per farm. This time, Taos County's farm sales averaged only $1,466, considerably below the level designated as farm poverty.[48]

It must be pointed out, too, that although the region has had a high percentage of New Mexico's farms, it has received considerably less agricultural aid than the state's other counties that have mostly large farms that raise wheat, sorghum, and cotton under the federal government's price-support program. Government payments amounted in 1964 to nearly $15 million for the farmers in four counties on New Mexico's Staked Plains, in contrast to only $1 million for the Río Arriba's farmers.[49] Spanish Americans could ill afford to put portions of their small acreages into any government farm program that limited production. Furthermore, their traditional crops of chiles, hay, beans, fruit, and vegetables were not included in the list of staples supported by the government.

Many Spanish Americans still farm. In fact, nearly 50 percent of the region's fifteen hundred farmers were Spanish Americans in 1978, and when over half the region's farms had sales of less than $2,500, most were actually under $1,500. Only 40 percent of the Spanish-American farmers had sales of $2,500 or more. Again, Taos County had the state's lowest average farm sales, only $4,200 per farm. When the percentage of Spanish-American farmers had declined in 1982 to only 46 percent of all farmers, it was the first time in the region's history of non-Indian settlement that they had constituted the minority of farmers. Approximately three-fifths of the region's farms, owned largely by Spanish Americans, had sales of less than $2,500. Taos County had the lowest average sales ($4,300) in New Mexico, where the average sales were more than $63,000 per farm. Only 10 percent of the Río Arriba's Spanish-American farmers had sales of $10,000 or more. More than half the region's farms (2,136) in 1987 had sales of less than $2,500.[50]

Besides their problems with small land sizes and inability to expand their operations, Spanish Americans found that they faced frustrations and competition in the marketing of their farm products. A case in point is their production of chile. Chile peppers (*Capsicum frutescens*) have long been a specialty crop, but the Río Arriba's growers have had problems marketing them. For a time, Spanish-American truckers peddled a considerable amount of chiles in Colorado, but that state's legislation, enacted in the 1930s, required them to have commercial licenses and liability insurance because they were involved in interstate commerce. In addition, they were charged a small fee per mile on tonnage.[51] Most could not afford these additional expenses, leading to the region's growers' return to marketing their produce locally, largely in the form of credit at regional stores, such as those owned by Bond and Nohl, Reuth and Kramer, and the Murrhage Brothers in Española. These merchants provided annually thousands of dollars in consumption credit that was secured largely by chiles. Bond and Nohl alone extended in the 1930s credit amounting to $15,000 a year. Each grower was allowed to accumulate credit up to $35.[52] Some growers peddled their green chiles by going door to door in Santa Fe, Albuquerque, and small towns or by selling them at roadside stands. Fresh chiles command a fairly good price because they are pungent and the milk stays in the skin, developing a desirable flavor. Much of the annual chile crop was, however, consumed in the growers' homes (Figure 22).

Chile growers in the Río Arriba were unable to develop external markets after World War II because they faced stiff competition from the large producers and processors in the lower Río Grande Valley near Las Cruces, New Mexico, and from California and Texas. Growers in southern New Mexico heavily fertilized their chile crop, grown on an average of 6.5 acres per grower, and harvested yields of nearly six tons per acre.

FIGURE 22

Spanish-American housewives were commonly seen cooking chile peppers in their kitchens. Photo taken in Córdova, Río Arriba County, September 1939.

Source: National Archives, Washington, D.C.

In contrast, the Río Arriba's small growers harvested in 1960 an average of only 1.1 acres of chile and obtained a yield of half that amount. Also, they relied heavily on hand labor and could invest neither in the machinery necessary to cultivate larger acreages nor in the dehydrators to process larger harvests.[53]

Small farmers, especially with the mindset of "farming as a way and means of life, rather than of amassing wealth," in general have been unable to cope with the trend toward agribusiness.[54] Population statistician Herman P. Miller claims that one major cause of American rural poverty has been "the perpetuation of the low-income farms."[55] Additional considerations include a region's "poverty linked characteristics" or social factors such as the population's low educational levels and advanced ages that limit off-farm employment opportunities, poor managerial knowledge, inability to adjust quickly, lack of assets or collateral to increase productivity, and limited accessibility to nonfarm employment. Relative isolation from large urban centers that could absorb portions of a surplus rural population is also a critical factor.[56]

Amenities associated with the social, physical, and scenic environments may hold people in a rural locale regardless of their low incomes, especially where there is a high percentage of landownership. Sociologist Michael Harrington pointed out in the early 1960s that the "property-owning poor" constituted a large segment of the "rural culture of poverty" while making reference to four centers of "property-owning poverty" in the United States, including the Río Arriba.[57] Various factors, therefore, contribute to the making of "insular poverty" in a region where a particular way of life has become "economically obsolete."

A national awareness developed after World War II over the relatively poor social and economic conditions found in both rural and urban areas of the United States. Not surprisingly, the Río Arriba emerged in various government studies as a region with pronounced rural poverty.[58] It stood out on maps depicting low farm-operator levels of living, low incomes, and areas eligible for redevelopment. Sandoval and Taos counties were listed in 1959 by the Bureau of the Census to be among the 182 poorest counties in the United States. They ranked 98th and 139th, respectively. Río Arriba and Taos counties were ranked in 1960 near the bottom of all U.S. counties, according to a five-factor economic index. Sandoval and Santa Fe counties also had pockets of chronic rural poverty.[59] Nearly half the region's families were below the poverty level in 1960, and 40 percent were found under the poverty level in 1970.[60] In the latter case, Spanish-American mean family annual income was slightly more than $2,100 for an average family size of 4.7 persons. Houses continued to lack modern conveniences. For instance, more than 60 percent of dwellings in Río Arriba, Sandoval, and Taos counties lacked some or all plumbing facilities (Figure 23). In 1980, one of five of the region's Spanish-American families was still listed below the poverty level, and in 1988 unemployment rates remained greater than 20 percent in many parts of the Río Arriba.[61]

By farming small and fragmented parcels of irrigable land that resulted from inheritance and subdivision, the economic scene on the neighboring Pueblo Indian grants and reservations has remained similar to that found

FIGURE 23

*Spanish-American children carried water from the Río Quemado to their homes in
Córdova, Río Arriba County, February 1939. All water for potable and other
domestic purposes for most homes came from the nearby stream. This was a
common practice as very few houses had indoor plumbing in the rural Río Arriba.
Some families still draw their water from shallow wells by using a rope and a pail.*
Source: National Archives, Washington, D.C.

in the Spanish-American communities. The Reverand J. Paul Stevens
described the situation in 1964:

> The Pueblo Indians use their land generally in much the same way as they
> have for generations, that is, for small farming activities and for grazing of
> livestock. With the increase of Indian population the average size of irrigated
> farm plots now ranges from 12 acres per capita for the Sandia Pueblo down
> to 1/2 acre per capita for the Laguna Pueblo [located immediately to the west
> of the Río Arriba]. Grazing land has suffered from overgrazing and erosion.

As a result the land base in all of the Pueblos is inadequate both in grazing and crop land to support the increasing numbers in the tribes. Thus there is increased dependence upon wage work away from the Pueblo or in nearby towns or upon welfare assistance.[62]

Government assistance programs in some way sustain most Pueblos who remained on their grants, especially on the isolated grants located some distance from Santa Fe, Albuquerque, or Los Alamos, such as Picurís.

It is no secret that many Spanish Americans have resented the federal government's purchases of land, including Spanish and Mexican grant land, to create or extend reservations added onto the original Pueblo Indian grants. For instance, a portion (5,914 acres) of the Ramón Vigil Grant was purchased in 1934 from one of the region's largest sheepmen, Frank Bond of Española, to be designated as a sacred area for the San Ildefonso Pueblos.[63] Historian George I. Sanchez complains that the United States acquired land for the Pueblos at the expense of the Spanish Americans.[64] Bodine found in the mid-1960s that the Spanish Taosaños "can always be counted on to oppose the claims of the [Taos] Indians to grazing, water, a right of way or even a cash settlement for past land grabs by either the Spanish or the Anglos. . . . Naturally the ire is raised when they see the Indians, who have received so many benefits from the Federal government, attempt to obtain even more."[65] Spanish Americans are also quite resentful about Indian lands being tax-exempt.

Various governmental agencies have pumped, however, millions of dollars in assistance funding into the Río Arriba to sustain the Spanish Americans and in many cases to keep them in the region. Much of the federal government's assistance started in the 1930s. Assistance from the State of New Mexico began largely in 1937 after the creation of the Department of Public Welfare. More than two-thirds of the families in numerous communities were on government relief of some sort during the 1930s. For instance, only two of the forty-four families in San Luis, Sandoval County, received no government assistance in 1939.[66] At first, many of the region's residents received cash welfare payments. Then, males were allowed to earn cash by working on local road construction and conservation-related jobs that were made available under federal programs such as the Works Projects Administration (WPA), National Youth Administration, and the Civilian Conservation Corps (CCC). About twenty vocational training programs were implemented to teach various skills to the region's residents.[67] The Farm Security Administration made loans available to help residents reacquire land grants, such as the case in 1942 of obtaining a large portion (92,000 acres) of the Sangre de Cristo Grant for the establishment of the Río Costilla Cooperative Livestock Association. Most Spanish Americans, however, preferred not to have debts because of fear of foreclosures, especially on their irrigated parcels.[68] The Forest Service worked with livestock owners on upgrading their animals, especially sheep. Under the Stock Reduction Program, the federal government bought livestock from the Spanish Americans in order to provide them with cash and to limit the numbers according to the suitability of the region's grazing capacities, which had been reduced drastically by drought and overgrazing. For instance, livestock owners in the communities of Leyden, Brady, and Claro were able to sell 20 percent of their cattle in 1934.[69] Many livestock, however, died of starvation. In addition, the Soil Conservation Service assisted farmers in improving their irrigation practices and lining many of their irrigation ditches with concrete, and with the Bureau of Reclamation it has had an ongoing program to build numerous check dams and levees for flood control.

Resettlement schemes were advocated in the 1930s by federal agencies and even by some Spanish-American leaders. Government studies showed there was serious overpopulation in the region's small mountain valleys. A 1935 study of 8,530 families living north of Santa Fe reported an excess of over 1,400 families in relation to the land resources able to support a family on $300 a year.[70] Because the resettlement schemes were not specific about where to relocate people, most residents did not favor moving from the security of their communities.[71]

Initially, Spanish Americans were hesitant about entering into agreements with governmental agencies. For instance, they were uncertain about placing their land into soil conservation districts and were also timid about accepting new crops and methods of production, despite the fact that the New Mexico Agricultural Extension Service has long had Spanish-American agricultural agents in each of the region's counties and an experimental station located north of Española for disseminating pertinent information to local farmers. These characteristics of uncertainty are, however, common in peasantries and, if the results are unfavorable, they could be disastrous to the family's welfare.[72]

World War II had a tremendous impact upon the Río Arriba in that it led to the exodus, mainly to distant urban cities, of a large number of young unskilled people who did not return and raise their families in the region. With the war under way, the region was identified again as a source of surplus labor. To upgrade this labor pool, the federal government established Schools for Vocational Training for War Production in Santa Fe, Albuquerque, and Las Vegas. Hundreds of their trainees migrated to the Pacific Coast states, mostly California, to work in shipyards, aircraft plants, and other industries.[73] It must not be overlooked that many Spanish-American males departed for the armed services (Figure 24). Their number in both world wars ranked, in fact, among the highest per capita of any American ethnic group.[74] Moreover, the acculturation of Spanish Americans was intensified by their leaving New Mexico.

Spanish-American men in both the military services and war-related

FIGURE 24

Buses provided commercial transportation in and out of Taos, Taos County. Spanish-American families often said farewell at this bus depot to their boys who left to join the army in World War II. Photo: *December 1941.*

Source: National Archives, Washington, D.C.

industries hesitated after World War II to return to the Río Arriba, where many families had annual cash incomes of less than $500.[75] Most did not return, which alleviated the region's unemployment problems, but some felt compelled to go back to their villages because of family bonds and their land. But out-migration had become recognized as a means of improving one's situation. Chain migrations were established where family members followed their relatives and even friends to certain urban centers where they were assisted in obtaining housing and employment. This is especially true of those who migrated to southern California and to Denver, where many remain grouped together, and these groups are reinforced by new migrants. As one might expect, persons in the age group of fifteen to forty-five migrated in the largest numbers, leaving behind relatively large and disproportionate young and elderly populations.[76]

Few industries had been established in the Río Arriba to hold the younger Spanish Americans at home. The construction in the 1940s of the world-renowned atomic energy facility at Los Alamos, thirty-five miles northwest of Santa Fe, was an economic boon for many residents.

Its initial construction, and later maintenance and continuous expansion absorbed a considerable amount of the region's supply of excess labor. Many Spanish Americans commute daily from their far-flung communities to what has become New Mexico's largest single employer. Others have moved to Los Alamos County, where today nearly one of ten residents is Spanish American. Other notable employment opportunities became available in the 1920s with the opening of an open-pit molybdenum mine north of Taos near Questa, Taos County. When the operation began to include underground extraction of the ore, employment grew steadily until Molycorp had become the Río Arriba's largest single private employer, hiring nearly five hundred workers by the mid-1980s. Molycorp closed its operation in 1986, but reopened it in 1989 with only 225 employees. The proliferation of the various county, state, and federal agencies has provided employment for numerous Spanish Americans, including hundreds of women who are employed largely in clerical or service-related jobs.

Many Spanish Americans have been able to find employment in recent years because of the continuous and rapid growth of the region's tourist industry. Thousands of tourists, largely Anglo Americans, have visited the region, which was made known to them as an interesting historical and cultural area dating back to various efforts during the late 1800s to attract settlers to New Mexico. Similar to the early efforts of the New Mexico Bureau of Immigration, the state's Tourist Bureau, established in 1934, began to advertise extensively in newspapers. Tourism was already in the 1930s Santa Fe's leading source of income and one of the state's largest revenue industries. The Tourist Bureau resumed advertising after World War II to increase interstate tourism by promoting accessibility via Route 66, the state's cultures, and its climate with the intent to create new employment opportunities. There was also an implicit message here of assuring travelers that New Mexico was not a part of Mexico.[77] According to the state's Highway Department, the number of out-of-state passenger cars, bearing nearly 16 million people, increased from 4.5 million in 1960 to nearly 6.5 million bearing over 20 million people in 1970.[78] Tourism had emerged in 1986 as the state's largest employer. Texas, California, and New York lead as the sources of tourists. Many of these tourists spent time in the Río Arriba, where by the 1960s they provided more annual income than agricultural sales. An estimated 2.5 million tourists visited "chic" Santa Fe alone in 1980.[79] They come to see and participate largely in the region's "living cultural museums," which are hosted by the Pueblos and the Spanish Americans in idyllic settings (Figure 25). Art galleries in Santa Fe and Taos, havens for early aesthetes and artists, are additional attractions, as is Bandelier National Monument west of Santa Fe.[80] Outdoor recreation in the national forests, particularly

FIGURE 25

Annual Indian Market around Santa Fe's plaza attracts thousands of tourists. Sponsored by the Southwest Association on Indian Affairs, it is today the largest Indian market in the American Southwest, featuring over 300 exhibitors who sell judged pottery, jewelry, rugs, baskets, and other arts and crafts. Santa Fe's first Indian market was held in 1922 in conjunction with the city's Fiesta; however, it became a separate event in the 1930s.
Source: Author, August 1971.

at the expanding number of ski resorts, is a growing year-round attraction. By nature, the employment of Spanish Americans in the motels, hotels, restaurants, and art and curio shops is largely seasonal. Many tourists eventually move to as well as retire in the Río Arriba.

Dependence upon seasonal off-farm work for supplemental income continued after World War II to be fairly important in the Río Arriba (Figure 26). For example, one-fourth of New Mexico's farmers who worked in 1964 off their farms resided in the region.[81] They were employed in various jobs, including since the early 1950s as firefighters to save national forests in the western states. Crews continued to leave the region as farm workers, largely to the San Luis Valley and Colorado's other specialty farming areas. Because entire families traveled in the late summer and early fall to the San Luis Valley to harvest potatoes, schools often closed temporarily in some communities to enable them to achieve maximum earnings. New Mexico's Department of Employment recruited

FIGURE 26

This Spanish-American farmer left his home in Córdova, Río Arriba County, in 1939 to herd sheep in Wyoming. Strings (ristras) of chiles hang from the roof to dry.

Source: National Archives, Washington, D.C.

regularly farm laborers within the Río Arriba because of its excess labor pool. Mexican and other seasonal laborers and mechanization had reduced by 1970 the need for Spanish Americans.[82] Even so, two-thirds of the region's farmers worked in the 1980s off their farms.[83] Consequently, the region had become a concentration of part-time farming operations, indicating that the farms did not provide adequate incomes and the landholdings were being used in the intermediate step of becoming rural nonfarm residences.

Both underemployment and unemployment have continued, however, to characterize the region. The following unedited responses gathered in a 1968 survey in the remote Spanish-American communities of Costilla and Amalia in northern Taos County provide insights into some of the resident's problems.

> Our man do not have jobs in the winter time with pay. They are all small farmers and hate to live homes, some go away as sheepherders and live their famileys in winter time.

Husband finds it very hard to find job to support family of three children. At present he couldn't find job, so he is training under HELP [Home Education Livelihood Program].

My husband and I don't know English. Its hard to find work.

They are poor familys and cant affort to move out with their famileys, since they are small farmers.

Its merely that there are no jobs to last all yr. around, but most of us owen a few acres of land and to much pride to abondone them.[84]

Many of the respondents indicated that they had no longer a high esteem for farming or farm labor. More than half of them wanted job training in mechanics and carpentry. Their responses confirm Claire Morrill's observation in 1973 that the Spanish Americans "will try everything before they will leave Taos—seasonal jobs harvesting potatoes or herding sheep in Colorado, fighting forest fires with organized crews. But finally, if they cannot find a permanent job, they will move away."[85]

Public welfare assistance is an entrenched characteristic of the region. For instance, Taos County had in 1957 the highest rate of public assistance in New Mexico. In the late 1960s more than one-third of Río Arriba County's residents were on some sort of welfare, while one-fifth of its labor force was unemployed, the highest rate in the state. The percentage of residents who received welfare payments was more than twice the state's average, and Río Arriba and Taos counties had the highest rates of participation in both the food stamp and food commodities programs.[86]

Because of the region's eligibility for the funding of rural redevelopment programs, a number of small community projects were developed in the 1960s to create employment. They included those sponsored by the Public Works and Economic Development Act and the Home Education Livelihood Program (HELP), which was funded primarily by the U.S. Office of Economic Opportunity with assistance from the Ford Foundation and the New Mexico Council of Churches. All were similar to the programs implemented in the 1930s and designed to revitalize village economies and help keep people in the region.

While the process of out-migration was ongoing, many Spanish Americans managed to retain ownership of their small landholdings because they wanted places to return to "if things do not go well elsewhere." They also maintained a special identification with their home villages. Both sentiments indicate the Spanish Americans' strong ties to the Río Arriba, their homeland. Knowlton put it well when he found that

even though many villages have been abandoned or depopulated by recent emigration, village identification is carried into the city. Many families resident in urban areas refuse to sell their village lands. There always exists among them the hope that someday they or their children will be able to return to

their village. The sense of belonging to a specific village with a distinctive per-
sonality and way of life is one of the basic characteristics of Spanish American
life.[87]

Elderly parents would also retain their land with the expressed intent of
keeping it for their children, even after the children had left the region.[88]
They believed commonly that out-migration was a temporary necessity
and at least one of their children would return to the region someday.
Numerous Spanish-American retirees have returned in recent years to
their landholdings.[89] Benedict Cuesta, a Catholic priest in Arroyo Hondo,
described in the early 1970s the situation in a way that I experienced in
my fieldwork when he stated, "Their families have lived here for centuries; their roots are in the land; their hearts and souls are there. The tie is
really mystical."[90] Fortunately or unfortunately, depending upon one's
viewpoint, many of these parcels could not be sold because of a lack of
marketable titles.

Their attachments to the land have made Spanish Americans concerned about what is happening to the region's physical environment.
They were joined, for instance, in 1982 by organized environmentalists in
a protest against the planned development of uranium mining near Canjilón in Río Arriba County. Their sense of reverence for the region's land
provides them with the good and reassuring feelings of a homeland.

In the past when a Spanish American sold land it was usually to someone within his or her community, as there was little demand by outsiders
for the small parcels until the 1960s. This attitude may have originated
early on the community land grants where land was precious and other
grantees were given first opportunity to acquire any abandoned or pur-
chasable land. It was acceptable for each landowner to sell his irrigated
land, but only to another Spanish American, particularly to someone who
had no land within the land grant.[91] Irrigable land was kept, therefore, in
the hands of Spanish Americans, who faced increasingly the competition
for land from Anglo Americans. Diecker found this to be the case, for
instance, in Córdova, where the small landholdings were perceived by the
Spanish American residents as "a home base, a fortress of ownership
which serves to keep the community free of non Spanish-American residents."[92] Parcels were traded occasionally within and between families to
derive desired housesites, the foremost assessment of many landholdings
today.

Outsiders, mainly Anglo Americans, have also assessed the Río Arriba
favorably because of its scenery, climate, quaint villages, and the awe of
living in a tricultural (Anglo, Indian, and Spanish) region that has vestiges
of a long and rich history. Beginning in the 1960s, several "beatniks"
purchased acreage in the vicinity of El Rito, Río Arriba County, and near
Taos. By the end of the 1960s, hundreds of "hippies" had moved into the

Taos area alone. Some resided in tepees and makeshift shelters on public land, including the Carson National Forest, and carried on communal livelihoods. Others, however, purchased land in nearby secluded mountain communities. Their presence caused considerable apprehension and dissension among the region's Spanish Americans. Those who sold land and their water rights, usually through a real estate agent because they lived elsewhere, were called *vendidos,* betrayers of the people.[93] Most Spanish Americans did not like the hippies' ability to live in self-proclaimed poverty and subsequently participate in the government assistance programs but yet be able to purchase land.[94] Small tracts have also been sold to other Anglo Americans, especially in the mountains for summer cabins. These sales to outsiders, however, indicate changing attitudes and values concerning landownership within the waning Spanish-American communities and the significance attached to buyers being able today to obtain clear titles.[95] Land values have increased accordingly.

In conclusion, the Río Arriba has remained not only a very distinct historic-cultural region, but it also has become identified with intense rural poverty. For Spanish Americans to blame their deficient economy upon the many rejected land-grant claims and loss of communal lands is an effort to divert attention from other problems that stem from the region's physical incompatibility with agriculture, as well as with its settlement and demographic patterns. Overpopulation, long associated with subsistence farming because it allowed low capital entry for too many people, became a problem. Consequently, insufficient accumulations of wealth combined with poor land resources prohibited the expansion and type of commercial agriculture needed to keep pace with national trends. Instead, the region's farm villages had produced a disproportionately high percentage of rural poor and unemployed people who became to a great degree dependent upon government welfare assistance and programs. Seasonal labor and out-migration have been ameliorating factors, but the Río Arriba continues to provide a sense of security for too many rural Spanish Americans.

Land Use in the
National Forests, 1910–1990

7

Spanish Americans' frustrations over their relatively poor economic situation and the continual influx of Anglo Americans became apparent when they began to physically contest the ownership and use of land, producing harassment, violence, and more controversy. Spanish Americans and Anglo Americans alike had implanted their own land policies, which were bound in both cases to affect the already settled population. The Spaniards' imposition of the *encomienda* system on the Pueblo Indians led eventually to the Pueblo Revolt of 1680, the greatest single occurrence of violence in the Río Arriba. After the reconquest, the Pueblos continued to wage lesser acts of harassment and violence against the Spanish Americans. In the late 1800s, groups of Spanish Americans started to torment Anglo Americans, especially the homesteaders, known also as nesters, whom they considered to be "land-grabbers."[1] The White Caps (Gorras Blancas) operated between the late 1800s and the 1920s, largely in neighboring eastern San Miguel County, to disrupt Anglo-American homesteading, land companies, and railroads from developing what they considered to be their rangeland. Another group, the Black Hand (Mano Negra), based in northwestern New Mexico during the 1920s and early 1930s, was responsible for limited harassment against Anglo Americans, some of whom lived in Río Arriba County.[2]

Although historians Robert J. Rosenbaum and Robert W. Larson claim that there was "long-term skirmishing" as evidenced in the form of Spanish Americans cutting the fences and burning the barns of Anglo Americans in northern New Mexico, little of it took place in the Río Arriba.[3] They concluded that the resistance against the Anglo Americans had less to do with the loss of land-grant claims and land grants than with the day-to-day conflicts of interest in regard to the use of land, especially that which comprised the open range.[4] Consequently, much of the overt resistance was found on the Río Arriba's periphery and on the plains east of the Sangre de Cristo Mountains. González has expressed surprise that no similar organized resistance group developed in the Río Arriba during the Depression of the 1930s, when Spanish Americans experienced very poor conditions.[5]

Organized resistance did not reappear in the Río Arriba until 1964, when a group of Spanish Americans sent eviction notices to landowners residing within the large (592,000 acres) and controversial Tierra Amarilla Grant. This group posted no trespassing signs and established an armed patrol around the grant's boundaries. After cases of suspected arson were reported to officials, a district court ordered in 1965 the group to discontinue its efforts and no subsequent trouble was attributed to it.[6]

Meanwhile, the militant organization, the Alianza Federal de Mercedes (Federated Alliance of Land Grants), later renamed the Alianza de los Pueblos Libres (Confederation of Free City-States), had been established in the Río Arriba by a Texan named Reies López Tijerina. Organized in 1963, the Alianza emphasized the rural Spanish Americans' poor and frustrating economic situation, especially for those who lived on the small parcels of land within rejected and patented Spanish and Mexican land-grant claims. In essence, its argument was that these residents had been illegally dispossessed of their grazing land. Tijerina sought help from the Mexican and American governments to investigate this claim. Both governments refused his requests.[7]

One condition of the Alianza was that it wanted the American government to purchase from the U.S. Forest Service the land that had been claimed by the Spanish Americans in the adjudication of the Spanish and Mexican land-grant claims—if pursued to the utmost this would have included almost all of the Río Arriba outside the Pueblo Indian grants. This land was to be given to the heirs of the original settlers as reparations for alleged past wrongdoings by the federal government. Furthermore, the Alianza wanted compensation for all the past profits gained from these lands.[8] In general, the organization was also against Anglo-American cultural and political influences in the region, despite the fact that the Spanish Americans had long dominated the region's elected political offices at both the county and state levels.[9] In addition, they had their own representatives in Congress and in the U.S. Senate.

Spanish Americans allegedly resented the fact that they needed permits from the Anglo-American established Forest Service (La Floresta) for grazing their livestock and cutting wood. Likewise, they also needed licenses for hunting and fishing, all on land that they argued was theirs from the outset of Spanish and Mexican colonization. Knowlton described the growing tension between Forest Service personnel and some Spanish Americans: "Forest Service personnel living in the rural villages of northern New Mexico began to move to the larger cities, as resentment against them spread. Rangers were shot at on mountain trails. Many fires were deliberately set on the National Forests in New Mexico."[10]

Under the leadership of Tijerina, 350 Alianzistas claimed land in October 1966 for the development of a free city-state (Pueblo Republica de San Joaquín del Río Chama) at Echo Amphitheatre in the Carson National Forest. This land was located within the rejected half-million acres of the San Joaquín del Río Chama land-grant claim, which had its irrigated portion (1,423 acres) patented as the Cañon de Chama Grant. They claimed that their action for establishing a city-state was allowed under the laws of the Indies (*La Recopilación de leyes de los reynos de las Indias*). Tijerina's intention was to use this case as the basis of a court test.[11]

A period of confrontation, however, ensued between the Alianzistas and the local authorities. Violence erupted on 5 June 1967, when an attempt was made by about twenty Alianzistas to release several of their arrested comrades and to make a citizen's arrest of the Río Arriba County district attorney in a raid at the county courthouse in Tierra Amarilla. Two county officials were wounded by gunfire. Tijerina was eventually arrested and spent two years in jail. Although the fervor for the Alianza has faded in the region, it not only renewed the land grant controversy but also focused attention upon the role of the Forest Service in the region's economy.[12] A flurry of sympathetic studies supporting the Alianza's position followed in various publications, and a nationally televised documentary in April 1969 probed the organization's activities and the poor conditions found in northern New Mexico. Most of the findings included the following sentiment: "The forced exodus of Hispano subsistence farmers and small cattlemen from their ancestral homes in the northern counties continues, because of their pauperization, the inevitable result of the loss of their primary resource, land."[13]

The Forest Service took the brunt of the blame for the Spanish Americans' plight because the region's Carson and Santa Fe national forests incorporate both rejected Spanish and Mexican land-grant claims and communal lands of patented land grants that were lost for taxes or purchased from heirs. Coincidentally, the Forest Service was accused of deliberately reducing the number of livestock grazing permits in 1965 by nearly 45 percent in order to oust small farmers from the program.[14] Knowlton reinforced this allegation: "Grazing permits for small herds of cattle and sheep upon which so many Spanish-Americans depend were sharply cut. The grazing season was reduced from nine to six months . . . Spanish-Americans dependent upon the National Forests that once were part of their land grants are today convinced that the National Forest Service would like to eliminate the Spanish-Americans and replace them with Anglo-American ranchers and tourists."[15] He further contended that when the Forest Service reduced the number of grazing permits it contributed to making malnutrition a serious problem in the Spanish-American villages because many of the permits were specifically for milch cows, which produced dairy products that the Spanish Americans could not afford to purchase in grocery stores.[16]

Others claimed that the Forest Service had given preferential treatment in providing livestock-grazing permits for Anglo Americans over the needs of the small Spanish-American landowners. Historian Myra Ellen Jenkins maintained that "one solution lies in the improvement of management practices of Forest Service lands; of more equitable grazing permits which will favor the local small livestock owners over the out-of-state large operators."[17] Her view was supported by Westphall: "Often the grazing policy incorporates the 'paperwork' efficiency of leasing land to owners with large herds, which is less trouble than working with more numerous small owners who barely produce enough food to nourish their bodies and who have little else than pride in their sturdy heritage to nurture their hope."[18] Frank Waters wrote that "land—formerly the common lands of community land grants—now comprising most of the Santa Fe and Carson National Forests, is used for the benefit of large business interests rather than for the people living in the villages on these grants."[19]

Because of the many adverse opinions and allegations that have been made against the Forest Service, some background information is necessary to gain a fuller appreciation of what took place in the Río Arriba. In 1891 Congress passed the Creative Act, which authorized the designation of forest reserves within the public domain. Concerns had arisen over the cutting of the nation's forests, the lack of reforestation, and the possible shortage of timber. In the Río Arriba the Pecos River Forest Reserve was set aside in 1892. It, with part of the Jémez Forest Reserve, established in 1905, became the Santa Fe National Forest in 1915. The Carson National Forest resulted in 1908 from the consolidation of the Taos Forest Reserve, set aside in 1906, and part of the Jémez Forest Reserve. By combining several forest reserves set aside after 1906, the Cíbola National Forest was created in 1931. (Two small extensions of the Cíbola National Forest are found today in southern Sandoval County.) By 1923 more than 161,000,000 acres had been set aside in the United States in national forests. Nearly 10,000,000 of these acres were in New

Mexico. Seven other states (Arizona, California, Colorado, Idaho, Montana, Oregon, and Washington) each had considerably more acreage withdrawn from the public domain for national forests than New Mexico.[20]

By 1910, the national forests had been opened as summer rangeland, under the multiple-use concept, to qualified owners of livestock under a permit policy directed by the U.S. Department of Agriculture. These owners were required to have sufficient base properties (land resources, water, and forage) to sustain their livestock for the rest of the year, maintain fire prevention in the national forests, and pay a small fee per head. This policy was implemented because of growing concern by agricultural officials and environmentalists in regard to overstocking and its impact upon flood control and other problems of erosion and entrenchment that could be created within watersheds. There had been a history of overgrazing in the Río Arriba that had destroyed much of the fragile vegetative cover of the region's watersheds and led to accelerated rates of erosion.[21] In 1985, DeBuys described the severity of the situation: "One hundred years ago, for instance, a great many relatively small decisions by stockmen to increase the size of their herds resulted in a debacle of overgrazing that seriously undermined the pastoral economy of the mountain villages."[22] Similar situations had developed elsewhere in New Mexico when record numbers of livestock grazed the state.[23] Extensive logging in the surrounding mountains during the turn of the century had also contributed to destroying watersheds.[24]

With the growing revelations, too, about the impact of the lingering drought and the creation of the dust bowl, Congress passed in 1934 the Taylor Grazing Act. This legislation organized the remaining public grasslands into grazing districts, and again livestock-grazing permits were issued to prevent overgrazing, soil deterioration, and other problems, including the animosity that had developed between sheepmen and cattlemen. This program was eventually placed in 1946 under the administration of the Bureau of Land Management (BLM), which merged the General Land Office and the Grazing Service. These policies had helped to bring an end to homesteading, especially as a means of acquiring large acreages of grazing land. In fact, sizable portions of the grasslands had been previous homestead claims and therefore all fences had to be removed.[25]

With the closing of the open range, pasturage other than that on one's farm was now available only through livestock-grazing permit programs administered by agencies of the U.S. government. Much of the Río Arriba's total land area (8,750,000 acres) is currently managed by federal agencies. The Forest Service alone administers approximately 2,545,000 acres (29 percent) and the BLM manages approximately 1,375,000 acres

(16 percent). Other land is included in the National Park Service system and state lands. The federal government continues to acquire land in the region, largely homesteads owned by private persons, particularly to expand and consolidate the acreage within the two national forests. For instance, approximately 130,000 acres are privately owned within the boundaries of the Santa Fe National Forest. The total acreage of the Carson and Santa Fe national forests, including that outside the Río Arriba, has been increased from 2,370,000 acres in 1945 to 3,080,000 acres in

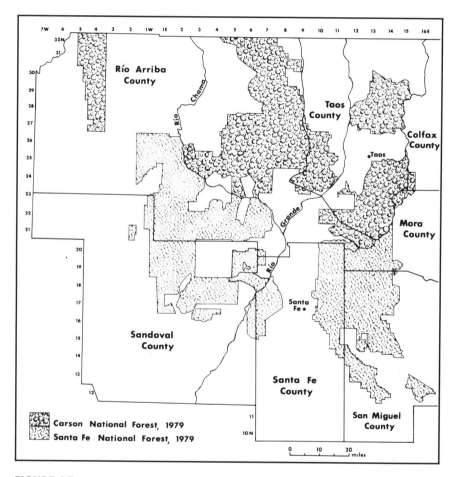

FIGURE 27

The Carson and Santa Fe national forests are located largely in the Río Arriba's counties of Río Arriba, Sandoval, Santa Fe, and Taos. Both national forests extend into the eastern neighboring counties of Colfax, Mora, and San Miguel (partially shown above).

Source: U.S. Department of Interior, Bureau of Land Management, "State of New Mexico Land Status Map, 1979."

1982 (Figure 27). According to census criteria, in 1982 less than 40 percent (3,283,000 acres) of the region was used as farmland, of which Spanish Americans farmed only 410,000 acres (13 percent).

An analysis is made here of the Forest Service's grazing permit program in the Río Arriba because of the numerous inferences that the establishment of the Carson and Santa Fe national forests seriously curtailed Spanish-American agriculture by the imposition of land-use controls. There is an underlying contention that if the Forest Service had not managed these lands the Spanish Americans would have been able to maintain a much more prosperous livestock industry. Despite the cited allegations and problems, my research indicates that the two national forests accommodated large numbers of Spanish-American livestock owners and their livestock. Hence, these forests must be considered as a factor in sustaining the region's Spanish-American subculture. This is not an attempt to condone all of the Forest Service's actions, but my findings do present conclusions different from those referred to in the allegations.

Census data were compiled from eight agricultural censuses between 1910 (used for 1915) and 1982 and for the same eight years from all paid grazing permits in the Carson and Santa Fe national forests that were held by permittees who had mailing addresses in the Río Arriba (Appendix I).[26] Data were not gathered on those permittees who lived outside the Río Arriba in adjacent counties of both New Mexico and Colorado or on the small number of distant out-of-state permittees, in both cases Anglo Americans and Spanish Americans who lived largely in California and Texas. In hindsight, some of these out-of-state permittees could have been included in this analysis because they, too, had to have owned or leased land as base property adjacent to or near the two national forests. It could not be determined, however, whether in these cases the base properties were located specifically within the Río Arriba. The compiled data also do not include those free grazing permits that exempted livestock, such as milch cows, used for household purposes (nearly all held by Spanish Americans); livestock owned by Pueblos; crossing or trailing privileges from one grazing district to another within a forest; and free use for owners of private property within a forest's boundaries.

Incidentally, the Bureau of the Census asked farmers for the first time in taking the 1982 agricultural census how many possessed livestock-grazing permits on public lands. According to unpublished data for the Río Arriba, 551 farmers reported having grazing permits, which represented more than one-third of the region's farmers who had livestock.[27] The Carson and Santa Fe national forests reported in 1982 a total of 895 paid grazing permits, of which my data show that 490 were held by farmers of the Río Arriba. The discrepancy between the census data and my data can be attributed partially to my exclusion of the previously mentioned permits. Moreover, nearly 600 residents had livestock grazing permits on BLM lands.[28] Obviously, many small livestock owners did not report these grazing permits in the census or, if they did, their operations did not qualify them as farmers. Then, too, some permittees who had grazing privileges under both programs probably reported them as a single permit. In addition, a growing number of Spanish-American livestock owners who each had only a few head have grouped together to form grazing associations in order to pool their resources. Because the New Mexican Livestock Board requires one bull per twenty cows on the public range, a considerable number of small operators cannot afford to keep bulls yearlong and hence have formed grazing associations where fewer bulls are needed. A grazing association is listed, however, as one grazing permit and was tabulated accordingly.[29] Therefore, the grazing permits represent more Spanish Americans than the data indicate.

Each grazing permit card provides a historical record of a permittee's allocation, which was normally for a period of ten years and could be renewed routinely. Although the grazing permit program started in 1910, many livestock owners did not comply with the policy until the 1920s. Also, not all the region's farmers had livestock. Approximately 80 percent of them owned livestock (cattle and sheep) between 1925 and 1982, and four out of five had cattle.

Since 1925, more than 90 percent of the Río Arriba's permittees have been persons with Spanish surnames (Spanish Americans) who also owned the vast majority of the permitted cattle and sheep that grazed in both national forests (Appendix I). Contrary to the allegations, their percentage of permitted cattle has increased significantly since 1945. Spanish Americans also possessed 90 percent or more of the grazing permits for sheep and goats and owned over 70 percent of those permitted. The rest were owned until 1945 largely by Frank Bond of Española, who for years operated a *partido* system by using grazing permits held by Spanish Americans in order to create large flocks in return for employing the permittees. This system was no longer attractive to Spanish Americans after World War II and it eventually faded from the region's economy. On permits between 1915 and 1945, Spanish Americans also grazed hundreds of draft horses annually, indicating their lack of mechanization—more than 1,100 alone in 1925 in comparison with only 130 for the permittees with non-Spanish (Anglo-American) surnames. Because the requests to graze horses dwindled to a very small number after 1954, data were not compiled on them thereafter for this analysis.

In comparing the number of the region's permittees to the number of farmers with livestock since 1925, the data show that the Carson and Santa Fe national forests have accommodated livestock in each decade for approximately one-third of the region's livestock owners. This was true in 1982 when they had 55 percent (490) of the total number (895) of paid grazing permits and grazed 60 percent (based upon 5 sheep = 1 cow) of the 28,000 head of permitted livestock. The other permittees, mostly Spanish Americans, resided in the neighboring rural counties within New Mexico and Colorado, especially the San Luis Valley, as well as in urban centers such as Albuquerque, Denver, and Los Angeles, but retained base properties. In 1954 and 1964, the region's livestock farmers possessed 75 percent (946 and 762, respectively) of all the paid grazing permits for cattle and owned 70 percent (12,250 and 13,175) of all paid-permit cattle. Over 70 percent (144 and 75) of all the sheep/goat permits in 1945 and 1954 were owned, too, by the region's livestock farmers, who grazed over 70 percent (61,900 and 33,800) of the paid-permit sheep and goats.

In addition to the livestock allowed onto the two national forests under paid grazing permits, livestock equivalent to over 4,400 cattle were permitted in 1945 to graze under exemptions. These exemptions were reduced to less than 2,500 in 1964 and they have since been reduced greatly, occurring especially when a base property is sold or transferred to another party. Many permittees did not use their full authorizations or did not use them at all, resulting in a total equivalence of nearly 2,200 cattle in 1945 and over 2,600 cattle in 1954. These nonuse authorizations were also reduced to a few hundred head of livestock in 1982.

Hundreds of Spanish Americans who had only a few livestock were given grazing permits in the Carson and Santa Fe national forests. Approximately 60 percent of the cattle permits from 1925 to 1954 were for farmers with one to nine head and another 20 percent were for farmers with ten to nineteen head (Appendix J). More than 70 percent of the permits were for farmers with one to nineteen head in 1964. As more small cattle owners dropped out of farming or entered grazing associations, the percentages of permits allowing one to nineteen head dropped to 60 percent in 1972 and to 55 percent in 1982. Agricultural economist Marlowe Taylor found in his 1956 study of three grazing districts that many small livestock owners had grazing permits.[30] This was also true in the mid-1940s in the case of livestock grazing permits on BLM lands in New Mexico. Of ten western states, New Mexico's farmers had the lowest average size grazing permit.[31] A large number of the state's Spanish Americans, who owned only a few livestock, had been given, therefore, access to BLM lands. Approximately 600 livestock owners, many of whom were Spanish American, possessed in the mid-1980s grazing permits for the equivalent of nearly 12,000 cattle on the Río Arriba's BLM land. In comparing the number of livestock according to the 1982 census with the number of grazing permits issued by both government agencies, the data show that these public lands accommodated one-third of the region's total livestock, which numbered an equivalent of about 90,000 cattle. The permitted livestock were owned overwhelmingly by Spanish Americans (Appendix I). It is interesting to note here that in the literature the BLM has not been the target of the same vehement accusations leveled against the Forest Service.[32] This may be because its lands include largely relinquished homesteads and unclaimed public lands rather than rejected Spanish and Mexican land-grant claims and purchased communal lands of patented land grants.

Large Anglo-American stockmen and corporations, therefore, have not dominated the grazing permit programs in the Río Arriba. DeBuys, too, found "no clear evidence that they benefited in their efforts from the connivance of the Forest Service."[33] It is not surprising, however, that the Anglo Americans continuously had larger grazing permits than the Spanish Americans, who owned the prevailing small land units or required base properties. Farms of under ten acres included only 1 percent of the Río Arriba's total farm acreage in 1964.[34]

Beginning in the 1940s, sizes of grazing permits were limited for all of New Mexico's national forests. Those for the Río Arriba's Carson and Santa Fe national forests were set the lowest. For instance, the Santa Fe National Forest's limit was set at fifty to one hundred cattle, depending upon circumstances. Agricultural historians Clyde Eastman and James R. Gray maintain that these "limits per owner were to give stability to established permittees consistent with economic operations, to make a fair division, and to prevent monopoly. The Carson and Santa Fe national forest limits were lower than those of other forests because of heavy local demand and heavy population pressures on the national forests."[35] Today, no permittee is allowed to put more than 400 head of livestock in either national forest. Only these two national forests in the American Southwest have had these low restrictions, which were designed to assure grazing opportunities for the Río Arriba's many small Spanish-American livestock owners. Requests to waive these restrictions have been disapproved.[36]

In analyzing the records of the grazing permits, it is apparent that the vast majority of the Spanish-American permittees had acquired their grazing permits based upon prior use of the range, which included the use of the rejected Spanish and Mexican land-grant claims and the purchased portions of patented land grants. Consequently, the small landowners continued to graze their livestock nearby. This enabled them to drive their livestock to pastures on the hoof, rather than creating the need to have them trucked to grazing districts some distance away. A commentary in the September 1931 issue of the *Carson Pine Cone* (Carson National Forest's newsletter) indicates not only this type of permitted grazing but also village dominance by a few extended families just as if they had owned the former land-grant claims or land grants.

> It's queer how certain Spanish American names run on this Forest. It would seem that years ago families by one name settled in one place and succeeding generations never moved around. For instance, we find almost all the Jaramillos, Peñas, and Ortegas on the Vallecitos District; on the Río Pueblo the Mascarenas are numerous and nowhere else; on the Tres Piedras District the Romeros, Lopez, and Atencios hold sway; at Canjilón, there are the Casados, Borregos, and Sanchez; on the Taos District we find many Raels, Cisneros, and Córdovas, and on the Jicarilla there are the Gómez families.[37]

On the whole, Spanish Americans and Anglo Americans have been given equitable grazing periods for their livestock in both national forests since 1925 (Appendix I). In recent years, approximately 80 percent of the cattle-grazing permits were for six months or 180 days, extending from mid-May through mid-October (Appendix J). A small percentage of the permittees have had winter grazing permits, and slightly under 10 percent had yearlong grazing permits. Grazing periods are determined by assessing local environmental conditions for each of the several districts within a national forest. Some districts are made up largely of high elevations and have very limited grazing capacities; hence, permittees near these districts have had shorter grazing periods than those who had their livestock assigned to districts with lower elevations and better pastures. Overall, there appears to have been fair treatment of the permittees when all the variables are taken into consideration; however, the grazing seasons for cattle have been shortened for both parties since the outset of the grazing permit program (Appendix J). Undoubtedly, this policy was implemented to maintain the pastures and prevent damage within the multiple-use concept.

It is true that the number of livestock grazing permits in the Río Arriba has declined in the past several decades. For instance, the number of paid grazing permits for cattle in 1982 was only half that of 1954. Only a few grazing permits remain for a greatly reduced number of sheep (Appendix I). On the other hand, fewer grazing permits have allowed a large increase in the number of cattle. Moreover, the decline in the number of grazing permits follows the national trend in agriculture as many permittees, like their counterparts elsewhere in the United States, have simply pulled out of unprofitable and time-consuming livestock operations.

The decline in the region's number of sheep (245,600 in 1945, 20,600 in 1982, and 13,400 in 1987) surely reflects the agricultural trends in the sheep industry. Since statistics started to be kept in 1876, the number of New Mexico's sheep first hit a record low in 1954. Since then, the number of sheep in the western states has declined by nearly 70 percent between 1960 and 1975.[38] The Forest Service decided in general not to renew grazing permits for sheep and goats from the mid-1950s onward. Sheep tend to damage a forest's vegetation more than cattle. Some of the forest land that sheep grazed in the higher elevations was closed for grazing altogether. Sheep grazing was finally discontinued in 1972 in the Santa Fe National Forest. In many cases, sheep permits became new cattle permits or they were merely consolidated with existing cattle permits. Essentially, sheepmen became cattlemen and the sizes of the grazing permits for cattle increased overall (Appendix J). Because new grazing permits are largely unavailable, they are valued and handed down when possible from one generation to the next in the transfer of land within families.

Horses and milch cows were also excluded, for the most part, from the Forest Service's grazing permit program in the 1960s because their numbers had declined steadily and there were far fewer requests for them. They also grazed near the villages and hence caused severe overgrazing in the immediate watersheds.[39] Knowlton's assertion that the Spanish Americans were greatly dependent upon milch cows is not borne out in the agricultural censuses. For instance, only 35 percent of the Río Arriba's farms had milch cows in 1925 and they averaged only two per farm. Before the Forest Service reduced the number of livestock grazing permits in the mid-1960s, only 12 percent of the region's farms had milch cows, and the average was again only two cows per farm. Less than 8 percent of the region's farms had milch cows in 1982, averaging two cows per farm, and only twenty farms sold dairy products.[40]

Forest Service records show that the agency has allowed more livestock to graze in the two national forests than allowable under ideal management. For example, nearly 2,900 more cattle and 15,000 more sheep were allowed in 1945 to graze on the national forests than what was figured to be the allowable grazing capacity. Almost 6,500 more cattle were allowed in 1964, when less than 50 percent of the combined acreage of the national forests was open to grazing, than what was figured to be ecologically sound.[41] This was again because the villages had too many livestock. Since then, portions of several grazing districts have been closed because of severe deterioration of the grazing conditions. The grazing capacity of the permitted land, often with improved vegetation, averaged about 50 acres per cow between 1945 and 1964.[42] Two-thirds (1,010,000) of the Santa Fe National Forest's total acreage (1,589,000) in 1982 were not open to grazing because of unsuitable vegetative cover, steepness, and mountains.[43] Today, this national forest's management still figures an average of 50 acres per cow for six months, but higher amounts are necessary in some grazing districts. The BLM also figures an average of about 50 acres, but carrying capacities on its lands range from 40 to more than 100 acres per cow.[44]

Grazing capacities of some Spanish and Mexican land grants could hardly support several families today, let alone an entire village. For example, the grazing capacity of the 2,668 acres of usable grazing land on the Ojo de San José Grant in 1945 was estimated to be for only 33 head of cattle—a carrying capacity of 81 acres per cow yearlong. If this grant's rejected portion (25,603 acres) of the land-grant claim were also included, the land grant would have been able to sustain a total of only 350 cattle. Likewise, the Ramon Vígil Grant's 20,296 usable grazing acres out of a patented grant of 31,210 acres were estimated to accommodate 167 cattle—a carrying capacity of 122 acres per cow.[45] These carrying capacities indicate clearly the extent of the region's poor land resources in a state where today's farmland is valued the lowest ($134 an acre) in the entire country and the livestock owners' need to use government pasturage.[46] Cattlemen in 1982 needed fifty or more cattle to provide even a minimum income. If a cattle operator in 1982 sold half his or her herd of fifty head at the region's average price of $380 per head and kept the other half for breeding purposes, the gross income would amount to only $9,500, hardly sufficient to support a family.[47]

Not only has the Forest Service accommodated as many of the region's livestock as possible, it has also from time to time shown considerable compassion for the permittees' problems. For instance,

> due to the grasshopper plague and the scarcity of water for irrigation during the season of 1931, the stockmen of Questa and vicinity were virtually without any feed when the first heavy snow fell in late November. In this extremity they appealed to the Forest Service for emergency winter range. The cattle were taken into the [Carson] Forest on December 1 and from all appearances the per cent of loss will be very small, and whatever losses will occur may be due to the extremely poor condition the stock were in at the time they entered the Forest. Stock kept at the ranches have suffered considerably and heavy losses are already taking place.[48]

The 1935 data on the permittees' grazing cards reveal, too, that the Forest Service accommodated nearly all the requests for livestock during the difficult times of the drought and Depression of the 1930s. Also during this time, hundreds of families did not need permits because they owned few or no livestock. In the case of twenty-four communities with a total of 2,260 families that owned livestock, each family owned an average of 1.7 head of cattle, 5.9 sheep, and 1.4 horses.[49] Most families had been engaged in seasonal labor and therefore depended only upon farmyard animals, which were readily accessible. This continues to be a common practice in the villages.

Permittees have been required to pay a nominal fee annually for each head of permitted livestock. At first, no fees were imposed for grazing livestock on the forest reserves and the national forests. This policy was changed in 1910, when there was apparent overgrazing of these lands by livestock owners who had little regard for the forests' ecological conditions. Grazing permits were introduced and fees charged not only to regulate the grazing activity but also to assure small landowners of equitable access to the national forests. The intent was to bring about some sort of economic stability in the Spanish-American communities by eliminating unfair and unregulated competition for the pastures or range. Each grazing permit had a Spanish translation explaining the grazing fees. There were also small monetary assessments for the placement of salt and snow drift fences in the forests. In lawsuits from California and Colorado, where permittees refused to pay grazing fees, the U.S. Supreme Court ruled unanimously in 1911 that the Forest Service (under the U.S. Department of Agriculture) could legally charge users' fees.[50] There is no indication from the data, when the length of the grazing period is considered, that the Spanish Americans had to pay higher fees than the Anglo Americans.

Grazing permit fees are used with large amounts of federal monies to revegetate thousands of acres in the national forests, to control rodents and poisonous plants, and to construct stock tanks, ponds, and corrals. Forest Service personnel also tag all permitted livestock for identification. Portable tagging chutes are taken to a permittee's corral where large legible tags are placed on the cattle before they are allowed to enter a national forest. All permitted livestock must also be branded. Some Spanish Americans resent paying these fees, but on the other hand they do not have to pay property taxes, which would be the case if the land were in their possession. It is apparent that the costly capital outlays for range improvements are in no way covered by the permittees' fees. Consequently, the federal government has long subsidized both the small and large livestock owners.[51] Incidentally, the Pueblo Indians also use the national forests, mostly, however, for religious purposes and to collect resources such as firewood and clays for making pottery.[52] Today only Nambé pueblo has a grazing permit (free use) in the Santa Fe National Forest.

Not only do some Spanish Americans look upon the Forest Service with disdain because of the grazing permit program, but they also dislike the fact that the agency controls and manages their previously claimed and owned lands for outdoor recreation, the fastest-growing use by the public (largely Anglo American), and for timber management.[53] For instance, the rugged Pecos Wilderness and Wheeler Peak Wilderness areas (between Las Vegas and Santa Fe and northeast of Taos, respectively) are largely unsuitable for livestock grazing and have been removed from any use but for recreation and wildlife management. The national forests in 1965 began to collect fees for recreational use under the Land and Water Conservation Fund Act. Special recreational projects, such as the Santa Fe

Ski Basin in the Santa Fe National Forest, have also been allowed. The
Forest Service manages thousands of acres of commercial timberland that
help to control surface runoff and subsequently provide flood control
within the Río Grande watershed. These various functions of the national
forests have been expanded under the mandate given to the Forest Service
by the Multiple Use–Sustained Yield Act of 1960. The Classification and
Multiple Use Act of 1964 provided a similar mandate for the use of lands
managed by the BLM. These policies, however controversial they may
seem to particular parties, were reaffirmed for both federal agencies by
the passage of the Federal Land Policy and Management Act of 1976.

In addition, the Carson and Santa Fe national forests have provided
considerable employment for many of the Río Arriba's Spanish Americans, especially after the Alianza movement. The Santa Fe National Forest
in the early 1970s employed 105 permanent employees and 130 seasonal
employees. In 1982 its employment had grown to 135 permanent full-
time positions, 82 permanent positions with a work year ranging from
six to eleven months, and approximately 100 temporary, seasonal
employees. Nearly 50 percent of the full-time employees were Spanish
Americans. They also held 85 percent of the other jobs. The annual payroll for all of these employees was $4,700,000. Meanwhile, the Carson
National Forest in the early 1970s employed over 100 permanent
employees and an additional 150 people on a seasonal basis. It employed
130 full-time employees, 54 permanent part-time employees, and 50 temporary seasonal employees in 1982 with a total payroll of $4,560,000.
Three-fourths of these employees were Spanish Americans. The combined
payrolls in 1982 equaled more than one-quarter of the region's total agricultural sales or one-third of its sales from livestock.[54] The payrolls did
not include the salaries that contractors and subcontractors paid their
employees for work done within the forests.

Timber harvested from the two national forests has provided employment for another several hundred Spanish Americans at local saw and
planing mills. For instance, the Duke City Lumber Company near Española began operations in 1966 with over two hundred employees and a
one million-dollar payroll. The Forest Service assured the sawmill of a
dependable supply of sawlogs. One-quarter of the income in 1977 for
120 households in the Gallina-Coyote area of Río Arriba County was
derived from working in the logging industry—the same percentage as
that derived from general government assistance payments. The logs were
taken from the surrounding Santa Fe National Forest.[55] Incidentally, a
considerable portion of the revenue from timber sales has been returned
to the counties. Several hundred Spanish Americans made at least part of
their livelihood by obtaining permits to cut firewood, posts, and *vigas*
(ceiling beams) for sale.[56] More than 17,300 Christmas trees were cut

annually for personal use during the 1970s in the Santa Fe National Forest alone. Consequently, the Forest Service carries on an extensive reforestation program. Furthermore, Spanish Americans continue to hunt, fish, and gather piñon nuts in the national forests. An economic study showed in the 1970s that recreation and timber each had a greater potential for increasing income from the region's national forests than did livestock grazing.[57] Despite this, Spanish Americans were allowed continual use of both national forests for their small numbers of livestock.

My fieldwork reveals that many of these rural Spanish-American permittees were wage earners in nearby urban centers who continued to keep a few livestock and their grazing permits for merely social reasons. Some of them can be overheard in summer explaining to their urban counterparts about their need to check, over an upcoming weekend, on their livestock in one of the national forests. The implied prestige is undoubtedly more important to many of these permittees than the livestock as a source of income. The importance of livestock to the region's Spanish Americans is reflected in a study done in 1979 by the Santa Fe National Forest, where the conclusion was drawn that

> there is an inordinate affinity for livestock among the residents of the region. This is not uncommon among people with recent agrarian antecedents. They feel incomplete, vaguely insecure, almost unfulfilled without a few animals. This may be true of many with good incomes from non-agrarian sources. What may appear at first observation to be an almost irrational desire for livestock and a place to graze them is indeed a pervasive and not uncommon cultural heritage. Anything which reduces livestock grazing is particularly incompatible to the traditional village culture.[58]

Overall, Spanish Americans have been able to maintain their rural presence in the Río Arriba not only by retaining their irrigable landholdings, but also by taking advantage of the opportunities in using the region's public lands as rangeland. On the whole, the Forest Service, contrary to the various allegations, accommodated the agricultural pursuits of many Spanish Americans within a region that has had, otherwise, serious environmental limitations and too many farmers.

PART THREE

The Maintenance of Culture

Architecture, Religion, and the Vernacular Landscape

8

Having been able to acquire land in the Río Arriba and fend for themselves against various obstacles, the Spanish Americans set about organizing and fashioning their region into usable landscapes.[1] Their decision-making processes and activities produced a folk environment of which some elements became manifested in vernacular landscapes. As John Brinckerhoff Jackson, a self-described "amateur geographer" and resident of the Río Arriba, has asserted, "A vernacular landscape reveals a distinct way of defining and handling time and space."[2] Vernacular landscapes are used here to delimit further the Spanish-American homeland. For instance, one such landscape resulted from the long-lot field pattern and the custom of partible inheritance. Common house types and methods of construction that rely heavily on local resources contributed to the development of a distinctive material culture that produced additional vernacular landscapes, all of which provided a sense of a homogeneous spatial behavior within the region.

Moreover, the Spanish Americans' history of subsistence livelihoods, seasonal labor, rural poverty, and slow out-migration is important in the enduring maintenance of their vernacular landscapes or of those retained in any other rural region of America. People in poor or disadvantaged economic situations find ways to cope with their limited capabilities until change and opportunities are introduced by external forces such as government programs or by out-migration. Consequently, a folk environment and its vernacular landscapes can change or disappear. Cultural geographer Fred B. Kniffen and folklorist Henry H. Glassie alluded to this when in the mid-1960s the federal government developed its campaign against rural poverty. They claimed that "the new attack on rural poverty will surely accelerate the destruction of unchronicled folk structures and practices to the point where their record is beyond recovery."[3] For the most part, the Río Arriba's vernacular landscapes and material culture can still be chronicled because of their continuing use.

Upon their arrival in the region, the Spaniards found the indigenous Pueblo Indians had built tiered structures consisting of aggregations of flat-roofed cells using wooden beams and clay soil to make walls of puddled mud or adobe.[4] With their own knowledge of Moorish building prototypes and techniques, they began to build flat-roofed adobe dwellings similar to those of the Pueblos. But unlike the Pueblos, they used bricks molded in wooden forms and strengthened by straw or grass as a bonding material to prevent cracking or crumbling in the drying process.[5] In time, the Pueblos also adopted the use of a binder. While the Indian pueblos were fascinating to Anglo Americans and Europeans, many at the same time wrote disparagingly about the Spanish-American adobe house. In general, they were described as crude, squatty, and unbecoming earthen structures and often referred to as "doby" houses. Santa Fe was described accordingly: "The town is a wretched collection of mud houses. . . . I can compare it to nothing but a dilapidated brick kiln or a prairie-dog town."[6] "It is true those are heaps of unburnt bricks, nevertheless they are houses."[7] On the other hand, they could not only be built cheaply but also provided ideal insulation against the winter cold and summer heat.

Spanish colonists built simple houses quickly by using adobe bricks and occasionally sod bricks (*terrones*). The bricks were normally placed upon a crude stone foundation in widths to achieve the desired wall thickness, usually two to three feet. Their flat roofs (*azoteas*) were supported by peeled ponderosa pine, spruce, or aspen ceiling beams (*vigas*) placed to taper toward one side, providing drainage via wooden troughs (*canales*). The exterior sides of the *vigas* were covered with an interlacing of peeled saplings or branches (*latias*) in a herringbone pattern and then covered with a combination of twigs, brush, straw, adobe mud, or dirt. Their exposed interior sides were occasionally carved with designs to make a decorative ceiling. Widths of ceilings were determined largely by the manageable lengths, usually no more than 13 to 15 feet, of the *vigas* and the strength of the walls to prevent buckling from the roof's weight. The result was the easy construction of low, rectangular, narrow, two- or three-room, one-room-deep, one-story houses (*ranchitos*) (Figure 28). Geographer Robert C. West maintains that, "except in the upper Rio Grande Valley . . . the flat-roofed farmhouse has practically disappeared from the rural scene in the United States."[8] And even though the region has been settled for centuries, Jackson points out that there is "no sophis-

FIGURE 28

A Spanish-American farmhouse (ranchito) in El Rancho, Santa Fe County.
Source: Author, July 1970.

tication of design here . . . no remarkable ingenuity of construction, and only a few simple variations on one or two basic forms."[9] This simplicity was exhibited in much of the early construction of housing in frontier areas of the West, where settlers used the nearest abundant, accessible, free, or cheap materials. Initially, imports of heavy, bulky building materials would have been too costly and difficult, especially considering the lack of transportation facilities.

After the construction of the first room, it was easy to add long, narrow rooms at either end. These rooms frequently accommodated a growing family or relatives. In the Spanish-American patriarchal system and where a landowner had sufficient land, married sons and their families would often remain at home and live in the extension of rooms. Consequently, rooms built perpendicular to the original elongated house resulted in an L-shaped or occasionally a U-shaped structure (Figure 29). The semienclosed space resulted in a small private courtyard (*placita* or *plazuela*) like those of houses found in Spain.[10] All doors and windows opened onto this courtyard (Figure 30). Frequently, there were no doors between the rooms, so families had to pass through the *placita* to visit one another. Architectural historian Roland F. Dickey described the lay-

FIGURE 29

An L-shaped house near Peñasco in Taos County, is an emergent style of what could become a U-shaped house, partially enclosing a placita *with a wellhouse. The original house remains with its flat roof, but its extensions of rooms have gable or pitched roofs, reflective of an Anglo-American influence on building in the region.*

Source: Author, July 1969.

out: "Beginning with a single room, the house grew like a game of dominoes. As each son brought home his bride, he added a room to one end of the paternal dwelling. Every room had its own outside door, and the system solved the in-law problem by giving privacy to the married couples in the family."[11]

This layout facilitated cooperation, companionship, and kin-related social events. An outdoor bake oven (*horno*), introduced from Spain, or multiple ovens and a wellhouse were located within the *placita* for common use (Figure 31).[12] The rear exterior walls of this housing complex were solid, giving the appearance of a small fortress that kept out strong winds. Adobe, but most often wood, outbuildings and even walled corrals were extended occasionally from the rear of the house to enclose and fortify a farmyard, forming a layout known as a *casa-corral,* but more commonly as a *hacienda,* in frontier days when defensive measures were needed against marauding Indians.[13] Some of the larger compounds were known locally by family surnames, such as Los Luceros, and later became accepted place-names. The vast majority of the settlers, however, lived in two- or three-room cheap adobe houses built in a straight line or

FIGURE 30

Framed ornate wooden doors showing Moorish-Spanish influence were found on some early Spanish-American houses. Photo was taken in Córdova, Río Arriba County, February 1939.

Source: National Archives, Washington, D.C.

FIGURE 31

Hornos *are still used by some Spanish Americans, especially to make* chicos *(roasted corn). Spanish colonists introduced the adobe bake ovens into the Río Arriba. They were used to bake bread and cook outdoors in summer and still are used for this purpose, largely, however, by the Pueblo Indians.*
Source: Author, Plaza Blanca, Río Arriba County, August 1981.

in the L-shaped arrangement. As late as 1935, 917 families living in twelve villages resided in houses with an average of three rooms.[14]

Although adobe brick construction distinguished rural houses in the Río Arriba, giving the region a Moorish-Pueblo appearance, wood was used extensively by Spanish-American settlers in building structures in the higher forested elevations (Figure 32).[15] Geographer Charles Gritzner has postulated that "it is possible that highland areas of northern New Mexico have the greatest concentration of historic log buildings remaining today anywhere in the United States."[16] These settlers chose to build their homes of poles and logs. For instance, many had walls of vertically placed unhewn but stripped (to prevent decay) poles made from the trunks of the nearby short juniper and piñon pine trees. This palisade construction can be traced to an earlier use by Spanish colonists in Mexico and even to Spain. Usually started as one room, these small, one-story, flat-roofed dwellings (*jacales*) were extended to two and three or more rooms of one room deep and arranged similarly to those built of adobe (Figure 33).[17]

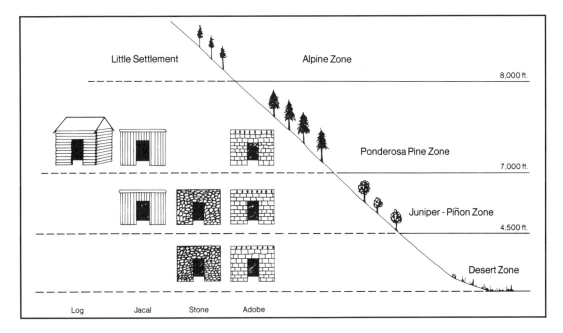

FIGURE 32

Types of construction and uses of available materials are shown by elevation in the Río Arriba.

Source: Gritzner, "Construction Materials in a Folk Housing Tradition" (see chap. 8, n. 16), 26. Permission granted by the Pioneer America Society.

FIGURE 33

The remains of an extended jacal *stand near Cebolla, Río Arriba County.*

Source: Author, August 1981.

Horizontal-log construction, using ponderosa pine logs that were in particular saddle-notched at the corners, was also used in building one-story, flat-roofed houses. Although horizontal-log construction was used in Spain and its earliest colonies, Spaniards did not employ the technique of corner notching. In the 1500s, Spaniards gained knowledge of log-notching techniques from German miners employed in Mexico. Subsequently, horizontal-log construction using corner notching became fairly widespread throughout the highlands of central Mexico by the 1800s, and from there it probably diffused northward into New Mexico.[18] Because log structures with corner notching began to appear in the Río Arriba by the mid-1800s, there is also a tendency to attribute the Spanish Americans' acceptance of this skill to Anglo Americans. Anglo Americans may have also introduced the technique, found in East Texas by the 1820s, into New Mexico during the era of the Santa Fe Trail trade.[19] It was common for these small log houses to be expanded in size by adding rooms built of vertically placed poles, logs, or even adobe resulting in houses of mixed construction. Similar to the adobe houses, the widths of the log houses were dependent largely upon the manageable lengths of the ceiling beams and the weight of the roof materials. Builders often had to take into consideration the weight of the heavy snowfall that occurred in the higher elevations.

Spanish Americans also used stone masonry in building houses in the Río Arriba, particularly in the Río Puerco Valley of western Sandoval County, where frequent sedimentary rock outcrops provided abundant building materials. Stone was used, too, as a building material in settlements found in eastern Santa Fe County and in the adjacent upper Pecos River Valley outside the Río Arriba but settled by Spanish Americans from the homeland. Adobe house construction appeared to be ubiquitous in the Río Arriba because it was accentuated by the common practice of applying a protective or insulating adobe plaster over the exterior of log and pole structures and even occasionally stone houses (Figure 34).

Like the exteriors, the interiors of the early Spanish-American houses were fairly similar throughout the region. Depending upon the availability of local resources, the walls were plastered with a mixture consisting largely of beige-yellow dirt (*tierra amarilla*) that normally contained particles of mica or a fawn-colored dirt (*tierra bayeta*). Many were also whitewashed with *caliche* or a solution (*yeso*) consisting of powdered gypsum rock (*tierra blanca*) and wheat paste to lighten up the interior space, which was usually fairly dark because of only one or two small windows. Then, too, these windows allowed little light because their panes were made of either *pergamino*, a translucent parchment made from sheepskins, or selenite.[20] Heat was provided in each room by a quarter-round adobe fireplace (*fogón*) built into a corner. This fireplace

FIGURE 34

*An abandoned Spanish-American house built in the late 1800s or early 1900s in
Gallina, Río Arriba County, depicts horizontal log construction covered with
adobe plaster held by diagonal wooden lathes. Chicken wire gradually replaced the
wooden lathes after World War II. The corner joists were covered with boards to
provide a finished appearance and the attic was built of milled lumber. Notice the
alto under the gable roof.*
Source: Author, August 1981.

had been commonly used in Spain and it can be traced to the Moorish
influence upon Spanish house construction.[21] Normally, the floors consisted of nothing more than packed earth, or a packed mixture of clay,
animal blood, and ashes. Consequently, there were seldom basements
(*soterranos*).

In the late 1800s, Anglo Americans, especially the homesteaders, began
to influence the region's house types and building techniques. Although
some built one-story log houses of horizontally placed notched logs and
occasionally chinked the exterior spaces between the logs with adobe,
they neither plastered the entire walls with adobe nor built adobe or sod
houses. Upon the establishment of nearby sawmills and the availability of
lumber, Anglo Americans quickly turned to building their familiar frame
house of milled and planed boards and rafters. Its pitched or ridge roof,
covered by shingles or sheets of corrugated metal over tar paper, allowed
for an attic and even dormers. Verandas with columns and occasionally
ballusters and trim around the windows and doors highlighted these
dwellings, which ushered in what became known as territorial architec-

ture (Figure 35).[22] A small number of Spanish Americans, largely prominent sheepmen especially in El Rito, Tierra Amarilla, and Brazos in northern Río Arriba County, adopted this architecture, but for the most part had their houses built of the traditional adobe or logs. Because heavy snow may fall in these locations, the pitched roofs were also more practical. Several of their houses were extended to enclose partially a courtyard or *placita*. Other Spanish Americans added a gable roof to their flat-roofed, one-story log and adobe houses or started to build gable-roofed houses. There is speculation, however, that a prototype for the Spanish-American gabled one-story farmhouse existed already in Mexico and Spain, but it did not appear in the Río Arriba until after the arrival of the Anglo Americans. The small attics (*altos*), with only exterior entrances in the cases of those added on, provided storage space, which was often used as a granary (Figure 34).[23] Many Spanish Americans also adopted the Anglo-Americans' plank floors and roofs, corrugated metal roofing, cast-iron stoves, and relatively large glass windows, improvements that the railroad made possible.[24]

Although Spanish Americans adopted certain building techniques and materials used by Anglo Americans, most continued to live in a very tra-

FIGURE 35

Territorial-style houses were built by Spanish Americans around 1900 in Brazos, Río Arriba County. Anglo Americans were responsible for introducing this two-story house into the Río Arriba, where they used milled lumber in such features as the gable roofs, verandas, and trim around the windows and doors.

Source: Author, August 1981.

ditional way. Sam Schulman, a public health worker in the Río Arriba, described the situation in 1960:

> In this village there are about 100 nuclear families, almost all living close to or sharing a common yard and well with their neighbors, related by blood or marriage. They live in homes of adobe, sun-dried mud-straw bricks. Most houses have flat roofs with a thick layer of adobe to hold them down; a few have pitched roofs of corrugated iron. Rooms are few. Beds are shared: by a conjugal pair, or by such a pair plus an infant, or by siblings, or by grandparents and grandchildren. In some homes the children sleep on individual soft sheepskins on the hard-packed mud floors. Heat is supplied by a small cast-iron stove and, perhaps, by a corner fireplace. In many homes cooking is still done on a large kitchen wood stove. Here the fuel is wood: chiefly dead *piñon* gathered in the local national forest. A few homes have stoves that burn propane or butane. Windows and doors are few; they are left open during the day, closed tightly at night.[25]

Many of the homes had electricity for lights, but few had electrical appliances. Water was still commonly taken from an irrigation ditch, stream, or from a hand-dug shallow well (Figure 23).

When younger Spanish Americans began to seek modern conveniences and facilities such as air conditioning and indoor plumbing in their houses, they turned to purchasing the affordable latest model of a two- or three-bedroom housetrailer. Beginning in the 1960s, housetrailers owned by married children placed near their parents' old adobe or log house became a rather common component of the residential yard (Figure 36). They comprised in the 1970s at least 10 percent of the housing units in a 10-mile radius of Española, and the percentage has increased steadily. In addition, they provide Spanish-American families with a sense of mobility in that housetrailers can be, if necessary, moved to new places of employment, such as to Albuquerque and out-of-state destinations. Incidentally, many Pueblo Indians also live today in modern and separate house units. In their case, it is the small bungalow house that is built away from the clustered pueblo, largely as a result of government programs that have provided Indians with on-the-job training in the building trades.

Before many of the Spanish-American land units became part-time farms and nonfarm residences, their owners had maintained several small outbuildings, mostly sheds and animal shelters, built of materials similar to those used in house construction (Figure 37).[26] Adobe was used in the lower elevations, but wooden poles were used in the higher elevations where farmsteads had relatively more if not larger outbuildings, partially because of the need to store fodder for the livestock. On the other hand, hardy livestock were allowed outdoors in the lower elevations and valley floors through much of the winter, creating localized overgrazing and

FIGURE 36

The old and new types of housing are placed side by side in a farmstead near Cerro, Taos County.
Source: Author, August 1971.

trampling of the vegetation near larger villages that had sizable numbers of animals. None of the barns or sheds (*fuertes* or *trojas*) was of the large size found, for instance, in the agricultural Middle West because there was no need for dairy barns and only a minimum number of breeding stock was kept over the winter.

Small storehouses (*trojas* or *dispensas*) for flour and other provisions were among the outbuildings that could be found in a farmstead. Some were built by placing an adobe mixture between two frame walls of diagonally arranged boards, somewhat similar to the rammed-earth (*Fachwerk*) construction of Germanic origin and found where Germans settled on the early frontiers of eastern Texas and western North Dakota (Figure 38). Because of the use of milled lumber in this construction, it was probably introduced by Anglo Americans. In addition, Anglo Americans apparently introduced a form of board-and-batten wall construction, which Spanish Americans covered with an adobe plaster (Figure 34).[27]

Spanish Americans used wood for many purposes other than in the construction of farm buildings. Field fences and corrals were commonly built by placing peeled and unpeeled poles in horizontal or vertical posi-

FIGURE 37

Logs and poles were used extensively in the construction of outbuildings and corrals in Truchas, Río Arriba County. February 1939.

Source: National Archives, Washington, D.C.

tions. Hand-hollowed logs were used as flumes (*cañoas*) to carry irrigation water across small canyons. Log gristmills (*molinos*), found only in the Río Arriba within New Mexico, were located on large irrigation ditches and streams where the water turned the horizontal water wheel in a counterclockwise direction, similar to the turning of mills in Spain. Firewood (*leña*) was the major fuel for domestic purposes.[28]

Unlike much of the rest of the country, where the isolated farmstead was dominant, Spanish-American farmsteads formed villages in the Río Arriba. Initially, the villages were of two types. In one layout, settlers built their houses on small lots (*solares*) around a *plaza* and journeyed to work on their outlying fields (*suertes*). This layout provided collective protection from the marauding Indians, and the *plaza*, enclosed by continuous houses and walls (*cordilleras*), provided a corral for the livestock, especially at night. Remnants of this layout remain today in Abiquiú in Río Arriba County, Chimayó in Santa Fe County, and Las Trampas in Taos County.[29] With the lessening of the Indian menace in the mid-1800s, many of these settlers moved their residences to their field locations. Consequently, a line village developed through a given valley

FIGURE 38

Spanish Americans frequently had storehouses, trojas *or* dispensas, *such as the one depicted here in Canjilón, Río Arriba County.*
Source: Author, July 1980.

along a major irrigation ditch or road. This layout was ultimately similar to the second and most common type of village, where the Spanish colonists settled initially upon their individual *suertes,* such as in the community land grants and on the Pueblo Indian grants. It resembled Europe's *Strassendorf,* which is characterized, too, by a row of continuous houses through a valley.[30]

Most Spanish-American rural villages had a Catholic church that was either impressive or inconspicuous and nondescript in size and design, reflecting both the size and wealth of a community (Figure 39). Unlike in Mexico, where there were larger settlements and more available labor, the churches lacked, for example, the tall steeples and corresponding sizes of cathedrals. They were at first usually not very wide, but a gable or pitched roof with a center ridge pole allowed later for a wider structure, up to about thirty feet or the length of two *vigas.* Churches were not oriented in any particular way in regard to the four cardinal directions, but they usually faced a village's *plaza* or the main road of a line village.[31]

No building distinguished the Spanish Americans' vernacular landscapes more than the Penitentes' (Los Hermanos de Jesús) unpretentious chapter meetinghouse or lodge (*morada*). Much has been written about this fraternal pious brotherhood that built its *moradas* to conceal partially its alleged fanatical, sanguinary methods of penance, particularly self-inflicted flagellation during the Easter Holy Week (La Semana Santa) when it re-enacted the suffering and crucifixion of Christ.[32] Historical evidence suggests that the brotherhood emerged in the Río Arriba in the late 1700s or early 1800s as a result of the lack of formal clerical attention to serve the religious needs of the rural, poor, devout Spanish Americans who were isolated spatially and socially in their microbasins. Under Spanish rule, the settlers had been serviced occasionally in their small mission churches or chapels (*visitas*) by priests from the larger churches in the *villas* of Santa Cruz, Santa Fe, and Albuquerque. After the reconquest in 1692, Spanish missionaries reestablished missions at the Indian pueblos. These missions were merely churches, not like the complexes that the Spaniards established later in California, where Indians were gathered together as transplanted neophyte populations into large industrial and manufacturing communities that required the services of many priests.[33] Interestingly enough, one of Spain's primary purposes in its efforts to

FIGURE 39

Las Trampas's relatively large Catholic church (San José de Graciá de Las Trampas), built in the mid-1700s, still dominates the village located in Taos County.

Source: Author, July 1970.

retain New Mexico was religious in nature. Yet there were few priests—an estimated twenty-five resident *padres* served the province's 12,700 Indians and 4,200 Spanish colonists in 1750.[34] No bishop visited New Mexico between 1760 and 1830. When the Mexican government took control of New Mexico in 1821, it proceeded to secularize its new territory by expelling the Franciscan priests. Secularization was complete by 1840. Approximately two-thirds of New Mexico's seventy-three churches, all Roman Catholic, were located in the Río Arriba in 1850.[35] The Franciscans did not return to New Mexico until 1897 and although nearly all the villages had their own Catholic church, most continued to be without resident priests. Some families had built small private chapels on their land to satisfy their immediate spiritual needs.

Surprisingly, the Penitente brotherhood is believed to have had its formal beginnings in 1810 in Santa Cruz, an important *villa* and religious center on the Santa Cruz Grant, located east of Española. It is also mentioned in the adjudication proceedings of the Rancho de Nuestra Señora de la Luz (Bishop John Lamy) Grant to have been in existence in 1818.[36] There is some evidence, however, that there may have been a forerunner of a Penitente organization in the mid-1790s in both Santa Cruz and Santa Fe, where the lay Venerable Third Order of Penitence was responsible for religious fiestas and processions that resembled later Penitente rituals.[37] If so, the Catholic Church must have been perceived as being unable to satisfy the spiritual needs of the people. Consequently, it is commonly suggested that the Río Arriba's Penitentes are an offshoot of the Franciscans' Third Order of St. Francis, which was devoted to the principles of St. Francis of Assisi, who was looked upon as an ideal penitent among the saints and archangels. In fact, the famous St. Francis of Assisi Church was built in 1772 by Franciscan missionaries near Ranchos de Taos and the brotherhood was known in some villages as the Third Order of the Penitentes in the late 1800s. Franciscan friars had instructed Spanish-American adult males on how to conduct lay services prior to their expulsion, and *moradas* were later established in many locations where they had had influence, but the Penitentes did not conduct mass.[38]

Fray Angélico Chávez, a well-known authority on the Catholic Church in the Río Arriba, argues, however, that the Penitentes arose in the region in the late 1700s as a result of the migration of members of lay penitential confraternities (*cofradías*) from Mexico. The origins of these *cofradías* can be traced to Spain.[39] Self-inflicted penance, especially flagellation, by religious or monastic groups to gain purification has antecedents in medieval Europe. It was practiced in Germany during the Black Plague of the 1300s and then spread to Spain and Portugal, where it became incorporated into festivals and was used by secretive brotherhoods that paid homage to their chosen saints and provided mutual aid within their com-

munities.[40] The *cofradías* followed Spanish colonization in the New
World, where they were established, for instance, in Mexican towns and
became known as *mayordomías,* associations that honored the local
patron saint and provided mutual aid.[41] Baxter claims that *cofradías* were
active in the Río Arriba before the reconquest.[42] It is reported that Oñate
and his men practiced flagellation in the presence of noncondemning
Franciscan friars to atone for their sins and transgressions after establishing their colony.[43] There is no evidence to suggest that penitential flagellation became a routine practice in the region during the 1600s and 1700s.
On the other hand, street processions still take place in Spain as a part of
the Holy Week's penitential rites, and similar commemorative processions
occur in Mexico.[44]

From the outset, the Catholic Church's hierarchy disavowed and
banned the Penitente brotherhood in the Río Arriba. The region's bishop,
don Juan Zuberiá, of Durango, Mexico, upon concluding his visit to the
Santa Cruz area in 1833, condemned its practices, particularly the flagellation or carnage (*carnicería*), and ordered that they be suppressed immediately. Both Archbishop John Lamy, who established the diocese of
Santa Fe in 1851, and Archbishop Jean Salpointe in the 1880s carried on
campaigns to rid the region of the Penitentes and excommunicated those
who refused to obey.[45] Despite these efforts, the brotherhood flourished
because its rituals were perceived to satisfy the precepts of the Catholic
Church and local needs for the most satisfying means of penance. (The
practice of penitential flagellation has also been attributed to the religious
rituals of the neighboring Pueblo Indians, but this contention is largely
dismissed as unlikely.)[46] Although flagellation has been mentioned in
association with All Saints' Day on November 1 and at the funerals of
Penitentes and relatives, it was practiced essentially around Eastertime.
Penitentes were at first quite open in conducting their rituals, but in time
they also came under harsh criticism and ridicule for being "barbaric,"
"masochistic," or "medieval" and for holding "orgies."

Much of this condemnation began to appear in the 1880s and 1890s
after Protestant Anglo Americans, many homesteaders, had settled in the
territory and coverage of the brotherhood appeared in their newspapers.
For instance, a Santa Fe newspaper reported unsympathetically on Good
Friday 1885 that "Penitentes are engaged in carrying out their barbaric
customs with all the blood-curdling hideousness imaginable."[47] Additional
local accounts of alleged deaths stemming from Penitente rituals height-
ened the criticism of the brotherhood.[48] Some of these deaths were attributed to Penitentes having been tied or nailed to a large erected cross to
resemble Christ's crucifixion (*Cristo*).[49] Non-Penitentes, however, did not
witness the dead bodies so there appears to have been no absolute proof
that there were actual deaths. On the other hand, folklore or fact has it

that if a Penitente died as a *Cristo* his shoes were laid quietly on the front steps of his house and the matter was not discussed in the village.[50] Villagers generally respected the Penitentes' rituals as private.

Books and travelogue magazines for national consumption contained more sensational accounts of the Penitentes. An example is that provided by Lummis, who complained in *The Land of Poco Tiempo*: "So late as 1891 a procession of flagellants took place within the limits of the United States. A procession in which voters of this Republic shredded their naked backs with savage whips, staggered beneath huge crosses, and hugged the maddening needles of the cactus; a procession which culminated in the flesh-and-blood crucifixion of an unworthy representative of the Redeemer. Nor was this an isolated horror. Every Good Friday, for many generations, it has been a staple custom to hold these barbarous rites in parts of New Mexico."[51] Eventually, novels such as Louis How's *The Penitentes of San Rafael,* published in 1900, appeared and continued to arouse the general public's interest and amazement.[52]

The flurry of negative and sensational reporting of their activities had led the Penitentes in the late 1800s to becoming a highly secretive organization that turned to building many chapter meetinghouses (*moradas*) where they could conduct their rituals without public scrutiny. The earlier Europeans who had also practiced penitential rituals constructed buildings for similar purposes. The secrecy that grew around the Penitentes in the Río Arriba was more intense, however, than that in the Spanish-colonized Philippine Islands or in parts of Spanish Latin America, especially Mexico, Colombia, and Peru.[53] In the case of the penitents in the Philippines, self-flagellation and the carrying of heavy wooden crosses are witnessed openly by all residents of the villages (*barrios*) and even outsiders, including this author, in somewhat of a carnivallike atmosphere. Persons are still nailed to erected crosses in *barrio plazas*.[54] These penitents, however, have no special building such as a *morada* in which to carry on their rituals in secrecy.[55]

A *morada* could be found by the late 1800s in nearly every village in the Río Arriba and in the surrounding villages that were settled by Spanish Americans, mainly in the upper Pecos River Valley to the east of the Sangre de Cristo Mountains and the San Luis and Purgatorie River valleys of southern Colorado.[56] A few Penitente *moradas* were also found in Spanish-American communities in the Río Grande Valley south of Albuquerque. None was reportedly built in the urban centers of Santa Fe and Albuquerque, where the Catholic Church may have served the people adequately, there was resistance to the brotherhood by the Catholic Church's hierarchy, and the growing Anglo-American population held the brotherhood in contempt.

There is no doubt that the Río Arriba was the core for the rapid growth and expansion of the brotherhood. Most rural adult Spanish-American males were Penitentes by 1890 and the height of *morada* construction occurred between 1890 and the 1920s.[57] Another impetus for its growth was the Spanish Americans' response to apprehensions about Anglo-American domination of New Mexico. It provided them with the means to band together to retain their identity and to procure a sense of emotional and cultural stability. Subsequently, the Penitentes developed in the early 1900s an incorporated hierarchy for the brotherhood (Cofradía de Nuestro Padre Jesús Nazareno) under the laws of New Mexico. It was headed by a supreme brother (*hermano mayor supremo* or *hermano supremo Arzobispal*) who governed the supreme council and coordinated chapters in designated districts. Several chapters had more than one hundred members each, and New Mexico had between 15,000 and 20,000 Penitentes who were also Catholics.

Locally, a chapter's membership usually included two groups: Los Hermanos de Luz (Brothers of Light) and Los Hermanos de Sangre (Brothers of Blood). The Brothers of Light were comprised of the brotherhood's officers and elders, while the Brothers of Blood were generally the younger members and initiates who allegedly carried on the more zealous and rigorous forms of penance that involved the symbolic letting of blood in remembrance of Christ's suffering.[58] These younger members were also known sometimes as the Brothers of Darkness because they covered their heads with black hoods during the reenactment of Christ's crucifixion. Both groups had existed in Spain's *cofradías*.

Because each Penitente chapter was autonomous and possessed independent decision-making capabilities, *moradas* were built with no particular architectural or ecclesiastical plan dictated by a central hierarchy. They were simple in layout, using the same materials and techniques used in the construction of houses found in any given village. My field analysis of sixty-one *moradas* in the early 1980s confirms architectural historian Bainbridge Bunting's conclusion that "morada design was by no means uniform; each chapter constructed its meeting house in accordance with site and such building materials, local resources, and technology as it commanded."[59] The concept of the *morada* probably started as a simple one- or two-room, linear or rectangular-shaped, one-story building.[60] Several were shaped with one end rounded or convergent for an apse or a chancel that accommodated the sanctuary or altar, similar to the shape of some Catholic churches (Figure 40). By adding rooms, most *moradas* were built like the L- and U-shaped houses and some were laid out in a T-shape and the shape of a cross.[61] Because the *moradas* were built largely after the Anglo Americans had arrived in the territory, many manifested the newcomers' pitched or ridge roofs covered with sheets of corrugated steel or metal.

FIGURE 40

The morada *at Llano, Taos County, has a rounded apse or chancel, similar to that built in some churches.*

Source: Author, July 1980.

A *morada*'s size depended greatly upon its chapter's number of members, functions, and financial situation. Normally, each *morada* by the early 1900s had two or three rooms: (1) a chapel (*oratorio*) that had a sanctuary; (2) a secret chamber or meeting room where the members held vigils, allegedly scourged themselves, prepared and ate their meals (if there were only two rooms), and slept during Holy Week; and (3) a storage room where the whips (*disciplinas*) made from the amole, soapweed, and yucca plants, metal flails, tub to cleanse wounds in herbal washes, crosses, and other paraphernalia were kept. If there were a fourth room, it was the kitchen, but separate cookhouses were also found (Figure 41). A large chapter would occasionally build a separate bunkhouse combined with a kitchen, but only twelve of the sixty-one *morada* sites had two or more buildings. Small quarter-round corner fireplaces heated the meeting room and occasionally the *oratorio,* but they were eventually replaced by cast-iron stoves.

Moradas epitomize secrecy. A few windows were included in the construction of new *moradas* and in the remodeling of older ones as glass

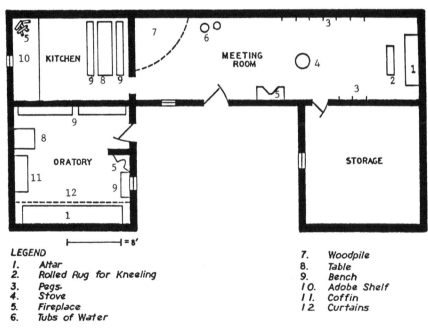

LEGEND

1.	Altar
2.	Rolled Rug for Kneeling
3.	Pegs.
4.	Stove
5.	Fireplace
6.	Tubs of Water

7.	Woodpile
8.	Table
9.	Bench
10.	Adobe Shelf
11.	Coffin
12.	Curtains

FIGURE 41

Layout of the morada *in Talpa, Taos County.*

Source: Ottaway, "The Penitente Moradas of the Taos, New Mexico Area" (see chap. 8, n. 45), 47. Permission granted by Harold Ottaway. *Photo:* Author, August 1981.

became more readily available in the Río Arriba.[62] Placed high on the walls, the small windows were covered with curtains and exterior shutters to permit privacy. None of the sixty-one *moradas* in this analysis had stained glass windows. *Moradas* have only one or two doors and they are locked securely when the buildings are not in use. Most *moradas* have no belfries, cupolas, or crosses that would readily identify them as religious structures. In many cases, however, a heavy wooden cross is erected less than 50 feet from the *morada*'s front entrance and a cross or crosses (*maderos*) are stored leaning against an exterior wall. Recently, identical small statues of Christ carrying a cross have been placed near the entrances of the *moradas* in Llano, Talpa, and Vadito. In several cases, Latin crosses, without ornamentation, and occasionally Celtic pommée crosses, painted on the exterior walls and doors, help to identify a *morada*.[63]

Generally, *moradas* were not conspicuous components of Spanish-American villages and they did not have an impact upon the villages' morphologies because most of them were located on or outside their peripheries. In fact, only sixteen of the sixty-one *moradas* were found within a village proper. Overall, their locations were based on two considerations. First, because the Catholic hierarchy did not approve of the brotherhood until after World War II, the Penitentes built their *moradas* varying distances from the churches, reflecting a local church's degree of tolerance for them. Only four *moradas* were located within 100 feet of a Catholic church, whereas nineteen were within 100 to 999 feet, fourteen within 1,000 to 2,999 feet, seventeen within 3,000 feet to 1 mile, and seven more than 1 mile away. Second, by locating a *morada* on the outskirts of a village, the brotherhood was able to find a site, especially in rough terrain, that offered a sense of seclusion and where a nearby hill could represent *calvario*. Chapters that built their *moradas* in highly secluded areas were suspected of practicing flagellation. Occasionally, a member of a local chapter allowed the *morada* to be built on his land, but in other cases the chapter bought the land. In either case, the *morada* is taxed as private property. Half of the sixty-one *morada* sites were fenced to keep livestock and outsiders from entering the grounds.

For a nonvillager, it is sometimes difficult to locate a *morada* in a village without making inquiry and even then there is considerable hesitation by Spanish Americans to reveal anything concerning the Penitentes. If one mentions Los Hermanos rather than Penitentes, villagers tend to respond more freely as they seem to be embarrassed today by the term Penitentes and the brotherhood's past activities. Some are undoubtedly apprehensive of spectacle-seeking "Penitente hunters." Furthermore, the term Penitentes appears to be Anglo American in origin and is not commonly used by the Spanish Americans. Penitentes may also refer to their

meetinghouse as La Casa de Dios (The House of God) rather than as a
morada.[64]

Moradas are used mostly during Lent, beginning on Ash Wednesday,
when the first of their weekly prayer meetings is held. Some chapters
have a nighttime confessional procession from the *morada* to *calvario*.
Initiation of new Penitentes, who renounce desires for great material
wealth and promise to practice charity by helping the chapter and the
community, may also take place during Lent. Males became Penitentes to
keep alive a family tradition or as a result of an experience that made a
person thankful for a favorable outcome of a difficult decision.

During Holy Week, meetings are often held nightly in the *morada*
until Good Friday. On Good Friday morning, Penitentes and their relatives and other villagers gather in the *morada*'s *oratorio* to begin the day-
long services and activities.[65] By disallowing photography and having a
disdain for nonvillagers, members maintain a sense of privacy. (I was an
invited participant observer at these services and activities in 1981.)
Paintings of Passion scenes and saints (*santos*) on pine boards or on skin
panels (*retablos*) line the plastered adobe walls. *Bultos,* wooden sculptured carvings of the saints, also adorn the *oratorio*.[66] The altar, placed
on a dais, often set off by a railing, is identified by life-size effigies of the
crucified Christ on a cross and the Virgin Mary. Placed near the altar is
the unusual two-wheeled cart (*carreta de la muerte*), a replica of a crude
oxcart, that carries the upright allegorical Angel of Death (La Doña
Sebastiana), a haunting carved wooden skeleton of four to five feet in
height with a black shawl over its shoulders and sometimes a blindfold
over its eyes. This skeleton figure usually holds a pulled bow with a
pointed arrow or sometimes an axe (Figure 42). Allegedly a surviving
aspect of the medieval European Cult of Death, a similar figure holding a
scythe was placed below a cross on religious floats during Good Friday
processions in sixteenth-century Spain. It represented Death having been
conquered by Christ's death.[67] In the case of the Penitentes, the skeleton
figure's drawn bow symbolizes death as omnipresent. Frequently, the cart
was pulled outdoors to be included in the day's rituals. Ramps to facilitate the movement of the cart can be seen at the front door of many
moradas.

Services begin with the singing of hymns (*alabados*) and the reciting of
biblical verses in Spanish.[68] They are followed by the outdoor dramatization of the encounter (*encuentro*) between Christ and his sorrowing
mother, which takes place at the cross located near the *morada*'s front
entrance. From here, the reader (*rezador*) leads those in attendance in
singing and praying in Spanish, accompanied sometimes by a flutist
(*pitero*), during the Procession of the Blood of Christ (La Procesión de la
Sangre de Cristo), which proceeds along the path or Way of the Cross

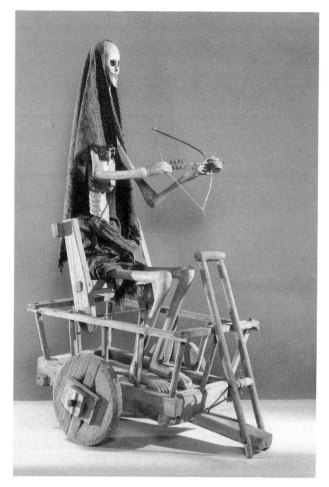

FIGURE 42

This death cart (carreta de la muerte), *built in the late 1800s, was formerly in the* morada *in El Rito, Río Arriba County.*

Source: Denver Art Museum, Denver, Colorado.

(Via Crucis) to stop and pray at each of the fourteen stations (*estaciones*) leading to Calvary. Normally, small white crosses or piles of stones mark the stations or resting places (*descansos*). It was during this part of the procession that the alleged flagellating and cross-bearing Penitentes would conceal their identities by wearing black hoods, cowls, or scarves. They would also wear white muslin pantaloon drawers and crowns of thorns and have their legs bound with ropes. Also, the path to *calvario* was allegedly made difficult by the placement of prickly pears and barbed cactus (*cholla*) for those Penitentes who chose to walk barefoot or crawl to remind them of Christ's ordeal. Guards (*guardiars*) were reportedly stationed in the surrounding area to keep away spectators or interlopers, especially if flagellation occurred.

After stopping at eleven stations, the procession returns to the *morada* to have a meatless lunch, consisting of red chile with red beans and salmon or *tortahuevo* (eggs in chile sauce), a sweet pudding made from sprouted wheat (*panocha*), rice, vegetables, and fruit. During this break, Penitentes will visit one or more nearby *moradas,* and non-Penitente villagers will also go to the opened *moradas* to pray and give offerings. Some of these villagers become observer participants of the Good Friday rituals because they believe that the brotherhood's reenactment of Christ's crucifixion serves their personal spiritual needs.

In mid-afternoon, the Penitentes resume their stops at the remaining three stations and proceed to *calvario,* arriving at approximately 3:00 P.M.—the alleged time of Christ's death—to bury a crucifix. They return to the *morada* for more singing and chanting, after which the non-Penitentes leave for their homes. Staying behind at the *morada,* the Penitentes wait for the evening rituals, particularly the loud *tinieblas* (earthquake) that is performed in complete darkness, symbolizing the chaos on earth after Christ's death. Normally, they will stay overnight in the *morada,* and some chapters conduct a brief business meeting on Saturday morning. Station crosses and frequently the cross or crosses at *calvario* are removed and the *santos* and *bultos* are sometimes removed from the *moradas* to discourage sightseers and loss by theft. The Penitentes return to their homes and will attend Easter services on Sunday morning at the local Catholic church.

Although Penitentes are best known for their Holy Week drama, they also provided a number of charitable services for their fellow villagers throughout the year. They were trusted to render assistance when necessary. González suggests that providing mutual aid within a village was actually the primary function of the Penitente chapters.[69] Members of a chapter can still be seen gathering at a *morada* on a Sunday afternoon once or twice a month to discuss village matters. They have prayer services not only for their members but also upon request for relatives and friends who are ill. Residents who experienced misfortunes were provided food and wood, and a disabled person's crops were cultivated, irrigated, and harvested. Penitentes were prominent in organizing religious feasts such as that honoring the village saint. If requested, they would conduct wakes (*velorios*), provide funeral services for one of their own or for a close relative of a member, defray funeral expenses, make coffins, and dig graves.[70] Services for the deceased person would often be conducted first in the *morada* and later in the Catholic church. The Penitentes normally did not maintain cemeteries (*camposantos*) exclusively for their members and relatives, probably because the land would not be consecrated by the

Catholic Church. Only eighteen of the sixty-one *moradas* had adjacent cemeteries (Figure 41). Graves were frequently surrounded by a small picket fence (*cerquita*), a practice used also in the Catholic cemeteries.[71] Members' widows and children were often given support until they were able to cope on their own.

Spanish-American cemeteries are another criterion that delimits the Río Arriba as a culture region. Landscape historian John R. Stilgoe, in writing about the sacredness associated with burial places prior to the Reformation in Europe, maintains that the graveyards found in the Río Arriba are unlike other American cemeteries. He concludes:

> Only in New Spain did the pre-Reformation burying ground survive almost intact. There a tall cross still ordered the sacred enclosure next to the church, and there the old traditions of care took root. Today such graveyards are concentrated in tiny Spanish-American villages in New Mexico. The ancient symbols—the cross, sheep, angels, tree of life, and heart—decorate the hand-carved wooden markers fenced off from grazing cattle. To be sure, the vegetation is different, but the rabbitbrush and tumbleweed cannot hide the eight-foot cross that announces the mysteries of Catholicism. Elsewhere in the United States such graveyards are virtually unknown.[72]

Although the image exists that all Penitentes were males, there were a few chapters, such as that found in Truchas in eastern Río Arriba County, that had female Penitentes (Carmelites).[73] Also, female auxiliaries (*auxiliadoras de la morada*) still help their male counterparts to maintain the *oratorio* and by preparing meals, including the Last Supper (*cena*) during Holy Week.[74]

The Penitente brotherhood was very influential in many aspects of village life. It became involved in politics, hence helping to elect its preferred candidates. (Several *moradas* were suspected of being gathering places for Alianzistas, discussed in Chapter 7, in the 1960s.) It is also claimed that there was little crime, if any, in the Spanish-American villages that had strong Penitente chapters because the brothers provided a sense of discipline. The brotherhood served as a sort of local court in determining justice in minor offenses as well as helping to resolve land and water disputes. In fact, there was suspicion that most Penitentes were also members of the village's irrigation ditch association, or *acequia*. This association may have provided the early organizational network for bringing together into the brotherhood the village's men who had the same values and beliefs. Although many Penitentes were poor, some prominent citizens belonged to chapters for political and social reasons without participating zealously in the rituals. Most chapters gained membership in the 1930s during the Depression when men had returned to the Río Arriba and remained year round because they could not find seasonal employment.

It was not until 1947 that the Catholic Church officially recognized and accepted the approximately 10,000 Penitentes in New Mexico and southern Colorado as a lay brotherhood, henceforth officially known as the Hermanos de Nuestro Padre Jesús Nazareno. Archbishop Edwin V. Byrne in his acclamation maintained the Penitentes had to disavow their alleged fanatical methods of penance, namely self-flagellation and placing cruciform scars on the backs of initiates.[75]

In 1952, the Penitentes' supreme brother revealed that there were approximately 90 active chapters with *moradas* in the Río Arriba out of an estimated 130 chapters in New Mexico. In addition, there were 5 active *moradas* in Río Arriba County that had no organized affiliation with the brotherhood's hierarchy. Río Arriba and Taos counties alone had over 80 of the state's *moradas*.[76] The supreme brother claimed in 1958 that there were 135 active *moradas* within his brotherhood in New Mexico and southern Colorado.[77]

The brotherhood had witnessed, however, serious losses in its membership resulting largely from:
- permanent out-migration during World War II;
- seasonal employment outside the Río Arriba;
- less dependence on an agrarian existence, which had given rise to homogeneous villages and common beliefs;
- improved means of mobility within the Río Arriba, allowing for regular attendance at mass in Catholic churches with resident priests;
- conversions to Pentecostal-type Protestant churches; and
- an acute awareness that the brotherhood was considered to be somewhat fanatical and that it did not complement the changing values of and therefore appeal to young Spanish Americans.[78]

Many Spanish Americans who had become Penitentes did so in sincerity because of their self-perceived pride in carrying on a tradition that was manly (*machismo*) and their belief that the brotherhood served their spiritual and personal needs. Older Penitentes claimed that the brotherhood's initiation rites and practices (bloodletting reportedly still occurred) were too arduous for young males and that people have lost interest in the importance of Holy Week. Moreover, they claimed that a greater emphasis was placed on material rather than on spiritual wealth. Government social welfare programs had fulfilled the needs of many residents and various clubs and organizations provided fellowship. Some claimed, too, that many young Spanish Americans do not know Spanish and therefore feel they cannot participate. Penitentes acknowledge that it has been difficult to increase or sustain their membership, and the Catholic Church does not actively promote building membership in Penitente chapters.

The decline in the number of active *moradas* became apparent when in

FIGURE 43

An abandoned morada, *constructed like a* jacal, *stands near Cebolla, Río Arriba County. Its chapter was disbanded in the 1940s after World War II, leaving the* morada *to be used to store agricultural tools and supplies.*

Source: Author, August 1980.

FIGURE 44

A newly refinished and enlarged morada *in El Duende, Río Arriba County, has the appearance of a modern ranch-style house, except for the cross on the front.*

Source: Author, August 1980.

1980 the Roman Catholic archbishop Robert Sanchez, New Mexico's first Spanish-American archbishop who is reportedly sympathetic to the brotherhood, estimated that there were fifteen hundred practicing Penitentes using about eighty *moradas,* mostly confined to northern New Mexico.[79] It is estimated that sixty of these *moradas* were found in the Río Arriba, and most were included in my field survey. The average size of a chapter is about twenty members, but the range is from five to over forty. The great majority of Penitentes today are more than fifty years of age—most in fact are older than sixty-five years of age.

In villages where the Penitentes have disbanded their chapters or merged with nearby chapters, the *moradas* stand abandoned or are used for nonreligious purposes. In at least two cases, *moradas* were sold to Anglo Americans who converted them into houses.[80] Abandoned *moradas* are used to provide shelter for livestock and store feed and equipment, reflecting their loss of sanctity in the villages (Figure 43). On the other hand, the remaining *moradas* are for the most part fairly well maintained, and the brotherhood continues to hold an annual regional meeting (Figure 44).

The Penitentes' demise was supposed to have been complete by now, but they persist, almost entirely in the Río Arriba. Several active *moradas* are maintained in adjacent areas, largely in the San Luis Valley, Purgatorie, and Las Animas river valleys of southern Colorado and in the upper Pecos River Valley. These were established by Spanish Americans who had migrated there from the Río Arriba. As Spanish Americans moved to the metropolitan areas of Denver and Los Angeles, some reportedly grouped together to establish chapters but, if so, they have since disbanded. Reports exist of a *morada* or two having been established at one time in Montana and Wyoming, where many Spanish-American men migrated seasonally to herd sheep and to work on railroads and in mines.[81] It has been common in past years for Spanish Americans to travel back to New Mexico to participate in Holy Week activities at their village's *moradas,* as in the cases of Pueblos who return to participate in their pueblo's annual feast day.

Penitentes contributed not only to the creation of a distinctive vernacular landscape by building self-styled *moradas,* they also developed an impressive religious folk art, expressed in *santos* and *bultos,* established mutual-aid and religious support systems, and provided a sense of civil leadership. In particular, it was the *morada* that manifested the will of the Spanish Americans and the relative simplicity of their villages. Bill Tate, a resident of Truchas, put it aptly: "If it is true that architecture is the mother of the arts, best relating the nature, environment, and the purpose of a people, then the Morada is the one structure in a Spanish village that fulfills these aesthetic prerequisites."[82]

On the one hand, the Penitentes represent a response to a perceived need by residents of a relatively isolated region rooted in the tenets of rural poverty. Not only did their various functions help the immediate needs of the Spanish Americans, but also they themselves provided a sense of identity, solidarity, and security for their own people against increasing Anglo-American domination.[83] On the other hand, the continuous, albeit slow, decline of the Penitentes represents the withering of a way of life that is contributing to the abandonment of a distinctive folk environment and therefore of a special type of building and land use in a vernacular landscape. Meanwhile, rural Spanish Americans have continued to a great degree to live in their old houses largely because of their personal economic situations. Surely, much of the region's remaining vernacular architecture can be attributed to lingering poverty.

The Town
of Abiquiú

9

Although common features can be found throughout the Río Arriba, such as its vernacular landscapes, rural poverty, and out-migration of rural Spanish Americans, each Spanish-American village is sustained by local circumstances. The next three chapters are vignettes of four villages that have been selected to illustrate their residents' assessments and adjustments in coping with different situations and yet persisting in the Río Arriba. These villages represent, therefore, the varying dynamics at play in determining to what extent the region will remain the homeland of the Spanish Americans. Much has been written about northern New Mexico, but local studies, especially those based upon fieldwork, that analyze and compare different rural villages to understand their pattern of human organization and land use are largely absent from the literature. In fact, Jackson has pointed out that "the history of these villages is largely unrecorded; all we usually know about them is roughly the decade of their settlement, the date of the first church, and place of origin of its first settlers."[1]

Abiquiú is a village located on the Town of Abiquiú Grant, one of the two land grants in the Río Arriba given to a combination of Spanish settlers and *genízaros,* Indian captives ransomed largely by the Spanish government from nomadic southwestern and Plains tribes.[2] These detribalized Indians, especially the children, were often half-breeds, or mestizos, who took Spanish surnames, learned to speak Spanish, and became acculturated in Spanish customs and in Christianity.[3] Some were servants and slaves for Spaniards. A similar land grant was given at not too distant Ojo Caliente, another peripheral settlement on the region's northwest frontier. Both were formed to promote buffer settlements between the outlying hostile tribesmen and the core of Spanish settlement in the Río Grande Valley. The Town of Abiquiú Grant has remained in the region's historiography of Spanish and Mexican land grants as one of the last functioning community grants owned by Spanish-American residents.[4] An analysis of this land grant explains not only how it was bestowed and how its residents have managed to retain control of it, but it reveals also the changing functions of the land grant and provides insights into whether its resources could have sustained a large resident farm population above the levels of poverty.

Spanish settlement in the Abiquiú area dates to 1744, when the Spanish government concentrated a small *genízaro* population at the site of an abandoned Moqui (Hopi) Indian pueblo located about three miles southeast of present-day Abiquiú. The site was abandoned and the colony, Pueblo de Santo Tomás Apóstol de Abiquiú, was relocated in the early 1750s at its present site of Abiquiú, located on a terraced, rocky mesa (elevation 6,060 feet) overlooking the Río Chama, approximately 20 miles upstream from the confluence of the Río Chama and the Río Grande. Various Indians—Utes, Comanches, Apaches, and Navajos— harassed and pillaged the frontier settlement, consequently putting it through a period of terror, abandonment, and resettlement. Settlers patrolled the area, but others gave up and moved to the Santa Cruz area, east of Española.

In order to encourage the permanency of this settlement, the Spanish government gave the settlers the Town of Abiquiú Grant. Governor Cachupin visited the site of the proposed land grant and reported in May 1754 that

> in regard to the assembling of the half breed Indians . . . and . . . giving [them] . . . sufficient cultivable lands . . . in accordance with law eight, title three, book six, of the *Recopilación of these Kingdoms of the Indies,* in which his Majesty directs that in the tracts in which Pueblos and settlements of converted Indians are to be established shall have a sufficiency of waters, lands, woods, entrances and exits and cultivable lands and one league in length of commons in order that they may keep their herds without interfering with those of the Spaniards. . . . I proceeded to the examination of all the lands, fields, woods, pastures and waters with the object of marking off for the said Pueblo of half breed Indians . . . on the south from the centre of the said Pueblo five thousand Castilian *varas* along the edge of a permanent creek (*arroyo permanete*) which descends in the said direction along the edge of the Pueblo with capacity to irrigate all the lands in the said direction. On the north also measuring from the centre there were marked off two thousand four hundred *varas* because of having come to the deep river (*río candeloso*) called Chama which runs from West to East and without a ford at this point which (river) serves as a boundary in the said direction. On the east starting

also from the center there were measured two thousand five hundred and fifty said Castilian *varas*. . . . On the west also measured from the center of the said Pueblo . . . another two thousand five hundred and fifty *varas* . . . and all said lands . . . are cultivable of good quality and all under irrigation with advantages of much water, forests and woods; on the south there was marked off and measured for them the league of commons its boundaries being on the north the south boundaries of the lands of the Pueblo, on the south the high road which goes to Navajo, on the east the source of the creek (*arroyo*) which descends along the edge of said Pueblo, and on the west the height (or hill) of the Rio de los Frijoles with most abundant pastures of fine quality because they are of grama grass and others of the same with much water.[5]

Abiquiú's estimated eight hundred residents, three-quarters Spanish and one-quarter Indian, began to abandon the site in the late 1760s only to have Governor Pedro Fermin de Mendinueta in 1770 order them to return and stay put or lose their land grant and face disciplinary action.[6] Upon their return, the settlers were reinforced by additional *genízaros* and stray Pueblo Indians as well as by Spanish settlers, including some from Chihuahua and Durango, Mexico. Abiquiú had become the military outpost for the upper Río Chama Valley. Although there was again some out-migration by Spanish settlers, this time to the Taos area, which was thought to be safer, Abiquiú had grown to nearly eighteen hundred people by 1800.[7] Spanish settlers far outnumbered the Indians, as Abiquiú was becoming less and less a *genízaro* settlement and many Indian half-breeds were counted as Spaniards as a result of miscegenation and inter-marriage. (Some of Abiquiú's children attended the Indian school in Santa Fe as late as 1930.)

Like other Spanish land grants in the Río Arriba, the Town of Abiquiú Grant contained a sizable area of irrigable floodplain along the Río Chama. This land was partitioned among the settlers into small parcels containing several acres. Rough, mountainous land with elevations of over 7,000 feet, covered with piñon, juniper, and live oak forests, comprised the rest of the land grant. The village of Abiquiú was laid out by fashioning a quadrangular *plaza* of 135 *varas* on each side. This layout fits one of the two types of Spanish villages, as discussed in Chapter 8, where settlers were instructed to build their houses contiguously around a *plaza* for defensive reasons. Space was left for four "good streets with entrances and exits free for those who might hereafter come to settle."[8] The Catholic church or mission, under the direction of the Franciscans, faced the *plaza*.

When the Mexican government took possession of the Río Arriba it found disputes over land claims in Abiquiú and some residents had no irrigable land. These disputes were probably the result of the settlement's history of abandonment and resettlement. To assure that each family had irrigable land, the government in 1825 ordered an investigation into possible reapportioning of landholdings and the partitioning of unimproved irrigable land into equitable shares.[9] Consequently, the local *alcalde,* Juan Cristobal Quintana, was instructed to evaluate the situation, and while in Abiquiú he

> ordered that there shall at once be measured a cord (*cordel*) of fifty Castillian *varas* and . . . began to measure the land and to see what might be given to each individual. . . . I found that a part of the said lands is useless and of no value, a part of it on account of its ridges and ravines (*arroyos*) could not be measured, and the discontent caused by this to the greater portion of the interested parties being seen . . . [they were asked] what arrangements would suit them, to which they replied unanimously that each person should keep the land which he had, and that (to) those who had no land, and (to) others, who had little there should be given a part of the lands of those who had . . . we agreed . . . to cut down the lands of the person who had, and to give part of them to the aggrieved parties, with which they were contented and satisfied . . . I directed the native residents and the legitimate heirs . . . of said Pueblo to proceed with a twenty-five *vara* cord (*cordel*) to segregate the good land from the bad in order that each one might enjoy for himself the lot which might fall to him and having delivered the first measurement by lot which each one drew, (each) receiving thirty-five *varas* of land in width and in length some more than others on account of the bends of the river. The second partition was not made by lot but by me . . . giving them a portion of thirty-five *varas* to designate them and to place them on an equality with those who were known to have received advantages in the lands in the first partition and on the part from north to south, there were measured to each one along the *cañon* forty *varas* of land in the same way as in the first (partitions) and in the fourth (partition). The partition of the gardens was continued in the same way by lot with fourteen *varas* to each one.[10]

People had the right to select vacant land around the *plaza* for new homesites. In addition, one parcel was designated for use by the mission. Several landowners filed litigation, without success, against the Mexican government for reassigning and reapportioning land. The unallocated upland (*dehesa*) continued to be used for communal grazing and for sources of firewood and building materials, as on other community land grants.

Abiquiú's situation as an important and large settlement was further revealed in an 1827 census by Col. Antonio Narvona, military commandant of the region. The village and its neighboring settlements had a total population of 3,560 (equally divided between males and females), the second largest area of Spanish settlement after Santa Fe, which had approximately 5,200 people. Almost half the people resided in Abiquiú proper. Nearly 60 percent of the area's 865 residents who had occupations were farmers, followed by another 35 percent who were day laborers. There

were six merchants, one priest, and one schoolteacher for Abiquiú's one
school.[11] The village was governed by an *ayuntamiento* (council).

163

The Town of
Abiquiú

Abiquiú was important for several reasons toward the middle of the
1800s. It served as an exploratory base for forays into northwestern New
Mexico and southern Colorado, a supply station in the 1830s and 1840s
on the Old Spanish Trail between Santa Fe and Los Angeles, and an
Indian trade center. It continued to be a military post (*puesto*) to protect
settlers against Indian raids into the Río Arriba.[12] In addition, it became
the source of settlers for new land grants, including the don José Manuel
Martínez family, who acquired in 1832 the large Tierra Amarilla Grant
in the upper Río Chama Valley.[13] José María Jácques and Crescencio Valdez led approximately two dozen or more of Abiquiú's families north in
1851 to settle along the Río Conejos in Colorado's San Luis Valley. Soon
thereafter, Jácques and Maj. Lafayette Head, a merchant, took a colony
of several hundred more people, many from Abiquiú, to the same area in
Colorado. More families from Abiquiú moved northwesterly to the San
Juan Basin of New Mexico, where a gold rush took place in 1860, and
after the Southern Ute Agency was established in the 1870s, which helped
to secure the area for permanent settlement. In this process, several villages were established within the large Tierra Amarilla Grant.[14] Partially
as a result of this out-migration, Abiquiú's population declined to about
eight hundred residents in the late 1800s, mostly Spanish Americans who
lived similarly to those found in other villages of the region. Anthropologist Richard E. Ahlborn has suggested that the remaining residents
wanted to preserve their life-style like others in the region against the
growing influence of the incoming Anglo Americans. Those who had
become Penitentes built two *moradas* in the village, one of which is still
used today.[15]

Meanwhile, much of the Town of Abiquiú Grant's approximately 800
acres of irrigable land on the floodplain of the Río Chama passed gradually and atypically into the possession of one landowner. Pedro Gonzáles,
a Spanish-American *rico,* began to acquire small parcels in the mid-1800s
as they were either abandoned and sold while becoming the largest sheep
owner in the lower Río Chama Valley. Fifteen of his sheep camps, with
an estimated 150,000 sheep, were scattered in the area with the herders
largely from Abiquiú. Miguel A. Gonzáles continued his father's extensive
sheep operations and expanded them in the early 1900s by acquiring
more of the Río Chama floodplain on the Town of Abiquiú Grant. All
these small parcels were consolidated into large fields for hay and winter
feeding of flocks. Those residents who persisted in retaining their small
parcels, mostly near the village proper, continued to be engaged primarily
in subsistence agriculture. They planted corn, wheat, beans, and chiles
and grazed a few head of livestock on the more than 15,000 acres of

communal land. These livestock were sold or exchanged for food staples and various goods in the regional trading centers of Española and Chama. In general there was little cash income in Abiquiú until the late 1800s and early 1900s, when men, here as elsewhere in the region, started to leave for seasonal work, primarily in other western states. Economic conditions were so poor in Abiquiú that the Catholic Church's records indicate that church marriages were free.[16]

The Town of Abiquiú Grant's validity was adjudicated with that of all the Spanish and Mexican land-grant claims. Confirmed in 1894, the residents—"Heirs of the Captive Indians of Abiquiú"—did not receive their patent until 1909 (there was a problem in discerning the course of the Río Chama as it existed in 1754). In addition to the land grant's patent for 16,708 acres, each of the grant's landowners received a deed to his individually owned land.

Abiquiú's families became increasingly dependent on seasonal labor in the early 1900s because of the limited economic opportunities in the Río Arriba. More than half the male labor force, representing more than one hundred families (530 people), left seasonally by 1930 to work in the mines and lumber camps of Nevada and Utah or the sugarbeet and potato fields of Colorado.[17] Nearly forty men alone were employed as sheepherders in Colorado and Utah. As throughout the Río Arriba, however, during the Depression Abiquiú's population increased slightly to 625 by 1940 as the men stayed home because of their inability to find work.[18] About forty families were largely dependent upon their small farms, averaging 4 acres each, and grazing a few livestock on the land grant.[19] Many other families owned only garden plots. Meanwhile, sheepman Miguel Gonzáles owned 60 percent of the land grant's Río Chama floodplain and rented small parcels to villagers while keeping the rest of it in alfalfa pasture or native hay.[20] He also pastured hundreds of sheep and cattle on the land grant's communal lands. All of Abiquiú's livestock owners witnessed overgrazing on their land grant, largely because of their strong dependence on livestock. Most families, nevertheless, still had to rely on some sort of public relief.

Abiquiú's residents paid real estate taxes on their homesites, but they had neglected to pay them on the land grant's communal land. They believed that taxes were not to be assessed on land "donated to them by the United States government," a perception stemming from the earlier land grant adjudication proceedings. When the land grant's communal land was declared tax delinquent, it was sold in 1941 by the Río Arriba County assessor to the State of New Mexico, which in turn sold it to the U.S. Department of Agriculture (Soil Conservation Service). It was to be placed eventually in the National Forest system.[21] Residents of other Spanish and Mexican land grants had been found in similar predicaments

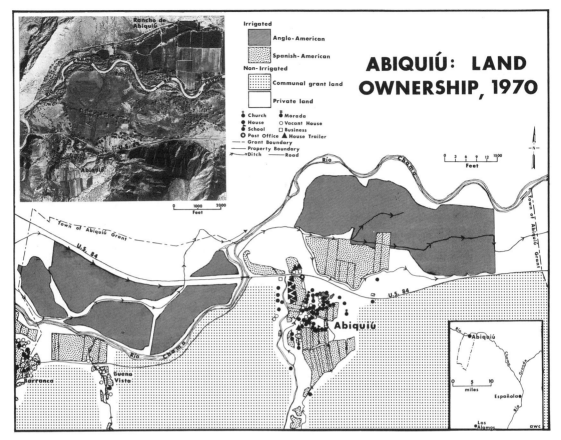

FIGURE 45

Source: State Engineer's Office, Santa Fe, ASCS, USDA, Salt Lake City, DXF-2CC-138 and 153, 22 October 1962, and fieldwork.

when they allowed their communal lands to become tax delinquent. In this case, the situation was resolved in 1943 when eighty residents formed the Abiquiú Cooperative Livestock Association, a nonprofit organization, which with the financial assistance of the federal government's Farm Security Administration purchased the communal rangeland (approximately 15,800 acres) for the amount of the delinquent tax bill.

During World War II, many of Abiquiú's males entered the military service while others returned to seasonal field work. Some left permanently, mostly to California for defense-related jobs. A few obtained employment 45 miles away, where the construction of the Los Alamos Atomic Laboratories was under way. Males responded likewise during the Korean War. Crops had become relatively unimportant and farming

continued to decline as a source of income and subsistence during the
1960s. Gonzáles's land on the floodplain was purchased by an Anglo
American and incorporated into a large livestock ranch, Rancho de
Abiquiú, which also included land in the Plaza Colorado Grant across the
Río Chama from Abiquiú (Figure 45).

Members of the Abiquiú Cooperative Livestock Association, many
descendants of the original group, continued to graze cattle on the Town
of Abiquiú Grant in the 1970s. They represented most of the approximately sixty resident families who were involved in part-time farming as
well as a few families who had moved away but continued to retain
membership and allowed others to graze their allocation. A total of about
two hundred cattle, a figure determined by a grazing committee but one
that demonstrates the land grant's poor carrying capacity, was allowed to
graze the communal rangeland. The residents' perception of the land
grant's poor rangeland was reflected also in their concern over taxes.
Grazing fees were assessed to pay the annual real estate taxes, approximately $1,500, but many residents thought that the land was not worth
the assessments. The Abiquiú Cooperative Livestock Association managed, however, to retain the communal rangeland, which was enclosed by
fences maintained by New Mexico's Department of Highways and the
Forest Service. Several residents possessed also the more preferred grazing
permits for cattle on the adjacent Santa Fe National Forest, where there
was better pasturage.[22]

Even though the Town of Abiquiú Grant had historically a low number of people, approximately four hundred in the early 1970s, it was
incapable of supporting this population. Besides the low number of livestock, its residents cultivated fewer than 20 acres, including gardens.
Employment opportunities continued to be sought in nearby and distant
locations. A small number of men worked on local ranches and in logging camps while others drove to work in Española and Los Alamos.
Others left in the summers to work as sheepherders in Idaho and Wyoming or on railroad crews throughout the West. Several worked in Utah
at a weapons storage facility. Young men even traveled to Wisconsin and
Minnesota to work seasonally in canneries and to Colorado's San Luis
Valley to work in the reliable potato harvests.[23] One-third of the families
received government financial assistance and a greater number benefited
from food stamps, especially in the winter months. Out-migration was
leaving behind not only a landscape of abandoned buildings but also an
aging population (Figure 46).

Reassessments of the residential and other land use possibilities in
Abiquiú and its surrounding area were becoming evident, however, by
the mid-1970s. For instance, the Corps of Engineers revealed plans in
1976 for creating a permanent reservoir at the nearby Abiquiú Dam,

FIGURE 46

Abandoned houses enclose Abiquiú's plaza, reflecting the village's decline in population during the 1960s.

Source: Author, September 1970.

which had been built originally in 1963 to control flooding in the Río Chama Valley. In addition to storing water for the Río Arriba's downstream residents, largely in Albuquerque, the reservoir was planned to provide recreational opportunities for residents and tourists. Some of the area's Spanish Americans were apprehensive about the new project because they feared higher land values, higher taxes, and the development of housing subdivisions for the influx of middle-income and weekend Anglo Americans. They argued, "This whole area will become a playground for outsiders. Our culture, our roots and our way-of-life will be lost."[24] County and other government officials generally approved of the project and the Corps proceeded with construction. The controversy reflected the Spanish Americans' desire to preserve the area as it had been—part of the old Spanish-American homeland. Abiquiú Dam's large reservoir, a permanent lake of 200,000 acre-feet of water, and limited recreational facilities have led to considerable touristic development in the area. Approximately 600,000 tourists and recreationists visited the site in 1986, but only half a dozen of Abiquiú's Spanish Americans are employed permanently there today.

Another aspect of the reappraisal of land use in the Abiquiú area resulted from a decision in 1980 by several Muslims to build a small Islamic mosque (*masjid*) and school (*madressa*) and establish Dar al-Islam, the country's first Islamic village, in northern New Mexico. Abiquiú was chosen as the appropriate site for this village largely because Abdullah Nurideen Durkee, an artist originally from New York and the planner of Dar al-Islam, was familiar with the Río Arriba as a result of his earlier founding in 1967 of another religious community, the Lama Foundation, near Taos. (More than two dozen religious or alternative groups have established similar communities or communes, such as that of Ashram Hacienda de Guru Ram Das owned by the Sikh Darma religious colony near Española, in the region since 1960. The Río Arriba has attracted the vast majority of these types of settlements in New Mexico, largely because of its different social environments, scenery, and climate.) Durkee conceived his idea while studying Islam in Saudi Arabia. Upon his return to New Mexico, he and his followers selected Abiquiú because of the nearby availability of a large tract of land whose location was coincidentally found to be in the same latitude (35° N) as that of other major Islamic centers. Durkee established a foundation that received considerable financial support from donors in Saudi Arabia. It purchased 1000 acres, 400 acres of mesa land and 600 acres of the Río Chama's bottomland, from the owner of the Rancho de Abiquiú for nearly $1.4 million. The bottomland was originally a part of the Town of Abiquiú Grant.[25]

Construction of the mosque started quickly on the mesa top under the supervision of the Egyptian architect Hassan Fathy. It was dedicated in 1981 and the construction of the school followed (Figure 47). Two of the twenty-five Muslim families lived at the complex in 1987 and several other families lived elsewhere on the foundation's land, which had been increased by the purchase of an additional 7000 acres of the Rancho de Abiquiú. Plans in 1987 called for thirty or forty additional houses to be built for housing nearly one hundred Muslim families, who will be sustained partially by producing saleable Islamic crafts such as woodwork, tile, and weaving and largely by charitable contributions from donors in Saudi Arabia.[26] The Muslims raise no livestock, but they do lease their land for limited livestock grazing.

Meanwhile, the Muslims had an immediate impact upon the village of Abiquiú. Eight families and seven single men lived there by June 1981.[27]

Consequently, old and abandoned Spanish-American houses were renovated and rented to them. Once they accepted the Muslims, Spanish-
American villagers also accepted several Anglo Americans, generally
retired people, who purchased deeded land and who also renovated their
properties' dilapidated adobe houses. Several residents of Abiquiú and the
immediate area became employed in the building trades, mostly as laborers, in the construction of the Muslim complex and in the renovation of
properties in Abiquiú. As Juan Mendez, a Catholic priest, of Española,
put it in 1986, "I don't think anyone realizes it yet, but the Muslim community has changed the face of Abiquiú as drastically as anything that
has happened in its history."[28]

Many of Abiquiú's remaining Spanish Americans continue to depend
on finding employment by commuting considerable distances, largely to
Española, Los Alamos, and Santa Fe. Others are retirees who live on their
small deeded parcels and derive their livelihoods from various retirement
benefits. Abiquiú is today a village that has grown to approximately five
hundred people. Incidentally, Spanish Americans who are members of the
land grant can still obtain assigned homesteads (*solares*) near the village.[29]
All of Abiquiú's houses are occupied, and the impact of the infusion of
external capital is very evident in providing an appearance of lessened
poverty.

FIGURE 47

*Dar al-Islam's mosque (*foreground*) and school are located near Abiquiú.*
Source: Author, April 1987.

When famous painter Georgia O'Keeffe died in 1986, several of the area's residents wanted her home to become a historic site for tourists. Having lived seasonally in the Río Arriba since 1929, O'Keeffe purchased her house in Abiquiú overlooking the Río Chama from the Catholic archdiocese in 1945. From it she was inspired by the scenery that was often incorporated into her paintings. She did not move to Abiquiú until 1949 and then lived there permanently in virtual seclusion. Earlier, her house had been occupied for many years by José María Chávez, a Union army general during the Civil War. After his death in 1902, the Chávez family owned the house until the mid-1920s when it was turned over to the Catholic Church.

When the U.S. Congress honored O'Keeffe in 1982 for her artistic contributions and designated her home as a national historic site, the National Park Service immediately made plans for the Georgia O'Keeffe National Historic Site and public visitation. The Park Service learned, however, that many of Abiquiú's residents were adamantly opposed to its plans, which would have made the village a tourist center. Their sentiments were summarized in the Park Service's report, which claimed that "Abiquiú is easily accessible to weekend vacationers attracted to the scenic Río Chama and to other recreational opportunities in the area. Sightseers, drawn to the traditional architecture and rural peacefulness of the village as well as by curiosity about the O'Keeffe house, are a source of irritation to many residents."[30] Consequently, the Park Service decided not to implement its plans. After O'Keeffe's death, interest was renewed in having her historic property turned into a tourist development, but again most residents wanted to preserve their privacy and Abiquiú as essentially a Spanish-American community.

However, the influx of non–Spanish Americans into Abiquiú and its immediate area is very pronounced. In fact, a check of telephone subscribers in 1986 for both the village and the immediate area revealed that one-third of them had Anglo-American surnames, over half of them had Spanish-American surnames, and the remaining subscribers had Arab (Muslim) surnames.[31] Of course, it may be argued that using such a technique undoubtedly omits many poor Spanish-American and other families who cannot afford telephones. Nevertheless, the numbers of Anglo Americans and Muslims do reflect the changes in the composition of the populations of the village and area as well as in land use.

In conclusion, it must be remembered that the Town of Abiquiú Grant was given to Spanish and *genízaro* settlers to provide them with self-sufficient livelihoods by utilizing the land grant's resources. Spanish officials, and later Mexican officials, made careful assessments of the resources when they partitioned the irrigable land and determined the extent of the communal rangeland. Subsistence agriculture coupled with overpopulation, despite considerable out-migration, found the land grant's residents by the late 1800s looking beyond its boundaries for employment opportunities. Most had become dependent upon seasonal labor. Parcels of privately owned irrigable land on the Río Chama floodplain were gradually acquired and consolidated by a Spanish-American *rico* whose descendant eventually allowed it to be incorporated into a large Anglo-American livestock ranch. The residents' continued interest in livestock united them to retain the remainder of the land grant. This rangeland, however, has been inadequate to provide the incomes necessary to avoid economic poverty in the 1900s. As a result, the land grant became merely the home base for a smaller and smaller number of Spanish-American families whose heads of households were willing to travel to distant places to work. Many other men and their families left permanently, leaving behind by the early 1970s a landscape of partial abandonment that became a feature of many rural communities in the Río Arriba.

Abiquiú has been transformed, beginning in the mid-1970s, into a slightly more prosperous village by the infusion of external capital, resulting from nearby tourist activity and the Muslims' construction of Dar al-Islam. Although the village's residents remain largely Spanish American and dependent upon commuting considerable distances to work, there is no doubt that significant change has taken place in the village and to such an extent that it raises the question of whether Abiquiú can remain a Spanish-American community. One factor in particular may keep Abiquiú a Spanish-American village—the Spanish Americans' interest in retaining ownership of the communal rangeland. Many continue to be involved today in the village's cooperative livestock association and use the rangeland for grazing a total of approximately 150 cattle, more than 50 sheep, and some horses, an indication of their determination to preserve aspects of their cultural heritage.[32] On the other hand, not all the Spanish Americans in the livestock association actually own livestock, but they allow others to use their grazing rights, which enable a few villagers to have sizable and somewhat profitable herds. In addition, the avid interest in livestock has declined steadily among younger Spanish Americans, who have realized the benefits of a wage economy and want to avoid the time-consuming care and work associated with livestock. They increasingly prefer to spend their idle time on the growing recreational opportunities throughout the Río Arriba. What impact these attitudes will have on the future of the Town of Abiquiú Grant remains to be seen.

10 The Villages of El Rancho and Vadito

Spanish Americans settled in large numbers on the Río Arriba's northern Pueblo Indian grants. As discussed in Chapter 3, they acquired titles in the late 1920s and 1930s to most of their land claims, largely irrigable cropland, through adjudication before the Pueblo Lands Board. An analysis here of the Spanish-American villages of El Rancho on the San Ildefonso Pueblo Grant and Vadito on the Picurís Pueblo Grant provides insights into the variables that have been at play in determining each village's continued existence without ever having been located within a Spanish or Mexican land grant and its role in sustaining the Spanish-American homeland.[1]

El Rancho is stretched out for two and one-half miles along the lower Pojoaque River in northwestern Santa Fe County. Despite government restrictions, Spanish settlers in the very early 1700s began to claim irrigable cropland here near the San Ildefonso Indians' pueblo (elevation 5,600 feet). They demanded at the outset of their encroachment that the San Ildefonso Pueblos prove ownership of their irrigable land and water rights, which was difficult for the Indians, who had no documents. Consequently, the San Ildefonso Pueblos took a trespassing case in 1736 to New Mexico's governor, who to their dismay ruled in favor of a Spanish encroacher. The Spaniard claimed he had inherited the land and had also bought land. Furthermore, he maintained he could therefore use the *acequia* and available water within the San Ildefonso Pueblo Grant. The San Ildefonso Pueblos argued that his original occupation of the land was attributed to their lending the defendant's ancestors a piece of land, not selling it.[2] Proof of ownership in these types of land disputes was made more complicated over time by partible inheritance, exchanges, and sales.

Spaniards continued to acquire land within the land grant throughout the 1700s and accelerated their acquisitions in the 1800s. Felipe Tafoya, a leader of the San Ildefonso Pueblos, complained in 1763 to Spanish Governor Tomás Vélez Cachupín that "the encroachments were so serious that some San Ildefonso families had virtually no agricultural lands at all."[3] Considerable litigation followed more complaints. The decisions rendered generally favored the San Ildefonso Pueblos, but they did not stop encroachments by non-Indians. Meanwhile, the pueblo's population declined, from nearly 500 residents in 1769 to approximately 200 in 1850, largely because of a smallpox epidemic.[4] Only 140 Indians resided in the pueblo in 1900, and that number dwindled further to only 91 in 1922.[5] Consequently, Pueblo agriculture had waned and the improved land, as well as the mostly unimproved but cultivable land, was sought by the growing number of nearby Spanish-American families who needed a means of subsistence. Small parcels were acquired from the remaining San Ildefonso Pueblos as well as from Spanish-American residents, of whom some had become become spouses of Indians, already located within the land grant. An 1890 report by the Department of the Interior claimed that "San Ildefonso by sales and thefts of lands maintains a precarious existence."[6] It further claimed that where the Pueblos did not use their land the "Mexicans . . . appropriated it."[7] The Board of Indian Commissioners in both 1900 and 1918 was alarmed by the continuous squatting on the San Ildefonso Pueblo Grant and how the Indians lacked not only irrigable land but also sources of water and wood for domestic fuel.[8]

Spanish Americans acquired their land parcels within the San Ildefonso Pueblo Grant in strips or long-lots, measured by *varas,* which were laid out to extend across the valley's floodplain to the Pojoaque River. This orientation allowed the non-Indian settlers to take irrigation water from the main ditches dug parallel to the river and have it flow by gravity across the fields and drain ultimately back into the river. To institute such a system, there had to be fairly large unoccupied sections of land to allow each parcel to extend the breadth of the floodplain so that there could be an uninterrupted flow of water. The farmsteads were situated on the upland immediately off the floodplain in order to maximize the utilization of the limited irrigable land, resulting in the formation of a linear settlement on each side of the river that was characterized by a sense of orderly field patterns in contrast to the Pueblo's irregular field patterns (Figure 48).

Spanish Americans acquired their land parcels within the San Ildefonso Pueblo Grant in exchange for various goods and livestock. Their transactions included in 1833, 25 *varas* for twelve goats; 1863, 19.5 *varas* for

FIGURE 48

El Rancho, 1935, is stretched out along the Pojoaque River.
Source: Río Grande Project, National Archives, Washington, D.C.

half a *fanega* of corn, half a *fanega* of wheat, and two milk goats; 1879, 42 *varas* for one mule, one horse, and one serape; and 1890, 18 *varas* and 29 *vigas* of a house for twenty goats, one burro, one burrito, and $29.50. They used more currency in the late 1800s after men had become seasonal laborers.[9] Some Spanish Americans worked parcels on a share basis and later assumed ownership of them, while others occupied land by verbal agreements with individual Pueblos, but a considerable number "appropriated" unused land by simply squatting on it. Spanish-American settlement did not take place on the north side of the Pojoaque River until the late 1880s because of the limited narrow floodplain there and only after a very serious shortage of irrigable cropland.

The extent of these acquisitions was revealed when non-Indian claims for 390 parcels, averaging less than four acres each, were presented in the late 1920s to the Pueblo Lands Board for adjudication. Spanish Americans acquired titles to nearly all their claims along the Pojoaque River. They ended up with 1,101 acres, mostly irrigable cropland.[10] San Ildefonso Pueblos reacquired 334 acres when funds were appropriated following the passage in 1933 of the Pueblo Lands Relief Act.[11] However, two-thirds of this acreage was "arid" upland, unsuitable for irrigation or dry farming.[12] Consequently, the San Ildefonso Pueblos ended up with a total of less than 300 acres of irrigable land. Approximately 130 Spanish-American families resided within the San Ildefonso Pueblo Grant in the mid-1930s in comparison to only 26 Pueblo families.[13]

Non-Indians, from the outset of settling within the San Ildefonso Pueblo Grant, acquired only small parcels because they had little cash or goods to consummate larger exchanges and, moreover, did not have the means to till large acreages. Their parcels became even smaller by their lengthwise subdivision among heirs, resulting in an intensified system of ribbon-shaped units. One *hijuela* in 1902 provided for each of five heirs to receive strips of land measuring only 10 *varas*. An average Spanish-American farm unit, comprised of one or more parcels, consisted of 4.9 acres in 1935.

Although subsistence agriculture prevailed in El Rancho, Spanish Americans sold on occasion small surpluses of hay, wheat, onions, chiles, and cabbages as well as a few livestock in Española and Santa Fe. Water shortages consistently limited crop production. Some Spanish Americans believed that the climate had changed, making the area drier.[14] But as settlement increased in the open Pojoaque River Valley, there was actually less water available downstream for El Rancho's farmers, who by 1930 were limited to irrigating their parcels only a few hours one day a week. Complicated by considerable evaporation, seepage, woody growth in the ditches, and a gravel loam soil that did not hold water well meant greater than normal amounts of water were needed.

When the non-Indian claimants received titles to their parcels, the remainder of the San Ildefonso Pueblo Grant, nearly all rangeland, was to be used solely by the Indians. Spanish-Americans landowners continued to graze several hundred head of livestock, mostly cattle, on the land grant, however. They were able to do so by obtaining permits from the Pueblos and by trespassing. Eventually, the San Ildefonso Pueblos took exclusive control of the rangeland when they increased their livestock numbers under the advice of the Bureau of Indian Affairs. The rangeland had, however, a low carrying capacity estimated to be only one cow per 100 acres. Consequently, El Rancho's Spanish Americans promptly sought new pastures on the nearby already overgrazed Town of Jacona Grant and on the Pajarito Plateau located to the west of the Río Grande. In 1943, the Pajarito Plateau was selected to be part of the site of the Los Alamos Scientific Laboratory (included later in Los Alamos County) and was put off limits for livestock pasture. Some obtained livestock grazing permits in the Santa Fe National Forest. Other Spanish Americans continued merely to graze small numbers of livestock in their so-called area on the open range, which was actually the public domain, or rented pasture on large ranches.

As elsewhere in the Río Arriba, Spanish-American men in El Rancho started in the late 1800s to leave their small farms to earn cash as seasonal laborers. Their summers were spent largely out of state in Colorado's potato and sugarbeet fields, Wyoming's sheep camps, and Utah's coal mines and on railroad crews throughout the West.[15] Meanwhile, their farms had become, in essence, part-time operations. When seasonal work was unavailable during the Depression, they returned to farming in the summers and took temporary jobs working on nearby projects created by the Works Projects Administration and the Civilian Conservation Corps.

The construction of the atomic laboratory facilities at Los Alamos changed dramatically the livelihoods of El Rancho's five hundred residents in the 1940s and 1950s. Steady employment on construction and maintenance crews was found now only 15 miles away. Most of the small farms became again part-time operations and eventually many became nonfarm residences. Those who could not find employment in Los Alamos County, which had in 1960 the highest median family income ($9,269) for counties west of the famous one hundredth meridian, soon sought it 18 miles to the south in Santa Fe. Approximately 80 percent of the employed persons residing in El Rancho in the early 1970s, however, worked in Los Alamos and the remainder, mostly women, was employed in Santa Fe. Several people also worked in Española.

Despite these local employment opportunities, El Rancho's growing population produced a larger labor force than jobs available. Aware of their parents' and relatives' economic benefits from both nearby steady employment and gains achieved through limited out-migration, some during World War II, many of El Rancho's younger Spanish Americans began to out-migrate permanently, mostly to California. For instance, seven siblings in one family of ten children moved to southern California, where several became laborers in Fontana's steel plant. Despite the out-migration, El Rancho's population increased because one or two of the children in a family would remain behind and have their own families. This continual, albeit slow, growth of the Spanish-American population coupled with in-migration by Anglo Americans, some of whom worked at Los Alamos, put El Rancho's population in the early 1970s at nearly 850 residents.

Although full-time farming was no longer practiced in 1970, about thirty of El Rancho's landowners, mostly elderly Spanish Americans, continued to practice part-time farming. They harvested and sold chiles and alfalfa hay from their long-lots. Young landowners considered the production of chiles and garden crops to be risky endeavors because of the seasonal water shortages and frost, lack of assured markets or prices, and too much stoop labor. Some even thought that the peddling of produce was a sign of poverty. Consequently, 60 percent of the irrigable acreage had lain fallow for years or it had been used merely for pasture. Only 20 percent of the acreage was in gardens and orchards and the remainder was in alfalfa hay.[16] Other farm income was derived from the sale of cattle, which were pastured in the summer on livestock grazing permits again on the surrounding San Ildefonso Pueblo Grant and 25 miles away in the Santa Fe National Forest, and on the leased pasture 80 miles away near Chama on the privately owned Tierra Amarilla Grant. Several livestock owners trucked a few cattle until the late 1960s to southern Taos County for grazing in the Carson National Forest. Many of El Rancho's Spanish Americans indicated their desire to own livestock but realized that they lacked large enough land units to provide for cattle year-round or even during part of the year. They considered, also, the trucking and the obtaining of the national forests' livestock grazing permits to be troublesome. In most Spanish-American villages, permitted grazing in a national forest is nearby, but in El Rancho the residents did not live on a rejected Spanish or Mexican land grant so there was no establishment of prior use. Their previous use of a rangeland was that found largely within the San Ildefonso Pueblo Grant and the land incorporated into Los Alamos County. The San Ildefonso Pueblos were very aware that some Spanish-American cattle continued to roam at will on their land grant in the winters as few of their owners winter fed livestock or had the capability of doing so. Despite the problems associated with the ownership of livestock, Spanish Americans sought prestige from owning cattle. Some enjoyed their summer weekends traveling to check on their cattle in the national forests.

El Rancho's Spanish-American landowners owned generally smaller parcels in 1970 than in 1935 because parents continued to give their children land and homesites and, here and there, they split parcels to sell to other Spanish Americans and Anglo Americans. The number of occupied houses nearly doubled from 101 in 1935 to 190 in 1970 while the number of land parcels increased from 118 to 177, splitting approximately 600 irrigable acres in the latter case (Figure 49). Although the Spanish Americans did not like to sell their land, they reported frequently that Anglo Americans in particular were willing to pay irresistible prices for a *rancho* with an old adobe house that could be renovated and found in reasonable proximity to their places of employment. As a result, Anglo

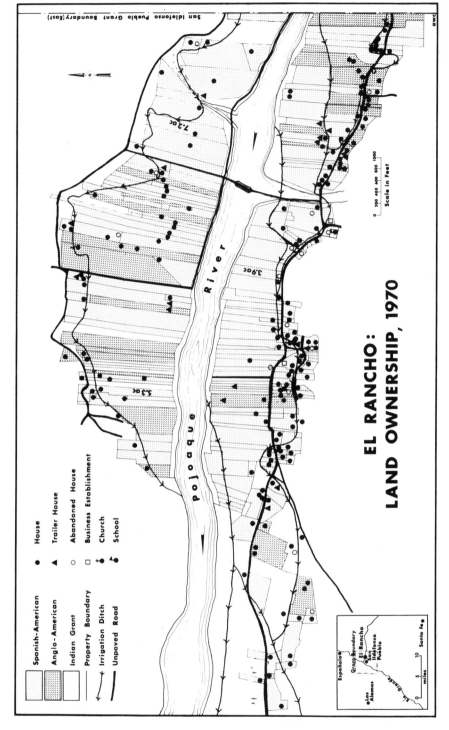

FIGURE 49

Source: Santa Fe County Assessor's Office, Santa Fe, and fieldwork.

Americans in 1970 owned more than 20 percent of the land in El Rancho. Most worked in Santa Fe and Los Alamos, although some were retirees who wanted to live in a bucolic, tricultural atmosphere. Land values
for homesites rose accordingly—from $40 to $50 an acre prior to the
establishment of Los Alamos to $700 an acre in the early 1940s during
the construction of Los Alamos to $1,500 to $2,000 an acre in the early
1970s. Spanish-American farmers could not pay these prices to consolidate and expand their agricultural operations. Likewise, these land values
made it difficult for the San Ildefonso Pueblos to buy land to consolidate
their holdings.[17]

Although external forces, such as those associated with Los Alamos,
had led to favorable assessments of El Rancho as a residential area in the
countryside, many older Spanish Americans retained their land for sentimental reasons, a sense of security, and their children. Even in cases
where their children had moved away, parents believed that their moves
were temporary by claiming that the children should have a place to
return to "when they get tired of California." Their expectations were
borne out then and now by El Rancho's considerable number of housetrailers, which reflect not only the need for quick, cheap, and modern
housing but also a sense of mobility. Overall, there was limited economic
poverty here in the early 1970s in comparison to other rural areas of the
Río Arriba. Of the more than fifteen hundred families who received welfare payments in rural Santa Fe County, only thirty families, mostly
elderly residents, were located in El Rancho. And, of the county's more
than thirteen hundred families who qualified for food stamps, only thirty-
two Spanish-American families qualified in El Rancho. "Hippies"
accounted for another twenty-five "voluntary cases."

El Rancho's population has continued to grow slowly since 1970. It
numbers approximately nine hundred residents today, half Spanish American and half Anglo American. In particular, the influx of Anglo Americans has had an impact on land values, which have increased to $20,000
to $25,000 for an irrigated acre and $16,000 to $19,000 for an acre of
dry upland. Longtime Spanish-American families continue to accommodate some of their children by allowing housetrailers to be located on
their long-lots. Others have sold parcels to Anglo Americans for building
sites in order to take advantage of the high land values. Anglo Americans
still acquire, if possible, properties with sizable old adobe houses that can
be renovated. The community's irrigable land lies mostly idle as residents
depend upon commuting to employment in Española, Los Alamos, and
Santa Fe.

Meanwhile, the San Ildefonso Pueblos numbered only two hundred in
1970. They also felt the impact of Los Alamos as almost one-fifth of
their labor force was employed there. Aside from a few gardens, the Indi-

ans had no crop farming. Consequently, much of their irrigable land was idle except for the pasturing of a few non-Indian livestock on leases and their own approximately 150 cattle and few horses, which also grazed the land grant's rangeland. As in the case of their Spanish-American neighbors, the livelihoods of the San Ildefonso Pueblos had been changed from dependence on subsistence agriculture to a dependence largely on wages and even in some cases the sales of pottery, such as that by the

FIGURE 50

Maria Martínez (right), *with the assistance of her husband, Julián* (left), *was largely responsible for reviving the making of pottery in the San Ildefonso pueblo. Their second son, John, posed between them in 1926.*

Source: Courtesy of Museum of New Mexico Library, Santa Fe.

well-known María Martínez (of black pot fame), who died in 1980 (Figure 50).

The number of resident San Ildefonso Pueblos had increased to more than five hundred by 1985 as there had been little out-migration and others retired back to their land grant. Although only slightly more than 40 percent of the potential labor force was employed, more than three-fourths of those employed had annual earnings of $7,000 or more—one of the higher percentages for earnings found on any of the Pueblo Indian grants in the Río Arriba.[18] Most are employed at facilities in Los Alamos. As one said to me in 1987, "If you can find a retired Indian, he worked at Los Alamos!" Others are employed by various state and federal government agencies and by the Indian hospital and school in Santa Fe. Fewer than five residents had livestock—a total of approximately 120 head of cattle—that grazed the grant's irrigable land and range. Meanwhile, tribal leaders have joined those of three other Pueblo Indian grants (Nambé, Pojoaque, and Tesuque) in the Pojoaque River Valley in a lingering lawsuit for their aboriginal water rights that have been diminished allegedly by the valley's Spanish-American settlers.[19]

Unlike El Rancho, Vadito in southern Taos County is located in a rather isolated area of the Río Arriba, but like El Rancho it is traversed by a perennial stream, the Río Pueblo, which originates in the Sangre de Cristo Mountains. Vadito lies in a small, high (elevation 7,450 feet) mountainous valley where the annual precipitation is slightly more than 17 inches. Situated within the Picurís (San Lorenzo) Pueblo Grant, the village is located 15 miles south of Taos and 3 miles north-northeast of the regional center of Peñasco, which is also located within the grant (Figure 51).

Spanish Americans had started to reside in and near the Picurís Pueblo Grant in the late 1700s. The Picurís Pueblos were quick to protest the Spanish Americans using their irrigable land and their assumption of water rights. More encroachments occurred and they filed more complaints, even to the American government in the early 1850s.[20] Their protests went largely unanswered because of the confusion over the Pueblos' legal status, which included the question of whether these Indians could alienate land. Meanwhile, additional Spanish Americans moved onto the grant after it was patented in 1864 and raids by Plains Indians had been subdued.[21]

Overgrazing and the scarcity of irrigable cropland in what had become the heavily populated Peñasco area led to some of the Spanish Americans acquiring uncleared land along the upper Río Pueblo and the establishment of Vadito. They were joined by other settlers who had come in search of land from the also heavily populated Santa Cruz Valley. Here, too, Spanish Americans acquired land within the Picurís Pueblo Grant by

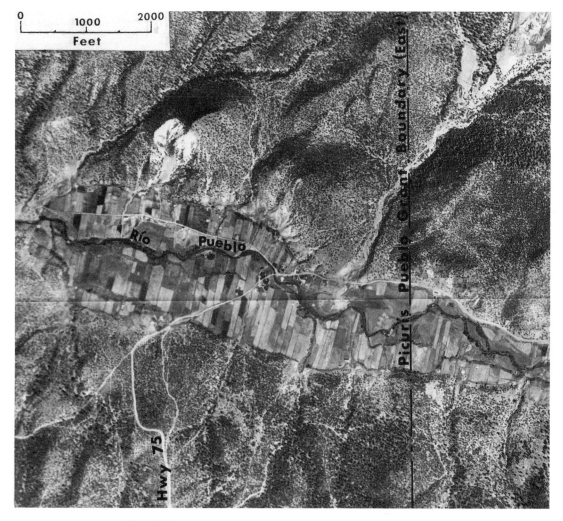

FIGURE 51

Vadito, 1935, is located along the Río Pueblo.

Source: Río Grande Project, National Archives, Washington, D.C.

squatting or exchanging goods, implements, grain, and livestock.[22] In time, intermarriage accounted for some of the Spanish Americans settling on different parts of the grant. It is important to emphasize that much of this non-Indian settlement took place during a decline in the Picurís Pueblo population from five hundred in 1830 to less than half that in 1860. Anthropologist Albert H. Schroeder has pointed out that "the presence of the Spaniards helped only to accelerate the decline through the introduction of disease and land aggression in a region where the native population depended largely on the surrounding country for game and wild food products."[23]

The demand for land in the overpopulated Peñasco area continued to a point where some Spanish Americans moved in the late 1800s northward to Colorado and eastward into the upper Mora River Valley, where an end had also been put to raids by marauding Indians. Meanwhile, the Picurís Pueblos' population continued to decline to where it numbered about one hundred in the early 1900s.[24] Their remaining land, largely unused, was left to facilitate the expansion of the established Spanish-American settlements.

Spanish Americans were required in the late 1920s to prove ownership of their land within the Picurís Pueblo Grant in the adjudication proceedings held by the Pueblo Lands Board. They ultimately received deeds to 2,550 acres by providing appropriate tax records or affidavits confirming their history of residency. The following excerpt, from the testimony of one of the claimants, provides an insight into Spanish-American thought as to why they frequently lacked tax records.

> Question. Did you ever pay any taxes. . . .
> Answer. No.
> Question. Why not?
> Answer. They did not send me any blanks, if you were not hired by the government you would not work for them.
> Question. Do you consider paying taxes working for the government?
> Answer. If one is not hired, one does not work.[25]

Others claimed they paid no taxes because they were away working as seasonal laborers.

Approximately three hundred Spanish Americans made claims on more than 670 parcels, averaging fewer than 4 acres each, within the Picurís Pueblo Grant. About forty-five of these Spanish Americans resided in Vadito, where they made claims on 380 acres, averaging 3.5 acres per parcel.[26] As in El Rancho, most of the Spanish-American acreage included irrigable cropland. The Picurís Pueblos were left 14,911 acres, of which only about 200 were irrigable. After the adjudication proceedings, they immediately reacquired 74 acres, of which 19 acres, half of them under cultivation, were in Vadito.[27] Again, they were to have exclusive use of the remainder of their land grant, mostly rangeland. As in the case of all Pueblos who lost land, the Pueblo Lands Relief Act of 1933 provided the Picurís Pueblos with funds to purchase back more parcels and their improvements such as irrigation facilities.[28] Vadito's Spanish Americans were not about to sell their parcels during the Depression, however. As a result, the Picurís Pueblos had reacquired a total of only 106 acres by 1941.[29]

Vadito's Spanish Americans had also acquired their parcels, for the most part, in long-lots extending across the breadth of the Río Pueblo's floodplain. This is especially true where many of the original parcels of approximately ten to fifteen acres had been subdivided by inheritance and sales to other Spanish Americans, mainly relatives. According to affidavits filed in 1915 by Spanish Americans on 293 parcels in both Vadito and adjacent non-Indian settlements, 26 percent of the parcels had been inherited and the remainder had been acquired by purchase. There is considerable evidence that by 1910 one son usually purchased the land inherited by his siblings, preventing greater subdivision and fragmentation. Two-thirds of the Spanish-American claimants were forty years of age and older, and all of them had owned their parcels for an average of nearly eighteen years.[30]

Vadito's underemployed subsistence farmers, like many Spanish-American males in the Río Arriba during the late 1800s and early 1900s, began to seek seasonal employment. They went off to work at various jobs throughout the western states and returned home during the winters. Consequently, land use in this high valley turned increasingly from crops of wheat, corn, and potatoes to hay and pasture, which required less labor. Chiles are difficult to raise here because of the high elevation and relatively short growing season, with frost-free days only between May 20 and September 28.

Vadito was a community of nearly 450 people during the Depression, when more than 70 percent of them were dependent upon different forms of relief.[31] Some of the men were employed in the Civilian Conservation Corps camps while others cut railroad ties and firewood in the nearby Carson National Forest. Subsistence agriculture prevailed again with marginal land put back into fairly extensive cultivation, largely by using hand implements. On occasion, small surpluses of onions and potatoes were sold outside the valley. Livestock overgrazed the surrounding area, including the lands owned by the Picurís Pueblos. Horses constituted 40 percent of the village's 180 head of livestock, reflecting their use for transportation and field work.

World War II reduced Vadito's underemployed labor force. Men not only left to serve in the military forces, but they also went to work in military installations such as the shipyards in Oakland, California. Many of them never returned to reside in Vadito and the village's population declined to slightly more than three hundred residents in 1950.[32] Vadito remained a source of seasonal laborers as several men ventured off to seek employment in western ranching, farming, and mining operations. Approximately ten men worked in a nearby sawmill until it closed in 1962. By the mid-1960s others had also out-migrated permanently, with most going to California, Colorado, Nevada, Utah, and Wyoming. There were cases where all the grown children of families left the valley. For instance, one family included nine children—two each resided in Nevada and Utah, four in Colorado, and one in West Virginia. In each case, a mining or a seasonal agricultural job had initially taken them or their spouses to these locations. As this out-migration progressed, little partitioning of parcels took place between 1940 and the 1980s (Figure 52). Yet because of a number of factors there was little consolidation or expansion of farms. One reason was the Spanish Americans' disdain for loans that mortgaged their land, and there was also the difficulty of obtaining loans from lending institutions except for the federal Farmers Home Administration.[33]

Vadito has survived because many of the elderly villagers customarily retained their birthright lands. When its population was only 150 in the early 1970s, much of the village's land was owned by elderly Spanish Americans as their form of security. Outsiders, particularly Anglo Americans, had been largely unsuccessful in acquiring land here despite the demand and enticement to sell it for $1,000 to $1,500 an acre. Only three parcels, totaling eleven acres, belonged to Anglo Americans (Figure 52). In checking the Taos County assessor's 1970 records, however, it was interesting to learn of the numerous parcels in the surrounding mountainous area that were owned largely by Anglo Americans—Texans and Nevadans.

None of the eighty-one landowners in Vadito in the early 1970s was a full-time farmer. Ten landowners were part-time farmers who sold at most a few cattle each year. Small numbers of cattle grazed the meadows and irrigated pastures on the floodplain, and approximately ninety cattle grazed in the nearby Carson National Forest from May 15 to September 30 under eight livestock-grazing permits. Several of the village's part-time farmers derived only $2,000 to $3,000 from agriculture while the others earned even less. A livestock sales yard was built with government funds between Peñasco and Vadito to help area farmers market their animals. In addition, the Home Education Livelihood Program (HELP), started in 1966, attempted to assist farmers throughout the Peñasco area in the cooperative marketing of their farm products and to encourage the men who worked seasonally elsewhere to remain in their villages with their families. Participating farmers placed approximately 300 acres, including 135 acres leased from the Picurís Pueblos, into the cooperative enterprise. Of this acreage, 50 acres were in Vadito, where seven landowners participated by planting potatoes, blue corn, oats, and barley. Participants received daily stipends in exchange for working at the cooperative's outlet in Peñasco and for attending adult education courses to improve their farming skills as well as to learn new skills for nonagricultural jobs.

Vadito's Spanish-American landowners maintained, however, that their

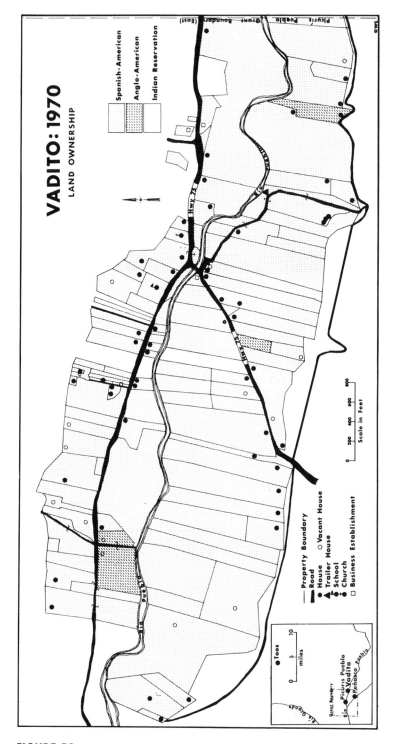

FIGURE 52

Source: Taos County Assessor's Office, Taos, and fieldwork.

land units, totaling 369 acres or averaging 4.5 acres each in 1970, were
too small for profitable farming and their potential value for seasonal recreational purposes had prevented any efforts to consolidate units for
large-scale agriculture. On the other hand, they would not move despite
the lack of nonfarm employment opportunities. Many thought that if
they sold their land neither they nor their children would ever have the
financial resources to reacquire it. Some resented, too, the possibility of
hippies acquiring land in the village. Residents claimed that the eight
absentee owners in the early 1970s also wanted to return to Vadito upon
their retirement. One expressed the idea that although some of these
absentee owners had permanent jobs and lived in Utah, "his people only
stay there and they are not settled until they return to Vadito." Ties to
the land remained strong and tended to hold the remaining residents in
the valley. Therefore, many continued to leave seasonally to work in mining operations near Grants, New Mexico (uranium); McGill, Nevada
(gold and silver); Butte, Montana (copper); and Gilman, Colorado (zinc).
Several worked at the large molybdenum mine north of Taos near
Questa, commuting a distance of fifty miles each way. Others joined fire-
fighting teams that traveled to wherever needed in the West, worked in
sheep camps in Idaho, or were employed on summer railroad crews in
Nevada.[34]

Vadito experienced considerable economic poverty in the 1970s when
more than 15 percent of its heads of households, mostly elderly residents,
were welfare recipients. An example of an elderly person receiving welfare assistance was the man who had become ill in Utah and returned to
Vadito to live "with his people." Nonelderly recipients fell largely into the
category of aid to families with dependent children.[35] Approximately 40
percent of its residents obtained federal food stamps for at least part of
the year. Nine out of ten houses had no indoor plumbing, and domestic
water was taken by pails from shallow wells and in a few cases directly
from the Río Pueblo, as was the case in the late 1920s, when only 20
percent of the villagers had wells.[36]

Similarly to what has occurred in Abiquiú and El Rancho, Anglo
Americans in the 1980s have increasingly reassessed Vadito and its surrounding area as a desirable place to live or especially to have seasonal
homes. (Natives speak disparagingly of the "Texan influence.") Consequently, Anglos have bought several of Vadito's *ranchos* and constitute
15 percent of the village's population. Meanwhile, a few Spanish-American retirees have returned to their land units. Because Vadito is located in
a relatively warm valley (the temperature is about 10° warmer on average
than elsewhere in Taos County), retirees in particular cite this amenity for
locating here. All of the villagers value the recreational opportunities in
the surrounding mountains and national forests. Land values range today

from $6,000 an acre for upland to $15,000 an acre for irrigable pastureland. Very little of the irrigable land is used for crops. Those few residents who are employed fulltime commute to distant places within the Río Arriba, but the closing in 1986 of Questa's molybdenum mine left several of them without jobs.[37] There is hardly any travel today to seasonal out-of-state jobs.

Meanwhile, the Picurís pueblo had fewer than one hundred residents in the 1970s. Its cropland remained idle or was leased to the neighboring non-Indians. Several Picurís Pueblos used the grant's rangeland to graze a small number of livestock. Lacking agricultural opportunities, the Indians turned to encouraging tourism by constructing a small museum and fishing ponds. Despite these efforts, economic poverty has prevailed in the pueblo, compounded by the fact that its population has increased to more than 150 residents in the mid-1980s. Only half the potential labor force in 1985 was employed doing seasonal construction and logging jobs created largely by government agencies, providing annual incomes of less than $7,000 for three-fourths of them.[38] None raised cattle, although some grazed a few horses and sheep on the grant.

The Pueblo Lands Board's adjudication of non-Indian claims within the Picurís and San Ildefonso Pueblo land grants, as well as those within other northern Pueblo Indian grants, had provided titles to substantial acreages of irrigable cropland for hundreds of Spanish Americans, leaving the particular Pueblos with not much more than upland suitable only for rangeland. Although they had adopted livestock grazing from the Spaniards, they had been horticulturalists who depended heavily upon irrigated crops and somewhat upon hunting and the gathering of wild plants.[39] On the other hand, the Spanish Americans relied upon the establishment of self-contained settlements that included both pastoral and irrigated agriculture. In essence, both groups ended up with land bases that were incongruent with their subsistence traditions. Also, neither possessed the desirable land to engage in large-scale, modern agriculture. They did realize, however, that their land gave them a sense of security and permanency—feelings commonly found among peasant societies. Ironically, the Pueblos cannot by law alienate their land and hence are confronted no longer with the loss of land, such as what the Spanish Americans are now experiencing in El Rancho and even in relatively isolated Vadito. This means that no Spanish-American village is immune to Anglo-American intrusions.

The Community
of Corrales

11

C orrales, located ten miles northwest of Albuquerque, has become
largely a fashionable bedroom community because of the availability of *ranchos* and its proximity to sprawling urban growth.
Originally, it was established as an early Spanish agricultural settlement
on the Town of Alameda Grant.[1] After the establishment of Villa de Albuquerque in 1706, this Spanish land grant was bestowed in 1710 upon
Capt. Francisco Montes y Vigil, originally of Zacatecas, Mexico, and his
large family of Santa Fe.[2] Having retired from the military service, Montes
y Vigil needed, in particular, pasture for his small herd of cattle.[3] Albuquerque's *alcalde,* Martin Hurtado, after working out an agreement with
the adjacent Sandía Pueblo Indians, who resided to the east of the Río
Grande, set the grant's boundaries: "On the North by the ruin of an old
pueblo, which of the two that there are is the most distant one from the
place of Alameda. . . . On the South a small hill which is the boundary
of Luis Garcia. . . . On the East the Rio Del Norte (el. 4,985 ft). . . . On
the West the prairies and hills for entrances and exits."[4] The western
boundary was actually the *ceja* (summit of hills) or divide (elevation 6,700
feet) between the watersheds of the Río Grande and the Río Puerco.

The petition to have this Spanish land grant confirmed was submitted
to New Mexico's surveyor-general in 1872. Considerable concern arose
over the grant's boundaries because the Río Grande had changed its
course that year and because Montes y Vigil may not have occupied the
land long enough according to Spanish law. Montes y Vigil had sold the
grant in 1712 to Capt. Juan José Gonzáles for 200 pesos.[5] The grant was
confirmed, however, in 1892 and patented in 1920. Only 89,346 acres

were included in the final survey instead of the 106,274 acres originally claimed by the grantees, heirs, and others. Both the Sandía Pueblos and the heirs of the nearby Elena Gallegos (Ranchos de Albuquerque) Grant objected to the original survey, contending it overlapped onto their land. Like many Spanish and Mexican grants, the Town of Alameda Grant fronted a stream, the Río Grande, and included uncultivated and unsettled bottomland or floodplain, which in this case amounted to approximately 2,500 acres. In fact, the Sandía Pueblos maintained during the confirmation proceedings that the Río Grande was a necessary boundary between their land grant and the Town of Alameda Grant because it provided both peoples with river frontage for irrigated agriculture.[6] Grassy sandhills made up the rest of the Town of Alameda Grant.

Captain Gonzáles quickly sold the northern half of the grant to his relative Salvatore Martínez in exchange for an estimated two hundred head of livestock.[7] The Gonzáles family had established the Rancho de Abajo in the southern half, while the northern half was subdivided after two families, the Montoyas and the Sandovals, acquired large portions.[8]

As elsewhere in the Río Arriba, the elderly Spanish Americans are proud of their ancestry. For example, Miguel Griego, a long-time resident of Corrales, explained his village's history in the following way:

> I tell you about this place . . . Juan Gonzáles sail from Spain, he and thirty-five other grandees, *patrones*. You understand, these were big men in Spain. They land in Vera Cruz and make their way to the mouth of the Bravo, now the Río Grande. They come up the Bravo by boat, not like the *conquistadores* for gold, but for land. They settle all along from Santa Fé to way down below here on the river. The names are all in the church in Old Albuquerque. The Gonzáles, Martínez, Sandoval, Greigo, Perea, all the old families here in Corrales, as we call it, trace their lineage back, through marriage and inter-marriage, to Captain Juan and his men.[9]

Spanish settlers considered the grant's floodplain as good agricultural land but difficult to clear because of the dense vegetation, consisting largely of cottonwoods. By 1740, they farmed small irrigated plots on the floodplain and pastured livestock on the surrounding hills. Fray Francisco Domínguez reported in 1776 that there were 36 families or 150 people on the grant.[10] Succeeding generations continued to clear the floodplain for garden plots and fields and to obtain firewood and building materials. They also extended the irrigation system to the new fields so that Corrales had a main ditch (*acequia madre*), lateral ditches, and a supervisor (*mayordomo*), who organized the community's work crews.[11]

When some of the settlers built extensive livestock corrals, which were used by Spanish, Mexican, and even American cavalry units because of their proximity to pastures, the community became known as Los Corrales de Alameda.[12] Its name was changed to Sandoval in the early 1900s when most of the Town of Alameda Grant was taken in 1903 from Bernalillo County and placed in Sandoval County, but was changed back to Corrales in 1966. Corrales's courthouse and jail were moved in 1904 to Bernalillo, a short distance north of Corrales and Sandoval County's seat, because of its location on a railroad line.

Corrales served as part of a line of defense against Navajo marauders who raided Spanish settlements, including nearby Albuquerque and Bernalillo. When necessary, its residents became militiamen who were assisted by Spanish cavalrymen and later Mexican and American troops. After the Indians were subdued in the 1870s and with the advent of the railroad into New Mexico, a few Anglo Americans started to purchase land near and on the Town of Alameda Grant. In addition, small numbers of Italian and French immigrants began in the late 1800s to acquire land in the Albuquerque area.[13] By the turn of the century, several Italians had also purchased largely uncultivated land from Spanish-American landowners in upper Corrales. Corrales remained, however, essentially a Spanish-American agricultural community of more than five hundred residents.

The Spanish-American farmers had acquired their land parcels by widths ranging from 50 to several hundred *varas*. These parcels extended usually from the Río Grande across the floodplain to the foothills so that landowners had access to pastures in the hills and frontage on the main irrigation ditch for water rights. The strips of land, therefore, amounted to as much as between thirty and fifty acres and generally took the shape of long-lots (Figure 53). Some of the larger tracts were later subdivided into smaller strips, usually 50 or 100 *varas,* and sold to the non-Spanish newcomers. For instance, an Italian paid $500 in 1898 for an unimproved strip of 100 *varas* amounting to 46.8 acres from a parcel of 141.4 acres.[14] The settlers assumed grazing rights on the remainder of the land grant.

Generally, farmsteads were centrally located here on the land parcels and were several feet above the flood stage of the Río Grande. The main road passed through the center of the broad floodplain and linked the farmsteads by forming a line settlement. Large cottonwoods in the wooded area (*bosque*) immediately along the Río Grande were difficult to clear and therefore this area was left unimproved.

Most of the community's Spanish landowners in the 1700s and early 1800s farmed fairly large garden plots and depended quite heavily upon livestock, which were tended to on the land grant by the village's herders, *pastores la communida,* who were normally young boys. Some of the livestock entered into the caravan trade carried on with the mining towns of northern Mexico. The nearest caravan market was Bernalillo. Livestock was also sold, or exchanged for goods, in Albuquerque and even in

FIGURE 53

*Corrales is laid out along the Río Grande. The Sandiá Pueblo Grant, where small
parcels were reorganized into square-shaped fields in the 1950s, is across the Río
Grande from Corrales. A few residents of Corrales built fences (on the lower left),
extending their long-lots to include mesa land.*
Source: ASCS, USDA, Salt Lake City, DFD-2DD-119 and 120, 4 May 1963.

Santa Fe. A number of farmers marketed their vegetables and fruit in
growing Albuquerque by the mid-1880s. Wheat was also made into flour
at the grist mills in nearby Alameda and sold in Albuquerque.

With the in-migration of non-Spanish settlers, particularly the Italians
and later in the early 1900s several Frenchmen who bought strips of
land, Corrales became northern New Mexico's center of vineyards and
wine production. Numerous hoers, including Navajo Indians, were
employed in these vineyards.[15] Wine and grape brandy were transported
primarily to northeastern New Mexico, where numerous Italians and others worked in the coal mines in Raton. By World War I, Corrales's population of over five hundred residents had developed mainly as a "wagon

garden" for Albuquerque (population 17,000).[16] Although there was considerable subsistence agriculture in Corrales, commercial crop production had become as important as livestock sales.

Problems developed in the early 1900s for many of the community's farmers. Serious flooding had occurred on occasion for over half a century, largely attributed to overgrazing upon the sparsely covered watershed. Runoff into the arroyos, especially in upper Corrales, brought considerable destruction to homes, irrigation facilities, and crops.[17] With the growing dependence upon crops, water shortages emerged, and intensive irrigation led in time to water-logged fields and alkali problems.

It was largely for these reasons that Corrales's landowners in 1927 agreed to put their land into the Middle Río Grande Conservancy District, which extended for 150 miles along the Río Grande from the Cochití Pueblo Grant in northern Sandoval County to San Marcial, a town south of Albuquerque. Assessments were levied for the construction of the retention dams and the maintenance of irrigation canals, ditches, and levees. The result was a highly controlled and regular supply of irrigation water as well as the elimination of Spanish-American ditch associations.[18] Crop farmers had been assured of sufficient irrigation water on the floodplain and many soon thereafter sold their grazing rights to the remainder of the Town of Alameda Grant to the Alameda Cattle Company.

Fieldwork was done in upper Corrales to determine the changing land use and landownership patterns in Corrales between the Depression of the 1930s and the 1970s. Significant change was already evident by 1930, as non-Spanish landowners, Italian, French, and Anglo American, owned two-fifths of the land in upper Corrales. Some Spanish Americans had sold their land in order to obtain money to pay higher taxes and the irrigation fees resulting from the improvements made by the Middle Río Grande Conservancy District.[19]

Spanish Americans usually subdivided their land lengthwise among their children upon inheritance or marriage, resulting in a more intensified ribbon or long-lot field pattern.[20] As an elderly Spanish-American farmer put it, this custom was to keep the very wealthy people from buying up large units, and for the children it offered "no trust, no bust, no hell"; that is, no financing system.[21] Relatives were also kept close together. A pattern where long-lots had been divided crosswise into small block patterns had developed in upper Corrales. In these cases, each child was normally given parcels both near and away from the river in order to provide equitable types of bottomland based upon intimate knowledge of productivity throughout the strip. This was particularly true of landowners who had no cattle and thus had no need of access to grazing lands. Interestingly enough, the French and Italian Americans subdivided their land likewise in order to achieve similar distributions.

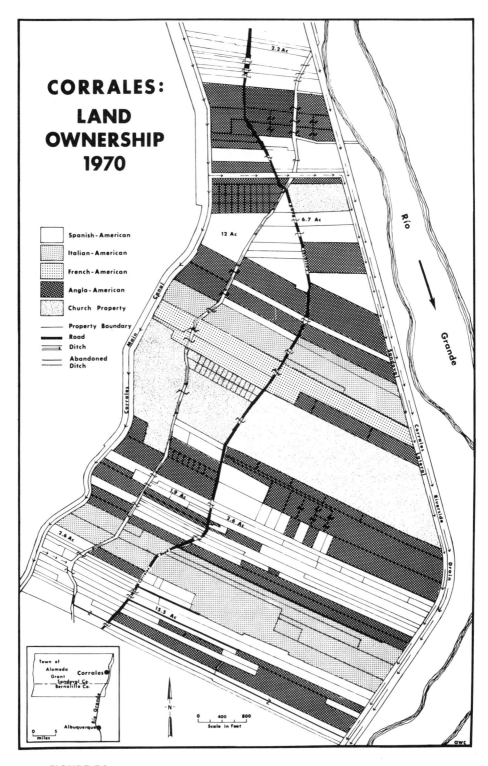

FIGURE 54

Source: Fieldwork, Middle Río Grande Conservancy District, Albuquerque, and Sandoval County Assessor's Office, Bernalillo.

Approximately 50 percent of the irrigable land in upper Corrales was in vineyards in the early 1930s. The French and Italian Americans continued to produce most of the grapes, but eventually many Spanish Americans had small vineyards, too, and they were selling grapes to local wineries or in the open markets of Albuquerque.[22] Wagon loads of grapes and other produce were taken also to Santa Fe in September to sell at the annual fiesta. Another 20 percent of the cropland was in orchards and vegetables with the remainder in hay, which was sold occasionally to northern New Mexico ranchers and dairymen or used locally to winter feed the few remaining livestock.

Actually, Corrales's viniculture had started to decline in the 1920s because of Prohibition, competition from California wines, and rising water tables that led to poor drainage in the vineyards.[23] Persistent vine diseases and pests were other factors. Some farmers claimed that the decline occurred after less acreage was planted in wheat. Birds that had formerly fed on grain turned to eating grapes and other fruit, thereby reducing yields. Wine production dropped dramatically during the Depression, especially when the Italians lost their principal market in Raton, where the coal mines had closed. In addition, the availability of field labor became a problem after the outbreak of World War II. Consequently, many farmers converted their vineyards into vegetable crops and orchards or simply into hay crops.[24]

Following World War II, Anglo Americans began to migrate into Corrales in increasing numbers. With the rapid growth of metropolitan Albuquerque (SMSA population of 155,000 in 1950; 262,000 in 1960; 314,000 in 1970; 454,000 in 1980; and 500,000 in 1990), many Anglo Americans sought country or rural residences with a few acres. They found them first in adjacent Alameda, but when land prices rose to be too high there, prospective buyers turned to Corrales. Here, Spanish Americans in particular but also other residents had subdivided their land into what Anglo Americans considered to be ideal units (Figure 54, Appendix K).

Meanwhile, Spanish Americans, especially youths, had been leaving Corrales since World War I. Although a few men worked seasonally as sheepherders in Arizona and under contract in the sugarbeet fields of Colorado in the early 1900s, Corrales was not an important source of seasonal labor as in the cases of many other Spanish-American villages.[25] Those who left went at first usually to Albuquerque. During and after World War II, out-migration increased to Albuquerque and notably to the Riverside–Los Angeles strip in southern California. Irrigable land in Corrales was for the most part no longer subdivided into strips for the purposes of farming. Some Spanish-American farmers sold their farms, or parts thereof, in their later years to Anglo Americans; or, if their children inherited a parcel, they would sell it as a unit or keep it, either renting it or leaving it idle. Others attempted to keep the land within their families, but Corrales had become in the late 1940s the base for a number of Anglo-American artists, photographers, and writers, prompting more Anglo Americans to move to the village where some developed additional amenities such as summer theater, galleries, and restaurants.[26]

Besides ideal-size *ranchos* with, in some cases, old adobe houses that could be renovated, Anglo Americans found in the 1950s low real estate taxes in Corrales in comparison to those found in adjoining Bernalillo County and Albuquerque. When Corrales's schools were incorporated into the Bernalillo County system in the mid-1950s, it provided what Anglo Americans considered an unwritten assurance of good educational opportunities for their children. Corrales, a community of thirteen hundred in 1960, was soon thought of as a community of country gentlemen living in a "delightful bit of antiquity" and billed to tourists and sightseers as "the charming art colony in the midst of fruit orchards."[27] Furthermore, it was known for lacking the alleged social problems, such as crime and drug peddling, found in Albuquerque's south Río Grande Valley. Thus, Corrales continued to lie in the path of Albuquerque's northward expansion. The uncleared *bosque* along the Río Grande offered wooded building sites that provided shade and privacy for new Anglo-American houses. Because paved highways provided easy access to employment opportunities in Albuquerque, Corrales had taken on the function of being a bedroom community of fifteen hundred by 1970. Unlike Abiquiú and Vadito, the village had little unemployment in 1970 and only a few people were on welfare or received food stamps. Any consolidation of small land units to enlarge farms was prohibited by suburban land values which had climbed from less than $1,000 an acre in 1950 to $1,500 to $2,000 an acre in the early 1960s and to $5,000 to $8,000 an acre in the 1970s.

Where there were approximately fifty full-time farmers in upper Corrales in 1930, there were seven in 1970: two Spanish Americans, two Italian Americans, two Anglo Americans, and one French American (Figure 54). Part-time farmers, mostly Spanish Americans, numbered about fifteen (Figure 55). Thus, only 15 percent of the landowners derived some income from agriculture. The land-use patterns had changed so that by 1970 20 percent of the land was in orchards, less than 10 percent in vegetables, 50 percent in hay and irrigated pasture, and 20 percent idle. Much of the hay, pasture, and idle acreage was held for speculation. Older Spanish Americans usually retained a portion of their farms because they felt more secure with land than with cash, but, in reality, they possessed considerable potential wealth.

Many Anglo Americans owned horses for recreation, breeding, and

FIGURE 55

An elderly Spanish-American farmer continued to use his traditional farming practices. The fairly modern house in the background did not belong to a farmer.
Source: Author, August 1969.

sale and planted an acre or two of their *ranchos* in alfalfa hay. Those landowners who had no horses derived some income from selling baled hay to the horsemen, dry-lot dairy farmers, livestock yards, and ranchers elsewhere in northern New Mexico. As one Spanish American put it: "Anglos have the horses, Spanish have the hay."[28] Aside from the horses, there was a general absence of livestock except for several cases where the livestock owners pastured a few cattle on BLM land in northern Sandoval County.

Corrales's few farmers sold, beginning in mid-July, most of their vegetables and fruit at about a dozen roadside stands along Corrales Road (State Road 46)—an indication of marginal agriculture. Supermarkets had put an end to the farmers' open markets in Albuquerque. As a result, possession of road frontage in Corrales had become an asset for these farmers as most of the customers were often sightseers from Albuquerque. Some fruit was sold to truckers or was marketed through wholesalers in Albuquerque. Vegetables and fruit produced, on average, about $1,000 an acre.[29]

In the 1970s, Corrales's transition to suburbia continued as the farmers reached retirement age and sold their remaining properties largely to Anglo Americans. Spanish-American youth did not like the seasonality and risks associated with specialized agriculture and claimed that the acreages were too small to allow buying the necessary equipment and labor. Several expressed the commonly held opinion among Spanish Americans that the climate had become drier during recent decades, diminishing the supply of irrigation water. They were also aware of the objections by new residents to the use of chemical sprays in the orchards for health reasons. Therefore, steady wage employment was an attractive alternative for them, and many have migrated from the community, leaving it to reassessment by newcomers.

The ongoing reassessment of quasi-rural Corrales has certainly had its impact upon the village's land-use patterns. The village's population had grown to twenty-eight hundred by 1980, nearly double that of 1970.[30] Farming continued to decline as the small parcels were evaluated more and more as residential sites with additional land used largely for equestrian purposes. One sees only two or three fruit and vegetable roadside stands. Land values have increased to where an acre of irrigable land with ditch rights and no buildings sold in 1987 for between $45,000 to $55,000, depending on whether it had road frontage or was near the *bosque*. An acre of upland sold for between $25,000 and $30,000. Because serious flooding continues to be a problem, much of the village has been designated as a flood zone, which forces landowners to possess flood insurance.[31]

To preserve the atmosphere of "uncrowded development" and a "leisurely, multicultural village life," most of Corrales was incorporated in 1971. Since then, it has been annexing the remaining parts of the community in order to control land-use patterns by zoning regulations and to block annexation attempts by sprawling Albuquerque.[32] As one resident in 1982 put it, "Compared to 50 years ago, the rural character of Corrales is indeed changed, but compared to most suburban areas, it is still rural."[33]

Urban developments are evident, however, with the construction of a small shopping center on the south end of Corrales, which after much controversy was annexed by Albuquerque.[34] A large shopping mall, River Walk Marketplace, opened in early 1990 near the center to serve northwest Albuquerque's growing population and that of incorporated Río Rancho Estates, a housing development started in the early 1960s, with a 1980 population of 10,000 but more than 30,000 in the late 1980s. Located on the mesa above Corrales, Río Rancho Estates is projected to have a population of approximately 60,000 by the year 2000.[35] Although most buyers have been young families, many from Albuquerque, who have entered the first-home market as well as some retirees from different states, developers have recently turned sections of Río Rancho Estates into houses for the luxury-home market, attracting "yuppies" and high-income families. Completed in 1988, a new and larger bridge over the Río Grande accommodates the dramatic increase in automobile traffic. These developments will certainly make Corrales even more desirable as a suburb where a new subdivision's houses were reported in 1987 to have an average value of $300,000, but where "no farm equipment, junk cars or travel trailers can be visible to residents."[36]

Corrales's Spanish-American population is declining rather rapidly as both the elderly and their heirs sell out at prices they "never dreamed could happen in Corrales." Younger Spanish Americans today can be found in "urban" Río Rancho Estates where they were able still to purchase in the mid-1980s new and modern, low to medium-priced standardized Anglo-American bungalows and townhouses for $40,000 to $70,000 each. These dwellings have been made available with small down payments and low taxes. Many Anglo Americans, meanwhile, prefer to renovate adobe Spanish-American houses or build similarly designed ones in "rural" Corrales, making for an interesting process of cross acculturation.[37] It is not surprising then that only one-third of the Corraleños in 1980 were of Spanish origin and that Sunbelt Albuquerque's population was less than 40 percent Spanish origin.[38] Both figures reflect the growing in-migration of Anglo Americans, who now dominate, as discussed in Chapter 6, migrational activity in the Río Arriba. Interestingly enough and maybe fortunately, most of the Anglo Americans who have sought out the environs of Abiquiú, El Rancho, Vadito, and Corrales want to preserve the quaint and pastoral ambience of the Spanish-American rural life-style.

PART FOUR

Clinging
to the
Homeland

The Río Arriba: A Waning Cultural Region

12

For four centuries New Mexico's semiarid upper Río Grande Valley has served as the homeland for Spanish Americans. The Río Arriba represents America's oldest European cultural region where a spatial behavior evolved that is manifested in the landscape in the form of certain settlement and land-use patterns that contributed to the creation of a persistent and distinctive folk environment. Many Spanish Americans have migrated from this region to surrounding areas and even out of New Mexico. A sizable concentration still exists here, however, reflecting the occupants' intriguing ability to acquire, occupy, and retain land under different governmental policies and legal confrontations as well as economic maladjustments and reappraisals. Their historic ethnic homeland, as any other, is based upon the continuous occupancy of land. Spanish Americans remain as the dominant rural population, especially in Taos and Río Arriba counties, but their number is declining throughout the region. Consequently, the Río Arriba as a culture region is on the wane, but it is, in comparison to the rest of rural America, still a relatively well-pronounced and easily identifiable region.[1]

Ancestors of the Spanish Americans settled permanently before 1600 in this isolated area of the upper Río Grande Valley. The extent of their settlement grew after the Spanish reconquest in 1692, following the Pueblo Indian Revolt of 1680. Both the Spanish and Mexican governments' strategic interests in having this frontier area occupied led to colonial land policies that involved agrarian planning and an orderly delivery system, based upon certain environmental perceptions and realities, to attract settlers who wanted land for livestock and crops. Floodplains found in numerous small microbasins or valleys tucked into the rough terrain offered irrigable land. Irrigation water was available by utilizing the Río Grande and its tributaries, all flowing within a drainage system maintained by surface runoff from the adjacent parallel mountain ranges, the Sangre de Cristos to the east, the San Juans and the Jémez to the west. Many of the tributaries are perennial streams, forming a concentration not found elsewhere in the arid Southwest.

Spanish and Mexican settlers and their heirs have occupied land in the Río Arriba under various governmental land policies implemented by either Spain, Mexico, or the United States. Until the late 1840s, the majority of the settlers had taken possession of small irrigable riverine long-lots on the limited floodplains within community land grants. In order to accommodate as many settlers as possible with cropland, this cadestral system provided for the egalitarian division of the irrigable land. It also allowed the settlers to reside in close proximity to one another, forming villages that enhanced both their ability to defend themselves and the maintenance of kin-related social and economic relationships. Each settler's grazing of a few livestock was an integral part of a community's agricultural traditions. Consequently, large expanses of uplands and woodlands were designated for pasturage and became functional parts of land grants. The unsettled areas outside the land grants were assumed to be usable as open range. Therefore, both extensive and intensive farming characterized Spanish-American agricultural practices. The continual issuance of new land grants allowed, also, for the Río Arriba's growing native-born Spanish population to acquire new lands and to expand its area of settlement. Many of the private land grants that were given to persons, largely for livestock pasture, also ended up being subdivided, especially if they contained any appreciable amounts of irrigable land, among settlers and heirs. There is no doubt that a distinctive, if not unique, human ecology had been developed.

Under the land policies of the United States, homesteading took the place of land grants in providing free land on the frontier to prospective settlers. Homesteading, as in the case of Spanish and Mexican land grants, involved certain settlement requirements that had to be met before the settlers received deeds to their land parcels. However, homesteads were not readily available to residents of the Río Arriba until the Spanish and Mexican land-grant claims had been surveyed, confirmed, and patented by the new government. It was necessary to determine the extent of the public domain that was available for alienating uncontested homesteads. Several thousand Spanish Americans filed for various homesteads and received patents. Homesteads, henceforth, provided equal amounts of land, but they were laid out in a grid pattern that did not provide equal types of land. The unclaimed land was also mostly suitable for dry farming as the irrigable land had already been settled. Spanish Americans were unfamiliar with this type of crop farming. It also required larger land units that necessitated investments in mechanization and dispersed settlement. They had, nevertheless, been given access by the U.S. government to the mechanisms for acquiring land from the public domain and therefore reinforcing their presence. Moreover, homesteading policies had allowed thousands of Anglo Americans to settle in the Río Arriba, a region where previously the land base had been used, including for the most part even the Pueblo Indian land grants, by Spanish Americans.

Meanwhile, Spanish Americans found unused irrigable cropland and water within the Pueblos' land grants, where the resident populations had declined dramatically. Their acquisitions of small parcels here amounted eventually to over half the floodplains of most northern Pueblo Indian grants during periods of ignoring Spanish decrees that prohibited non-Indian encroachment and confusing legalities lasting from the Mexican era into the early 1900s.

Furthermore, the limited opportunities to acquire scarce irrigable lands for a growing resident population led to extensive subdivision of Spanish-American farm units through inheritance and sales. Because permanent out-migration was for the most part negligible up to World War I, heirs of Spanish-American landowners turned their subdivided portions into smaller family farms, resulting in a more intensified pattern of long-lots and considerable fragmentation that further aggravated agricultural production but allowed more people to remain and farm with low capital entry. All these processes were self-restrictive and contrary to the trends of consolidation and expansion underway elsewhere in American agriculture.

Not surprisingly, subsistence agriculture has prevailed in the Río Arriba for centuries, undoubtedly longer here than in any other part of the American West, if not in the country, outside of the Indian reservations. Potential markets were too distant even if agricultural surpluses could have been derived from the small farms. There was little trickling down of the economic gains from sheep ranching or the Santa Fe Trail trade to the region's populace. With no incentives and innovations to improve techniques before the Treaty of Guadelupe Hidalgo, agricultural production lagged steadily in comparison to that found in much of the United States. Village life was sustained largely by a local barter economy that operated between communities and family support systems within the communities. An almost communal type of life-style based upon an "economy of scarcity" was nurtured when the United States acquired the region.[2] Spanish Americans were impoverished in terms of material possessions and living standards, with high infant mortality rates being an indicator of their plight. Families had a sense of security, however, because they had full possession of at least small plots of irrigable cropland, no mortgages, and a strong social network. Under these conditions, there was little individual accumulation of capital that would have permitted the expansion of agricultural production and the improvement of living standards.

Each generation was trapped by its economic and cultural history in a situation that could have been alleviated by depopulation of its villages. Undoubtedly, an overpopulated peasantry had developed in relation to the available natural and human resources. It consisted of cultivators who engaged in subsistence production, lived in villages where they depended upon each other, allowed for "equalized allocation of cultivation rights" on the arable land, and provided for partible or equal division of land among heirs—all customs of peasant societies.[3] This situation was found by the United States, not implanted by the United States, and was part of the continuum of factors that influenced later developments such as endemic rural poverty and no emergence of a sizable middle class.

Anglo-American economic precepts based upon wage economies, introduced in the later half of the 1800s, had dramatic consequences in the Río Arriba. Cash and credit became important and wages could be earned from off-farm seasonal employment. Spanish Americans determined, too, that their small acreages were incapable of producing the necessary surpluses that would gross incomes comparable to wages and the attractive steady flow of money for at least part of each year. Even before the adjudication of many of the complex land-grant claims and the loss of communal lands, a growing number of underemployed and unemployed laborers from the overpopulated villages had penetrated the veil of economic isolation by working first on the nearby rail lines and then in the region's lumber camps and sawmills, all established with Anglo-American capital. This unskilled labor force grew steadily and sought additional opportunities, leading males eventually to more distant employment. Their families remained behind on the small plots, as it was too difficult and expensive to transport them, particularly large ones, from areas of employment. Many of the numerous land units were placed, therefore, in a state of transition, gradually becoming largely non-farm residences. Other landowners who did not depend upon external employment continued with their traditional operations and production.

During the early transition from subsistence agriculture to dependence upon seasonal wage labor, Spanish Americans were confronted with major problems involving their ownership and utilization of land. Their claims to Spanish and Mexican land grants had to be validated by the U.S. legal system along with accurate or precise surveys, rather than by the vague and impermanent metes-and-bounds survey in order to be included in the American land system. Americans also brought a new system of taxation based largely upon acreage rather than on production or land use. Although all the land-grant claims had to be surveyed and adjudicated, some were contested in lengthy court proceedings. Of the 176 claims involving land in the Río Arriba, 100 were rejected and 76 were patented, including both community and private land grants of various acreages. In some cases, however, the claimed amounts of communal lands were reduced or rejected outright. Other claims to communal land were not only lost in court proceedings, but communal land was also used to pay shrewd lawyers in cases involving extreme exaggerations of claims and unfortunate legal manipulations. On the whole, the U.S. government made judicious efforts, considering the paucity of valid evidence, to follow Spanish and Mexican laws in adjudicating the complicated land-grant claims. After adjudication and in time, communal land was also sold for various reasons, including the nonpayment of taxes. The residents clung tenaciously, however, to their individually owned long-lots. There was, despite the condemnation of Anglo Americans as callous land grabbers, no mass eviction, physical displacement, or banishment of Spanish-American families.

Another question had arisen in the Río Arriba over the ownership or occupancy of land. This time it involved Spanish Americans who resided within the Pueblos' land grants. They were compelled to prove legal ownership of their individual plots. Most Spanish Americans were eventually able to do so by using the American legal system and receiving the generosity of the Pueblo Lands Board, but the outcome prevented further encroachment and restricted their use of the surrounding Pueblo Indian lands. If they were to continue livestock grazing, they had now to obtain permission from the Pueblos. Again, there was no mass eviction of the Spanish-American claimants, who included many middle-aged heads of household, but the Pueblos, who had already been relegated to small land grants, ended up with even less land, consisting primarily of dry upland.

Having had their land claims generally settled, Spanish Americans relied upon their villages in the Río Arriba as havens or refuges, especially during the Depression, when many of the land units became full-time farms again. Fortunately, these unemployed seasonal laborers had security because they had irrigable land with no mortgages as a result of their custom of partible inheritance and their inability to obtain loans. The subdividing of land was no longer a widespread practice as the return to the farms in the 1930s was temporary and there was increasing disinterest in farming. This retreat to the Río Arriba, moreover, reinforced the Spanish Americans' perception of the region as their homeland.

Spanish-American out-migration resumed during World War II, in larger numbers than ever before and on a more permanent and continued basis. Their relatively high rate of natural increase, however, offset out-migration or the push effect, resulting in continued overpopulation for the region's resources. For those who remained, farm sizes were considered to be insufficient to produce incomes that could assure those material goods and services now thought to be necessities.

Basically, the Spanish Americans' egalitarian settlement practices had encouraged overpopulation. Compensating factors to correct this maladjustment were limited and subsistence agriculture had thus become intractable poverty, reflecting the region's longtime functions. Historian Carey McWilliams maintains that "poverty is always relative to historical and social circumstances" and points out, too, that "many of the mountain villages have never known anything but poverty."[4] In particular, the long-lot settlement pattern had been flexible enough to allow adaptations to the physical environment and to population growth for many years, but this symbiosis eventually had outlived its practicality and was incongruent with agricultural trends. Colonial planning and policy were not directed toward overall regional economic prosperity, but rather toward successful occupation of the region, a legacy that had left an indelible imprint upon ensuing economic activity.[5]

Even if the communal portions of land-grant claims had not been lost in legal adjudication or sold, it is doubtful the Spanish and Mexican land grants could have supported these overpopulated communities and sustained viable economies of scale. This contention is not to advocate that the land-grant claims should have been rejected, but the inability of a land grant to support its residents is apparent today, of course in hindsight, in the Town of Abiquiú Grant, which did not lose its communal lands. This grant has been unable to keep all its families above the poverty levels of the twentieth century. Despite the allegations concerning the losses of rangeland, the U.S. government has allowed the Spanish Americans to use most of this land, albeit under the controlled conditions imposed by the Forest Service and the Bureau of Land Management. Not only are the grazing capacities of this land low, as is the case throughout the Río Arriba, but also the Spanish Americans have been constrained by their small base properties, which did not allow each of them to maintain large herds of livestock even if they had resided on land grants. (It must not be overlooked that large numbers of Spanish Americans never owned land within Spanish and Mexican land-grant claims but rather resided within Pueblo Indian grants, where they merely assumed grazing rights. Therefore, sweeping generalizations about the losses of rangeland applying to all, or even most, Spanish Americans are simply untrue. Moreover, there is no way that the Pueblos' small land grants could have sustained the pastoral pursuits, introduced by the Spaniards, of both peoples above the levels of poverty.) Although the Forest Service had intended to provide economic stability for the villages by assuring the region's livestock owners access to summer pastures, it had instead and unfortunately, according to DeBuys, "helped to perpetuate the traditional subsistence way of life in the villages."[6] Rather than studying allegations about how Anglo Americans dominated the grazing permit program and the use of the rangeland, the question arises whether the program was in the long term beneficial to the Spanish Americans who may otherwise have sought economic alternatives. Incidentally, Anglo Americans were not given gross preferential treatment in the livestock grazing program, as alleged.

Spanish Americans who argue that they have received unfair treatment from the Forest Service fail to explain how the two national forests could have accommodated additional livestock without gross overgrazing and land abuse, creating severe ecological imbalances and consequences. Loud outcries would have been heard, too, if floods had swept away cropland and human life in the small microbasins. There is sufficient documentation of the failed settlements in the neighboring upper Río Puerco Valley because of flooding and extensive erosion due to overgrazing in the first half of the 1900s.[7]

Arguments, too, that the Anglo-American legal system did not recognize the Spanish land tenure system because it emphasized the communal occupancy and use of land rather than the ownership of land by fee simple, which allows land to be bought and sold as a commodity for exploitation and profit, are questionable.[8] They are counter to the fact that Spanish settlers were given individual tracts within community land grants that had to be settled for a certain number of years, usually ten, before they could be sold and inherited. Heirs occasionally sold their parcels to their siblings, where again a value was determined according to the particular situation. In addition, hundreds of Spanish Americans acquired land within the Pueblo Indian land grants, claiming for the most part that they had purchased it. They exploited their land, too, by extensive overgrazing for economic reasons. To claim that Spanish Americans were unaware of the value of land as a commodity is simply contrary to their settlement history.

Another argument is that the Spanish Americans did not receive the same "protection" from the U.S. government as that awarded to the Pueblo Indians.[9] For instance, they resent the fact that the U.S. government reacquired in 1970 the Blue Lake area of 48,000 acres in the Sangre de Cristo Mountains from the Forest Service for the Taos Pueblos. It is interesting to note, however, that no other European population has received this type of special treatment as that accorded the aboriginal peoples. Ironically, Gilberto Espinosa, a well-known Spanish-American lawyer and authority on Spanish and Mexican land grants, has argued that "the U.S. was not obligated under the Treaty of Guadalupe Hidalgo . . . to become a 'guardian' for its new citizens" and the United States was not responsible for protecting the Spanish Americans in holding their patented land grants.[10]

Legal attempts to regain the land lost in the adjudication of the land-grant claims and losses of "thefts" of land because of duplicity, misinterpretation of the Treaty of Guadalupe Hidalgo, or whatever do little more than raise the hopes of some Spanish Americans. (I discovered in my fieldwork that many of the young Spanish Americans knew very little, if anything, about the region's land grants.) A small group of scholars and academicians, several associated with the Center for Land Grant Studies, has actually called for a Hispanic Lands Claims Commission or congressional action to reopen the land-grant cases.[11] This call continues to champion the cause that the Spanish Americans have been the subjects of perpetual victimization and that there must be remedial action. For example, Knowlton's emotional charge epitomizes this rationale: "They were left defenseless before the invading, dynamic, ruthless, legalistic, lawless, and competitive Anglo-American civilization that did nothing to prepare them for adequate citizenship; that stripped them of most of their land; that reduced them to the situation of a conquered people without enforceable rights, and left them in extreme poverty."[12] Ideally, this group wants to help the Spanish Americans regain the land in the land-grant claims, but more realistically it wants to help obtain monetary reparations for the descendants of the early grantees—actually echoing the demands and allegations of the activist Alianza Federal de Mercedes.

Despite the harsh criticism leveled against the U.S. government of aggravating bureaucratic and legalistic procrastination in determining the validity of the land-grant claims and of unfair decisions, there is doubt now among scholars over whether all the Spanish and Mexican land grants were conveyed in perpetuity and with water rights.[13] These ongoing controversies have been characteristic of the Río Arriba's history, and surely some of their antecedents can be attributed to what took place in the region during the Spanish and Mexican eras. Too many scapegoats, including the Anglo-American surveyor-generals, the Court of Private Land Claims, the U.S. Forest Service, Santa Fe Ring lawyers, and land grabbers, have been used to explain the Spanish Americans' plight. Interestingly enough, no similar condemnations exist of the Spanish and Mexican governments for any wrongs and noncompliance with procedures or of the Spanish Americans themselves, who in many cases grossly exaggerated their claims to land grants, necessitating long legal disputes.[14] Certainly, ongoing controversy will continue to be part of the rhetorical scenario that characterizes the Río Arriba in years ahead. There will always be those, particularly academicians, who will tendentiously place the burden of accusation and guilt upon the U.S. government and Anglo Americans and who appear to romanticize the region's past and apply their perceptions of past centuries to what the region should be like today—quaint villages dependent mostly upon a pastoral economy. There is the fallacious tendency to assume that the Spanish Americans want to be full-time farmers.

Meanwhile, the neighboring Pueblos, who maintain that the Spanish Americans acquired considerable water rights from them, are naturally interested in any court cases brought on behalf of the Spanish Americans. There could be an unraveling of the region's land tenure patterns as well as those concerning water rights in which the Spanish Americans, not all blood related to Pueblos so they can conveniently label themselves Indians when desired, could find themselves in complicated and disadvantageous positions. It was, after all, the Pueblos' use of the region and its water that initially attracted Spanish colonizers and settlers to the Río Arriba. It was also Spanish law, yet unchallenged, that allowed them to expropriate, without remorse, both resources from the aboriginal peoples, limiting their ancestral lands to comparatively small land grants. As Morrill put the Pueblo Indians' position, "Go ahead and get the land back . . . and when you get it, we'll be right there waiting to take it back from you."[15]

Expectedly, the call exists, too, for a Pueblo Lands and Water Claims Commission that would have the federal government purchase or condemn with compensation those water or land rights assumed by both Spanish and Anglo-American settlers and their heirs.[16] A precedent was set for this procedure when the U.S. Indian Claims Commission in 1965 awarded compensation to the Nambé Pueblos for their claim of 45,000 acres in the Santa Fe National Forest.[17] They maintained that they had lost the right of aboriginal use to this acreage.

The basic question is: What kept the large number of Spanish Americans in the Río Arriba after they had been cast into the Anglo-American economic system and realized the limited potential of their land, which had been further diminished by abuse, especially that of overstocking? Opportunities for employment in urban centers were restricted by their lack of skills and education. Family ties and lingering village consciousness tended to hold others who realized, too, that their land units were unmarketable because of the lack of surveyed and recorded titles. Middle-aged and older people with large families realized that a move was expensive and involved risk. Equally important as any one of these reasons, landowners continued to cling to their long-lots not only because of sentimental reasons, but also for economic and emotional security, reflecting a mentality found in peasant societies. This security was available only within familiar environs found among their relatives, villages, and homeland. Thus, many accepted low wages that were supplemented by limited agricultural sales, which together amounted to low per capita incomes because of large families. The Río Arriba's dysfunctional economy led the federal and state governments to designate the region as having endemic rural poverty and therefore eligible for various types of assistance and benefits, which became an entrenched characteristic contributing immeasurably to sustaining the Spanish Americans. In addition, numerous programs were implemented to revitalize village economies and culture.[18]

Moreover, it has been the significant proportion of residents whose willingness to commute or travel considerable distances from their villages to seasonal or permanent in-state or out-of-state employment that has kept the Spanish Americans in the region and alleviated the severity of rural poverty. This has been an ongoing economic adjustment dating back before 1900, more important to some Spanish-American villages than others. Many Spanish Americans since the 1940s have commuted great distances on a daily basis, in some cases more than 60 miles each way, as exemplified in Vadito, Abiquiú, and El Rancho. More than three thousand workers, many Spanish Americans, commuted to Los Alamos County alone in the 1970s. Most of them were semiskilled or unskilled laborers who worked, for instance, on the county's highway maintenance crews. Others work in various government bureaucracies, including the Forest Service. In essence, autos and improved highways that allowed Spanish Americans to out-migrate have also helped those who have remained to keep the Río Arriba as their homeland. Commuting has led, however, to less self-reliance upon the land and community interdependence and cooperation.

Spanish-American youth today will not pursue agriculture as an occupation, for, if they were to do so, their chances of success would be marginal, as reflected in the case studies of Abiquiú, Corrales, El Rancho, and Vadito. It would be almost a financial impossibility for them to acquire and consolidate land units of sufficient size to produce an adequate annual farm income. Relatively high values have always been placed on the irrigable cropland, but land in this semiarid, elevated environment has been reappraised by the region's recent newcomers. Anglo Americans seek out available small farms, *ranchos* with old adobe houses, often in run-down condition because of the residents' impoverished situations, but that can be renovated with the inclusion of modern conveniences—usually costly projects. Consequently, land values have increased because of this process of gentrification, which includes living in the sophisticated Santa Fe life-style that embodies the region's cross-cultural, artistic, and traditional values, beyond what Spanish Americans themselves can afford to expand or consolidate their farms, even if their home property is inherited acreage. It is interesting to witness, also, how many Spanish Americans have accepted the rather inexpensive Anglo-American housetrailer. An estimated 40 percent of the inhabited dwellings found today between Española and Abiquiú are housetrailers owned almost totally by Spanish Americans. Anglo Americans, on the other hand, have become increasingly responsible for preserving the appearance and ambience of the Spanish-American landscape.

Unmistakably, given the trends of American agriculture and rural life, one can foresee the continuing erosion of the old way of life identifiable with the Spanish-American folk culture. This is evident in the declining number of Penitentes (Los Hermanos), who were not only an integral part of a community's support system but who also contributed to the villagers' sense of security. After centuries of not having been confronted with the need for change, this way of life will disappear rather quickly, largely with the passing on of the older generations and the alienation of their landholdings to non–Spanish Americans. The farming of the small acreages will eventually cease altogether as they offer no hope to the younger generation. Land reform is not an American tradition to solve rural poverty, despite Knowlton's assertion in 1985 that "the potential for violence will continue to exist in northern New Mexico until land reform takes place."[19] Rather, farmsteads will continue to be abandoned with the land left idle or they will become rural nonfarm residences for those Spanish Americans who reside within commuting distances of steady employment, depend on government assistance payments, or are retirees. Major industries are unlikely to locate in the region for various spatial and economic reasons, such as considerable distances to large markets and the lack of skilled labor.

Unfortunately, an excess supply of rural unskilled laborers will continue to exist until out-migration eliminates the problem. Until then, the Río Arriba will continue to be perceived from elsewhere as a source, albeit on a smaller scale, of agricultural laborers. This is apparent in the following advertisement which appeared in 1987 in Santa Fe's newspaper, the *New Mexican*:

> SHEEPHERDER WITH minimum of 30 days experience. Attends sheep grazing on range, herds sheep using trained dogs. Guards flock from predators and from eating poisonous plants. May assist in lambing, docking, and shearing. Large flocks with a single-pair herder. Food, housing, tools, supplies, and equipment provided. Hours variable, on call 24 hours—7 days. Term of employment from 11 months up to 3 years. Employment for 3/4 of work days guaranteed. Transportation to job and subsistence advanced. Minimum salary is $589 in CO., NV., WY. Minimum salary is $600 in AZ., CA., ID., MT., OR., UT., and WA. Contact: Employment Security Department, P.O. Box 4218, Santa Fe, 87502.[20]

Similar surpluses of labor have developed in other areas of rural America, including the Finnish communities of Michigan's Upper Peninsula and northern Minnesota and the "hillbilly" settlements of Appalachia's Cumberland Plateau and of the Ozark Mountains, and out-migration was necessary to alleviate the problem.

Meanwhile, Anglo Americans will continue to reappraise the Río Arriba as a region ideal for recreation, tourism, retirement, and simply for real estate investment. The counterculture youth who flocked here in the 1960s and 1970s to establish idealistic livelihoods were also aware of the region's numerous amenities. The region offers spectacular mountainous scenery, high elevations for both summer and winter recreational activities, aridity, and (as compared with Denver, Phoenix, and Tucson) clean air (perceptions going back to the healthseekers of the late 1800s), plus authentic cultural diversities. All these factors have pushed up land values so that they are irresistible to Spanish-American landowners. Others, however, simply have not sold their landholdings. History has shown that once they relinquish their lands they are unable to reacquire them.

Anglo-American economic values have permeated the Río Arriba, and their demands to use the region continue to be not only relentless but also resented by Spanish Americans. This is evident, for instance, in the case of the Carson and Santa Fe national forests, which provide a growing number of recreational opportunities. Spanish Americans look upon the Anglo Americans as those who derive the major benefits from the forests' water and land resources—an assertion made also by the Alianza Federal de Mercedes. Texans, in particular, are looked upon with almost universal disdain by Spanish-American residents with longtime roots in the Río Arriba. They are perceived to have the financial resources to eventually "buy" the region.[21] This resentment is revealed on auto bumper stickers, including "Texans Ski Texas!" Nevertheless, the Spanish-American core, although weakened, exists. Aside from the aforementioned reasons for remaining in the region, this core can be attributed chiefly to the lingering attachments to their land and inexpensive living, especially in the northern isolated villages and in Española and Taos, where Spanish Americans comprised approximately 60 percent or more of each town's population in 1980.[22]

Many Spanish Americans today are cognizant of the fact that tourism and recreation, involving largely Anglo-American capital, will provide new jobs for them. In fact, the tourism and travel industry had become by 1986 New Mexico's largest private sector employer, accommodating over 23,000,000 travelers annually. The industry is also one of the state's largest producers of revenue, generating monies from both personal expenditures and from state and local taxes. Visitors to New Mexico's eleven national parks and monuments numbered in 1986 over 2,000,000 for the first time, while visitors to its forty-three state parks numbered nearly 7,000,000. Meanwhile, New Mexico's number of skier days at its eleven ski areas during the 1986–87 season was 1,130,000, two-thirds of them at the Río Arriba's seven ski areas, which in total set a record.[23]

New Mexico has become a favorite tourist state for Southwesterners. Nearly two-thirds of the out-of-state tourists in the mid-1980s had origins in the Southwest, largely from Texas, but California is also now a major source.[24] Although the Río Arriba constitutes a small part of New Mexico, it is one of the most heavily visited parts of the state. Tourists seek out the aforementioned physical and cultural amenities as well as its numerous state parks, Bandelier National Monument, Río Grande Gorge, and campgrounds. Their needs have contributed to a dramatic building boom in hotels and motels. Santa Fe's number of rooms nearly doubled between 1983 and 1985. Nearby Albuquerque, the distribution hub for interstate motorists (80 percent of the tourists traveled in 1985 by auto, truck, or camper) and air travelers in New Mexico, increased its room capacity by one-third, adding two thousand rooms.[25] As a result, Santa Fe and Albuquerque alone added approximately 90 percent of the new rooms statewide, indicating the importance of tourism and recreation in northern New Mexico.

Aside from the numerous roadside tourist information centers, the importance of tourism is especially realized when travelers enter Santa Fe. A large interstate highway billboard informs them that the city has "53 modern gas stations, 193 restaurants, 36 motels and 6 campgrounds." Tourism has created most of the jobs in Taos. And, when the Río Arriba's residents have no employment alternatives, they readily accept tourist-related jobs. In fact, Questa's residents quickly sought tourism-related employment in nearby Taos and in Red River's ski area, designed in a Swiss chalet style, as an economic cure after many of them had lost their jobs in 1986 with the closing of the area's molybdenum mine. The village's search for survival was reflected in the comment of a local restauranteur: "We're lucky . . . because we're on the main throughway. Maybe we can pick up the Albuquerque–Denver traffic . . . If we can make it through March and April, then in May come the fishermen. And then we'll get the summer season."[26] Although tourism is growing in the Río Arriba as a year-round industry, it does experience seasonal fluctuations like tourism in most parts of the country, which, of course, does not contribute to job security.[27]

It is appropriate to point out here that not all Spanish Americans favor tourist or related recreational development, such as the proposed Georgia O'Keeffe historic site, in the region because they perceive it will have a negative impact on the unspoiled environment and their value system.[28] They have staged protests such as that in the case of the group opposed in 1982 to the construction of a condominium complex in Valdez, north of Taos.[29] The recent compassionate but fictitious movie, *The Milagro Beanfield War,* which was filmed partly in the Río Arriba's community of Truchas and directed by Robert Redford, illustrates the feelings of some Spanish Americans toward taking land and water rights for recreational development, especially when it is intended for Anglo Americans. Incidentally, several of the neighboring Pueblo Indian tribes have, on the other hand, actively sought tourism. The Taos Pueblos garner entry and photography fees from visitors, and the Santa Clara Pueblos charge a fee for photographing their festivals. Meanwhile, the Pojoaque, San Juan, and Tesuque Pueblos have sizable bingo operations. Many individual Pueblos have long sold their hand-crafted jewelry and pottery to tourists.

Undoubtedly, more land will be purchased by the increasing number of Anglo Americans who visit the Río Arriba as a playground and decide to relocate to this interesting part of the Sunbelt. (Ironically, Redford is now the owner of more than 200 acres of land near Santa Fe.[30]) As a result, the transition of turning the small *ranchos* into nonfarm residences is being completed. In reverse roles, Spanish Americans seek the advantages of an engulfing, dynamic Anglo-American economic system while Anglo Americans partake in amenities that were partially implanted by the Spanish Americans. Past Spanish-American sentiments about their landholdings will not be enough to hold future generations, interested in pulling themselves above the economic positions of their forefathers, in the rural communities. Consequently and as in other rural subcultures mentioned above, the abandonment and depopulation of these communities are almost a necessary, but unfortunate, compromise. In the process, these villages will be left either to history or be rejuvenated largely by Anglo Americans, who had indicated they will attempt to preserve some semblance of the Spanish-American culture. For instance, Crawford points out that "the fashionable developers in Santa Fe and Taos, pay lip service to it [the Spanish language] by giving Spanish names to their streets and businesses and subdivisions. . . . As time passes the real-estate Spanish of Santa Fe and its new suburbs may be all that survives of the colorful variants of the villages of northern New Mexico—like the old Santa Fe *acequias* which no longer carry water but which are now and then still cleaned out for their historic interest or curiosity value."[31]

Spanish Americans will continue then gradually to forsake, voluntarily and involuntarily, aspects of their rural culture and homeland as they lose their land base and sense of traditional communities, in spite of their history of adaptability and activism in retaining the rural region by using legal means to substantiate their land-grant claims, encroaching upon Pueblo Indian grants and assuming their water rights, filing for thousands

of homesteads and livestock grazing permits, migrating seasonally and
commuting long distances for employment, developing a religious brotherhood to serve as part of a local support system, and accepting various
types of government assistance. Even if attempts were made today to preserve the Spanish-American culture by declaring, for instance, that the
Río Arriba be designated a historic rural culture region, there is little that
can be done to thwart the incessant in-migration of Anglo Americans.
(Very few Mexican or other Spanish-speaking foreign immigrants choose
the Río Arriba as their destination. Instead, they head for urban areas
where they create new ethnic cores.) The question is whether the Spanish
Americans want to reside within a living museum.

It must be noted here that although Simmons concluded in 1979 that
"in spite of a shared language and a common religion, the Hispano
[Spanish American] is as different from the Mexican-American as an
American is from a Canadian" and "time has elapsed since 1848 . . . for
wholly divergent cultures to emerge,"[32] cultural landscapes in the region
have revealed signs of becoming Mexicanized during the 1980s. For
instance, a growing number of old and new restaurants, owned by both
national chains and local entrepreneurs, feature Mexican food specialties
and dining atmospheres in their advertisements. Some use Mexico or
Mexican in the names of their establishments. Apparently, these operators
figure that tourists relate more readily to what is Mexican food because

FIGURE 56

*Holiday Inn's Pyramid Hotel, shaped after Aztecan pyramids, was opened in 1986
in northern Albuquerque. It has 311 rooms.*
Source: Author, October 1989.

of its national acceptance or fad than to food that has been traditionally called Northern New Mexican, Native New Mexican, or Spanish-American. Then, too, Holiday Inn opened a large pyramid-shaped hotel in 1986 in northern Albuquerque, imposing an element of Mexico's Aztecan mystique upon the landscape (Figure 56). Aside from the changing landscapes, the celebrating of Mexico's Cinco de Mayo is also being introduced into the Río Arriba, much to the resentment of older Spanish Americans. These marketing strategies and commemorative activities will help to bring the region into what both Americans and Mexicans have perceived as Mex-America, the Mexican-American Southwest.[33] Interestingly enough, New Mexico feels obligated in 1990 to remind its residents and other Americans that it is still an American state by labeling its automobile license plates "New Mexico, U.S.A."

Yet most of the remaining Spanish Americans strive to retain certain aspects of their folk culture, such as celebrating historical events like "La Conquistadora" and "Los Moros y Cristianos," making the pilgrimage on Good Friday to the shrine of Santuario de Chimayó, preparing their cuisine, speaking their Spanish dialect, conducting Penitente services, and distinguishing themselves from other persons of Spanish origin.[34] Admirable activities like these will help to preserve their identity for at least themselves. They recognize, however, that a gradual conquest of their homeland is well underway. As the twentieth century was bound to reach the Spanish Americans, the twentieth-first century will also reach them.[35] The test of time will determine whether the Río Arriba as America's oldest rural European cultural region will endure to be the country's last one.

APPENDIXES

NOTES

GLOSSARY

INDEX

Appendixes

APPENDIX A Patented Spanish and Mexican Grants that Included Land within the Río Arriba (Río Arriba, Sandoval, Santa Fe, and Taos Counties)[a]

Land Grant	Approved	Confirmed (SG/CPLC)	Patented	Acreages Rejected by CPLC	Patented Acres[b]
1. Agua Salada (Luis Jaramillo)	1769 S	CPLC	1909	7,306	10,694[c]
2. Alamitos (Juan Salas)	1840 M	CPLC	1914	2,202	298
3. Angostura	1745 S	CPLC	1906	720	1,580
4. Antoine Leroux	1742 S	SG	1911	—	56,428
5. Antonio de Abeytia	1736 S	CPLC	1910	7,279	721
6. Antonio Martínez (Lucero de Godoi)	1716 S	CPLC	1896	0	61,606
7. Arroyo Hondo	1815 S	CPLC	1908	2,371	20,629
8. Baca Location No. 1 (Luis María Cabeza de Baca)	1825 M	SG	1860	—	99,289[c]
9. Bartolome Sanchez	1707 S	CPLC	1914	5,530	4,470
10. Bernabe Montaño	1753 S	CPLC	1909	106,929	44,071**
11. Bishop John Lamy (Rancho de Nuestra Señora del la Luz)	1820 S	SG	1874	—	16,547
12. Black Mesa (Medina)	1743 S	CPLC	1907	5,829	19,171
13. Caja del Río	1742 S	CPLC	1897	0	66,849
14. Cañada de Cochití	1728 S	CPLC	1901	85,441	19,113
15. Cañada de los Alamos	1785 S	CPLC	1896	1,638	12,068

APPENDIX A *continued*

Land Grant	Approved	Confirmed (SG/CPLC)	Patented	Acreages Rejected by CPLC	Patented Acres[b]
16. Cañada de los Alamos	1768 S	CPLC	1911	144,755	4,107
17. Cañon de Chama	1806 S	CPLC	1905	472,737	1,423
18. Cañon de San Diego	1798 S	SG	1881	—	116,287
19. Cañon del Agua	1844 M	SG	1875	—	3,501
20. Cieneguilla (Francisco de Anaya Almazan)	1714 S	CPLC	1916	42,042	3,203
21. City of Santa Fe	1715 S	CPLC	1901	0	17,361
22. Cristoval de la Serna	1715 S	CPLC	1903	7,767	22,233
23. Cuyamungue	1731 S	CPLC	1909	4,396	604
24. E. W. Eaton (Domingo Fernandez)	1827 M	SG	1880	—	81,633
25. Felipe Gutierrez (Bernallilo)	1742 S	CPLC	1900	8,270	3,405
26. Francisco Montes Vigil	1754 S	CPLC	1899	26,746	8,254
27. Gijosa	1715 S	CPLC	1908	3,759	16,241
28. Ignasio Chávez (Chaca Mesa)	1768 S	CPLC	1899	195,797	47,259**
29. Juan Bautista Valdez	1807 S	CPLC	1913	58,531	1,469
30. Juan de Gabaldón	1752 S	CPLC	1902	929	10,690
31. Juan José Lobato	1740 S	CPLC	1902	0	205,616
32. La Majada	1695 S	CPLC	1908	0	54,404
33. Las Trampas	1751 S	SG	1903	—	28,132
34. Los Cerrillos	1788 S	CPLC	1897	805	1,479
35. Miguel and Santiago Montoya	1766 S	CPLC	1925	1,372	2,968
36. Mesita de Juana Lopez	1782 S	SG	1879	—	42,023
37. Mora	1835 M	SG	1876	—	827,621**
38. Nuestra Señora de la Luz de Las Lagunitas (Antonio Baca)	1762 S	CPLC	1902	4,469	39,185
39. Nuestra Señora del Rosario San Fernando y Santiago	1754 S	CPLC	1905	5,213	14,787
40. Ojo Caliente	1793 S	CPLC	1895	37,755	2,245
41. Ojo de San José	1768 S	CPLC	1912	25,663	4,340
42. Ojo del Borrego	1768 S	CPLC	1913	58,920	16,080
43. Ojo del Espíritu Santo	1815 S	SG	1916	—	113,141
44. Ortiz Mine	1833 M	SG	1876	—	69,458
45. Pacheco	1769 S	CPLC	1913	0	581
46. Petaca	1836 M	CPLC	1910	185,585	1,392
47. Piedra Lumbre	1766 S	CPLC	1902	0	49,748
48. Plaza Blanca	1739 S	CPLC	1914	7,045	8,955
49. Plaza Colorado	1739 S	CPLC	1907	11,622	7,578

50. Polvadera	1766 S	CPLC	1900	0	35,761
51. Ramón Vigil	1742 S	SG	1898	—	31,210
52. Rancho del Río Grande	1795 S	CPLC	1909	17,230	91,813
53. Salvador Gonzáles (Cañada Ancha)	1742 S	CPLC	1917	24,799	201
54. San Antonio de las Huertas	1767 S	CPLC	1907	125,236	4,764
55. San Fernando de Taos	1796 S	CPLC	1909	72	1,817
56. San Marcos Pueblo	1754 S	CPLC	1896	0	1,895
57. San Pedro	1839 M	SG	1875	—	35,911**
58. Sangre de Cristo	1843 M	SG	1880	—	998,781*
59. Santa Barbara	1796 S	CPLC	1905	0	30,638
60. Santa Cruz	1703 (1695)ᵈ S	CPLC	1910	43,432	4,568
61. Santa Rosa de Cubero	1815 S	CPLC	1914	3,055	1,945
62. Santiago Ramirez	1744 S	CPLC	1912	5,893	272
63. Santo Domingo de Cundiyó	1743 S	CPLC	1903	0	2,137
64. Sebastian Martínez	1712 S	SG	1893	—	51,388
65. Sebastian de Vargas	1710 S	CPLC	1900	28,566	13,434
66. Sitio de Juana Lopez	1762 S	CPLC	1897	280	1,086
67. Sitio de Los Cerrillos	1788 S	CPLC	1897	0	572
68. Talaya Hill	1731 S	CPLC	1914	923	319
69. Tierra Amarilla	1832 M	SG	1881	—	594,516*
70. Town of Abiquiú	1754 S	CPLC	1909	0	16,708
71. Town of Alameda	1710 S	CPLC	1920	16,928	89,346**
72. Town of Cebolleta	1800 S	SG	1882	—	199,568**
73. Town of Galisteo	1814 S	CPLC	1927	21,739	261
74. Town of Jacona	1702 S	CPLC	1909	39,288	6,953
75. Town of San Isidro	1736 S	SG	1936	—	11,477
76. Town of Tejon	1840 M	SG	1882	—	12,802
Total					4,501,080

Source: J. J. Bowden, "Private Land Claims in the Southwest" (Master's thesis, Southern Methodist University, 1969), 272–808 (Santa Fe County), 811–1031 (Taos County), 1035–1214 (Río Arriba County), 1225–1478 (Sandoval County); Richard W. Bradfute, *The Court of Private Land Claims: The Adjudication of Spanish and Mexican Land Grant Titles, 1891–1904* (Albuquerque: University of New Mexico Press, 1975), 245–53; Bureau of Land Management (BLM), *Plat Books,* Public Room, Federal Building, Santa Fe; David J. Miller, "Private Lane Claims Reported," File RI 2172, Ritch Collection, Huntington Library, San Marino, Calif.; Victor Westphall, *Mercedes Reales: Hispanic Land Grants of the Upper Rio Grande Region* (Albuquerque: University of New Mexico Press, 1983), 285–88; and White, Koch, Kelley, and McCarthy, *Land Title Study* (Santa Fe: State Planning Office, 1971), 222–34. Records on each claim are given in Albert J. Díaz, *A Guide to the Microfilm of Papers Relating to New Mexico Land Grants* (Albuquerque: University of New Mexico Press, 1960).

*Patented grant extends into Colorado.

**Patented grant extends into adjacent county.

ᵃAbbreviations: S, Spain; M, Mexico; SG, Surveyor General; CPLC, Court of Private Land Claims.

ᵇAll patented acreages are those given in the plat books found in the Bureau of Land Management, Santa Fe.

^cGrant was confirmed in 1860 in exchange for land granted in San Miguel County in 1825.
^dSettlers were placed on tracts of land in the Santa Cruz Valley by don Diego de Vargas in 1695; however, the petition for a grant including grazing land was not approved officially until 1703.

APPENDIX B Acreages of Unconfirmed and Patented Grants, Including Land within the Río Arriba (Río Arriba, Sandoval, Santa Fe, and Taos Counties)

Size of Grant (acres)	Unconfirmed Grants	Patented Grants	No. (%) of Patented Acres	
<1,000	25	9	3,829	(0.1)
1,000–2,999	20	12	21,436	(0.5)
3,000–4,999	4	8	32,358	(0.7)
5,000–9,999	12	4	31,740	(0.7)
10,000–19,999	12	14	207,173	(4.6)
20,000–49,999	12	12	426,800	(9.5)
50,000–99,999	7	10	722,214	(16.0)
100,000–499,000	8	4	634,612	(14.1)
>500,000	0	3*	2,420,918	(53.8)
Total	100	76	4,501,080	(100.0)

Source: See Appendix A.

*These three grants (Mora, Sangre de Cristo, and Tierra Amarilla) have large acreages outside of the Río Arriba.

APPENDIX C Private Non-Indian Lands within the Río Arriba's Pueblo Indian Grants, 1940

Pueblo	Date of Patent	Patented Acreage of Grant	Private Non-Indian Land Claims confirmed *(acres)*	Private Non-Indian Claims Reacquired by Pueblo Indians *(acres)*
1. Cochití	1864	24,257	651	206
2. Jémez	1864	17,510	19	4
3. Nambé	1864	13,586	1,235	103
4. Picurís	1864	17,461	2,550	74
5. Pojoaque	1864	13,520	1,857	37
6. San Felipe	1864	34,767	2,797	379
7. San Ildefonso	1864	17,293	1,101	334
8. San Juan	1864	17,545	4,108	70
9. Sandía	1864	24,187	887	274
10. Santa Ana	1883	17,361	—	—
11. Santa Clara	1864	17,369	4,309	256
12. Santo Domingo	1864	74,743	632	133

13. Taos	1864	17,361	2,820	—	
14. Tesuque	1864	17,471	252	—	
15. Zia	1864	17,515	—	—	**Appendixes**
Total		341,946	23,218	1,870	

Source: UPA, Real Property Management Records, Albuquerque, "Land Status Reports—Pueblos," File 385.0, 1 April 1940, 18; and BLM, *Plat Books,* Public Room, Federal Building, Santa Fe.

APPENDIX D Pueblo Indian Populations on Grants/Reservations in the Río Arriba: 1945 and 1980

Indian Populations	1945	1980	Percentage of Total Population: 1980*
Northern Pueblos	2,770	4,855	21
Nambé	150	188	17
Picurís	125	125	8
Pojoaque	30	94	8
San Ildefonso	160	488	33
San Juan	730	851	21
Santa Clara	555	1,839	21
Taos	870	1,034	25
Tesuque	150	236	64
Total acreage of grants/reservations	187,500	241,941**	
Average size of grants/reservations	23,438	30,243	
Southern Pueblos	3,710	7,203	70
Cochití	480	613	73
Jémez	815	1,504	99
Sandía	135	227	9
San Felipe	730	1,789	79
Santa Ana	290	407	99
Santo Domingo	1,010	2,139	99
Zia	250	524	100
Total acreage of grants/reservations	233,677	413,673**	
Average size of grants/reservations	33,382	59,096	

Source: 1945 data: Sophie D. Aberle, *The Pueblo Indians of New Mexico: Their Land, Economy, and Civil Organization* (Menasha: American Anthropological Association, 1948), 69–90; and UPA, Real Property Management Records, Albuquerque, "Land Use Extension Report, 1945," 1945. 1980 data: U.S. Department of Commerce, Bureau of the Census, *1980 Census of Population,* American Indian Areas and Alaska Native Villages (Washington: GPO, 1984), 23–24. The 1974 acreages were obtained from U.S. Department of Commerce, *Federal and State Indian Reservations and Indian Trust Areas* (Washington: GPO, 1974), 341–97.
*Indians represent this percentage of the grant's/reservation's total population.
**1974 data.

APPENDIX E Homesteads in the Río Arriba Owned by Persons with Spanish Surnames, 1860–1949

Decade	Homesteads No. (%)	Acres (%)	Additional Homesteads No. (%)	Acres (%)	Stock-raising Homesteads No. (%)	Acres (%)	Desert Land Homesteads No. (%)	Acres (%)	Timber Culture Homesteads No. (%)	Acres (%)	Cash Entries No. (%)	Acres (%)
Patented land												
1860–69												
1870–79												
1880–89	53 (2)	7,742 (3)									8 (28)	851 (27)
1890–99	256 (12)	37,936 (12)					1 (20)	160 (20)	1 (50)	145 (48)	10 (35)	1,489 (46)
1900–09	248 (12)	35,601 (11)					1 (20)	160 (20)	1 (50)	160 (52)	5 (17)	303 (9)
1910–19	595 (28)	78,720 (25)									5 (17)	544 (17)
1920–29	825 (38)	128,630 (41)			171 (39)	78,229 (39)	3 (60)	480 (60)			1 (3)	15 (1)
1930–39	141 (7)	22,118 (7)			242 (55)	109,855 (55)						
1940–49	31 (1)	4,284 (1)			26 (6)	12,439 (6)						
Total	2,149	315,031			439	200,523	5	800	2	305	29	3,202
Average no. of acres		147				457		160		153		110
Unpatented land												
1860–69												
1870–79	1 (—)*	80 (—)										
1880–89	69 (6)	9,807 (6)					1 (7)	640 (25)	6 (86)	960 (86)		
1890–99	82 (7)	11,149 (7)					3 (21)	320 (12)	1 (14)	160 (14)		
1900–09	184 (17)	25,175 (15)	1 (—)	80 (—)			6 (43)	1,161 (45)				
1910–19	504 (45)	74,749 (45)	37 (26)	7,163 (19)	12 (3)	6,113 (3)	4 (29)	480 (18)				
1920–29	241 (22)	40,433 (24)	86 (61)	26,242 (68)	314 (74)	178,326 (77)						
1930–39	25 (2)	4,273 (3)	18 (13)	4,914 (13)	98 (23)	46,867 (20)						
1940–49	2 (—)	79 (—)										
Total	1,108	165,745	142	38,399	424	231,306	14	2,601	7	1,120		
Average no. of acres		150		270		546		186		160		

Source: Plat Books, BLM, Santa Fe and Tract Books, National Archives, Washington, D.C.
*Less than 1 percent.

APPENDIX F Homesteads in the Río Arriba Owned by Persons with Non–Spanish Surnames, 1860–1949

Decade	Homesteads		Additional Homesteads		Stock-raising Homesteads		Desert Land Homesteads		Timber Culture Homesteads		Cash Entries	
	No. (%)	Acres (%)	No. (%)	Acres (%)	No. (%)	Acres (%)	No. (%)	Acres (%)	No. (%)	Acres (%)	No. (%)	Acres (%)
Patented land												
1860–69											42 (14)	4,932 (12)
1870–79	3 (–)*	461 (–)									8 (3)	860 (2)
1880–89	44 (4)	6,747 (3)									26 (9)	3,567 (9)
1890–99	49 (4)	7,232 (3)									70 (23)	10,601 (25)
1900–09	426 (38)	87,616 (36)			1 (–)	320 (–)	2 (14)	280 (11)			144 (48)	21,549 (51)
1910–19	498 (44)	115,534 (48)			545 (63)	281,641 (65)	1 (7)	293 (12)			7 (2)	467 (1)
1920–29	102 (9)	20,835 (9)			303 (35)	139,604 (33)	10 (72)	1,824 (72)			2 (1)	57 (–)
1930–39	9 (1)	1,929 (1)			21 (2)	9,491 (2)	1 (7)	120 (5)				
1940–49												
Total	1,131	240,354			870	431,056	14	2,517			299	42,033
Average no. of acres		213				495		180				141
Unpatented land												
1860–69	1 (–)	138 (–)										
1870–79	4 (–)	629 (–)										
1880–89	47 (3)	7,488 (3)					12 (10)	2,913 (12)	61 (91)	9,340 (93)		
1890–99	46 (3)	5,585 (2)					11 (9)	2,080 (9)	4 (6)	496 (5)		
1900–09	623 (40)	97,853 (33)	4 (1)	440 (1)			62 (49)	11,499 (49)	2 (3)	260 (2)		
1910–19	460 (29)	92,889 (31)	42 (15)	7,111 (10)	22 (2)	13,586 (3)	40 (32)	6,764 (29)				
1920–29	291 (19)	69,870 (24)	185 (68)	54,153 (75)	687 (77)	372,043 (78)	1 (–)	160 (–)				
1930–39	93 (6)	21,661 (7)	42 (16)	10,457 (14)	184 (21)	93,693 (19)						
1940–49	2 (–)	320 (–)										
Total	1,567	296,433	273	72,161	893	479,322	126	23,416	67	10,096		
Average no. of acres		189		264		537		186		151		

Source: Plat Books, BLM, Santa Fe and Tract Books, National Archives, Washington, D.C.

* Less than 1 percent.

APPENDIX G Populations of the Río Arriba and New Mexico for Decennial Census Years 1910–1980

Río Arriba	1910	1920	1930	1940	1950	1960	1970	1980
Río Arriba County	16,620	19,550	21,380	25,350	25,000	24,190	25,170	29,280
Sandoval County	8,580	8,860	11,140	13,900	12,440	14,200	17,490	34,800
Santa Fe County	14,770	15,030	19,570	30,830	38,150	44,970	54,770	75,360
Taos County	12,010	12,770	14,390	18,530	17,150	15,930	17,520	19,460
Total	51,980	56,210	66,480	88,610	92,740	99,290	114,950	158,900
% of New Mexico's population	16	16	16	17	14	10	11	12
City of Santa Fe	5,070	7,240	11,180	20,330	28,000	33,390	41,170	48,950
Urban (%)	10	13	17	23	30	38	41	50
Rural Nonfarm (%)	n/a[c]	n/a	40	38	40	57	56	47
Rural farm (%)	n/a	n/a	43	39	30	5	3	3
Pueblo Indians (%)	9	9	8	7	8	9	9	9
Spanish Americans (%)[a]	n/a	n/a	76	84	69	57	71	42[b]
New Mexico								
Total population	327,300	360,350	423,320	531,820	681,190	951,020	1,017,060	1,302,890
Urban (%)	14	18	25	33	30	66	70	72
Rural Nonfarm (%)	n/a	37	38	34	40	28	26	26
Rural Farm (%)	n/a	45	37	33	30	6	4	2

Source: U.S. Department of Commerce, Bureau of the Census, *Thirteenth Census of the United States: 1910, Population* (Washington: GPO, 1913), 3: 176–81; *Fourteenth Census of the United States: 1920, Population* (Washington: GPO, 1923), 3: 667, 669–70; *Fifteenth Census of the United States: 1930, Population* (Washington: GPO, 1932), 3: part 2, 227, 244; *Sixteenth Census of the United States: 1940, Population* (Washington: GPO, 1943), 2: part 4, 955, 994; *Census of Population: 1950* (Washington: GPO, 1952), 2: part 31, 7, 16, 58; *Census of Population: 1960* (Washington: GPO, 1962), 1: part 33, 8, 50–51, 64, 140–41; *1970 Census of Population* (Washington: GPO, 1973), 1: part 33, 237–45; *1980 Census of Population, General Population Characteristics* (Washington: GPO, 1982), 1: part 33, 12, 112–16; *1980 Census of Population, General Social and Economic Characteristics* (Washington: GPO, 1983), 1: part 33, 11, 259–60; and

1980 Census of Population, Number of Inhabitants (Washington: GPO, 1982), 1: part 33, 8–9. Sources for the data on the Río Arriba's Spanish-American population include 1930: Sigurd Johansen, *Rural Social Organization in a Spanish-American Culture Area* (Albuquerque: University of New Mexico Press, 1942), 18; 1940; Allen J. Beigle, Harold F. Goldsmith, and Charles P. Loomis, "Demographic Characteristics of the United States–Mexican Border," *Rural Sociology* 25 (March 1960): 107–62; George I. Sanchez, *Forgotten People, a Study of New Mexicans* (Albuquerque: Calvin Horn Publishers, 1967), 30; 1950: U.S. Department of Commerce, Bureau of the Census, *United States Census of Population: 1950*, Persons of Spanish Surname (Washington: GPO, 1953), 4: part 3, 44; 1960: *United States Census of Population: 1960*, Persons of Spanish Surname (Washington: GPO, 1963), Report PC (2)-1B: 197; 1970: *1970 Census of Population*, 1: part 33, 226–27; and 1980: *1980 Census of Population*, 1: part 33, 12.

[a] Data on Spanish Americans are based upon identifiers (Spanish surname, Spanish origin, Spanish language, other Spanish) in the decennial census reports.

[b] "Other Spanish" identifier equals 42 percent. If use Spanish origin identifier equals 55 percent.

[c] Not available.

APPENDIX H Farm Sizes in the Río Arriba, 1910–1982

	1910	1925	1935	1945	1954	1964	1974	1982
No. of farms	5062 (179)[a]	5695 (258)	8845 (199)	5801 (676)	4544 (835)	2583 (1480)	1291 (2577)	1943 (1690)
<10 acres	31% (n/a)[b]	33%	43% (5.3)	31% (5.6)	41% (5.1)	23% (5.2)	14% (n/a)	20% (4.5)
10–49 acres	33% (n/a)	31% >(14.1)	32% (20.1)	38% (21.4)	34% (21.0)	38% (21.9)	28% (n/a)	32% (23.3)
Total % of farms	64	64	75	69	75	61	42	52

Source: U.S. Department of Commerce, Bureau of the Census, *Thirteenth Census of the United States, Agriculture, 1910* (Washington: GPO, 1913), 7: 163–64; *1925 Census of Agriculture* (Washington: GPO, 1927), 3: 266–67, 290–91; *United States Census of Agriculture: 1935* (Washington: GPO, 1936), 2: part 3, 865–66; *1945 Census of Agriculture* (Washington: GPO, 1946), 1: part 30, 67–68; *1954 Census of Agriculture* (Washington: GPO, 1956), 1: part 30, 51–52; *1964 Census of Agriculture* (Washington: GPO, 1967), 1: part 42, 236–37; *1974 Census of Agriculture* (Washington: GPO, 1977), 1: part 31, 121, 133, 151, 169; and *1982 Census of Agriculture* (Washington: GPO, 1983), 1: part 31, 123–24, 133–34, 143–44, 146–47.

[a] ( ) denote average size

[b] Not available.

APPENDIX I Grazing Permits Held by Persons with Spanish Surnames and Persons with Non-Spanish Surnames: Carson and Santa Fe National Forests, ca. 1915–1982*

	ca. 1915 (%)	1925 (%)	1935 (%)	1945 (%)	1954 (%)	1964 (%)	1974 (%)	1982 (%)
Cattle								
No. of permits								
Spanish surnames	349 (89)	761 (92)	1,075 (91)	859 (94)	890 (94)	707 (93)	540 (93)	447 (94)
Non-Spanish surnames	42 (11)	67 (8)	100 (9)	52 (6)	56 (6)	55 (7)	42 (7)	31 (6)
No. of cattle								
Spanish surnames	3,955 (76)	6,657 (77)	7,447 (73)	7,457 (84)	10,439 (85)	11,052 (84)	13,499 (87)	13,522 (88)
Non-Spanish surnames	1,255 (24)	2,003 (23)	2,793 (27)	1,412 (16)	1,809 (15)	2,123 (16)	2,010 (13)	1,848 (12)
Average size permit								
Spanish surnames	11	9	7	9	12	16	25	30
Non-Spanish surnames	30	30	28	27	32	39	48	60
Average grazing period (days)								
Spanish surnames	282	219	270	205	187	188	176	178
Non-Spanish surnames	249	196	225	214	205	171	184	203
Sheep								
No. of permits								
Spanish surnames	270 (95)	157 (92)	139 (95)	130 (90)	65 (87)	22 (100)	16 (100)	12 (100)
Non-Spanish surnames	13 (5)	13 (8)	8 (5)	14 (10)	10 (13)	0	0	0
No. of sheep								
Spanish surnames	151,259 (86)	63,604 (68)	58,264 (74)	48,422 (78)	29,123 (86)	11,446 (100)	11,402 (100)	6,564 (100)
Non-Spanish surnames	25,327 (14)	29,342 (32)	20,508 (26)	13,478 (22)	4,691 (14)	0	0	0
Average size permit								
Spanish surnames	560	405	419	372	448	520	712	547
Non-Spanish surnames	1,948	2,257	2,564	963	469	0	0	0

Average grazing period (days)	ca. 1915	1925	1935	1945	1954	1964	1974	1982
Spanish surnames	160	144	133	127	128	148	259	218
Non-Spanish surnames	157	135	258	142	93	0	0	0

Source: Compiled from records in the Headquarters of the Carson National Forest, Taos, and the Santa Fe National Forest, Santa Fe.
*Permittees resided in Río Arriba, Sandoval, Santa Fe, and Taos counties.

APPENDIX J Sizes of Cattle-Grazing Permits: Carson and Santa Fe National Forests, ca. 1915–1982[a]

No. of Cattle	ca. 1915 (%)	1925 (%)	1935 (%)	1945 (%)	1954 (%)	1964 (%)	1974 (%)	1982 (%)
1–9	61%[b]	71%	70%	69%	60%	48%	34%	25%
10–19	23	16	16	20	22	24	26	30
20–29	7	6	7	6	9	12	15	14
30–49	5	4	4	3	5	8	11	15
50–99	3	2	3	2	4	7	11	10
>100	1	1	—[c]	—	—	1	3	6
Total No. of cattle permits	391	828	1,175	911	946	762	582	478
Total No. of cattle	5,210	8,660	10,240	8,869	12,248	13,175	15,509	15,370
Average size of grazing permit	13	11	9	10	13	17	27	32
Average grazing period (days)	274	214	258	206	189	185	177	181

Source: Compiled from records in the Headquarters of the Carson National Forest, Taos, and the Santa Fe National Forest, Santa Fe.
[a]Permittees resided in Río Arriba, Sandoval, Santa Fe, and Taos counties.
[b]Percentages are rounded to nearest whole percent.
[c]Less than 1 percent.

APPENDIX K Landownership in Corrales, 1930–1970[a]

	1930	1970
No. of landowners		
Spanish American	90	80
Anglo American	5	51
Italian American	11	9
French American	6	2
Total acreages owned		
Spanish American	530.7	297.5
Anglo American	82.3	282.2
Italian American	167.8	125.8
French American	110.4	38.9
Church	—	147.7[b]
Average acreage owned/landowner		
Spanish American	5.9	3.7
Anglo American	16.0	5.5
Italian American	15.2	14.0
French American	18.4	19.4
Range of acreage owned/landowner		
Spanish American	41.1–0.5	19.3–0.3
Anglo American	36.9–2.5	28.9–0.3
Possession of ≥2 parcels (%)[c]		
Spanish American	15	6
Anglo American	0	0

Source: Fieldwork, Records of the Middle Río Grande Conservancy District, and Sandoval County Assessor's Office, Bernalillo.

[a]Study area includes 891.2 acres. See Figures 53 and 54.

[b]138.1 acres were owned by the Sandía Academy, a Seventh-Day Adventist institution. This acreage until 1970 was farmed by the church.

[c]Parcels across the road or a ditch were figured as one parcel if owned by the same person.

Notes

Preface

1. Charles L. Briggs and John R. Van Ness, "Introduction," in *Land, Water, and Culture: New Perspectives on Hispanic Land Grants,* ed. Charles L. Briggs and John R. Van Ness (Albuquerque: University of New Mexico Press, 1987), 3–12 (quotation, 4).

2. Ibid., 8; and Alvar W. Carlson, "An Analysis of the Spanish Americans' Geographical Problems as Cited in the Literature," paper presented at Western Social Science Association Meetings, Reno, 25 April 1986.

1 Spanish and Mexican Land Grants

1. These early expeditions (Francisco Vásquez de Coronado, 1540; Francisco Sánchez Chamuscado and Fray Augustin Rodriquez, 1581; Antonio de Espejo, 1582; and Gaspar Castaño de Sosa, 1590) are discussed in Hubert H. Bancroft, *History of Arizona and New Mexico, 1530–1888,* vol. 17 (San Francisco: History Company, 1889), 75–93; Warren A. Beck and Ynez D. Haase, *Historical Atlas of New Mexico* (Norman: University of Oklahoma Press, 1969), map 14; Herbert E. Bolton, *The Spanish Borderlands, a Chronicle of Old Florida and the Southwest* (New Haven: Yale University Press, 1921), 165–69; Arthur L. Campa, *Hispanic Culture in the Southwest* (Norman: University of Oklahoma Press, 1979), 10–17; Linda S. Cordell, *A Cultural Resources Overview of the Middle Rio Grande Valley, New Mexico* (Washington: GPO, 1979), 113–14; and Charles W. Hackett, ed., *Historical Documents Relating to New Mexico, Nueva Viscaya, and Approaches Thereto, to 1773,* vol. 1 (Washington: Carnegie Institution of Washington, 1923), 7–196.

2. Carl O. Sauer, *Seventeenth Century North America* (Berkeley: Turtle Island Foundation, 1980), 37–47, 218–19.

3. Oñate's colonization scheme and colony are discussed in Bolton, *The Spanish Borderlands,* 171–75; Campa, *Hispanic Culture in the Southwest,* 19–21; George

P. Hammond, "Oñate's Effort to Gain Political Autonomy for New Mexico," *Hispanic American Historical Review* 32 (August 1952): 321–30; Elizabeth A. H. John, *Storms Brewed in Other Men's Worlds* (College Station: Texas A & M University, 1975), 17–19, 41–56; Oakah L. Jones, Jr., *Los Paisanos: Spanish Settlers on the Northern Frontier of New Spain* (Norman: University of Oklahoma Press, 1979), 110; David B. Quinn, "Juan de Oñate and the Founding of New Mexico, 1595–1609," in *The Extension of Settlement in Florida, Virginia and the Spanish Southwest,* ed. David B. Quinn (New York: Arno Press, 1979), 437–86; and Julian Samora and Patricia V. Simon, *A History of the Mexican–American People* (Notre Dame: University of Notre Dame Press, 1977), 41–42.

4. Sauer, *Seventeenth Century North America* (quotation, 59); J. Manuel Espinosa, "Out Debt to the Franciscan Missionaries of New Mexico," *Americas* 1 (July 1944): 79–87; Quinn, "Juan de Oñate and the Founding of New Mexico, 1595–1609," 482; and France V. Scholes, "Civil Government and Society in New Mexico in the Seventeenth Century," *New Mexico Historical Review* 10 (April 1935): 71–111.

5. Eric Beerman, "The Death of an Old Conquistador: New Light on Juan de Oñate," *New Mexico Historical Review* 54 (October 1979): 305–19; Sauer, *Seventeenth Century North America,* 54–58; and George P. Hammond and Agapito Rey, *Don Juan de Oñate, Colonizer of New Mexico, 1595–1628* (Albuquerque: University of New Mexico Press, 1953), 1109–13.

6. Dora P. Crouch, Daniel J. Garr and Axel I. Mundigo, *Spanish City Planning in North America* (Cambridge: The MIT Press, 1982), 9, 13, 74; Clarence H. Haring, *The Spanish Empire in America* (New York: Oxford University Press, 1947), 159–61; Dan Stanislawski, "Early Spanish Town Planning in the New World," *Geographical Review* 37 (January 1947): 94–105; and Ralph E. Twitchell, *Spanish Colonization in New Mexico in the Oñate and DeVargas Periods,* no. 22 (Santa Fe: Historical Society of New Mexico, August 1919), 5–7.

7. Thomas R. Lopez, Jr., *Prospects for the Spanish American Culture of New Mexico* (San Francisco: R & E Research Associates, 1974), 2–3; and Joseph V. Metzgar, "The Ethnic Sensitivity of Spanish New Mexicans: A Survey and Analysis," *New Mexico Historical Review* 49 (January 1974): 49–73. For varying definitions of the Río Arriba, see T.M. Pearce, *New Mexico Place Names: A Geographical Dictionary* (Albuquerque: University of New Mexico Press, 1965), 133; Thomas J. Steele, S.J., and Rowena A. Rivera, *Penitente Self-Government: Brotherhoods and Councils, 1797–1947* (Santa Fe: Ancient City Press, 1985) 34, n. 23; and Jerry L. Williams, *New Mexico in Maps* (Albuquerque: University of New Mexico Press, 1986), 56, 96. For background information on the Río Abajo, see Michael P. Marshall and Henry J. Walt, *Río Abajo: Prehistory and History of a Río Grande Province* (Santa Fe: New Mexico Historic Preservation Program, 1984); and Joseph P. Sánchez, *The Río Abajo Frontier, 1540–1692: A History of Early Colonial New Mexico* (Albuquerque: The Albuquerque Museum, 1987).

8. Jessie B. Bailey, *Diego De Vargas and the Reconquest of New Mexico* (Albuquerque: University of New Mexico Press, 1940), 207–9; Peter Gerhard, *The North Frontier of New Spain* (Princeton: Princeton University Press, 1982), 320–23; Myra E. Jenkins, "Spanish Land Grants in the Tewa Area," *New Mexico Historical Review* 47 (April 1972): 113–34; Jones, *Los Paisanos,* 119–20; Lopez, *Prospects for the Spanish American Culture of New Mexico,* 15–26; and Sauer, *Seventeenth Century North America,* 60, 67.

9. François Chevalier, *Land and Society in Colonial Mexico: The Great Haci-*

enda (Berkeley: University of California Press, 1963), 52–53; Michael C. Meyer, "The Legal Relationship of Land to Water in Northern Mexico and the Hispanic Southwest," *New Mexico Historical Review* 60 (January 1985): 61–79; Manual C. Stampa, "The Evolution of Weights and Measures in New Spain," *Hispanic American Historical Review* 29 (February 1949): 2–24; Twitchell, *Spanish Colonization in New Mexico in the Oñate and De Vargas Periods,* 8; and David Weeks, "The Agrarian System of the Spanish American Colonies," *Journal of Land and Public Utility Economics* 23 (May 1947): 153–68.

10. H. Allen Anderson, "The Encomienda in New Mexico, 1598–1680," *New Mexico Historical Review* 60 (October 1985): 353–77; Lansing B. Bloom, "A Glimpse of New Mexico in 1620," *New Mexico Historical Review* 3 (October 1928): 357–89; Lansing B. Bloom, "The Vargas Encomienda," *New Mexico Historical Review* 14 (October 1939): 366–417; Robert S. Chamberlain, "Castilian Backgrounds of the Repartimiento-Encomienda," *Contributions to American Anthropology and History* (Washington: Carnegie Institution of Washington, 1939), 23–53; Henry F. Dobyns, "The Study of Spanish Colonial Frontier Institutions," in *Spanish Colonial Frontier Research,* no. 1, ed. Henry F. Dobyns (Albuquerque: Center for Anthropological Studies, Spanish Borderlands Research, 1980), 5–25; George M. McBride, *The Land System of Mexico* (New York: Octagon Books, 1971), 43–50; Samora and Simon, *A History of the Mexican-American People,* 22–24; Lesley B. Simpson, *The Encomienda in New Spain: The Beginning of Spanish Mexico* (Berkeley: University of California Press, 1950); Weeks "The Agrarian System of the Spanish American Colonies," 155–59; and Silvio Zavala, *New Viewpoints on the Spanish Colonization of America* (Philadelphia: University of Pennyslvania Press, 1943), 69–92.

11. George P. Hammond and Agapito Rey, "The Crown's Participation in the Founding of New Mexico," *New Mexico Historical Review* 32 (October 1957): 293–309; and Sauer, *Seventeenth Century North America,* 60.

12. Lansing B. Bloom, "Spain's Investment in New Mexico under the Hapsburgs," *Americas* 1 (July 1944): 3–14; J. Manuel Espinosa, trans., *First Expedition of Vargas into New Mexico, 1692* (Albuquerque: University of New Mexico Press, 1940), 9–10; Peter P. Forrestal, trans., *Benavides' Memorial of 1630* (Washington: Academy of American Franciscan History, 1954), 24; Hackett. *Historical Documents Relating to New Mexico, Nueva Vizcaya, and Approaches Thereto, to 1773,* vol. 3, 249–52; and Jones, *Los Paisanos,* 136–37.

13. Van H. Garner, "Seventeenth Century New Mexico," *Journal of Mexican American History* 4 (1974): 41–70; Charles W. Hackett, "The Revolt of the Pueblo Indians of New Mexico in 1680," *Quarterly of the Texas State Historical Association* 15 (October 1911): 93–147; Charles W. Hackett, ed., and Charmion C. Shelby, trans., *Revolt of the Pueblo Indians of New Mexico and Otermín's Attempted Reconquest, 1680–1682* (Albuquerque: University of New Mexico Press, 1942), 8: xxix–lii, 9: 3–16; Arley Sanchez, "Pueblos Celebrate Revolt That Saved Way of Life," *Albuquerque Journal,* 3 August 1980, pp. A-1, A-4; Scholes, "Civil Government and Society in New Mexico in the Seventeenth Century," 78–82; and Marc Simmons, "The Pueblo Revolt: Why Did It Happen?" *El Palacio* 86 (Winter 1980–81): 11–15.

14. Sauer, *Seventeenth Century North America,* 239.

15. Bolton, *The Spanish Borderlands,* 179–80; and Ralph E. Twitchell, *The Leading Facts of New Mexican History,* vol. 1 (Cedar Rapids: Torch Press, 1911), 361.

16. Bailey, *Diego De Vargas and the Reconquest of New Mexico,* 10–36, 88–93; and J. Manuel Espinosa, "The Recapture of Santa Fé, New Mexico, by the Spaniards—December 29–30, 1693," *Hispanic American Historical Review* 19 (November 1939): 443–63.

17. John, *Storms Brewed in Other Men's Worlds,* 112, 155.

18. Sauer, *Seventeenth Century North America,* 68.

19. John, *Storms Brewed in Other Men's Worlds,* 134.

20. Alvar W. Carlson, "Environmental Overview," *Borderlands Sourcebook: A Guide to the Literature on Northern Mexico and the American Southwest,* ed. Ellwyn R. Stoddard, Richard L. Nostrand, and Jonathan P. West (Norman: University of Oklahoma Press, 1983), 75–80; W. E. Hale, L. J. Reiland, and J. P. Beverage, *Characteristics of the Water Supply in New Mexico,* Report 31 (Santa Fe: New Mexico State Engineer, 1965); Earle L. Hardy, "New Mexico Climatic Summary," *Climate and Man* (Washington: GPO, 1941), 1011–24; Yi-Fu Tuan, Cyril E. Everard, and Jerold G. Widdison, *The Climate of New Mexico* (Santa Fe: State Planning Office, 1969); and J. R. Watson, "Plant Geography of North Central New Mexico," *Botanical Gazette* 54 (September 1912): 194–217.

21. Sauer, *Seventeenth Century North America* (quotation, 220).

22. Fray Angélico Chávez, *Origins of New Mexico Families* (Santa Fe: Historical Society of New Mexico, 1954), xii–xv, 1–114, 119–335; Iris W. Engstrand, "Land Grant Problems in the Southwest: The Spanish and Mexican Heritage," *New Mexico Historical Review* 53 (October 1978): 317–36; Scholes, "Civil Government and Society in New Mexico in the Seventeenth Century," 96–97; Clevy L. Strout, "The Resettlement of Santa Fe, 1695: The Newly Found Muster Roll," *New Mexico Historical Review* 53 (July 1978): 261–70; and Twitchell, *Spanish Colonization in New Mexico in the Oñate and De Vargas Periods,* 29–39.

23. Scholes, "Civil Government and Society in New Mexico in the Seventeenth Century," 98–100.

24. Bailey, *Diego De Vargas and the Reconquest of New Mexico,* 213–14; J. J. Bowden, "Private Land Claims in the Southwest" (Masters thesis, Southern Methodist University, 1969), 319, 430; Meyer, "The Legal Relationship of Land to Water in Northern Mexico and the Hispanic Southwest," 66; and Stampa, "The Evolution of Weights and Measures in New Spain," 13–20.

25. Bailey, *Diego De Vargas and the Reconquest of New Mexico,* 213–14; Bowden, "Private Land Claims in the Southwest," 319; and Stampa, "The Evolution of Weights and Measures in New Spain," 13, 15–16, 19. A *cuartilla* and an *almud* equaled one-fourth and one-twelfth of a *fanega,* respectively. An *arroba* weighed 25 pounds of grain.

26. These laws are discussed by Gustavus Schmidt, *The Civil Law of Spain and Mexico* (New Orleans: Thomas Rea, 1851). Information on the *tierras realengas* is found in David E. Vassburg, "The *Tierras Baldías*: Community Property and Public Lands in 16th Century Castile," *Agricultural History* 48 (July 1974): 383–401.

27. William W. Morrow, *Spanish and Mexican Private Land Grants* (San Francisco: Bancroft-Whitney Company, 1923), 15–17; and White, Koch, Kelley, and McCarthy, *Land Title Study* (Santa Fe: State Planning Office, 1971), 10–11. The *alcaldías* that included land in the Río Arriba were Taos, Santa Cruz de la Cañada, Queres, Albuquerque, Santa Fé, and Sandía.

28. Malcolm Ebright, "Introduction: Spanish and Mexican Land Grants and the Law," *Journal of the West* 27 (July 1988): 3–11.

29. Bowden, "Private Land Claims in the Southwest," 272–808, 811–1031,

1035–1214, 1225–1478; Richard W. Bradfute, *The Court of Private Land Claims: The Adjudication of Spanish and Mexican Land Grant Titles, 1891–1904* (Albuquerque: University of New Mexico Press, 1975), 9–11; Michael J. Rock, "Anton Chico and Its Patent," *Journal of the West* 19 (July 1980): 86–91; Andrew T. Smith, "The Founding of the San Antonio de las Huertas Grant," *Social Science Journal* 13 (October 1976): 35–43; and Weeks, "The Agrarian System of the Spanish American Colonies," 162.

30. Bowden, "Private Land Claims in the Southwest," 272–808, 811–1031, 1035–1214, 1225–1478; and Myra E. Jenkins, "Land Tenure History in New Mexico," *El Cuaderno,* n.v. (1976): 32–46.

31. Howard R. Lamar, *The Far Southwest, 1846–1912, a Territorial History* (New Haven: Yale University Press, 1966), 49–52; and Marianne L. Stoller, "Grants of Desperation, Lands of Speculation: Mexican Period Land Grants in Colorado," *Journal of the West* 19 (July 1980): 22–39.

32. Bradfute, *The Court of Private Land Claims,* v; and Mathew G. Reynolds, *Spanish and Mexican Land Laws, New Spain and Mexico* (St. Louis: Buston and Skinner Company, 1895), 122. For background information on Mexican colonization laws, see *Laws and Decrees of the Republic of Mexico in Relation to Colonization and Grants of Land, More Particularly in New Mexico and California, from 1823 to 1846* (New York: New York Printing Company, 1871); and John A. Rockwell, *A Compilation of Spanish and Mexican Law in Relation to Mines and Titles to Real Estate in Force in California, Texas and New Mexico,* vol. 1 (New York: John S. Voorhies, 1851). A Spanish league measured 2.6 miles; see Roland Chardon, "The Elusive Spanish League: A Problem of Measurement in Sixteenth-Century New Spain," *Hispanic American Historical Review* 60 (May 1980): 294–302; Roland Chardon, "The Linear League in North America," *Annals, Association of American Geographers* 70 (June 1980): 129–53; and Peter M. Enggass, "The Spanish League: A Geographical Conspiracy," *Journal of Geography* 70 (October 1971): 407–10.

33. White, Koch, Kelley, and McCarthy, *Land Title Study,* 27–28.

34. Ibid., 28–33. Unlike in California, where Congress established a board of land commissioners to render final determination in the cases of private land claims, the task was left to the surveyor-general to research and recommend claims in New Mexico. Congress may have done this because of economic reasons, but it led to lengthy delays in the adjudication process. Frank Springer, *Land Titles in New Mexico* (Washington: Gibson Bros., Printers, 1889), 7.

35. Bureau of Land Management, U.S. Surveyor-General Records of Private Land Claims Adjudicated, 1855–1890, Federal Building, Santa Fe, Report 10, File 25, Reel 13, Frame 20.

36. Adolf F. A. Bandelier, "Why New Mexico Does Not Flourish," *Nation,* 28 January 1886, pp. 70–71 (quotation, 70).

37. George W. Julian, "The Redemption of a Territory," *Magazine of Western History* 10 (July 1889): 238–46 (quotation, 240).

38. White, Koch, Kelley, and McCarthy, *Land Title Study,* 33–46.

39. Data on the confirmation and patent dates and acreages of the 176 land-grant claims are found in Bowden, "Private Land Claims in the Southwest," 272–808 (Santa Fe County), 811–1031 (Taos County), 1035–1214 (Río Arriba County), 1225–1478 (Sandoval County); Bradfute, *The Court of Private Land Claims,* 245–53; Bureau of Land Management (BLM), *Plat Books,* Public Room, Federal Building, Santa Fe; David J. Miller, "Private Land Claims Reported," File

RI 2172, Ritch Collection, Huntington Library, San Marino, California; Victor Westphall, *Mercedes Reales: Hispanic Land Grants of the Upper Rio Grande Region* (Albuquerque: University of New Mexico Press, 1983), 285–88; and White, Koch, Kelley, and McCarthy, *Land Title Study,* 222–34. Records on each claim are given in Albert J. Diaz, *A Guide to the Microfilm of Papers Relating to New Mexico Land Grants* (Albuquerque: University of New Mexico Press, 1960).

40. Bowden, "Private Land Claims in the Southwest," 272–808, 811–1031, 1035–1214, 1225–1478; Arie Poldervaart, *Manual for Effective New Mexico Legal Research* (Albuquerque: University of New Mexico Press, 1955), 26; and White, Koch, Kelley, and McCarthy, *Land Title Study,* 40–43.

41. Bowden, "Private Land Claims in the Southwest," 1094–99; and Ira G. Clark, *Water in New Mexico: A History of Its Management and Use* (Albuquerque: University of New Mexico Press, 1987), 35.

42. White, Koch, Kelley, and McCarthy, *Land Title Study,* 31–33.

43. Westphall, *Mercedes Reales,* 98–99, 232–36.

44. Lance Chilton, Katherine Chilton, Polly E. Arango, James Dudley, Nancy Neary, and Patricia Stelzner, *New Mexico: A New Guide to the Colorful State* (Albuquerque: University of New Mexico Press, 1984), 36–37.

45. John O. Baxter, *Las Carneradas: Sheep Trade in New Mexico, 1700–1860* (Albuquerque: University of New Mexico Press, 1987), 28–30, 44.

46. W. A. Keleher, "Law of the New Mexico Land Grant," *New Mexico Historical Review* 4 (October 1929): 350–71; J. Paul Stevens, "Changes in Land Tenure and Usage among the Indians and Spanish American in Northern New Mexico," in *Indian and Spanish American Adjustments to Arid and Semiarid Environments,* ed. Clark S. Knowlton (Lubbock: Texas Technological College, 1964), 38–43; and White, Koch, Kelley, and McCarthy, *Land Title Study,* 31–32.

47. Clark S. Knowlton, "Land-Grant Problems among the State's Spanish-Americans," *New Mexico Business* 20 (June 1967): 1–13.

48. White, Koch, Kelley, and McCarthy, *Land Title Study,* 21–22.

49. Ibid., 20–22.

50. Bowden, "Private Land Claims in the Southwest," 324–42; Bradfute, *The Court of Private Land Claims,* 122–23; and Bureau of Land Management, U.S. Court of Private Land Claims Records of Private Land Claims Adjudicated, 1891–1904, Federal Building, Santa Fe, Report 88, File 166, Reel 21, Frames 1–53. For information on grants given as town sites, see Richard E. Greenleaf, "Land and Water in Mexico and New Mexico 1700–1821," *New Mexico Historical Review* 47 (April 1972): 85–112.

51. Bowden, "Private Land Claims in the Southwest," 350–54, 361–70, 375–85, 390–418.

52. Ibid., 619–33.

53. Ibid., 980–85.

54. Stephen K. Williams, "United States v. Julian Sandoval," *Cases Argued and Decided in the Supreme Court of the United States,* Book 42 (Rochester: Lawyers Co-operative Publishing Company, 1901), 168–74 (quotation, 168). Also, see Ebright, "Introduction," 5.

55. See note 39.

56. Bowden, "Private Land Claims in the Southwest," 342–50; George W. Julian, "Land Stealing in New Mexico," *North American Review* 145 (1 July 1887): 17–31; Bureau of Land Management, U.S. Surveyor-General Records, Report 82, File 157, Reel 21, Frames 6–47, 215–16; and U.S. Congress, Senate, *Report of the*

*Surveyor-General of New Mexico on the Land Claim called Salvador Gonzales,
No. 82,* Ex. Doc. No. 127, 49th Cong., 1st sess., 21 August 1886, 1–6.

57. Bowden, "Private Land Claims in the Southwest," 1231–44; and Julian,
"Land Stealing in New Mexico," 22.

58. Bowden, "Private Land Claims in the Southwest," 637–42.

59. Bureau of Land Management, U.S. Surveyor-General Records, Report 3, File
33, Reel 12, Frames 29–33. For background discussion, see Malcolm Ebright, *The
Tierra Amarilla Grant: A History of Chicanery* (Santa Fe: Center for Land Grant
Studies, 1980), 3, 8; Gilberto Espinosa, "About New Mexico Land Grants," *State
Bar of New Mexico Bulletin* 6 (2 November 1967): 258–63; Frankie McCarty,
Land Grant Problems in New Mexico (Albuquerque: Albuquerque Journal, 1969),
10–11; and Victor Westphall, "Fraud and Implications of Fraud in the Land
Grants of New Mexico," *New Mexico Historical Review* 49 (July 1974): 189–218.

60. Herbert O. Brayer, "The Place of Land in Southwestern History," *Land Pol-
icy Review* 4 (December 1941): 15–20; and Clark S. Knowlton, "The Town of Las
Vegas Community Land Grant: An Anglo-American Coup D'Ètat," *Journal of the
West* 19 (July 1980): 12–21.

61. Morrow, *Spanish and Mexican Private Land Grants,* 14–15.

62. Bradfute, *The Court of Private Land Claims,* 12.

63. Iris H. W. Engstrand, "An Enduring Legacy: California Ranchos in Historical Perspective," *Journal of the West* 27 (July 1988): 36–47.

64. Andrew F. Rolle, *California, a History* (New York: Thomas Y. Crowell
Company, 1963), 111–12, 298–300 (quotation, 112). California's land grants are
discussed in R. H. Allen, "The Spanish Land-Grant System as an Influence in the
Agricultural Development of California," *Agricultural History* 9 (July 1935): 127–
42; Rose H. Aviña, *Spanish and Mexican Land Grants in California* (New York:
Arno Press, 1976); David Hornbeck, "The Patenting of California's Private Land
Claims, 1851–1885," *Geographical Review* 69 (October 1979): 434–48; and
White, Koch, Kelley, and McCarthy, *Land Title Study,* 39–40.

65. Bradfute, *The Court of Private Land Claims,* 214.

66. These forty-five grants averaged 112,531 acres each. Sizes ranged from 319
acres (Ojito del Río de las Gallinas) to 1,714,765 acres (Maxwell-Beaubien/Mir-
anda), of which 1,470,000 acres were located in New Mexico. One-half (twenty-
three) of them were given to grantees during the Mexican era. Bureau of Land
Management, *Plat Books,* Public Room, Federal Building, Santa Fe.

67. Jenkins, "Spanish Land Grants in the Tewa Area" (quotation, 114); and
Clark, *Water in New Mexico,* 12.

68. Francis L. Quintana, "Land Grants and Grazing Grants of New Mexico,"
paper presented at Western Social Science Association Meetings, Reno, 24 April
1986.

69. See Donald C. Cutter, "The Legacy of the Treaty of Guadalupe Hidalgo,"
New Mexico Historical Review 53 (October 1978): 305–15; Engstrand, "Land
Grant Problems in the Southwest," 333; Malcolm Ebright, "The Embudo Grant: A
Case Study of Justice and the Court of Private Land Claims," *Journal of the West*
19 (July 1980): 74–84; John R. Van Ness and Christine M. Van Ness, "Introduc-
tion: Spanish Land Grants in New Mexico and Colorado," *Journal of the West* 19
(July 1980): 3–11; and Westphall, *Mercedes Reales,* 145, 216, 273.

70. William deBuys, "Fractions of Justice: A Legal and Social History of the Las
Trampas Land Grant, New Mexico," *New Mexico Historical Review* 56 (January
1981): 71–97 (quotation, 92).

71. Clark S. Knowlton, "The Mora Land Grant: A New Mexican Tragedy," *Journal of the West* 27 (July 1988): 59–73 (quotation, 71).

72. Marc Simmons, *Spanish Government in New Mexico* (Albuquerque: University of New Mexico Press, 1968). Also see Beck and Haase, *Historical Atlas of New Mexico,* map 21; and Greenleaf, "Land and Water in Mexico and New Mexico 1700–1821," 92.

73. Brief acknowledgments that Spanish Americans were also involved in fraud and the like can be found in Stephen W. Dorsey, " 'Land Stealing in New Mexico': A Rejoinder," *North American Review* 145 (October 1887): 396–409; Bruce T. Ellis, "Fraud without Scandal: The Roque Lovato Grant and Gaspar Ortiz y Alarid," *New Mexico Historical Review* 57 (January 1982): 43–62; Julian, "Land-Stealing in New Mexico," 18–28; and Wayne S. Scott, "Spanish Land Grant Problems Were Here before the Anglos," *New Mexico Historical Review* 20 (July 1967): 1–9.

2   Community Land Grants, Long-Lots, and Irrigation

1. Much of this chapter is based upon my article "Long-Lots in the Río Arriba," *Annals, Association of American Geographers* 65 (March 1975): 48–57. Permission to reproduce Figures 5 and 7 is granted by the Association of American Geographers.

2. Clark, *Water in New Mexico* (see chap. 1, n. 41), 19; and Twitchell, *Spanish Colonization in New Mexico in the Oñate and De Vargas Periods* (see chap. 1, n. 6), 24–25.

3. Crouch, Garr, and Mundigo, *Spanish City Planning in North America* (see chap. 1, n. 6), 11–12; and Twitchell, *Spanish Colonization in New Mexico in the Oñate and De Vargas Periods* (see chap. 1, n. 6), 6.

4. Bowden, "Private Land Claims in the Southwest" (see chap. 1, n. 24), 272–808, 811–1031, 1035–1214, 1225–1478; Bureau of Land Management, U.S. Surveyor-General Records (see chap. 1, n. 35); and U.S. Court of Private Land Claims Records (see chap. 1, n. 50).

5. Virginia H. T. Houston, "Surveying in Texas," *Southwestern Historical Quarterly* 65 (October 1961): 204–33; and Stampa, "The Evolution of Weights and Measures in New Spain" (see chap. 1, n. 9), 10–11.

6. Alvar W. Carlson, "Rural Settlement Patterns in the San Luis Valley: A Comparative Study," *Colorado Magazine* 44 (Spring 1967): 111–28; and Daniel Tyler, "Ejido Lands in New Mexico," *Journal of the West* 27 (July 1988): 24–35.

7. Rowena Martinez, ed., *Land Grants in Taos Valley* (Taos: Taos County Historical Society, 1968), 7–9. For background information on this grant, see William deBuys, "Fractions of Justice" (see chap. 1, n. 70).

8. Bureau of Land Management, U.S. Surveyor-General Records, Report 77, File 156, Reel 21, Frames 16–19. The settlers' names are found on Frames 19–21.

9. Frances L. Swadesh, *Los Primeros Pobladores: Hispanic Americans of the Ute Frontier* (Notre Dame: Notre Dame University Press, 1974), 134–35.

10. Paul Kutsche, John R. Van Ness, and Andrew T. Smith, "A Unified Approach to the Anthropology of Hispanic Northern New Mexico: Historical Archaeology, Ethnohistory, and Ethnography," *Historical Archaeology* 10 (1976): 1–16; and John R. Stilgoe, *Common Landscapes of America, 1580 to 1845* (New Haven: Yale University Press, 1982), 40–43.

11. Bureau of Land Management, U.S. Court of Private Land Claims Records, Report 149, File 152, Reel 48, Frames 134, 150.

12. Marc Simmons, "Settlement Patterns and Village Plans in Colonial New Mexico," *Journal of the West* 8 (January 1969): 7–21.

13. Alvar W. Carlson, "Rural Settlements and Land Use," in *Borderlands Sourcebook: A Guide to the Literature on Northern Mexico and the American Southwest*, ed. Ellwyn R. Stoddard, Richard L. Nostrand, and Jonathan P. West (Norman: University of Oklahoma Press, 1983): 105–10; and Jerold G. Widdison, "Historical Geography of the Middle Rio Puerco Valley, New Mexico," *New Mexico Historical Review* 34 (October 1959): 248–84.

14. Wells A. Hutchins, "The Community Acequia: Its Origins and Development," *Southwestern Historical Quarterly* 31 (January 1928): 261–84 (quotation, 273–74).

15. Vassberg, "The *Tierras Baldiás*" (see chap. 1, n. 26).

16. Herbert E. Bolton, "French Intrusions into New Mexico, 1749–1752," in *The Pacific Ocean in History*, ed. H. Morse Stephens and Herbert E. Bolton (New York: Macmillan Company, 1917), 389–407; William E. Dunn, "Spanish Reaction against the French Advance toward New Mexico, 1717–1727," *Mississippi Valley Historical Review* 2 (December 1915): 348–62; and Henri Folmer, "Contraband Trade between Louisiana and New Mexico in the Eighteenth Century," *New Mexico Historical Review* 16 (July 1941): 249–72. Fur trappers and traders did not arrive in the Río Arriba until the early 1800s; see Ray A. Billington, *The Far Western Frontier, 1830–1860* (New York: Harper and Row, 1956), 41–68.

17. Richard C. Harris, *The Seigneurial System in Early Canada: A Geographical Study* (Madison: University of Wisconsin Press, 1966), 119–21.

18. Francis P. Burns, "The Spanish Land Laws of Louisiana," *Louisiana Historical Quarterly* 11 (October 1928): 557–81; R. Louis Gentilcore, "Vincennes and French Settlement in the Old Northwest," *Annals, Association of American Geographers* 47 (September 1957): 285–97; John W. Hall, "Sitios in Northwestern Louisiana," *North Louisiana Historical Association Journal* 1 (Spring 1970): 1–9; and Michael Roark, "Imprint of the French in North America: Long-Lots in the Mid-Mississippi Valley," in *French and Germans in the Mississippi Valley: Landscape and Cultural Tradition*, ed. Michael Roark (Cape Girardeau: Southeast Missouri State University, 1988), 111–23.

19. Terry G. Jordan, "Antecedents of the Long-Lot in Texas," *Annals, Association of American Geographers* 64 (March 1974): 70–86 (quotation, 72).

20. Ibid., 71–74, 82. Also see Edwin J. Foscue, "Historical Geography of the Lower Rio Grande Valley of Texas," *Texas Geographic Magazine* 3 (Spring 1939): 1–15; Houston, "Surveying in Texas," 206–7; and Florence J. Scott, "Spanish Land Grants in the Lower Rio Grande Valley" (Master's thesis, University of Texas, Austin, 1935), 56–57.

21. Marc Simmons, "Spanish Irrigation Practices in New Mexico," *New Mexico Historical Review* 47 (April 1972): 135–50.

22. Alvar W. Carlson, "Commentary: Long-Lots in the Rio Arriba," *Annals, Association of American Geographers* 65 (December 1975): 593–94. Long-lots appear not to have been used in Mexico. Chevalier, *Land and Society in Colonial Mexico* (see chap. 1, n. 9).

23. Clark, *Water in New Mexico* (see chap. 1, n. 41), 9–12; Greenleaf, "Land and Water in Mexico and New Mexico 1700–1821" (see chap. 1, n. 50), 85; and

Michael C. Meyer, *Water in the Hispanic Southwest: A Social and Legal History,
1550–1850* (Tucson: University of Arizona Press, 1984), 109–11.

24. Crouch, Garr, and Mundigo, *Spanish City Planning in North America* (see
chap. 1, n. 6), 8.

25. Meyer, "The Legal Relationship of Land and Water in Northern Mexico
and the Hispanic Southwest" (see chap. 1, n. 9), 63–65, 68; and Meyer, *Water in
the Hispanic Southwest*, 117–18.

26. Robert E. Clark, "Water Rights Problems in the Upper Rio Grande Watershed and Adjoining Areas," *Natural Resources Journal* 11 (January 1971): 48–86;
and Meyer, *Water in the Hispanic Southwest*, 120.

27. Meyer, *Water in the Hispanic Southwest,* 120.

28. Bureau of Land Management, U.S. Court of Private Land Claims Records,
Report 107, File 110, Reel 45, Frame 8.

29. Meyer, *Water in the Hispanic Southwest,* 133.

30. In Texas, under Spanish and Mexican law until 1836, large grants intended
for ranching purposes, *tierras de agostadero,* allowed for surface water to be used
only for livestock. Only landowners of a *tierras de riego* grant, a small grant for
the purpose of crop agriculture, could legally divert surface water for irrigation.
The remaining *tierras de temporal* included no water rights for irrigation and were
understood to be used only for dry farming. These terms do not appear, however,
in the documentation of grants in the Río Arriba. Terry G. Jordan, John L. Bean,
Jr., and William M. Holmes, *Texas: A Geography* (Boulder: Westview Press,
1984), 151; and Meyer, "The Legal Relationship of Land to Water in Northern
Mexico and the Hispanic Southwest," 68, 70.

31. Meyer, "The Legal Relationship of Land to Water in Northern Mexico and
the Hispanic Southwest," 63–65, 71–72.

32. Meyer, *Water in the Hispanic Southwest,* 136–37.

33. Malcolm Ebright, "The San Joaquín Grant: Who Owned the Common
Lands? A Historical-Legal Puzzle," *New Mexico Historical Review* 57 (January
1982): 5–26; and Meyer, "The Legal Relationship of Land to Water in Northern
Mexico and the Hispanic Southwest," 72.

34. Meyer, "The Legal Relationship of Land to Water in Northern Mexico and
the Hispanic Southwest" (quotation, 72); and Meyer, *Water in the Hispanic Southwest,* 129–30.

35. Meyer, *Water in the Hispanic Southwest,* 71, 154.

36. Meyer, "The Legal Relationship of Land to Water in Northern Mexico and
the Hispanic Southwest," 72–73.

37. Hutchins, "The Community Acequia: Its Origins and Development," 274;
Meyer, *Water in the Hispanic Southwest,* 41; and Dorothy L. Pillsbury, "Ditches:
America's Oldest Co-operatives," *Christian Science Monitor,* 12 October 1946, 2.

38. Marc Simmons, "An *Alcalde's* Proclamation: A Rare New Mexico Document," *El Palacio* 75 (Summer 1968): 5–9.

39. Simmons, "Spanish Irrigation Practices in New Mexico," 142.

40. F. Lee Brown and Helen M. Ingram, *Water and Poverty in the Southwest*
(Tucson: University of Arizona Press, 1987), 48–50; Clark, *Water in New Mexico,*
15–16; 25–31; Hutchins, "The Community Acequia," 271; and Simmons, "Spanish Irrigation Practices in New Mexico," 140.

41. Campa, *Hispanic Culture in the Southwest* (see chap. 1, n.1), 189; and
Meyer, *Water in the Hispanic Southwest,* 69–70.

42. Hutchins, "The Community Acequia," 267.

43. Simmons, "Spanish Irrigation Practices in New Mexico," 141, 144. For a

discussion of a dispute, albeit not involving a *mayordomo,* see Malcolm Ebright, "Manuel Martínez's Ditch Dispute: A Study in Mexican Period Custom and Justice," *New Mexico Historical Review* 54 (January 1979): 21–34.

44. Clark, *Water in New Mexico,* 31; and Meyer, *Water in the Hispanic Southwest,* 67–68.

45. Clark, *Water in New Mexico,* 30; Clark, "Water Rights Problems in the Upper Rio Grande Watershed and Adjoining Areas," 56–57, 61; and Hutchins, "The Community Acequia," 266–67.

46. Stanley Crawford, *Mayordomo: Chronicle of an Acequia in Northern New Mexico* (Albuquerque: University of New Mexico Press, 1988).

47. For information on *acequias,* see *Acequias y Sangrias: Course of New Mexico Waters, Guidebook to Photo Exhibit* (Albuquerque: University of New Mexico, Southwest Hispanic Research Institute, 1986); and Phil Lovato, *Las Acequias del Norte* (Taos: Kit Carson Memorial Foundation, 1974).

3 The Pueblo Indian Grants

1. This chapter is based largely upon my article "Spanish American Acquisition of Cropland within the Northern Pueblo Indian Grants, New Mexico," *Ethnohistory* 22 (Spring 1975): 95–110. Permission is granted by *Ethnohistory* to reproduce Figure 13 and by the *Annals, Association of American Geographers* (see chap. 2, n. 1) to reproduce Figure 11.

2. Florence H. Ellis, "Where Did the Pueblo People Come From?" *El Palacio* 74 (Autumn 1967): 35–43; Stephen C. Jett, "Pueblo Indian Migrations: An Evaluation of the Possible Physical and Cultural Determinants," *American Antiquity* 29 (January 1964): 281–300; Deric O'Bryan, "The Abandonment of the Northern Pueblos in the Thirteenth Century," in *Indian Tribes of Aboriginal America,* ed. Sol Tax (Chicago: University of Chicago Press, 1952), 153–57; and Fred Wendorf and Erik Reed, "An Alternative Reconstruction of Northern Rio Grande Prehistory," *El Palacio* 62 (May-June 1955): 133–73.

3. Sauer, *Seventeenth Century North America* (see chap. 1, n. 2), 50.

4. Erik K. Reed, "Sources of Upper Rio Grande Pueblo Culture and Population," *El Palacio* 56 (June 1949): 163–84.

5. Albert H. Schroeder, "Shifting for Survival in the Spanish Southwest," *New Mexico Historical Review* 43 (October 1968): 291–310.

6. Kirk Bryan, "Pre-Columbian Agriculture in the Southwest, as Conditioned by Periods of Alluviation," *Annals, Association of American Geographers* 31 (December 1941): 219–42; Bruce D. Dickson, "Settlement Pattern Stability and Change in the Middle Northern Rio Grande Region, New Mexico: A Test of Some Hypotheses," *American Antiquity* 40 (April 1975): 159–71; and Dietrich Fliedner, "Pre-Spanish Pueblos in New Mexico," *Annals, Association of American Geographers* 65 (September 1975): 363–77.

7. John, *Storms Brewed in Other Men's Worlds* (see chap. 1, n. 3), 49; and Sauer, *Seventeenth Century North America* 38, 46, 54, 233.

8. Jack D. Forbes, *Apache, Navaho and Spaniard* (Norman: University of Oklahoma Press, 1960), 98–99, 107.

9. Sophie D. Aberle, *The Pueblo Indians of New Mexico: Their Land, Economy, and Civil Organization* (Menasha: American Anthropological Association, 1948), 7; Adolph F. Bandelier, *Final Report of Investigation among the Indians of the Southwestern United States,* part 1 (Cambridge: University Press, 1890), 160–61; Adolph F. Bandelier and Edgar L. Hewitt, *Indians of the Rio Grande Valley*

(Albuquerque: University of New Mexico Press, 1937), 35; and Ralph M. Linton, "Land Tenure in Aboriginal America," in *The Changing Indian,* ed. Oliver LaFarge (Norman: University of Oklahoma Press, 1942), 42–54.

10. Sauer, *Seventeenth Century North America,* 49.

11. Jenkins, "Spanish Land Grants in the Tewa Area" (see chap. 1, n. 8), 115–16.

12. Clark, *Water in New Mexico* (see chap. 1, n. 41), 17–19; and Crouch, Garr, and Mundigo, *Spanish City Planning in North America* (see chap. 1, n. 6), 17.

13. Herbert O. Brayer, *Pueblo Indian Grants of the "Rio Abajo," New Mexico* (Albuquerque: University of New Mexico Press, 1938), 10; and Ralph E. Twitchell, *The Spanish Archives of New Mexico,* vol. 1 (Cedar Rapids: Torch Press, 1914), 397.

14. Baxter, *Las Carneradas* (see chap. 1, n. 45), 23–24.

15. Frank W. Blackmar, *Spanish Insititutions of the Southwest* (Baltimore: Johns Hopkins Press, 1891), 252; Brayer, "The Place of Land in Southwestern History" (see chap. 1, n. 60), 16; and Twitchell, "Pueblo Indian Land Tenures in New Mexico and Arizona," *El Palacio* 12 (1 March 1922): 31–33, 38–61.

16. Brayer, *Pueblo Indian Land Grants of the "Rio Abajo," New Mexico,* 10; and Jenkins, "Land Tenure History in New Mexico" (see chap. 1, n. 30), 36.

17. Simmons, "An Alcalde's Proclamation: A Rare New Mexico Document" (see chap. 2, n. 38), 8.

18. Merton L. Miller, *The Pueblo of Taos, New Mexico* (Chicago: University of Chicago Press, 1898), 15.

19. Chardon, "The Elusive Spanish League" (see chap. 1, n. 32), 302; and Chardon, "The Linear League in North America" (see chap. 1, n. 32), 147–51.

20. Brayer, *Pueblo Indian Land Grants of the "Rio Abajo," New Mexico,* 13; Leo Crane, *Desert Drums: The Pueblo Indians of New Mexico, 1540–1928* (Boston: Little, Brown and Company, 1928), 81–82; and G. Emlen Hall and David J. Weber, "Mexican Liberals and the Pueblo Indians, 1821–1829," *New Mexico Historical Review* 59 (January 1984): 5–32.

21. Bureau of Land Management, U.S. Surveyor-General Records (see chap. 1, n. 35), Case I, File 534, Reel 7, Frame 6.

22. Brayer, *Pueblo Indian Land Grants of the "Rio Abajo," New Mexico,* 86–88; Charles C. Royce, *Indian Land Cessions in the United States,* part 2 (Washington: GPO, 1899), 539–41; and Twitchell, *The Spanish Archives of New Mexico,* 9, 437–39.

23. A. B. Renehan, "Extension of Remarks," *Congressional Record,* House of Representatives, 64 (14 December 1922), part 1, 497–99.

24. John L. Kessell, *Kiva, Cross, and Crown: The Pecos Indians and New Mexico, 1540–1840* (Washington: U.S. Department of the Interior, National Park Service, 1979), 455.

25. O'Bryan, "The Abandonment of the Northern Pueblos in the Thirteenth Century," 156–57; and G. Emlen Hall, *Four Leagues of Pecos: A Legal History of the Pecos Grant, 1800–1933* (Albuquerque: University of New Mexico Press, 1984), 274–77.

26. Hall and Weber, "Mexican Liberals and the Pueblo Indians, 1821–1829," 20.

27. For the extent of the Comanche terror, see Daniel Tyler, "Mexican Indian Policy in New Mexico," *New Mexico Historical Review* 55 (April 1980): 101–20. For information on encroachments on the Taos Pueblo Grant, see Crane, *Desert Drums,* 300; Myra E. Jenkins, "Taos Pueblo and Its Neighbors, 1540–1847," *New*

Mexico Historical Review 41 (April 1966): 85–114; and Twitchell, *The Spanish Archives of New Mexico,* 428–32.

28. Clark, *Water in New Mexico,* 21; Charles F. Coan, *A History of New Mexico,* vol. 1 (Chicago: American Historical Society, 1925), 45–46; and Bureau of Land Management, U.S. Surveyor-General Records, Case I, File 534, Reel 7, Frames 11–13.

29. Bill Hume, "Taos Pueblo Seeks Return of Sacred Tribal Lands," *Albuquerque Journal,* 15 November 1970, G-1; and Alvin M. Josephy, Jr., *Now That the Buffalo's Gone: A Study of Today's American Indians* (Norman: University of Oklahoma Press, 1984), 117. Josephy claims this incident occurred in 1910, but the Taos Pueblo Indians claim it took place in 1919.

30. Witter Bynner," 'From Him That Hath Not,' " *Outlook* 133 (17 January 1923): 125–27 (quotation, 126).

31. Hall and Weber, "Mexican Liberals and the Pueblo Indians, 1821–1829," 20–21.

32. United Pueblo Agency (UPA), Real Property Management Records, Albuquerque, "Pueblo of Pojoaque—Abstracts, Testimony and Receipts for Deeds (P.C. 417)," File 300.7-9-5, 1929; and "Pueblo of Taos vs. Priceliano Garcia, et al.," File 300.16-8, 1929.

33. Henry R. Poore, "Conditions of 16 New Mexico Indian Pueblos, 1890," *Report on Indians Taxed and Indians Not Taxed in the U.S. at the Eleventh Census: 1890* (Washington: GPO, 1894), 407.

34. Hall and Weber, "Mexican Liberals and the Pueblo Indians, 1821–1829," 6–10; Myra E. Jenkins, "The Pueblo of Nambe and Its Lands," in *The Changing Ways of Southwestern Indians,* ed. Albert H. Schroeder (Glorieta, N.M.: Rio Grande Press, 1973), 98; and Tyler, "Mexican Indian Policy in New Mexico," 104–5.

35. William T. Otto, "United States v. Joseph," *United States Reports, Supreme Court, Volume 94: Cases Argued and Adjudicated in the Supreme Court of the United States, October Term, 1876* (New York: Banks Law Publishing Company, 1909), Vol. 4, sections 616–17.

36. U.S. Congress, House, *Titles to Lands within Pueblo Indian Land Grants,* 67th Cong., 4th sess., Report 1748 (Washington: GPO, 1 March 1923), 3. Also see "United States v. Felipe Sandoval," *Cases Argued and Decided in the Supreme Court of the United States,* Book 58 (Rochester: Lawyers Co-operative Publishing Company, 1914), 107–15.

37. John Collier, "The American Congo," *Survey* 50 (1 August 1923): 467–76 (quotation, 469). For similar complaints, see Alois B. Renehan, *The Pueblo Indians and Their Land Grants: The Pioneers and Their Families, Their Descendants and Grantees Occupying Parts of the Pueblo Indian Land Grants in New Mexico* (Albuquerque: T. Hughes, 1923).

38. Lawrence C. Kelly, "John Collier and the Pueblo Lands Board Act," *New Mexico Historical Review* 58 (January 1983): 5–34; and Kenneth Philip, "Albert B. Fall and the Protest from the Pueblos, 1921–23," *Arizona and the West* 12 (Autumn 1970): 237–54.

39. UPA, Real Property Management Records, "Field Notes of Surveys in New Mexico, Affidavits of Applicants, San Juan Pueblo Grant," volumes 308–9, 1915.

40. UPA, Real Property Management Records, "Field Notes of Surveys in New Mexico, Affidavits of Applicants, Taos Pueblo Grant," volumes 288–289, 1915; "Field Notes of Surveys in New Mexico, Affidavits of Applicants, San Juan Pueblo Grant," volumes 308–9, 1915; "Field Notes of Surveys in New Mexico, Affidavits

of Applicants, Taos Pueblo Grant," volumes 228–29, 1915; "Pueblo of Picuris—
Abstracts, Claims, Testimony and Receipts for Deeds," Files 300.6-9-18, 1928–29;
"Pueblo of Pojoaque—Abstracts, Testimony and Receipts for Deeds," Files 300.7-
9-3, 5, 1928–29; and "Pueblo of San Ildefonso—Abstracts, Testimony and Records
for Deeds," Files 300.10-9-12, 16, 17, 1929.

41. UPA, Real Property Management Records, "Field Notes of Surveys in New
Mexico, Affidavits of Applicants, San Juan Pueblo Grant," volumes 308–9, 1915.

42. UPA, "Field Notes of Surveys in New Mexico, Affidavits of Applicants,
Taos Pueblo Grant," volumes 288–89, 1915.

43. Ralph E. Twitchell, "Points in re Matter of Pueblo Land Titles," *Congressional Record* 64 (16 December 1922): 569–72; Bynner, " 'From Him That Hath
Not,' " 125–27; and Collier, "The American Congo," 467–76.

44. U.S. Congress, House, *Titles to Land within Pueblo Indian Land Grants*, 3.

45. Myra E. Jenkins, "The Baltasar Baca 'Grant': History of an Encroachment,"
El Palacio 68 (Spring 1961): 47–64.

46. Aberle, *The Pueblo Indians of New Mexico*, 69–84, UPA, Real Property
Management Records, "Land Status Reports—Pueblos," File 385.0, 1 April 1940,
18; and Hugh G. Calkins, *Tewa Basin Study* (Albuquerque: USDA, Soil Conservation Service, 1939) vol. 3, 80–89. For losses on the Santa Clara Pueblo Grant, see
G. Emlen Hall, "Land Litigation and the Idea of New Mexico Progress," *Journal
of the West* 27 (July 1988): 48–58.

47. UPA, Real Property Management Records, "Appraiser's Report of Taos
Pueblo Grant," Map 11159-8, 1927 and "Pueblo of Taos—Appraisals," File
300.16-1, 1927; "Pueblo of San Juan—Report of Appraisers," File 300.11-1c,
1928; and "San Juan Pueblo Land Classification," Map 11159-13, 1929.

48. James A. Vlasich, "Transitions in Pueblo Agriculture, 1938–1948," *New
Mexico Historical Review* 55 (January 1980): 25–46.

49. Edward P. Dozier, *The Pueblo Indians of North America* (New York: Holt,
Rinehart and Winston, 1970); Margaret Meaders, *The Indian Situation in New
Mexico* (Albuquerque: University of New Mexico, Bureau of Business Research,
1963); and Anne M. Smith *New Mexico Indians: Economic, Educational and
Social Problems* (Santa Fe: Museum of New Mexico Press, 1969). For a bibliography on the Pueblos, see Tim Wehrkamp, "A Selected Guide to Sources on New
Mexico Indians in the Modern Period," *New Mexico Historical Review* 60 (October 1985): 435–44.

50. Coan, *A History of New Mexico*, vol. 1, 46; and Meyer, *Water in the Hispanic Southwest* (see chap. 2, n. 23), 53–55, 151. For other cases, see Charles T.
DuMars, Marilyn O'Leary, and Albert E. Utton, *Pueblo Indian Water Rights:
Struggle for a Precious Resource* (Tucson: University of Arizona Press, 1984), 119–
26.

51. Bynner, " 'From Him That Hath Not,' " 126; and Vlasich, "Transitions in
Pueblo Agriculture," 28, 33.

52. Brown and Ingram, *Water and Poverty in the Southwest* (see chap. 2, n.
40), 70–71, 180; Clark, "Water Rights Problems in the Upper Rio Grande Watershed and Adjoining Areas" (see chap. 2, n. 26), 68; and Joe S. Sando, *The Pueblo
Indians* (San Francisco: Indian Historian Press, 1976), 100–10.

53. Alvar W. Carlson, "Review of *Pueblo Indian Water Rights: Struggle for a
Precious Resource*, by Charles T. DuMars, Marilyn O'Leary, and Albert E. Utton,"
Professional Geographer 37 (August 1985): 366–67. For a discussion of recent
concerns about Pueblo Indian water rights, see Clark, *Water in New Mexico* (see
chap. 1, n. 41), 654–56, 668–69.

54. Charles Bowden, *Killing the Hidden Waters* (Austin: University of Texas Press, 1977); and Josephy, *Now That the Buffalo's Gone,* 173.

4 U.S. Land Policies and Homesteading

Note: Research for this chapter was funded by the National Science Foundation, Award SES-8006996.

1. Roy M. Robbins, *Our Landed Heritage, the Public Domain, 1776–1970* (Lincoln: University of Nebraska Press, 1976), 153–54.

2. Benjamin H. Hibbard, *A History of the Public Land Policies* (New York: Macmillian Company, 1924), 352–54; and Victor Westphall, *The Public Domain in New Mexico, 1854–1891* (Albuquerque: University of New Mexico Press, 1965), 37–38. The duties of New Mexico's surveyor-general are described in Thomas Donaldson, *The Public Domain: Its History with Statistics* (Washington: GPO, 1884), 394–401.

3. Donaldson, *The Public Domain,* 1026–27; Samuel Herrick, *Herrick's Manual of the United States Homestead and Other Public Land Laws* (Seattle: Adams Publishing Company, 1909); and U.S. General Land Office, *Circular from the General Land Office* (Washington: GPO, 1904).

4. E. Louise Peffer, *The Closing of the Public Domain* (Stanford: Stanford University Press, 1951), 12–13; and Robbins, *Our Landed Heritage,* 207.

5. Donaldson, *The Public Domain,* 1092; Hibbard, *A History of the Public Land Policies,* 441–56; and Robbins, *Our Landed Heritage,* 218–19, 325, 361.

6. Peffer, *The Closing of the Public Domain,* 22–24; and Robbins, *Our Landed Heritage,* 325.

7. Hibbard, *A History of the Public Land Policies,* 391–96; Peffer, *The Closing of the Public Domain,* 147–48; and Robbins, *Our Landed Heritage,* 363, 375.

8. Harvey B. Fergusson, *Speech of Hon. Harvey B. Fergusson on the Bill to Provide for Stock-Raising Homesteads,* House of Representatives, 15 June 1914 (Washington: GPO, 1914), 2; Hibbard, *A History of the Public Land Policies,* 398–402; Peffer, *The Closing of the Public Domain,* 160; and Robbins, *Our Landed Heritage,* 387.

9. Examples of this literature include A. Avery, *Hand-Book and Travelers' Guide of New Mexico* (Denver: E. Price and Company, 1881); William M. Berger, *Berger's Tourists' Guide to New Mexico* (Kansas City: House of Ramsey, Millett and Hudson, 1883); William Blackmore, *Investments in Land in Colorado and New Mexico* (London: Witherby and Company, 1876); Elias Brevoort, *New Mexico, Her Natural Resources and Attractions* (Santa Fe: Author, 1874); Theo. C. Camp, *Taos County* (Santa Fe: Bureau of Immigration of New Mexico, 1881); Max Frost, ed., *New Mexico, Its Resources, Climate, Geography, and Geological Conditions* (Santa Fe: New Mexican Publishing Company, 1890); F. C. Nims, *Health, Wealth and Pleasure in Colorado and New Mexico* (Chicago: Belford, Clarke and Company, 1881); William G. Ritch, *The Resources of New Mexico* (Santa Fe: Bureau of Immigration, New Mexican Book and Job Printing Department, 1881); and Cyrus Thomas, *The Agricultural and Pastoral Resources of Southern Colorado and Northern New Mexico* (London: John King and Company, 1872).

10. John E. Baur, "The Health Seeker in the Westward Movement, 1830–1900," *Mississippi Valley Historical Review* 46 (June 1959): 91–110; Billy M. Jones, *Health-Seekers in the Southwest, 1817–1900* (Norman: University of Oklahoma Press, 1967), 38–41, 168; and Karen D. Shane, "New Mexico: Salubrious El

Dorado," *New Mexico Historical Review* 56 (October 1981): 387–99.

11. Cleve Hallenbeck, "Climate and Health," *New Mexico* 9 (December 1931): 9–12, 44–47; and Yi-Fu Tuan and Cyril E. Everard, "New Mexico's Climate: The Appreciation of a Resource," *Natural Resources Journal* 4 (October 1964): 268–308.

12. Paul M. Carrington, "The Climate of New Mexico, Nature's Sanatorium for Consumptives," *New York Medical Journal* 84 (6 July 1907): 1–10; George Halley, "New Mexico as a Health Resort," *Kansas City Medical Record* 5 (February 1888): 41–44; J. J. Jones, "New Mexico as a Health Resort for Consumptives," *Medical and Surgical Reporter* 37 (15 September 1877): 201–3; and H. B. Masten, "New Mexico as a Health Resort," *New York Medical Journal* 77 (6 September 1902): 414–17. For surveys on this promotion, see Stephen D. Fox, "Healing, Imagination, and New Mexico," *New Mexico Historical Review* 58 (July 1983): 213–37.

13. Francis W. Gallagher, "The Climate of New Mexico," *New York Medical Record* 49 (13 June 1896): 847–48; Jones, *Health-Seekers in the Southwest, 1817–1900,* 151, 168; Shane, "New Mexico: Salubrious El Dorado," 388–91; and Williams, *New Mexico in Maps* (see chap. 1, n. 7), 123, 129–31.

14. Charles P. Clever, *New Mexico: Her Resources; Her Necessities for Railroad Communications with the Atlantic and Pacific States; Her Great Future* (Washington: McGill and Witherow, 1868), 7.

15. Brevoort, *New Mexico, Her Natural Resources and Attractions,* ix. Also see Julian, "The Redemption of a Territory" (see chap. 1, n. 37), 238.

16. Donaldson, *The Public Domain,* 1214–15.

17. Although homesteading in the Río Arriba has been mentioned occasionally in the literature, no study has specifically analyzed homesteading by the region's Spanish Americans. This is even true in the studies on the alienation of the public domain by Westphall, *The Public Domain in New Mexico, 1854–1891*; and Victor Westphall, "The Public Domain in New Mexico, 1854–1891," *New Mexico Historical Review* 33 (January 1958): 24–52, (April 1958): 128–43.

18. Bowden, "Private Land Claims in the Southwest" (see chap. 1, n. 24), 1107–11.

19. Ibid., 1136–40.

20. Ibid., 1094–99; and Bureau of Land Management, U.S. Surveyor-General Records (see chap. 1, n. 35), Report 140, File 143, Reel 48, Frames 99, 102, 108, 116.

21. "Stanley Making Rapid Strides," *Santa Fe New Mexican,* 21 December 1907, 1; Matt Telin, "Stanley Commercial Center of Northern Estancia Valley," *Santa Fe New Mexican,* 4 June 1908, 3; "Town of Stanley Coming Metropolis," *Santa Fe New Mexican,* 17 February 1908, 8; "Town of Stanley Growing Steadily," *Santa Fe New Mexican,* 29 August 1907, 1; and "Town of Stanley Growing Steadily," *Santa Fe New Mexican,* 25 March 1908, 8.

22. Personal interview, Vernon Shupe, Carson, New Mexico, 21 July 1980.

23. Kalervo Oberg, "Cultural Factors and Land-Use Planning in Cuba Valley, New Mexico," *Rural Sociology* 5 (December 1940): 438–48.

24. Allan G. Harper, Andrew R. Cordova, and Kalervo Oberg, *Man and Resources in the Middle Rio Grande Valley* (Albuquerque: University of New Mexico Press, 1943), 21.

25. Hibbard, *A History of the Public Land Policies,* 396–98, 402; and Peffer, *The Closing of the Public Domain,* 321–24.

26. Paul W. Gates, "The Homestead Law in an Incongruous Land System,"

American Historical Review 41 (July 1936): 652–81; Robbins, *Our Landed Heritage,* 240, 247–48; Fred A. Shannon, "The Homestead Act and the Labor Surplus," in *The Public Lands,* ed. Vernon Carstensen (Madison: University of Wisconsin Press, 1963), 307; and White, Koch, Kelley, and McCarthy, *Land Title Study* (see chap. 1, n. 27), 30–31.

27. Sarah Deutsch, *No Separate Refuge: Culture, Class, and Gender on an Anglo-Hispanic Frontier in the American Southwest, 1880–1940* (New York: Oxford University Press, 1987), 31.

28. Gates, "The Homestead Law in an Incongruous Land System," 655. Also see Robbins, *Our Landed Heritage,* 236, 297.

5 A Region of Self-sufficiency, 1600–1930

1. John P. Andrews, "History of Rural Spanish Settlement and Land Use in the Upper Culebra Basin of the San Luis Valley, Costilla County, Colorado" (Master's thesis, University of Colorado, 1972), 33–34; Campa, *Hispanic Culture in the Southwest* (see chap. 1, n. 1), 142–48; Carlson, "Rural Settlement Patterns in the San Luis Valley" (see chap. 2, n. 6), 113–15; Fray Angélico Chávez, "Early Settlements in the Mora Valley," *El Palacio* 62 (November 1955): 318–23; and Richard L. Nostrand, "The Century of Hispano Expansion," *New Mexico Historical Review* 62 (October 1987): 361–86.

2. Richard L. Nostrand, "The Hispano Homeland in 1900," *Annals, Association of American Geographers* 70 (September 1980): 382–96.

3. Oberg, "Cultural Factors and Land-Use Planning in Cuba Valley, New Mexico" (see chap. 4, n. 23), 440.

4. Lynn I. Perrigo, *Texas and Our Spanish Southwest* (Dallas: Banks Upshaw and Company, 1960), 370. For more information on Spanish-American inheritance practices, see Deutsch, *No Separate Refuge* (see chap. 4, n. 27), 45.

5. Nancie L. González, *The Spanish-Americans of New Mexico: A Heritage of Pride* (Albuquerque: University of New Mexico Press, 1969), 55, n. 3; Thomas D. Hall, *Social Change in the Southwest, 1350–1880* (Lawrence: University Press of Kansas, 1989), 154; and Gary D. Libecap and George Alter, "Agricultural Productivity, Partible Inheritance, and the Demographic Response to Rural Poverty: An Examination of the Spanish Southwest," *Explorations in Economic History* 19 (April 1982): 184–200.

6. González, *The Spanish-Americans of New Mexico: A Heritage of Pride,* 55, n. 3; Frances L. Swadesh, "Hispanic Americans of the Ute Frontier from the Chama Valley to the San Juan Basin, 1694–1960" (Ph.D. dissertation, University of Colorado, 1966), 188, 227; and Frances L. Swadesh, "Property and Kinship in Northern New Mexico," *Rocky Mountain Social Science Journal* 2 (March 1965): 209–14. For inheritance customs in southern Spain, see Julian A. Pitt-Rivers, *The People of the Sierra* (New York: Criterion Books, 1954), 103–4.

7. Personal interview, Gilberto A. Espinosa (lawyer), Albuquerque, 6 August 1969.

8. Ernest E. Maes, "The World and the People of Cundiyo," *Land Policy Review* 4 (March 1941): 8–14.

9. Carlson, "Long-Lots in the Rio Arriba" (see chap. 2, n. 1), 55–56; and Crane, *Desert Drums* (see chap. 3, n. 20), 285–86.

10. UPA (see chap. 3, n. 32), "Pueblo of San Juan, Report of Appraisers," File 300.11-1C, 1928; and "Pueblo of Taos, Appraisals," File 300.16-1, 1928.

11. Ward A. Minge, "The Last Will and Testament of Don Severino Martinez,"

New Mexico Quarterly 33 (Spring 1963): 33–56; Claire Morrill, *A Taos Mosaic: Portrait of a New Mexico Village* (Albuquerque: University of New Mexico Press, 1973), 21; José D. Sena, "Archives in the Office of the Cadastral Engineer at Santa Fe," *El Palacio* 36 (11–18 April 1934): 113–21; and Louis H. Warner, "Wills and Hijuelos," *New Mexico Historical Review* 7 (January 1932): 75–89.

12. UPA (see chap. 3, n. 32), "Pueblo of San Ildefonso—Abstracts, Testimony and Receipts for Deeds, F. Roybal through P. Roybal," File 300.10-9-16, PC 71, P1, 1929. Also see UPA, "Pueblo of Pojoaque—Abstracts, Testimony and Receipts for Deeds, J thru L," File 300.7-9-4, 1929; and "Pueblo of Pojoaque—Abstracts, Testimony and Receipts for Deeds-G," File 300.7-9-3, PC 52, 64, 1929.

13. Marc Simmons, "The Chacón Economic Report of 1803," *New Mexico Historical Review* 60 (January 1985): 81–88 (quotation, 84–85).

14. H. Bailey Carroll and J. Villasana Haggard, ed. and trans., *Three New Mexico Chronicles* (Albuquerque: University of New Mexico Press, 1942), 38; and E. H. Ruffner, *Lines of Communication between Southern Colorado and New Mexico,* U.S. Congress, House Ex. Doc. 172, 44th Cong. 1st sess. (Washington: GPO, 8 June 1876), 11.

15. Bailey, *Diego de Vargas and the Reconquest of New Mexico* (see chap. 1, n. 8), 19, 215, 224–25, 252; and Alfred B. Thomas, ed., *Forgotten Frontiers: A Study of the Spanish Indian Policy of Don Juan Bautista de Anza, Governor of New Mexico, 1777–1787* (Norman: University of Oklahoma Press, 1932), 383, n. 89.

16. Elliott Coues, ed., *The Expeditions of Zebulon Montgomery Pike during the Years 1805–6–7* (New York: Frances P. Harper Company, 1895), 741. Also see Max L. Moorhead, ed., *Commerce of the Prairies, by Josiah Gregg* (Norman: University of Oklahoma Press, 1954), 107.

17. For information on the Spanish-American diet, see William W. H. Davis, *El Gringo: Or, New Mexico and Her People* (New York: Harper and Brothers, 1857), 340–41; and Arthur Goss, *Dietary Studies in New Mexico in 1895,* USDA Bulletin 40 (Washington: GPO, 1897).

18. "Report of Trinidad Alarid, Auditor, of the Territory of New Mexico," *Official Reports of the Territory of New Mexico, for the Years 1882 and 1883* (Santa Fe: New Mexican Printing Company, 1884), 14 ff.; and U.S. Department of Commerce, Bureau of the Census, *Twelfth Census of the United States: 1900, Agriculture,* vol. 5, part 1 (Washington: GPO, 1902), 106. Also see Alvin R. Sunseri, "Agricultural Techniques in New Mexico at the Time of the Anglo-American Conquest," *Agricultural History* 47 (October 1973): 329–37.

19. John, *Storms Brewed in Other Men's Worlds* (see chap. 1, n. 3), 231–32, 243, 312.

20. Charles F. Coan, *A Shorter History of New Mexico* (Ann Arbor: Edwards Bros., 1928), 125; and Alfred B. Thomas, *The Plains Indians and New Mexico, 1751–1778* (Albuquerque: University of New Mexico Press, 1940), 168–73.

21. Thomas, *The Plains Indians and New Mexico,* 53–55; and Thomas, *Forgotten Frontiers,* 96, 101.

22. John, *Storms Brewed in Other Men's Worlds,* 330. Also see Catherine Price, "The Comanches' Threat to Texas and New Mexico in the Eighteenth Century and the Development of Spanish Indian Policy," *Journal of the West* 24 (April 1985): 34–45.

23. Hall, *Social Change in the Southwest, 1350–1880,* 160–61; and John, *Storms Brewed in Other Men's Worlds,* 670–74.

24. David H. Snow, "A Note on Encomienda Economics in Seventeenth-Cen-

tury New Mexico," *Hispanic Arts and Ethnohistory in the Southwest,* ed. Marta Weigle (Santa Fe: Ancient City Press, 1983), 347–48.

25. James I. Culbert, "Distribution of Spanish-American Population in New Mexico," *Economic Geography* 19 (April 1943): 171–76; Richard R. Greer, "Origins of the Foreign-Born Population of New Mexico during the Territorial Period," *New Mexico Historical Review* 17 (October 1942): 281–87; Richard L. Nostrand, "Mexican Americans Circa 1850," *Annals, Association of American Geographers* 65 (September 1975): 378–90; Paul Horgan, *The Centuries of Santa Fe* (New York: E. P. Dutton and Company, 1956); and Victor Westphall, "Albuquerque in the 1870's," *New Mexico Historical Review* 23 (October 1948): 253–68.

26. David J. Weber, "Spanish Fur Trade from New Mexico, 1540–1821," *Americas* 24 (October 1967): 122–36 (quotation, 124).

27. Coan, *A Shorter History of New Mexico,* 112; Lawrence Kinnaird, "The Spanish Tobacco Monopoly in New Mexico, 1766–1767," *New Mexico Historical Review* 21 (October 1946): 328–39; Moorhead, *Commerce of the Prairies,* 111; Twitchell, *The Spanish Archives of New Mexico* (see chap. 3, n. 13), 169; and Leslie A. White, "Punche: Tobacco in New Mexico History," *New Mexico Historical Review* 18 (October 1943): 386–93.

28. Bolton, "French Intrusions into New Mexico, 1749–1752" (see chap. 2, n. 16), 389–407; Dunn, "Spanish Reaction against the French Advance toward New Mexico, 1717–1727" (see chap. 2, n. 16), 348–62; and Folmer, "Contraband Trade between Louisiana and New Mexico in the Eighteenth Century" (see chap. 2, n. 16), 263–72.

29. Bancroft, *History of Arizona and New Mexico* (see chap. 1, n. 1), 277; Cheryl Foote, "Spanish-Indian Trade along New Mexico's Northern Frontier in the Eighteenth Century," *Journal of the West* 24 (April 1985): 22–23; Hall, *Social Change in the Southwest, 1350–1880,* 95; Thomas, *The Plains Indians and New Mexico,* 2–3; and Ralph E. Twitchell, *The Leading Facts of New Mexican History,* vol. 1 (Cedar Rapids: Torch Press, 1911), 453–54.

30. Weber, "Spanish Fur Trade from New Mexico, 1540–1821," 122. Also see David J. Weber, *The Taos Trappers: The Fur Trade in the Far Southwest, 1540–1846* (Norman: University of Oklahoma Press, 1971).

31. Mrs. Edward E. Ayer, *The Memorial of Fray Alonso de Benavides, 1630* (Chicago: Privately printed, 1916), 217.

32. Carroll and Haggard, *Three New Mexico Chronicles,* 90.

33. Beck and Haase, *Historical Atlas of New Mexico* (see chap. 1, n. 1), map 35.

34. Max L. Moorhead, *New Mexico's Royal Road, Trade and Travel on the Chihuahua Trail* (Norman: University of Oklahoma Press, 1958), 32–34; and France V. Scholes, "The Supply Service of the New Mexico Missions in the Seventeenth Century," *New Mexico Historical Review* 5 (January 1930): 93–115, (April 1930): 186–210, (October 1930): 386–404.

35. Max L. Moorhead, "Spanish Transportation in the Southwest, 1540–1846," *New Mexico Historical Review* 32 (January 1957): 107–22 (quotation, 113).

36. Ibid., 112–17; and Marc Simmons, "Carros y Carretas: Vehicular Traffic on the Camino Real," in *Hispanic Arts and Ethnohistory in the Southwest,* ed. Marta Weigle (Santa Fe: Ancient City Press, 1983): 325–34.

37. Lansing B. Bloom, "The Chihuahua Highway," *New Mexico Historical Review* 12 (July 1937): 209–16; Lansing B. Bloom, "Early Weaving in New Mexico," *New Mexico Historical Review* 2 (July 1927): 228–38; Lansing B. Bloom, "A

Trade-Invoice of 1638 for Goods Shipped by Governor Rosas from Santa Fe," *New Mexico Historical Review* 10 (July 1935): 242–48; and Moorhead, *New Mexico's Royal Road*, 34–36.

38. Moorhead, *Commerce of the Prairies,* 332.

39. Seymour V. Connor and Jimmy M. Skaggs, *Broadcloth and Britches: The Santa Fe Trade* (College Station: Texas A & M University Press, 1977), 70.

40. Colonel Henry Inman, *The Old Santa Fé Trail* (New York: Macmillan Company, 1899), 45; and Joan Myers and Marc Simmons, *Along the Santa Fe Trail* (Albuquerque: University of New Mexico Press, 1986), 21.

41. Connor and Skaggs, *Broadcloth and Britches,* 199–200.

42. Moorhead, *Commerce of the Prairies,* 332.

43. Hall, *Social Change in the Southwest, 1350–1880,* 154–55, 190.

44. Lewis E. Atherton, "The Santa Fe Trader as Mercantile Capitalist," *Missouri Historical Review* 77 (October 1982): 1–12; and Samora and Simon, *A History of the Mexican American People* (see chap. 1, n. 3), 73.

45. Connor and Skaggs, *Broadcloth and Britches,* 204.

46. F. T. Cheetham, "El Camino Militar," *New Mexico Historical Review* 15 (January 1940): 1–11; Jones, *Los Paisanos* (see chap. 1, n. 3), 143–45; and Williams, *New Mexico in Maps* (see chap. 1, n. 7), 123–25.

47. Baxter, *Las Carneradas* (see chap. 1, n. 45), 20; and Alvar W. Carlson, "New Mexico's Sheep Industry, 1850–1900: Its Role in the History of the Territory," *New Mexico Historical Review* 44 (January 1969): 25–49.

48. LeRoy R. Hafen and Ann W. Hafen, *Old Spanish Trail Santa Fe to Los Angeles* (Glendale: Arthur H. Clark Company, 1954), 19; and Eleanor Lawrence, "Mexican Trade between Santa Fe and Los Angeles, 1830–1848," *California Historical Society Quarterly* 10 (March 1931): 27–39.

49. Baxter, *Las Carneradas,* 103; and Alvin R. Sunseri, "Sheep Ricos, Sheep Fortunes in the Aftermath of the American Conquest, 1846–1861," *El Palacio* 83 (Spring 1977): 3–8.

50. Carlson, "New Mexico's Sheep Industry, 1850–1900," 29.

51. Baxter, *Las Carneradas,* 24–25.

52. Ibid., 28.

53. Ibid., 30.

54. Sunseri, "Sheep Ricos, Sheep Fortunes in the Aftermath of the American Conquest, 1846–1861," 5.

55. Carlson, "New Mexico's Sheep Industry, 1850–1900," 37–38.

56. Baxter, *Las Carneradas,* 68.

57. Davis, *El Gringo,* 195.

58. Baxter, *Las Carneradas,* 69–71.

59. James W. Thompson, *A History of Livestock Raising in the United States, 1607–1860* (Washington: GPO, 1942), 111.

60. William M. Denevan, "Livestock Numbers in Nineteenth-Century New Mexico, and the Problem of Gullying in the Southwest," *Annals, Association of American Geographers* 57 (December 1967): 691–703; and Widdison, "Historical Geography of the Middle Rio Puerco Valley, New Mexico" (see chap. 2, n. 13), 272–73.

61. Ruffner, *Lines of Communication between Southern Colorado and Northern New Mexico,* 11.

62. Arthur L. Campa, "Piñon as an Economic and Social Factor," *New Mexico Business Review* 1 (October 1932): 144–47; and John A. Gjevre, *Chili Line* (Española: Rio Grande Sun Press, 1969), 18–19.

63. Thomas, *Forgotten Frontiers,* 113–14; and Louis H. Warner, "Conveyance of Property, the Spanish and Mexican Way," *New Mexico Historical Review* 6 (October 1931): 334–59.

64. Deutsch, *No Separate Refuge,* 120.

65. Calkins, *Tewa Basin Study,* vol. 2 (see chap. 3, n. 46), v–vi, 126–31; Calkins, *Village Dependency on Migratory Labor in the Upper Rio Grande Area* (Albuquerque: USDA, Soil Conservation Service, Bulletin 47, 1937), 1–4, 7; Alvar W. Carlson, "Seasonal Farm Labor in the San Luis Valley," *Annals, Association of American Geographers* 63 (March 1973): 97–108; and Deutsch, *No Separate Refuge,* 164.

66. Deutsch, *No Separate Refuge,* 88.

67. Ibid., 40.

68. *A Complete Business Directory of New Mexico and Gazetteer of the Territory for 1882* (Santa Fe: New Mexican Printing and Publishing Company, 1882), 17–34.

69. John P. Bloom, "New Mexico Viewed by Anglo-Americans, 1846–1849," *New Mexico Historical Review* 34 (July 1959): 165–98; Arthur L. Campa, "Mañana Is Today," *New Mexico Quarterly* 9 (February 1939): 3–11; and John C. Russell, "State Regionalism in New Mexico," *Social Forces* 16 (December 1937): 268–71.

70. Baxter, *Las Carneradas,* 68.

71. H. T. Wilson, *Historical Sketch of Las Vegas* (Chicago: Hotel World Publishing Company, 1880), 21.

72. Charles F. Lummis, *The Land of Poco Tiempo* (New York: Charles Scribner's Sons, 1902), 5–6.

73. Marc Simmons, "New Mexico's Spanish Exiles," *New Mexico Historical Review* 59 (January 1984): 67–79; and Twitchell, *The Leading Facts of New Mexican History,* vol. 2, 54–55.

74. Chávez, *Origins of New Mexico Families* (see chap. 1, n. 22), 119–335; Greer, "Origins of the Foreign-Born Population of New Mexico during the Territorial Period," 282; Strout, "The Resettlement of Santa Fe, 1695" (see chap. 1, n. 22), 261–70; and Alicia V. Tjarks, "Demographic, Ethnic and Occupational Structure of New Mexico, 1790," *Americas* 35 (July 1978): 45–88.

75. Superintendent of the U.S. Census, *The Seventh Census of the United States: 1850* (Washington: Robert Armstrong, 1853), xxxvi, 988–89, 993, 996.

76. Harvey Fergusson, *Rio Grande* (New York: Alfred A. Knopf, 1933), 184; Hall, *Social Change in the Southwest, 1350–1880,* 101–2; and Sanford A. Mosk, "The Influence on Tradition on Agriculture in New Mexico," *Journal of Economic History* 2 (December 1942): 34–51.

6   A Region of Poverty, 1930–1990

1. For instance, see Deutsch, *No Separate Refuge* (see chap. 4, n. 27), 137.

2. John J. Bodine, "A Tri-Ethnic Trap: The Spanish Americans in Taos," in *Spanish-Speaking People in the United States,* ed. June Helm (Seattle: University of Washington Press, 1968), 145–53 (quotation, 150). Also see González, *The Spanish-Americans of New Mexico* (see chap. 5, n. 5), 78.

3. Thomas J. Steele, "Naming of Places in Spanish New Mexico," in *Hispanic Arts and Ethnohistory in the Southwest,* ed. Marta Weigle (Santa Fe: Ancient City Press, 1983), 293–302. Also see Fray Angélico Chávez, "Saints' Names in New Mexico Geography," *El Palacio* 56 (November 1949): 323–35.

4. Teresa Marquez, "The Condition of Hispanics in the U.S. Today," *Special Libraries Association Geography and Map Division Bulletin 142* (December 1985): 73. Also see Robert Coles, *The Old Ones of New Mexico* (Albuquerque: University of New Mexico Press, 1973), 68; Culbert, "Distribution of Spanish-American Population in New Mexico" (see chap. 5, n. 25), 171–72; Erna Fergusson, *New Mexico: A Pageant of Three Peoples* (New York: Alfred A. Knopf, 1955), 217–18; Metzgar, "The Ethnic Sensitivity of Spanish New Mexicans" (see chap. 1, n. 7), 50–51; Richard L. Nostrand, "Commentary: The Hispano Homeland in 1900," *Annals, Association of American Geographers* 71 (June 1981): 282–83; and Richard L. Nostrand, " 'Mexican American' and 'Chicano': Emerging Terms for a People Coming of Age," *Pacific Historical Review* 42 (August 1973): 389–406.

5. Aurelio M. Espinosa, *The Spanish Language in New Mexico and Southern Colorado* (Santa Fe: New Mexican Printing Company, 1911); and Juan B. Rael, "Alternate Forms in the Speech of the Individual: Phonology and Morphology of New Mexican Spanish," *Studies in Philology* 36 (October 1939): 664–70.

6. Campa, *Hispanic Culture in the Southwest* (see chap. 1, n. 1), 201; Arthur L. Campa, *Spanish Folk-Poetry in New Mexico* (Albuquerque: University of New Mexico Press, 1946); Arthur L. Campa, "Superstition and Witchcraft along the Rio Grande," in *1949 Brand Book* (Denver: Westerners, 1950), 165–82; Rubén Cobos, *A Dictionary of New Mexico and Southern Colorado Spanish* (Santa Fe: Museum of New Mexico Press, 1983); Deutsch, *No Separate Refuge,* 59; Aurelio M. Espinosa, "Traditional Spanish Ballads in New Mexico," *Hispania* 15 (March 1932): 89–102; Aurelio M. Espinosa and J. Manual Espinosa, *The Folklore of Spain in the American Southwest: Traditional Spanish Folk Literature in Northern New Mexico and Southern Colorado* (Norman: University of Oklahoma Press, 1985); Laura Gilpin, "La Conquistadora," *New Mexico Sun Trails* 6 (September 1953): 21–23; José Griego y Maestas and Rudolfo A. Anaya, *Cuentos: Tales from the Hispanic Southwest* (Santa Fe: Museum of New Mexico Press, 1980); Lummis, *The Land of Poco Tiempo* (see chap. 5, n. 72), 23–24; Pedro R. Ortega, "Fiesta Theme Is Religious Tribute," *New Mexican* (Santa Fe), 30 August 1972, 4; Juan B. Rael, *Cuentos Españoles de Colorado y Nuevo Mexico* (Santa Fe: Museum of New Mexico Press, 1977); and John D. Robb, *Hispanic Folk Music in New Mexico and the Southwest: A Self-Portrait of a People* (Norman: University of Oklahoma Press, 1980).

7. U.S. Department of Commerce, Bureau of the Census, *Thirteenth Census of the United States: 1910, Population* (Washington: GPO, 1913), 3: 176–81; *Fourteenth Census of the United States: 1920, Population* (Washington: GPO, 1923), 3: 667, 669–70; *Fifteenth Census of the United States: 1930, Population* (Washington: GPO, 1932), 3: part 2, 227, 244; *Sixteenth Census of the United States: 1940, Population* (Washington: GPO, 1943), 2: part 4, 955, 994; *Census of Population: 1950* (Washington: GPO, 1952), 2: part 31, 7, 16, 58; *Census of Population: 1960* (Washington: GPO, 1962), 1: part 33, 8, 50–51, 64, 140–41; *1970 Census of Population* (Washington: GPO, 1973), 1: part 33, 237–45; *1980 Census of Population,* General Population Characteristics (Washington: GPO, 1982), 1: part 33, 12, 112–16; *1980 Census of Population,* General Social and Economic Characteristics (Washington: GPO, 1983), 1: part 33, 11, 259–60; and *1980 Census of Population,* Number of Inhabitants (Washington: GPO, 1982), 1: part 33, 8–9. Sources for the data on the Río Arriba's Spanish-American population include 1930: Sigurd Johansen, *Rural Social Organization in a Spanish-American Culture Area* (Albuquerque: University of New Mexico Press, 1942), 18; 1940: Allan J. Beigle, Harold F. Goldsmith, and Charles P. Loomis, "Demographic Characteristics

of the United States–Mexican Border," *Rural Sociology* 25 (March 1960): 107–62 and George I. Sanchez, *Forgotten People, a Study of New Mexicans* (Albuquerque: Calvin Horn Publishers, 1967), 30; 1950: U.S. Department of Commerce, Bureau of the Census, *United States Census of Population: 1950, Persons of Spanish Surname* (Washington: GPO, 1953), 4: part 3, 44; 1960: *United States Census of Population: 1960, Persons of Spanish Surname* (Washington: GPO, 1963), Report PC(2)-1B: 197; 1970: *1970 Census of Population*, 1: part 33, 226–27; and 1980: *1980 Census of Population*, 1: part 33, 12.

8. U.S. Department of Commerce, Bureau of the Census, *Thirteenth Census of the United States, Agriculture, 1910* (Washington: GPO, 1913), 7: 163–64; *1925 Census of Agriculture* (Washington: GPO, 1927), 3: 266–67, 290–91; *United States Census of Agriculture: 1935* (Washington: GPO, 1936), 2: part 3, 865–66; *1945 Census of Agriculture* (Washington: GPO, 1946), 1: part 30, 67–68; *1954 Census of Agriculture* (Washington: GPO, 1956), 1: part 30, 51–52; *1964 Census of Agriculture* (Washington: GPO, 1967), 1: part 42, 236–37; *1974 Census of Agriculture* (Washington: GPO, 1977), 1: part 31, 121, 133, 151, 169; and *1982 Census of Agriculture* (Washington: GPO, 1983), 1: part 31, 123–24, 133–34, 143–44, 146–47.

9. Marlowe M. Taylor, *Rural People and Their Resources: North-Central New Mexico* (Las Cruces: Agricultural Experiment Station, 1960), 8–13 (quotation, iii); Sigurd Johansen, *The Population of New Mexico: Its Composition and Change* (State College: New Mexico College of Agriculture and Mechanic Arts, 1940), 13, 18, 55–56; and U.S. Department of Commerce, Bureau of the Census, *County and City Data Book, 1962* (Washington: GPO, 1962), 252.

10. Margaret Mead, "The Spanish Americans of New Mexico, U.S.A.," in *Cultural Patterns and Technical Change* (New York: New American Library, 1955), 151–77.

11. U.S. Department of Commerce, Bureau of the Census, *County and City Data Book, 1962*, 252.

12. U.S. Department of Commerce, Bureau of the Census, *1980 Census of Population*, Gross Migration for Counties: 1975 to 1980 (Washington: GPO, 1984), 75, 195. For accounts on migration to and from the Río Arriba, see Clyde Eastman, *Assessing Cultural Change in North-Central New Mexico* (Las Cruces: New Mexico State University, 1972), 31; Ralph L. Edgel, "New Mexico Population: Its Size and Its Changing Distribution," *New Mexico Business* 12 (October 1958): 1–13; Thomas J. Maloney, "Recent Demographic and Economic Changes in Northern New Mexico," *New Mexico Business* 17 (September 1964): 2–14; David W. Varley, *Migration Patterns: New Mexico and Adjoining States* (Santa Fe: State Planning Office, 1967), 17–19; and Kenneth R. Weber, "Rural Hispanic Village Viability from an Economic and Historic Perspective," in *The Survival of Spanish American Villages*, ed. Paul Kutsche (Colorado Springs: Colorado College, 1979), 79–89.

13. Richard L. Nostrand, "Growth and Decline of the Hispano Ethnic Island," paper presented at Association of American Geographers Meetings, Baltimore, 22 March 1989.

14. George M. Foster, "Cofradía and Compadrazgo in Spain and Spanish America," *Southwestern Journal of Anthropology* 9 (Spring 1953): 1–28; Clark S. Knowlton, "Changes in the Structure and Roles of Spanish-American Families of Northern New Mexico," *Proceedings of the Southwestern Sociological Association* 15 (April 1965): 38–48; Clark S. Knowlton, "Changing Spanish-American Villages of Northern New Mexico," *Journal of Mexican American Studies* 1 (Fall 1970):

31–43; and Sidney W. Mintz and Eric R. Wolf, "An Analysis of Ritual Co-Parenthood (*Compadrazgo*)," *Southwestern Journal of Anthropology* 6 (Winter 1950): 341–68.

15. Carolyn Zeleny, "Relations between Spanish-Americans and Anglo-Americans in New Mexico" (Ph.D. dissertation, Yale University, 1944), 69.

16. Tómas C. Atencio, "The Human Dimensions in Land Use and Land Displacement in Northern New Mexico Villages," in *Indian and Spanish American Adjustments to Arid and Semiarid Environments,* ed. Clark S. Knowlton (Lubbock: Texas Technological College, 1964), 44–52; Brown and Ingram, *Water and Poverty in the Southwest* (see chap. 2, n. 40), 48, 73; Paul Kutsche and John R. Van Ness, *Cañones: Values, Crisis, and Survival in a Northern New Mexico Village* (Albuquerque: University of New Mexico Press, 1981), 141; and Sanchez, *Forgotten People, a Study of New Mexicans,* 11.

17. Lou S. Batchen, "La Curandera," *El Palacio* 81 (Spring 1975): 20–25; Campa, *Hispanic Culture in the Southwest,* 190–91; Tibo J. Chávez, *New Mexican Folklore of the Rio Abajo* (Portales: Bishop Printing Company, 1972), 2–4; Tibo J. Chávez, "A Remedio a Day Keeps the Doctor Away," *New Mexico Magazine* 56 (January 1978): 7, 9, 11–12; Leonara S. M. Curtin, *Healing Herbs of the Upper Rio Grande* (Santa Fe: Rydal Press, 1947); Christine A. Heller, "Regional Patterns of Dietary Deficiency: The Spanish Americans of New Mexico and Arizona," *Annals, American Academy of Political and Social Sciences* 225 (January 1943): 49–51; Sam Schulman, "Rural Healthways in New Mexico," *Annals, New York Academy of Sciences* 84 (8 December 1960): 950–58; and Annette H. Thorp, "The Curandera," WPA File 5-5-52, No. 70, 19 and 26 November 1940, History Library, Museum of New Mexico, Santa Fe.

18. John H. Burma, *Spanish-Speaking Groups in the U.S.* (Durham: Duke University Press, 1954), 22; Johansen, *The Population of New Mexico,* 47; Russell, "State Regionalism in New Mexico" (see chap. 5, n. 69), 270; and Paul Walter and M. A. Saxton, *Social Pathology of New Mexico* (Albuquerque: University of New Mexico Press, 1936), 9.

19. González, *The Spanish-Americans of New Mexico,* 41–42; Juan B. Rael, "New Mexican Spanish Feasts," *California Folklore Quarterly* 1 (January 1942): 83–90; and Sanchez, *Forgotten People, a Study of New Mexicans,* 7–8, 10.

20. Lopez, *Prospects for the Spanish American Culture of New Mexico* (see chap. 1, no. 7), 59–60; and Superintendent of the Census, Secretary of the Interior, *Population of the United States in 1860* (Washington: GPO, 1864), 4: 506; and *The Seventh Census of the United States: 1850* (see chap. 5, n. 75), 1003.

21. Deutsch, *No Separate Refuge,* 27, 65–67.

22. Lopez, *Prospects for the Spanish American Culture of New Mexico,* 84–86; and J. E. Seyfried, *Illiteracy Trends in New Mexico* (Albuquerque: University of New Mexico Press, 1934), 34–35.

23. U.S. Department of Commerce, Bureau of the Census, *Census of Population: 1950,* 2: part 31, 31–62; and U.S. Department of Commerce, Bureau of the Census, *County and City Data Book, 1952* (Washington: GPO, 1953), 283–84. Also see Sanchez, *Forgotten People, a Study of New Mexicans,* 71–73.

24. U.S. Department of Commerce, Bureau of the Census, *1964 Census of Agriculture,* 1: part 42, 248–51.

25. Lopez, *Prospects for the Spanish American Culture of New Mexico,* 84–86; and Seyfried, *Illiteracy Trends in New Mexico,* 34–35.

26. George I. Sanchez, "New Mexicans and Acculturation," *New Mexico Quarterly Review* 11 (February 1941): 61–68.

27. Leo Horton, *Indian Lands in New Mexico* (Santa Fe: New Mexico State Planning Board, 1936), 133–35. (The villages were Chupadero, Cuartelas, Córdova, El Guache, Tierra Azul, El Rito, Barranca, Velarde, Ojo Sarco, and Las Trampas.) Also see Calkins, *Tewa Basin Study* (see chap. 3, n. 46), 2: 176; *Reconnaissance Report on Barranca Project, New Mexico* (Amarillo: Bureau of Reclamation, 1965), 20; and *Reconnaissance Report on El Rito Project, New Mexico* (Amarillo: Bureau of Reclamation, 1965), 30.

28. Jimmy C. Diecker, "Culture Change in Cordova, New Mexico" (Masters thesis, University of Oklahoma, 1971), 49.

29. White, Koch, Kelley, and McCarthy, *Land Title Study* (see chap. 1, n. 27), 70; and Morrill, *A Taos Mosaic* (chap. 5, n. 11), 22. Extreme cases were also identified on 1940 aerial photography of Cerro and Questa, Taos County. Olen E. Leonard, *The Role of the Land Grant in the Social Organization and Social Processes of a Spanish-American Village in New Mexico* (Ann Arbor: Edwards Brothers, 1948), 95–96.

30. Burma, *Spanish-Speaking Groups in the United States*, 14.

31. U.S. Department of Commerce, Bureau of the Census, *1982 Census of Agriculture*, 1: part 31, 143–44, 146–47.

32. U.S. Department of Commerce, Bureau of the Census, *1987 Census of Agriculture* (Washington: GPO, 1989), Advance Reports AC87-A-35-039, 043, 049, 055.

33. Definitions of farms by the Bureau of the Census were generally based upon a combination of acreages and sales until 1974. In 1925 and 1935, a farm was three or more acres if used for farming or under three acres if the land produced farm products valued at $250 or more. A farm in 1945 and 1954 had at least three acres used for agriculture and it could be less than three acres if it had $150 or more in annual sales. In 1964, a farm could be under ten acres but had sales of $250 or it could be more than ten acres with sales of at least $50. The definition was changed in 1974 whereby a farm had to have sales of $1,000 or more of agricultural products. This 1974 definition was used in 1982 and 1987.

34. Hugh G. Calkins, *Notes on Community-Owned Land Grants in New Mexico* (Albuquerque: USDA, Soil Conservation Service, 1937), 12–15, 16–19; Clark, *Water in New Mexico* (see chap. 1, n. 41), 37; Leonard, *The Role of the Land Grant in the Social Organization and Social Processes of a Spanish-American Village in New Mexico*, 85; and J. T. Reid, *It Happened in Taos* (Albuquerque: University of New Mexico Press, 1946), 68–69.

35. For further discussion, see Ebright, "The San Joaquín Grant" (see chap. 2, n. 33), 5–26; Michael J. Rock, "The Change in Tenure New Mexico Supreme Court Decisions Have Effected upon the Common Lands of Community Land Grants in New Mexico," *Social Science Journal* 13 (October 1976): 53–63; and Scott, "Spanish Land-Grant Problems Were Here before the Anglos" (see chap. 1, n. 73), 3.

36. Westphall, *Mercedes Reales* (chap. 1, n. 39), 229.

37. "Spanish Grants Held Taxable in U.S. Court," *Albuquerque Journal*, 21 December 1939, 1.

38. Federal legislation included the National Industrial Recovery Act of 1933, the Emergency Relief Act of 1935, and the Bankhead-Jones Farm Tenant Act of 1936.

39. U.S. Department of Agriculture, *The National Forests of New Mexico* (Washington: GPO, 1922), 7–8.

40. U.S. Forest Service, Headquarters of the Santa Fe National Forest Records,

"Annual Grazing Statistical Report (Form 438), Ojo de San José Grant and Ramon Vigil Grant," Santa Fe, 1945.

41. U.S. Department of Commerce, Bureau of the Census, *1925 Census of Agriculture*, 3: 270–71; *1964 Census of Agriculture*, 1: part 42, 246–47; and *1978 Census of Agriculture* (Washington: GPO, 1981), 1: part 31, 120–21.

42. White, Koch, Kelley, and McCarthy, *Land Title Study*, 64.

43. Charles T. DuMars and Michael J. Rock, "The New Mexico Legal Rights Demonstration Land Grant Project—An Analysis of the Land Title Problems in the Santo Domingo de Cundiyo Land Grant," *New Mexico Law Review* 8 (Winter 1977–78): 1–37; Frankie McCarty, *Land Grant Problems in New Mexico* (Albuquerque: Albuquerque Journal, 1969), 19–21; Morrill, *A Taos Mosaic*, 21–23; and White, Koch, Kelley, and McCarthy, *Land Title Study*, 65.

44. Taylor, *Rural People and Their Resources*, iii.

45. White, Koch, Kelley, and McCarthy, *Land Title Study*, 79–80.

46. Ibid., 66–80. Also see Roxanne D. Ortiz, *Roots of Resistance, Land Tenure in New Mexico, 1680–1980* (Los Angeles: University of California, Chicano Studies Research Center and American Indian Studies Center, 1980), 115–16.

47. U.S. Department of Commerce, Bureau of the Census, *1945 Census of Agriculture*, 1: part 30, 61, 70, 76–78; and *1954 Census of Agriculture*, 1: part 30, 53–54.

48. U.S. Department of Commerce, Bureau of the Census, *1964 Census of Agriculture*, 1: part 42, 244–47.

49. Eldon G. Marr, "Agriculture in New Mexico," *New Mexico Business* 20 (October 1967): 1–12.

50. U.S. Department of Commerce, Bureau of the Census, *1978 Census of Agriculture*, 1: part 31, 153, 299; *1982 Census of Agriculture*, 1: part 31, 130–34, 151–52, 251; and *1987 Census of Agriculture*, Advance Reports AC87-A-35-039, 043, 049, 055.

51. Hugh G. Calkins, *Handling of a Cash Crop (Chili) in the Tewa Basin* (Albuquerque: USDA, Soil Conservation Service, 1937), 12–13. Also see Deutsch, *No Separate Refuge*, 167.

52. Ibid., 6–7.

53. Gerald M. Burke, *Marketing Chile in the Rio Grande Valley* (Las Cruces: New Mexico State University, 1966), 1, 4, 7; Arthur L. Campa, "Chile in New Mexico," *New Mexico Business Review* 3 (April 1934): 61–63; Chilton, Chilton, Arango, Dudley, Neary, and Stelzner, *New Mexico* (see chap. 1, n. 44), 87–88; John Crenshaw, "New Mexico's Fiery Soul," *New Mexico Magazine* 54 (May 1976): 33–35; Lynell Rubright, "A Sequent Occupance of the Española Valley, New Mexico" (Masters thesis, University of Colorado, 1967), 142–45, 150; and Ruth Sneed, *Chile* (Las Cruces: New Mexico State University, 1966), 1–3. For a discussion of recent marketing problems of agricultural crops, such as apples, produced in the Río Arriba, see Brown and Ingram, *Water and Poverty in the Southwest*, 90.

54. Charles M. Wilson, *The Landscape of Rural Poverty* (New York: Henry Holt and Company, 1940), 25.

55. Gordon E. Reckord, "The Geography of Poverty in the United States," in *Problems and Trends in American Geography*, ed. Saul B. Cohen (New York: Basic Books, 1967), 92–112 (quotation, 95).

56. Dale E. Hathaway, *Problems of Progress in the Agricultural Economy* (Chicago: Scott, Foresman and Company, 1964), 110–12; James G. Maddox, "An His-

Journal of Agricultural Economics 50 (December 1968): 1351–61; Oscar Ornati, "The Convergence of Poverty-Linked Characteristics," in *Poverty in Affluence,* ed. Robert E. Will and Harold G. Vatter (New York: Harcourt, Brace and World, 1965), 184–89; and Oscar Ornati, *Poverty amid Affluence* (New York: Twentieth Century Fund, 1966), 58.

57. Michael Harrington, *The Other America: Poverty in the United States* (New York: Macmillan Company, 1962), 43–44.

58. Alan R. Bird, *Poverty in Rural Areas of the United States* (Washington: GPO, 1964), 7; Margaret J. Hagood, *Farm-Operator Family Level-of-Living Indexes for Counties of the United States, 1930, 1940, 1945 and 1950* (Washington: GPO, 1952), 2, 5; President's National Advisory Commission on Rural Poverty, *The People Left Behind* (Washington: GPO, 1967), 4; U.S. Department of Agriculture, *Development of Agriculture's Human Resources: A Report on Problems of Low-Income Farmers* (Washington: GPO, 1955), 7; U.S. Department of Commerce, Area Redevelopment Administration, "Eligible Redevelopment Areas Approved Projects" (Washington: GPO, 1964), map; and John Zimmer and Elsie S. Manny, *Farm Operator Level-of-Living Indexes for Counties of the United States, 1950, 1959, and 1964* (Washington: GPO, 1967), 1, 9–10.

59. U.S. Department of Commerce, Bureau of the Census, "The 182 Lowest Ranking Counties in the U.S. Ordered by Per Capita Income in 1959," Washington (unpublished data); and U.S. Department of Agriculture, Human Resources Branch, Economic Development Division, "Data on Rural Poverty by County," Washington (unpublished data).

60. Marlowe M. Taylor, *Selected Statistics Relating to Agriculture in New Mexico* (Las Cruces: New Mexico State University, 1959), 56–58; U.S. Department of Commerce, Bureau of the Census, *1970 Census of Population, Poverty Status in 1969 and 1959 of Persons and Families, for States, SMSA's, Central Cities, and Counties 1970 and 1960* (Washington: GPO, 1975), 77.

61. Don Laine, "Getting Serious about Development," *New Mexico Business Journal* 12 (May 1988): 31–35; Alan Murray, "Unemployment Tops 25% in Some Regions Mired in Deep Poverty," *Wall Street Journal,* 21 April 1988, 1, 22; U.S. Department of Commerce, Bureau of the Census, *1970 Census of Population,* 1: part 33, 235–36; and *1980 Census of Population,* General Social and Economic Characteristics, 1: part 33, 249–51.

62. Stevens, "Changes in Land Tenure and Usage among the Indians and Spanish Americans in Northern New Mexico" (see chap. 1, n. 46), 39–40. Also see Ortiz, *Roots of Resistance,* 111–12; and Sando, *The Pueblo Indians* (see chap. 3, n. 52), 122–27.

63. Horton, *Indian Lands in New Mexico,* 131.

64. Sanchez, *Forgotten People, a Study of New Mexicans,* 60.

65. Bodine, "A Tri-Ethnic Trap," 150–51.

66. Widdison, "Historical Geography of the Middle Rio Puerco Valley, New Mexico" (see chap. 2, n. 13), 281. Also see Deutsch, *No Separate Refuge,* 167.

67. Hugh G. Calkins, *Village Livelihood in the Upper Rio Grande Area* (Albuquerque: USDA, Soil Conservation Service, 1937); Eshref Shevky, "Rural Rehabilitation in New Mexico," *New Mexico Business Review* 5 (January 1936): 5–9; and William Wroth, "New Hope in Hard Times: Hispanic Crafts Are Revised during Troubled Years," *El Palacio* 89 (Spring 1983): 22–31.

68. Charles Loomis and Glen Grisham, "The New Mexican Experiment in Vil-

lage Rehabilitation," *Applied Anthropology* 2 (April–June 1943): 13–37.

69. Calkins, *Tewa Basin Study* (see chap. 3, n. 46), 166–71.

70. U.S. Forest Service, Division of Forest Land Planning, Northern New Mexico Planning Unit, "Population Dependency" (map), ca. 1935, National Archives, Washington.

71. George I. Sánchez, "Community Education in Taos County, a Critical Review and a Proposal" (Albuquerque, January 1940), 5–6; and Paul Walter, Jr., "The Spanish-Speaking Community in New Mexico," *Sociology and Social Research* 24 (November–December 1939): 150–57.

72. Anacleto Apodaca, "Corn and Custom: The Introduction of Hybrid Corn to Spanish American Farmers in New Mexico," in *Human Problems in Technological Change,* ed. Edward H. Spicer (New York: Russell Sage Foundation, 1952), 35–39; and Reid, *It Happened in Taos,* 64–65.

73. Charles P. Loomis, "Wartime Migration from the Rural Spanish-Speaking Villages of New Mexico," *Rural Sociology* 7 (December 1942): 384–95; and Charles P. and Nellie H. Loomis, "Skilled Spanish-American War-Industry Workers from New Mexico," *Applied Anthropology* 2 (October–December 1942): 33–36.

74. Lopez, *Prospects for the Spanish American Culture of New Mexico,* 80–81.

75. Reginald Fisher, "Hispanic People of the Rio Grande," *El Palacio* 49 (August 1942): 157–62.

76. John H. Burma and David E. Williams, *An Economic, Social and Educational Survey of Rio Arriba and Taos Counties* (El Rito: Northern New Mexico College, 1961), 6–8.

77. Deutsch, *No Separate Refuge,* 196; Julie Dunleavy, "New Mexico: A Pioneer in Southwestern Tourism," *New Mexico Magazine* 62 (November 1984): 61–65; Mary I. Severns, "Tourism in New Mexico: The Promotional Activities of the New Mexico State Tourist Bureau, 1935–1950" (Masters thesis, University of New Mexico, 1951), ii, 29–42.

78. Unpublished data from the New Mexico State Highway Department, Santa Fe, 1971.

79. Paul Logan, "More Tourists Ask about New Mexico," *Albuquerque Journal,* 22 May 1988, D1; and "Will Desert Chic Spoil Old Santa Fe?" *U.S. News & World Report,* 15 June 1981, 57–58.

80. Arrell M. Gibson, *The Santa Fe and Taos Colonies: Age of the Muses, 1900–1942* (Norman: University of Oklahoma Press, 1983); and Blanche C. Grant, *When Old Trails Were New: The Story of Taos* (New York: Press of the Pioneers, 1934), 254–71.

81. U.S. Department of Commerce, Bureau of the Census, *1964 Census of Agriculture,* 1: part 42, 248–51.

82. Carlson, "Seasonal Farm Labor in the San Luis Valley" (see chap. 5, n. 65), 100–104.

83. U.S. Department of Commerce, Bureau of the Census, *1987 Census of Agriculture,* Advance Reports AC87-A-35-039, 043, 049, 055. Also see Brown and Ingram, *Water and Poverty in the Southwest,* 53.

84. *An Opinion Survey of Costilla-Amalia Perceived Problems,* Taos County Community Planning, New Mexico Health and Social Services Department, May 1968, 23–24, 28 (unpublished report). Also see Taylor, *Rural People and Their Resources,* 13–22.

85. Morrill, *A Taos Mosaic,* 34.

86. Data were obtained from the New Mexico Health and Social Services

Department, Santa Fe, July 1969. Also see Taylor, *Selected Statistics Relating to Agriculture in New Mexico,* 24–25, 85–99; and U.S. Department of Commerce, Bureau of the Census, *1964 Census of Agriculture,* 1: part 42, 248–51.

87. Knowlton, "Changes in the Structure and Roles of Spanish-American Families of Northern New Mexico," 39. Also see Deutsch, *No Separate Refuge,* 9–10, 197.

88. John H. Burma, "The Present Status of the Spanish-Americans of New Mexico," *Social Forces* 28 (December 1949): 133–38; and personal fieldwork.

89. For instance, see Crawford, *Mayordomo* (see chap. 2, n. 46), 51, 62, 91, 223.

90. Morrill, *A Taos Mosaic,* 34. Also see Burma, "The Present Status of the Spanish-Americans of New Mexico," 134; and C. Lynn Reynolds, "Economic Decision-Making: The Influence of Traditional Hispanic Land Use Attitudes on Acceptance of Innovation," *Social Science Journal* 13 (October 1976): 21–34.

91. Calkins, *Notes on Community-Owned Land Grants in New Mexico,* 12–15.

92. Diecker, "Culture Change in Cordova, New Mexico," 65. This perception is confirmed by personal fieldwork and by Knowlton, "Land-Grant Problems among the State's Spanish Americans" (see chap. 1, n. 47), 4; and Kutsche and Van Ness, *Cañones,* 217.

93. Brown and Ingram, *Water and Poverty in the Southwest,* 56, 79.

94. "Flower Children Buy Land Worth $500,000 in New Mexico," *San Francisco Examiner and Chronicle,* 4 May 1969, 4A; "The Hippie Scene in Taos," *New Mexico Review and Legislative Journal* 2 (May 1970): 1–4; "Hippies," *Time,* 20 June 1969, 55; Morrill, *A Taos Mosaic,* 40–42; and Rose-Mary Schouten and Donna Osgood, *The Impact of Tourism on Regional Development: A Case Study of Taos, New Mexico* (Dallas, Tex.: Southern Methodist University, 1975), xxiv–xxv.

95. For discussions on changing cultural values among the Spanish Americans, see Eastman, *Assessing Cultural Change in North-Central New Mexico,* 1–47; and Kutsche and Van Ness, *Cañones,* 217–20.

7 Land Use in the National Forests, 1910–1990

1. Marc Simmons and Buddy Mays, *People of the Sun* (Albuquerque: University of New Mexico Press, 1979), 57. About nesters, see Conrad Richter, *Sea of Grass* (New York: Knopf, 1937), 88, 94.

2. Deutsch, *No Separate Refuge* (see chap. 4, n. 27), 24–26; Gonzáles, *The Spanish-Americans of New Mexico* (see chap. 5, n. 5), 90; Robert J. Rosenbaum and Robert W. Larson, "Mexicano Resistance to the Expropriation of Grant Lands in New Mexico," in *Land, Water, and Culture: New Perspectives on Hispanic Land Grants,* ed. Charles L. Briggs and John R. Van Ness (Albuquerque: University of New Mexico Press, 1987), 269–310; and Simmons and Mays, *People of the Sun,* 57.

3. Rosenbaum and Larson, "Mexicano Resistance to the Expropriation of Grant Lands in New Mexico," 279–81, 295.

4. Ibid., 282–83.

5. Gonzáles, *The Spanish-Americans of New Mexico,* 104.

6. Doyle Akers, "Controversial Tierra Amarilla Land Grant Flares," *New Mexican* (Santa Fe), 26 September 1965, B1–B2.

7. John R. Chávez, *The Lost Land: The Chicano Image of the Southwest* (Albuquerque: University of New Mexico Press, 1984), 139.

8. Gonzáles, *The Spanish-Americans of New Mexico,* 100.

9. Chávez, *The Lost Land,* 141; and Deutsch, *No Separate Refuge,* 26–27.

10. Clark S. Knowlton, "Tijerina: Hero of the Militants," *Texas Observer* 61 (28 March 1969): 1–4 (quotation, 3).

11. Chávez, *The Lost Land,* 139.

12. A small skirmish occurred in July 1979 when heirs of the same San Joaquín del Río Chama Grant set up a roadblock to prevent trucks from taking logs from the Santa Fe National Forest. They claimed the forest belonged to them because it was included in the land-grant claim that was largely rejected. Ebright, "The San Joaquín Grant" (see chap. 2, n. 33), 21, n. 11.

13. "How the Hispanos Lost Their Lands," *New Mexico Review and Legislative Journal* 2 (January 1970): 1, 5–6 (quotation, 5). Also see Deutsch, *No Separate Refuge,* 20; Richard Gardner, *Grito! Reies Tijerina and the New Mexico Land Grant War of 1967* (Indianapolis: Bobbs-Merrill Company, 1970); McCarty, *Land Grant Problems in New Mexico* (see chap. 6, n. 43), 14–17; Peter Nabokov, "Reflections on the Alianza," *New Mexico Quarterly* 37 (Winter 1968): 343–56; and Frances L. Swadesh, "The Alianza Movement: Catalyst for Social Change in New Mexico," in *Spanish-Speaking People in the United States,* ed. June Helm (Seattle: University of Washington Press, 1968), 162–77.

14. Patricia B. Blawis, *Tijerina and the Land Grants* (New York: International Publishers, 1971), 40.

15. Knowlton, "Tijerina," 3.

16. Clark S. Knowlton, "Violence in New Mexico: A Sociological Perspective," *California Law Review* 58 (October 1970): 1054–84.

17. Jenkins, "Land Tenure History in New Mexico" (see chap. 1, n. 30), 46.

18. Westphall, *Mercedes Reales* (see chap. 1, n. 39), 272.

19. Ebright, *The Tierra Amarilla Grant* (see chap. 1, n. 59), xii.

20. Hibbard, *A History of the Public Land Policies* (see chap. 4, n. 2), 532–34. Also see William D. Rowley, *U.S. Forest Service Grazing and Rangelands: A History* (College Station: Texas A & M University Press, 1985), 17.

21. William deBuys, *Enchantment and Exploitation: The Life and Hard Times of a New Mexico Mountain Range* (Albuquerque: University of New Mexico Press, 1985), 217–26, 232; and Rebecca Menaul, "Plant Resources of New Mexico, S-162," WPA File 5-5-55, No. 28, 3 July 1936, History Library, Museum of New Mexico, Santa Fe, 12.

22. DeBuys, *Enchantment and Exploitation,* xix.

23. P. W. Cockerill, *Recent Trends in New Mexico Agriculture* (Las Cruces: New Mexico College of Agriculture and Mechanic Arts, April 1956), 19.

24. DeBuys, *Enchantment and Exploitation,* 226–30.

25. Robbins, *Our Landed Heritage* (see chap. 4, n. 1), 421.

26. U.S. Forest Service, Headquarters of the Carson National Forest Records, Taos, 1915–82; Headquarters of the Santa Fe National Forest Records (see chap. 6, n. 40), 1915–82; U.S. Department of Commerce, Bureau of the Census, *Thirteenth Census of the United States, Agriculture, 1910* (see chap. 6, n. 8), used for ca. 1915; *1925 Census of Agriculture* (see chap. 6, n. 8); *United States Census of Agriculture: 1935* (see chap. 6, n. 8); *1945 Census of Agriculture* (see chap. 6, n. 8); *1954 Census of Agriculture* (see chap. 6, n. 8); *1964 Census of Agriculture* (see

chap. 6, n. 8); *1974 Census of Agriculture* (see chap. 6, n. 8); *1982 Census of Agriculture* (see chap. 6, n. 8).

27. U.S. Department of Commerce, Bureau of the Census, unpublished tabulated data for the *1982 Census of Agriculture,* Washington, 12 June 1985.

28. Letters from BLM Area Managers: Dwain W. Vincent, Río Puerco Resource Area Office, Albuquerque (3 November 1986); Taos Resource Area Office, Taos (6 November 1986); Farmington Resource Area Office, Farmington (21 November 1986); and BLM District Manager Robert T. Dale, Albuquerque (6 July 1988).

29. Clyde Eastman and James R. Gray, *Community Grazing: Practice and Potential in New Mexico* (Albuquerque: University of New Mexico Press, 1987), 37, and personal fieldwork.

30. Taylor, *Rural People and Their Resources* (see chap. 6, n. 9), 7. Also see *Analysis of the Management Situation, 1980, Santa Fe National Forest* (Santa Fe: USDA, Forest Service, Southwestern Region, 1980), 4.9 and Appendix J.

31. Peffer, *The Closing of the Public Domain* (see chap. 4, n. 4), 253.

32. A minor confrontation between cattlemen and motorcyclists did occur in 1976 on BLM land in Sandoval County. Judith Friedlander, "Struggles on the Rio Puerco: Environmental Stress and Ethnic Conflict in Northern New Mexico," *Révue Française d'Etudes Américaines* 5 (April 1980): 67–77. For more information on New Mexico's BLM lands, see Clark, *Water in New Mexico* (see chap. 1, n. 41), 588–92.

33. DeBuys, *Enchantment and Exploitation,* 246.

34. U.S. Department of Commerce, Bureau of the Census, *1964 Census of Agriculture,* 234–37.

35. Eastman and Gray, *Community Grazing,* 37.

36. DeBuys, *Enchantment and Exploitation,* 246.

37. *The Carson Pine Cone* (newsletter of the Carson National Forest, Taos), 5 September 1931, 1.

38. Cockerill, *Recent Trends in New Mexico Agriculture,* 19–20; P. W. Cockerill, *A Statistical History of Crop and Livestock Production in New Mexico* (Las Cruces: New Mexico State University, 1959), 6; Richard L. Polese and James Sachse, "New Promise for a Timeless Resource: New Mexico's Sheep Industry Today," *El Palacio* 83 (Spring 1977): 25–27; and U.S. Department of Commerce, Bureau of the Census, *1987 Census of Agriculture* (see chap. 6, n. 32).

39. DeBuys, *Enchantment and Exploitation,* 258–59.

40. U.S. Department of Commerce, Bureau of the Census, *1925 Census of Agriculture,* 276–77, 286–88; *1964 Census of Agriculture,* 260–63; and *1982 Census of Agriculture,* 135–39, 184–85.

41. U.S. Forest Service, Headquarters of the Carson National Forest Records, "Animal Grazing Statistical Report (Form 438)," Taos, 1945, 1964; and Headquarters of the Santa Fe National Forest Records, "Animal Grazing Statistical Report (Form 438)," Santa Fe, 1945, 1964.

42. Ibid. Also see Donald C. Henderson and H. R. Stucky, *Agricultural Land and Water in New Mexico* (Santa Fe: State Planning Office, 1966), 42.

43. Letter from Maynard Rost, Headquarters of the Santa Fe National Forest, Santa Fe, 14 October 1986; and Headquarters of the Santa Fe National Forest Records, "Annual Grazing Statistical Report (Form 438)," Santa Fe, 1982.

44. Letters from Alan Uchida, BLM, Taos, 27 August 1986; Maynard T. Rost, Headquarters of the Santa Fe National Forest, Santa Fe, 29 August 1986; and Robert T. Dale, BLM District Manager, Albuquerque, 6 July 1988.

45. Headquarters of the Santa Fe National Forest Records, "Annual Grazing Statistical Report (Form 438), Ojo de San José Grant and Ramón Vigil Grant," Santa Fe, 1945.

46. "Less Green for Green Acres," *U.S. News and World Report,* 12 May 1986, 13.

47. U.S. Department of Commerce, Bureau of the Census, *1982 Census of Agriculture,* 184–85.

48. *Carson Pine Cone,* 5 February 1932, 1.

49. Horton, *Indian Lands in New Mexico* (see chap. 6, n. 27), 133–35.

50. *Carson Pine Cone,* June 1911, 1, 28 March 1921, 1, and 6 February 1925, 1.

51. This is also confirmed by deBuys, *Enchantment and Exploitation,* 268–69.

52. *Analysis of the Management Situation 1980, Santa Fe National Forest,* 2.22; and Eva Friedlander and Pamela J. Pinyan, *Indian Use of the Santa Fe National Forest: A Determination from Ethnographic Sources* (Albuquerque: Center for Anthropological Studies, 1980), vi, 19–29, 32.

53. J'Wayne McArthur, William R. Summitt, and Robert O. Coppedge, *Outdoor Recreation in North-Central New Mexico, 1967* (Washington: GPO, 1971).

54. Letters from John C. Bedell, Headquarters of the Carson National Forest, Taos, 23 September 1986; Maynard Rost, Headquarters of the Santa Fe National Forest, Santa Fe, 29 August 1986; and U.S. Department of Commerce, Bureau of the Census, *1982 Census of Agriculture,* 133–34, 184–85, 189–90.

55. "Final Environmental Statement—Gallina Planning Unit, Santa Fe National Forest" (Albuquerque: USDA, Forest Service, 1977), 36–37.

56. DeBuys, *Enchantment and Exploitation,* 275–76; and Morrill, *A Taos Mosaic* (see chap. 5, n. 11), 39.

57. James R. Gray and Burton C. English, *Local Benefits of National Forest Resources in North-Central New Mexico* (Las Cruces: New Mexico State University, 1976), 8, 11, 32–35.

58. Brown and Ingram, *Water and Poverty in the Southwest* (see chap. 2, n. 40), 95; Eastman and Gray, *Community Grazing,* 42; and Clyde Eastman and James Gray, *Social Analysis Model for the Santa Fe National Forest* (Santa Fe: Santa Fe National Forest, 1979), 18.

8   Architecture, Religion, and the Vernacular Landscape

1. For a discussion of the literature on the region's cultural landscapes, see Charles F. Gritzner, "Cultural Landscapes," in *Borderlands Sourcebook: A Guide to the Literature on Northern Mexico and the American Southwest,* ed. Ellwyn R. Stoddard, Richard L. Nostrand, and Jonathan P. West (Norman: University of Oklahoma Press, 1983), 116–20.

2. John B. Jackson, *Discovering the Vernacular Landscape* (New Haven: Yale University Press, 1984), 150.

3. Fred B. Kniffen and Henry H. Glassie, "Building in Wood in the Eastern United States: A Time-Place Perspective," *Geographical Review* 56 (January 1966): 40–66 (quotation, 41).

4. See J. B. Jackson, "Pueblo Architecture and Our Own," *Landscape* 3 (Winter 1953–54): 20–25; Roy A. Keech, "Pueblo Dwelling Architecture," *El Palacio* 36 (14–21 February 1934): 49–53; Wayne Mauzy, "Architecture of the Pueblos," *El Palacio* 42 (27 January/3–10 February 1937): 21–30; and Cosmos Mindeleff,

"Origin of the Cliff Dwellings," *Journal of the American Geographical Society* 30 (1898): 111–23.

5. E. Boyd, Ronald Stewart, and William Lumpkins, *Adobe: Past and Present* (Santa Fe: Museum of New Mexico Press, 1974); Bainbridge Bunting, Jean Lee Booth, and William R. Sims, Jr., *Taos Adobes: Spanish Colonial and Territorial Architecture of the Taos Valley* (Santa Fe: Museum of New Mexico Press, 1964); Randall Fleming, "Architecture of Earth," *Pacific Discovery* 27 (September–October 1974): 16–22; Jones, *Los Paisanos* (see chap. 1, n. 3), 157–59; Irving Rusinow, "Spanish-Americans in New Mexico: A Photographic Record of the Santa Cruz Valley," *Survey Graphic* 27 (February 1938): 95–99; and Robert C. West, "The Flat-Roofed Folk Dwelling in Rural Mexico," *Geoscience and Man* 5 (10 June 1974): 111–32.

6. "Prairie Dog Town," *Albuquerque Journal,* 7 July 1984, E-1. Also see Agnesa Lufkin Reeve, *From Hacienda to Bungalow: Northern New Mexico Houses, 1850–1912* (Albuquerque: University of New Mexico Press, 1988), 5.

7. Moorhead, *Commerce of the Prairies, by Josiah Gregg* (see chap. 5, n. 16), 77. Also see Jones, "New Mexico as a Health Resort for Consumptives" (see chap. 4, n. 12), 202.

8. West, "The Flat-Roofed Folk Dwelling in Rural Mexico," 111.

9. Steven A. Yates, ed., *The Essential Landscape: The New Mexico Photographic Survey with Essays by J. B. Jackson* (Albuquerque: University of New Mexico Press, 1985), 13.

10. J. J. Brody and Anne Colberg, "A Spanish-American Homestead near Placitas, New Mexico," *El Palacio* 73 (Summer 1966): 11–20; Bainbridge Bunting and John P. Conron, "The Architecture of Northern New Mexico," *New Mexico Architecture* 8 (September–October 1966): 14–49; Roland F. Dickey, *New Mexico Village Arts* (Albuquerque: University of New Mexico Press, 1949), 41–42; and Winsor Soule, *Spanish Farm Houses and Minor Public Buildings* (New York: Architectural Book Publishing Company, 1924), 1–24.

11. Dickey, *New Mexico Village Arts,* 42. Also see Robert Adams, *The Architecture and Art of Early Hispanic Colorado* (Boulder: Colorado Associated University Press, 1974), 37.

12. Tibo Chavez, "In Search of the Horno," *New Mexico Magazine* 55 (January 1977): 28–33.

13. A. W. Conway, "Southwestern Colonial Farms," *Landscape* 1 (Spring 1971): 6–9; and Reeve, *From Hacienda to Bungalow,* 23–28.

14. Horton, *Indian Lands in New Mexico* (see chap. 6, n. 27), 133–35.

15. For instance, see Beverly Spears, *American Adobes: Rural Houses of Northern New Mexico* (Albuquerque: University of New Mexico Press, 1986).

16. Charles Gritzner, "Hispanic Log Construction of New Mexico," *El Palacio* 85 (Winter 1979–80): 20–29 (quotation, 21). Also see Charles Gritzner, "Construction Materials in a Folk Housing Tradition: Considerations Governing Their Selection in New Mexico," *Pioneer America* 6 (January 1974): 25–39.

17. Gritzner, "Construction Materials in a Folk Housing Tradition," 29–31; Robert J. Torrez, "The Jacal in the Tierra Amarilla," *El Palacio* 85 (Summer 1979): 14–18; and West, "The Flat-Roofed Folk Dwelling in Rural Mexico," 121–24.

18. Gritzner, "Construction Materials in a Folk Housing Tradition," 33; Gritzner, "Hispanic Log Construction of New Mexico," 26; Charles Gritzner, "Hispano Gristmills in New Mexico," *Annals, Association of American Geographers* 64

(December 1974): 514–24; Charles Gritzner, "Log Housing in New Mexico," *Pioneer America* 3 (July 1971): 54–62; and John J. Winberry, "The Log House in Mexico," *Annals, Association of American Geographers* 64 (March 1974): 54–69.

19. Richard E. Ahlborn, "The Wooden Walls of Territorial New Mexico," *New Mexico Architecture* 9 (September–October 1967): 20–23; Gritzner, "Construction Materials in a Folk Housing Tradition," 37; Kutsche, Van Ness, and Smith, "A Unified Approach to the Anthropology of Hispanic Northern New Mexico" (see chap. 2, n. 10), 14, n. 6; and Winberry, "The Log House in Mexico," 59, 67. For a discussion of log construction in Texas, see Terry G. Jordan, *Texas Log Buildings: A Folk Architecture* (Austin: University of Texas Press, 1978).

20. For the interior arrangements of Spanish-American homes, see Jean E. Hess, "Domestic Interiors in Northern New Mexico," *Heresies* 11 (Winter 1981): 30–33; and Sytha Motto, *Old Homes of New Mexico and the People Who Built Them* (Albuquerque: Calvin Horn Publisher, 1972), 5–6.

21. E. Boyd, "Fireplaces and Stoves in Colonial New Mexico," *El Palacio* 65 (December 1958): 219–24; and Motto, *Old Homes of New Mexico and the People Who Built Them*, ix.

22. Bunting and Conron, "The Architecture of Northern New Mexico," 21–24; Reeve, *From Hacienda to Bungalow*, 17–18; and Nancy H. Warren, *New Mexico Style: A Source Book of Traditional Architectural Details* (Santa Fe: Museum of New Mexico Press, 1986), x.

23. A. W. Conway, "A Northern New Mexico House-Type," *Landscape* 2 (Autumn 1951): 20–21; and West, "The Flat-Roofed Folk Dwelling in Rural Mexico," 117–18.

24. Bainbridge Bunting, "The Architecture of the Embudo Watershed," *New Mexico Architect* 4 (May–June 1962): 19–26.

25. Schulman, "Rural Healthways in New Mexico" (see chap. 6, n. 17), 952.

26. "A Catalog of New Mexico Farm-Building Terms," *Landscape* 1 (Winter 1952): 31–32.

27. Ahlborn, "The Wooden Walls of Territorial New Mexico," 22–23.

28. Gritzner, "Hispano Gristmills in New Mexico," 514–24.

29. For a discussion of Chimayó, see Stilgoe, *Common Landscapes of America, 1580 to 1845* (see chap. 2, n. 10), 40–43.

30. A. W. Conway, "Village Types in the Southwest," *Landscape* 2 (Spring 1952): 14–19; and Stephan F. deBorhegyi, "The Evolution of a Landscape," *Landscape* 4 (Summer 1954): 24–30.

31. J. B. Jackson, *Landscape Autoguide, Tour I: Santa Fe to Taos* (Santa Fe: Landscape Magazine, 1962), 26.

32. Marta Weigle, *A Penitente Bibliography* (Albuquerque: University of New Mexico Press, 1976).

33. Henry W. Kelly, "Franciscan Missions of New Mexico, 1740–1760," *New Mexico Historical Review* 15 (October 1940): 345–68. Also see Earle R. Forrest, *Missions and Pueblos of the Old Southwest* (Cleveland: Arthur H. Clark Company, 1929), 33–206; Cleve Hallenbeck, *Spanish Missions of the Old Southwest* (Garden City: Doubleday, Page and Company, 1926), 17–37; and Bradford L. Prince, *Spanish Mission Churches of New Mexico* (Cedar Rapids: Torch Press, 1915).

34. Carroll and Haggard, *Three New Mexico Chronicles* (see chap. 5, n. 14), 50–54; Edgar L. Hewett and Reginald G. Fisher, *Mission Monuments of New Mexico* (Albuquerque: University of New Mexico Press and the School of Ameri-

can Research, 1943), 109–10; and Kelly, "Franciscan Missions of New Mexico, 1740–1760," 362–63.

35. Barnabas C. Diekemper, "The Catholic Church in the Shadows: The Southwestern United States during the Mexican Period," *Journal of the West* 24 (April 1985): 46–53; and Samora and Simon, *A History of the Mexican-American People* (see chap. 1, n. 3), 56; and Superintendent of the U.S. Census, *The Seventh Census of the United States: 1850* (see chap. 5, n. 75), 1013.

36. Bowden, "Private Land Claims in the Southwest" (see chap. 1, n. 24), 302.

37. Richard E. Ahlborn, *The Penitente Moradas of Abiquiú* (Washington: Smithsonian Institution Press, 1968), 126; Barron B. Beshoar, "Western Trails to Calvary," *1949 Brand Book* (Denver: Denver Posse of the Westerners, 1950), 119–48; E. Boyd, "The New Mexico Santero," *El Palacio* 76 (Spring 1969): 1–24; Reginald Fisher, "Notes on the Relation of the Franciscans to the Penitentes," *El Palacio* 48 (December 1941): 263–71; Forrest, *Missions and Pueblos of the Old Southwest,* 205–6; Alice C. Henderson, *Brothers of Light: The Penitentes of the Southwest* (New York: Harcourt, Brace and Company, 1937), 65–68; and Prince, *Spanish Mission Churches of New Mexico,* 369–70.

38. W. Thetford LeViness, "The Truth about the Penitentes," *Empire Magazine* (Denver Post), 22 March 1970, 8–11.

39. Fray Angélico Chávez, *My Penitente Land* (Santa Fe: William Gannon, 1979), xiii; and Fray Angélico Chávez, "The Penitentes of New Mexico," *New Mexico Historical Review* 29 (April 1954): 97–123. Also see Bainbridge Bunting, Thomas R. Lyons, and Margil Lyons, "Penitente Brotherhood Moradas and Their Architecture," in *Hispanic Arts and Ethnohistory in the Southwest,* ed. Marta Weigle, Claudia Larcombe, and Samuel Larcombe (Santa Fe: Ancient City Press, 1983), 31–80; and Steele and Rivera, *Penitente Self-Government* (see chap. 1, n. 7), 7.

40. Campa, *Hispanic Culture in the Southwest* (see chap. 1, n. 1), 205–6; Chávez, "The Penitentes of New Mexico," 112–14; and Prince, *Spanish Mission Churches of New Mexico,* 365–68.

41. George C. Barker, "Some Aspects of Penitential Processions in Spain and the American Southwest," *Journal of American Folklore* 70 (April–June 1957): 137–42; and Foster, "Cofradía and Compadrazgo in Spain and Spanish America" (see chap. 6, n. 14), 10–19.

42. Baxter, *Las Carneradas* (see chap. 1, n. 45), 29.

43. Campa, *Hispanic Culture in the Southwest,* 205; and Chávez, "The Penitentes of New Mexico," 98.

44. Barker, "Some Aspects of Penitential Processions in Spain and the American Southwest," 137–38.

45. Fray Angélico Chávez, *Archives of the Archdiocese of Santa Fe, 1678–1900* (Washington: Academy of American Franciscan History, 1957), 182–185; Chávez, "The Penitentes of New Mexico," 99–101; Paul Horgan, *Lamy of Santa Fe: His Life and Times* (New York: Farrar, Straus and Giroux, 1975), 149–50, 204, 241; Harold N. Ottaway, "The Penitente Moradas of the Taos, New Mexico Area" (Ph.D. dissertation, University of Oklahoma, 1975), 13–15, 153; and "The Penitentes," *Santa Fe Daily New Mexican,* 8 April 1886, 1.

46. Campa, *Hispanic Culture in the Southwest,* 205; Marta Weigle, *Brothers of Light, Brothers of Blood* (Albuquerque: University of New Mexico Press, 1976), 26–51; and Dorothy Woodward, "The Penitentes of New Mexico" (Ph.D. dissertation, Yale University, 1935), 43–70.

47. "The 'Blood Atonement'—Barbaric Practices of Self Torture Indulged in

Today," *Santa Fe New Mexican Review,* 3 April 1885, 4.

48. "The Brutal and Revolting Practice of the Penitentes Graphically Pictured," *Santa Fe Daily New Mexican,* 25 March 1883, 1; "Penitente Horrors," *Weekly New Mexican Review,* 17 April 1884, 4; and "Penitentes Rites End in Tragedy," *Santa Fe New Mexican,* 15 April 1908, 1.

49. Inigo Deane, S.J., "The New Flagellants: A Phase of New Mexican Life," *Catholic World* 39 (June 1884): 300–311.

50. Tricia Hurst, "Painting the Penitentes," *Impact/Albuquerque Journal Magazine* 8 (2 April 1985): 4–9.

51. Lummis, *The Land of Poco Tiempo* (see chap. 5, n. 72), 79. Also see Alexander M. Darley, *The Passionists of the Southwest, or the Holy Brotherhood* (Pueblo: Author, 1893), 44.

52. Louis How, *The Penitentes of San Rafael* (Indianapolis: Bowen-Merrill, 1900). Other novels on the Penitentes include Alcie Eyre, *Torture at Midnight, the Mystery of the Penitentes* (New York: House of Field, 1942); Donald J. Hall, *Perilous Sanctuary* (New York: Macmillan, 1937); and Raymond Otis, *Miguel of the Bright Mountain* (London: Victor Gallancz, 1936).

53. Robert S. Fetrow, "The Penitentes of Santo Tomas," *Explorers Journal* 51 (September 1973): 164–66.

54. Fernando Del Mundo, "Six Filipinos Re-enact Crucifixion," *Sentinel-Tribune* (Bowling Green, Ohio), 9 April 1982, 10; and "Filipinos Begin Their Bloody Easter Rituals," *Sentinel Tribune* (Bowling Green, Ohio), 13 April 1990, 8.

55. Letter from Dominador Z. Rosell, editor, *Philippine Geographical Journal* (Manila), 18 October 1982.

56. William W. Bundy, "The Mexican Minority Problem in Otero County, Colorado" (Masters thesis, University of Colorado, 1940), 81–86; Rev. D. Convers, "The Flagellants of Southern Colorado," *Spirit of Missions* 42 (July 1877): 329–31; José M. Romero, *El Valle de los Rancheros* (Denver: Author, 1978), 33–35; and E. R. Vollmar, "Religious Processions and Penitente Activities at Conejos, 1874," *Colorado Magazine* 31 (June 1954): 172–79.

57. "The Mexican Penitentes," *Rocky Mountain News* 30 (5 July 1888): 17; and Weigle, *Brothers of Light, Brothers of Blood,* 7.

58. For background information on this symbolism, see William Wroth, "La Sangre de Cristo: History and Symbolism," in *Hispanic Arts and Ethnohistory in the Southwest,* ed. Marta Weigle, Claudia Larcombe, and Samuel Larcombe (Santa Fe: Ancient City Press, 1983), 283–92. For information on these two groups, see Barker, "Some Aspects of Penitential Processions in Spain and the American Southwest," 138; Chávez, "The Penitentes of New Mexico," 118–19; and Steele and Rivera, *Penitente Self-Government,* 8.

59. Bainbridge Bunting, "The Penitente Upper Morada, Arroyo Hondo," *New Mexico Architect* 4 (September–October 1962): 15–17 (quotation, 15). Also see George Kubler, *The Religious Architecture of New Mexico in the Colonial Period and since the American Occupation* (Albuquerque: University of New Mexico Press for the School of American Research, 1972), 142. Locations of the sixty-one *moradas:* Río Arriba: Abiquiú (upper), Abiquiú (lower), Alcalde, Amalia, Arroyo Hondo (lower, inactive), Arroyo Hondo (upper, inactive), Arroyo Seco, Canjilón (north), Canjilón (south), Cañon, Cebolla (inactive), Cerro, Chamisal, Chamita, Chimayó, Córdova, Coyote, Cuba (inactive), El Duende, El Rito, Gallina, La Jara, La Madera, La Puente, Las Trampas, Llano, Los Pachecos, Lyden, Ojo Caliente (inactive), Peña Blanca, Peñasco, Ranchitos, Ranchos de Taos, Rodarte (inactive), San Luis, Santa Cruz, Talpa, Taos (inactive), Truchas, and Vadito. Southern Colo-

rado: Fort Garland, Garcia, San Francisco, San Pablo, Segundo (inactive), and Vigil (inactive). Adjacent New Mexico counties: Bibo, Chacon, Cleveland, Cubero, Holman, Moquino, Mora, Rociada (inactive), San José, San Mateo, San Rafael, San Ysidro, Tecolote, Veguita, and Villaneuva.

60. Henderson, *Brothers of Light,* 116; and "Mystery of the Penitentes," *Colorful Colorado* 3 (Spring 1968): 18–22, 97–98. For descriptions of early *moradas,* see Betty Applegate, "Los Hermanos Penitentes," *Southwest Review* 17 (Autumn 1931): 102–7; Beshoar, "Western Trails to Calvary," 124; Bainbridge Bunting, "An Architectural Guide to Northern New Mexico," *New Mexico Architecture* 12 (September–October 1970): 13–50; Juan Hernandez, "Cactus Whips and Wooden Crosses," *Journal of American Folklore* 76 (July–September 1963): 216–24; Charles F. Lummis, "The Penitente Brothers," *Great Divide* 1 (August 1889): 76–78; and Raymond Otis, "Medievalism in America," *New Mexico Quarterly* 6 (May 1936): 83–90.

61. Ahlborn, *The Penitente Moradas of Abiquiú,* 129–35; and Ottaway, "The Penitente Moradas of the Taos, New Mexico Area," 46.

62. Bunting, "The Penitente Upper Morada, Arroyo Hondo," 16.

63. Bunting, Lyons, and Lyons, "Penitente Brotherhood Moradas and Their Architecture," 38; and Roy Rosen, "Crosses of the Country People," *New Mexico Magazine* 43 (November–December 1965): 34–38.

64. For the origins of the word *morada,* see Bunting, Lyons, and Lyons, "Penitente Brotherhood Moradas and Their Architecture," 31; and Martin Rist, "Penitentes of New Mexico in the 1870's According to Thomas and Emily Harwood," *Denver Westerners Monthly Roundup* 26 (January 1970): 3–14.

65. For descriptions of the Penitentes' activities during Holy Week, see Mary Austin, "The Trail of the Blood," *Century Magazine* 108 (May 1924): 35–44; Lorenzo de Córdova, *Echoes of the Flute* (Santa Fe: Ancient City Press, 1972); Susan E. Door, "Pagan Easter in New Mexico," *Desert Magazine* 7 (April 1944): 4–8; D. J. Flynn, "Holy Week with the Penitentes," *Harper's Weekly* 38 (26 May 1894): 489–90; Forrest, *Missions and Pueblos of the Old Southwest,* 200–205; Susan Hendrix, "Procession to Calvario," *Empire, the Magazine of the Denver Post* 10 April 1955, 6–7; Hernandez, "Cactus Whips and Wooden Crosses," 220–22; Jo Roybal Hogue, "The Penitentes: Unique New Mexico Easter Rites," *Santa Fe New Mexican,* 11 April 1971, D1; Ida L. Kenney, "Cross Bearers of New Mexico," *Overland Monthly* 56 (10 September 1910): 292–95; Sam Marler, "Privileged Few Visitors Watch Devout Penitente Good Friday Rites, Services," *New Mexican* (Santa Fe), 15 April 1963, 6; "The Penitentes," *Santa Fe Daily New Mexican,* 25 March 1883, 1; C. Bryson Taylor, "The Penitentes of New Mexico," *Everybody's Magazine* 10 (April 1904): 501–10; and Nancy H. Warren, *Villages of Hispanic New Mexico* (Santa Fe: School of American Research Press, 1987), 70–74.

66. The Penitentes' religious art is discussed in E. Boyd, *The New Mexican Santero* (Santa Fe: Museum of New Mexico Press, 1969); Charles L. Briggs, "What Is a Modern Santo?" *El Palacio* 79 (March 1974): 40–49; Dickey, *New Mexico Village Arts,* 138; Roland F. Dickey and E. Boyd, "Early New Mexican Art: Santos," *New Mexico Quarterly* 23 (Spring 1953): 68–72; José E. Espinosa, *Saints in the Valleys: Christian Sacred Images in the History, Life, and Folk Art of Spanish New Mexico* (Albuquerque: University of New Mexico Press, 1960), 4; W. Thetford LeViness, "He Carves the Santos—In the Land of the Penitentes," *Desert Magazine* 21 (January 1958): 10–12; Alan C. Vedder, "Conservation of an Altar Screen from a Penitente Brotherhood Morada," in *Hispanic Arts and Ethnohistory in the Southwest,* ed. Marta Weigle, Claudia Larcombe, and Samuel Larcombe (Santa Fe:

Ancient City Press, 1983), 219–27; and William J. Wallrich, "The *Santero* Tradition in the San Luis Valley," *Western Folklife* 10 (April 1951): 151–61.

67. Ahlborn, *The Penitente Moradas of Abiquiú*, 138; Chávez, *My Penitente Land*, 94–95; Dickey, *New Mexico Village Arts*, 182; Henderson, *Brothers of Light*, 32; Louisa R. Stark, "The Origin of the Penitente 'Death Cart,'" *Journal of American Folklore* 84 (July–September 1971): 304–10; Thomas J. Steele, "The Death Cart: Its Place among the Santos of New Mexico," *Colorado Magazine* 55 (Winter 1978): 1–14; and Weigle, *Brothers of Light, Brothers of Blood*, 168–70.

68. Beshoar, "Western Trails to Calvary," 139–41; Lorin W. Brown, Charles L. Briggs, and Marta Weigle, *Hispano Folklife of New Mexico* (Albuquerque: University of New Mexico Press, 1978), 235–37; "Los Hermanos Penitentes," *El Palacio* 8 (31 January 1920): 2–20; and Juan B. Rael, *The New Mexican Alabado* (Palo Alto: Stanford University Press, 1951).

69. González, *The Spanish-Americans of New Mexico* (see chap. 5, n. 5), 115, n. 3. Also see Applegate, "Los Hermanos Penitentes," 102; Beshoar, "Western Trails to Calvary," 123; Deutsch, *No Separate Refuge* (see chap. 4, n. 27), 26; Paul Kutsche and Dennis Gallegos, "Community Functions of the *Cofradía de Nuestro Padre Jesús Nazareno*," in *The Survival of Spanish American Villages*, ed. Paul Kutsche (Colorado Springs: Colorado College, 1979), 91–98; and Ottaway, "The Penitente Moradas of the Taos, New Mexico Area," 77.

70. Diekemper, "The Catholic Church in the Shadows," 48; Lorayne A. Horka-Follick, *Los Hermanos Penitentes* (Los Angeles: Westernlore Press, 1969), 116–17; and Juan B. Rael, "Arroyo Hondo: Penitentes, Weddings, Wakes," *El Palacio* 81 (Spring 1975): 4–19.

71. Dorothy Benrimo, E. Boyd, and Rebecca S. James, *Camposantos* (Fort Worth: Amon Carter Museum of Western Art, 1966).

72. John R. Stilgoe, "Folklore and Graveyard Design," *Landscape* 22 (Summer 1978): 22–28 (quotation, 27). For a full discussion of the historical development of designed cemeteries in the United States, see David Charles Sloane, *The Last Great Necessity: Cemeteries in American History* (Baltimore: Johns Hopkins University Press, 1990).

73. Eleanor Adams, "The Penitent Brothers," *Sunset: The Pacific Monthly* 38 (April 1917): 26–28, 88; and Bill Tate, *The Penitentes of the Sangre de Cristos* (Truchas: Tate Gallery, 1966), 15–16.

74. Deutsch, *No Separate Refuge*, 50; Horka-Follick, *Los Hermanos Penitentes*, 119; Ottaway, "The Penitente Moradas of the Taos, New Mexico Area," 126–31; William Wallrich, "Auxiliadoras de la Morado," *Southwestern Lore* 16 (June 1950): 4–10; and Weigle, *Brothers of Light, Brothers of Blood*, 144–46.

75. "Archbishop Grants Church Blessing to Penitente Order in New Mexico," *Santa Fe New Mexican*, 29 January 1947, 1, 7.

76. John B. Curtis, "Holy Week Climaxes Penitente Lenten Rites," *New Mexican* (Santa Fe), 11 April 1952, 1; and Weigle, *Brothers of Light, Brothers of Blood*, 111.

77. "Penitentes Get *Time* Writeup," *Albuquerque Journal*, 28 August 1958, 11.

78. Bunting, Lyons, and Lyons, "Penitente Brotherhood Moradas and Their Architecture," 33–34; Knowlton, "Changing Spanish-American Villages of Northern New Mexico" (see chap. 6, n. 14), 41; and Ottaway, "The Penitente Moradas of the Taos, New Mexico Area," 150–58.

79. Arley Sanchez, "Charity, Mercy Modern Rituals for Penitentes," *Albuquerque Journal*, 13 April 1980, A-4.

80. Vera D. Hahn, "Lively Living in a Sanctuary," *American Home* 73 (March 1970): 56–63.

81. Bunting, Lyons, and Lyons, "Penitente Brotherhood Moradas and Their Architecture," 35; and Jo Roybal Hogue, "Miguel Archibeque, the King in My Closet," *La Luz* 3 (April 1974): 26–27.

82. Tate, *The Penitentes of the Sangre de Cristos*, 27.

83. González, *The Spanish-Americans of New Mexico*, 115, n. 3.

9 The Town of Abiquiú

1. Yates, *The Essential Landscape* (see chap. 8, n. 9), 4.

2. This chapter is a revision of my article "Spanish Colonization and the Abiquiú Grant, New Mexico, 1754–1970," *Philippine Geographical Journal* 20 (April–May–June 1976): 61–68. Permission is granted by the Philippine Geographical Society.

3. For discussions of the *genízaros* and early Abiquiú, see Cordell, *A Cultural Resources Overview of the Middle Rio Grande Valley, New Mexico* (see chap. 1, n. 1), 119; Frances L. Quintana and David H. Snow, "Historical Archaeology of the Rito Colorado Valley, New Mexico," *Journal of the West* 19 (July 1980): 40–50; and Swadesh, *Los Primeros Pobladores, Hispanic Americans of the Ute Frontier* (see chap. 2, n. 9), 39–46.

4. John L. Kessell, "Sources for the History of a New Mexico Community, Abiquiu," *New Mexico Historical Review* 54 (October 1979): 249–85.

5. Bureau of Land Management, U.S. Surveyor-General Records (see chap. 1, n. 35), Report 140, File 199, Reel 26, Frames 73–74.

6. Bureau of Land Management, U.S. Court of Private Land Claims Records (see chap. 1, n. 50), Report 97, File 100, Reel 43, Frame 87; Twitchell, *The Leading Facts of New Mexican History* (see chap. 5, n. 29), 3: 521; and Twitchell, *The Spanish Archives of New Mexico* (see chap. 3, n. 13), 1: 25–26.

7. Twitchell, *The Leading Facts of New Mexican History*, 1: 455; and Twitchell, *Spanish Archives of New Mexico*, 1: 26.

8. Bureau of Land Management, U.S. Court of Private Land Claims Records, Report 140, File 143, Reel 48, Frame 357.

9. Bureau of Land Management, U.S. Surveyor-General Records, Report 140, File 199, Reel 26, Frames 76–81.

10. Bureau of Land Management, U.S. Court of Private Land Claims Records, Report 52, File 55, Reel 38, Frames 28–30.

11. Carroll and Haggard, *Three New Mexico Chronicles* (see chap. 5, n. 14), 88.

12. Gilberto B. Córdova, *Abiquiú and Don Cacahuate: A Folk History of a New Mexican Village* (Los Cerrillos: San Marcos Press, 1973), 31–32; Don Devereux, "Julian Chavez: An Early Rio Arriba Emigrant," *El Palacio* 74 (Winter 1967): 35–36; Fray Francisco Atanasio Domínguez, *The Missions of New Mexico, 1776*, trans. Eleanor B. Adams and Fray Angélico Chávez (Albuquerque: University of New Mexico Press, 1956), 252–53; and Frank C. Spencer, "Old Abiquiu—Crossroads of History," *New Mexico Magazine* 26 (May 1948): 22–23, 31–33.

13. John R. Van Ness, "The Juan Bautista Valdez Grant: Was It a Community Land Grant?" in *Spanish and Mexican Land Grants in New Mexico and Colorado*, ed. John R. and Christine M. Van Ness (Manhattan: Sunflower University Press, 1980): 107–16; and John R. Van Ness, "The Polvadera Grant: Hispanic Settlement in the Cañones Region," in *Spanish Colonial Frontier Research*, ed. Henry F. Dobyns (Albuquerque: Center for Anthropological Studies, Spanish Borderlands Research, No. 1, 1980), 79–84.

14. Nostrand, "The Century of Hispano Expansion" (see chap. 5, n. 1), 374; and Robert J. Torrez, "The San Juan Gold Rush of 1860 and Its Effects on the Development of Northern New Mexico," *New Mexico Historical Review* 63 (July 1988): 257–72.

15. Ahlborn, *The Penitente Moradas of Abiquiú* (see chap. 8, n. 37), 129.

16. Swadesh, "Hispanic Americans of the Ute Frontier from the Chama Valley to the San Juan Basin, 1694–1960" (see chap. 5, n. 6), 269.

17. Calkins, *Tewa Basin Study* (see chap. 3, n. 46), 2: 141–45.

18. U.S. Department of Commerce, Bureau of the Census, *Census of Population: 1950*, Number of Inhabitants (Washington: GPO, 1952), 1: 31–9; and *Fifteenth Census of the United States: 1930, Population*, Number and Distribution of Inhabitants (Washington: GPO, 1931), 1: 736.

19. Calkins, *Tewa Basin Study*, 2: 141–45; and Horton, *Indian Lands in New Mexico* (see chap. 6, n. 27), 133–35.

20. Arthur D. Hollis, "New Mexico's Lost Pueblo," *Santa Fe Magazine* 29 (March 1935): 25–29.

21. "FSA to Determine Needs of Abiquiu," *Albuquerque Journal*, 10 September 1941, 1, 9; and personal interview, Joseph Ferron (landowner), Abiquiú, 19 August 1970.

22. George Chirmack, "A Day in Land of the 'Genizaros'—Historic Abiquiu," *Albuquerque Tribune*, 10 February 1973, A-4; and Eastman and Gray, *Community Grazing* (see chap. 7, n. 29), 81.

23. Personal interviews with Ferron, Abiquiú, 19 August 1970; Juan M. Martinez (landowner), Barranca, 18 August 1970; and Paul Trujillo (Río Arriba County Agricultural Agent), Española, 17 August 1970.

24. Arturo Sandoval, "Abiquiu Dam Causes Controversy," *Seers* (Albuquerque), 24 September–8 October 1976, 1, 3 (quotation, 1).

25. Karen Evans, "Islam in the American Southwest," *Denver Post Magazine*, 27 April 1986, 13–16; and Mary Frei and Larry Calloway, "Muslims Dedicate Abiquiu Mosque," *Albuquerque Journal*, 16 June 1981, A-1, A-3; and Williams, *New Mexico in Maps* (see chap. 1, n. 7), 316–18.

26. Evans, "Islam in the American Southwest," 16.

27. Frei and Calloway, "Muslims Dedicate Abiquiu Mosque," A-3.

28. Evans, "Islam in the American Southwest," 16.

29. Eastman and Gray, *Community Grazing*, 81.

30. Mary Frei, "Plan for O'Keeffe Home Considers Effect on Abiquiu," *Albuquerque Journal (North)*, 29 May 1982, 9.

31. *Abiquiu, Canjilon, Chama, Chimayo, Cuba, Dixon, Dulce, El Rito, Española, Gallina, Jemez Springs, Lindrith, Lybrook, Ojo Caliente, San Ysidro, Tierra Amarilla, Truchas, Vallecitos, Velarde Telephone Directory* (Española: Continental Telephone Company of the West, 1986).

32. Letter from Max D. Martinez, Río Arriba County Extension Agent, Española, 5 August 1986.

10   The Villages of El Rancho and Vadito

1. This chapter is a revision of my article "El Rancho and Vadito: Spanish Settlements on Indian Land Grants," *El Palacio* 85 (Spring 1979): 28–39. Permission is granted by the Museum of New Mexico.

2. Meyer, *Water in the Hispanic Southwest* (see chap. 2, n. 23), 147–48. For similar cases concerning the San Ildefonso Pueblos, see Clark, *Water in New Mex-*

ico (see chap. 1, n. 41), 20; and Jenkins, "Spanish Land Grants in the Tewa Area" (see chap. 1, n. 8), 124–28.

3. Jenkins, "Spanish Land Grants in the Tewa Area," 125.

4. For background information on the San Ildefonso Pueblos and their early land use, see Bureau of Land Management, U.S. Surveyor-General Records (see chap. 1, n. 35), Report M, File 539, Reel 7, Frame 3.

5. Crane, *Desert Drums* (see chap. 3, n. 20), 225, 303. Also see Edgar L. Hewett, "Present Condition of the Pueblo Indians," *El Palacio* 19 (1 July 1925): 3–11; and Thomas, *Forgotten Frontiers* (see chap. 5, n. 15), 95.

6. Poore, "Condition of 16 New Mexico Indian Pueblos, 1890" (see chap. 3, n. 33), 425. A similar observation was made by Bynner, " 'From Him That Hath Not' " (see chap. 3, n. 30), 126.

7. Poore, "Condition of 16 New Mexico Indian Pueblos, 1890," 428.

8. William Whitman III, *The Pueblo Indians of San Ildefonso: A Changing Culture* (New York: Columbia University Press, 1947), 5.

9. United Pueblo Agency (UPA), Real Property Management Records (see chap. 3, n. 32), "Pueblo of San Ildefonso—Abstracts, Testimony and Receipts for Deeds," Files 300.10.9-16, 17, 1929.

10. Ibid., "Pueblo of San Ildefonso—Appraisals," File 300.10-1a, 1929.

11. Ibid., "List of Purchases with Compensation Funds and Exchanges," File 367.0, 17 October 1945.

12. Ibid., "List (by Pueblos) of Lands Awarded to Indians by Adjudication of Pueblo Lands Board for which Non-Indian Claimants Received Compensation," File 367.2—San Ildefonso Pueblo, ca. 1942.

13. For background information on the San Ildefonso Pueblos in the 1930s, see Calkins, *Tewa Basin Study* (see chap. 3, n. 46), 2: 19–33.

14. This is a common belief held by many Spanish-American old-timers. For instance, see deBuys, *Enchantment and Exploitation* (see chap. 7, n. 21), 215.

15. Personal interviews with J. R. Chávez (Santa Fe County agricultural agent), Santa Fe, 11 September 1970; Elizardo Roybal (landowner), El Rancho, 11 September 1970; and J. Trujillo (landowner), El Rancho, 23 July 1970.

16. State Engineer's Office Records, Santa Fe, 1970.

17. Personal interview with Abel Sanchez (governor), San Ildefonso Pueblo Grant, 11 September 1970.

18. U.S. Department of the Interior, Bureau of Indian Affairs, "Report on Service Population and Labor Force—Pueblo of San Ildefonso," Santa Fe, 21 August 1986; and "Indian Service Population and Labor Force Estimates," Santa Fe, January 1987, 3.

19. Ortiz, *Roots of Resistance* (see chap. 6, n. 46), 120.

20. Albert H. Schroeder, *A Brief History of Picuris Pueblo* (Alamosa: Adams State College, Series in Anthropology, 1974), 14–15.

21. Bureau of Land Management, U.S. Surveyor-General Records, Report D, File 531, Reel 7, Frames 1–11.

22. UPA, Real Property Management Records, "Pueblo of Picuris—Abstracts, Claims, Testimony and Receipts for Deeds," File 300.6-9-18, 1928.

23. Schroeder, *A Brief History of Picuris Pueblo,* 17.

24. Crane, *Desert Drums,* 225; Hewett, "Present Condition of the Pueblo Indians," 3–4; and Schroeder, *A Brief History of Picuris Pueblo,* 16.

25. UPA, Real Property Management Records, "Pueblo of Picuris—Abstracts, Claims, Testimony and Receipts for Deeds," File 300.6-9-1, 1928, PC. 292.

26. Ibid., "Pueblo of Picuris—Report of Appraisers—1928," File 300.6-1d, 1928.

27. Ibid., "List of Purchases with Compensation Funds and Exchanges," File 367.0; and "Pueblo of Picuris—Report of Appraisers," File 300.6-1d, Folder 1, 1928.

28. C. Kuipers, "The New Deal for the Indian," *New Mexico Business Review* 2 (July 1933): 101–6. For a discussion of the poor agricultural situation on the Picurís Pueblo Grant, see "Agronomic and Farm Analysis Survey of Picuris Indian Grant," Rio Grande Project (Albuquerque: Soil Conservation Service, August 1936), 1–9.

29. UPA, Real Property Management Records, "List (by Pueblos) of Lands Awarded to Indians by Adjudication of Pueblo Lands Board for which Non-Indian Claimants Received Compensation," File 367.2—Picuris Pueblo, ca. 1942.

30. Ibid., "Field Notes of Surveys in New Mexico, Picuris Pueblo Grant with Small Holding Proofs in Association with the Joy Survey," volumes 330–333— Affidavits of Applicants, 1915.

31. U.S. Department of Commerce, Bureau of the Census, *Fifteenth Census of the United States* (see chap. 6, n. 7), 3: part 2, 254. For background information on Vadito, see Calkins, *Tewa Basin Study*, 2: 203–9; and Horton, *Indian Lands in New Mexico* (see chap. 6, n. 27), 133–35.

32. Vadito was a separate minor civil division for the four censuses of population between 1920 and 1950. U.S. Department of Commerce, Bureau of the Census, *Census of Population: 1950* (see chap. 9, n. 18), 1: 31-10.

33. *Reconnaissance Report on Embudo Creek Basin, New Mexico* (Amarillo: Bureau of Reclamation, February 1962), 19.

34. Personal interviews with Abad Martinez (Taos County agricultural agent), Taos; Nick Montoya (landowner), Vadito, 7 August 1970; and J. Romero (landowner), Vadito, 6 August 1970.

35. Personal interview with E. M. Sanchez (caseworker for Vadito, Taos County Welfare Office), Taos, 3 August 1970.

36. UPA, Real Property Management Records, "Pueblo of Picuris—Report of Appraisers."

37. Inez Russell, "When the Work Ends," *New Mexican* (Santa Fe), 2 March 1986, B1–B3.

38. U.S. Department of the Interior, Bureau of Indian Affairs, "Report on Service Population and Labor Force—Pueblo of Picuris," Santa Fe, 21 August 1986; and "Indian Service Population and Labor Force Estimates," 3.

39. Elsie C. Parsons, "Picurís, New Mexico," *American Anthropologist* 41 (April–June 1939): 206–22.

11   The Community of Corrales

1. This chapter is a revision of my article "Corrales, New Mexico: Transition in a Spanish-American Community," *Red River Valley Historical Review* 4 (Summer 1979): 88–89. Permission is granted by the Red River Valley Historical Association.

2. Twitchell, *The Spanish Archives of New Mexico* (see chap. 3, n. 13), 1: 166.

3. Bowden, "Private Land Claims in the Southwest" (see chap. 1, n. 24), 1666.

4. Register of Deeds, Bernalillo County, New Mexico, "Alameda Grant, Report of George H. Pradt, U.S. Deputy Surveyor, 1893," Book 64, 18 August 1920, 412. Also see Bureau of Land Management, U.S. Surveyor-General Records (see chap. 1,

n. 35), Report 91, File 144, Reel 22, Frame 10; and Keleher, "Law of the New
Mexico Land Grant" (see chap. 1, n. 46), 354–55.

275

**Notes to Pages
189–195**

5. Bowden, "Private Land Claims in the Southwest," 1669–70. Also see U.S.
Congress, Senate, *Report of the Surveyor-General of New Mexico on the Alameda
Tract, No. 91,* Ex. Doc. 9, 50th Cong., 1st sess. (Washington: GPO, 8 December
1887).

6. Bowden, "Private Land Claims in the Southwest," 1673–74.

7. Twitchell, *The Spanish Archives of New Mexico,* 99.

8. Cora Headington, "Los Corrales" (Corrales, N.M.: Corrales Community
Council, May 1957), 1–3; Lezzanddro L. M. Silva, "Tales from an Old Spanish
Village," *New Mexico Magazine* 59 (November 1981): 8, 58–59, 66–67; and Betty
Woods, "Corrales," *New Mexico Magazine* 35 (June 1957): 6.

9. Cora Headington, "The Old Houses of Sandoval," *New Mexico Magazine* 25
(October 1947): 16, 35, 37, 39 (quotation, 35). Miguel Griego related parts of the
same account to me. He was considered by his contemporaries to be the village
historian. Personal interview with Miguel Griego (landowner), Corrales, 26 August
1969.

10. Domínguez, *The Missions of New Mexico, 1776* (see chap. 9, n. 12), 144.

11. Silva, "Tales from an Old Spanish Village," 66.

12. Woods, "Corrales," 6.

13. Frederick G. Bohme, "The Italians in New Mexico," *New Mexico Historical
Review* 34 (April 1959): 98–116; and Greer, "Origins of the Foreign-Born Population of New Mexico during the Territorial Period" (see chap. 5, n. 25), 284–86.

14. Personal interview with Dulcelina Salce Curtis (landowner), Corrales, 25
August 1969.

15. Personal interview with Miguel Griego, 26 August 1969.

16. U.S. Department of Commerce, Bureau of the Census, *Fourteenth Census of
the United States: 1920, Population,* Number and Distribution of Inhabitants
(Washington: GPO, 1921), 1: 525, 528.

17. Ernest L. Alary, "Alary Family Growing Grapes—A Recollection," *New
Mexico Grapevine* 2 (August 1976): 5–6; Howard Bryan, "Off the Beaten Path,"
Albuquerque Tribune (5 October 1965): 3; Headington, "Los Corrales," 1–3; "El
Rio del Norte," *New Mexican* (Santa Fe), 7 July 1868, 4; Silva, "Tales from an
Old Spanish Village," 59; and personal interview with Julio Tenorio (landowner),
Corrales, 31 July 1969.

18. For background information on the problems between the Middle Río
Grande Conservancy District and the Spanish-American landowners, see Clark S.
Knowlton, "Cultural Impacts of New Mexico and West Texas Reclamation Proj-
ects," *Southwestern Review* 5 (Spring 1986): 13–29.

19. Paul A. F. Walter, Jr., "A Study of Isolation and Social Change in Three
Spanish Speaking Villages of New Mexico" (Ph.D. dissertation, Stanford University, 1938), 156.

20. Personal interview with Anastacio C. deBaca (landowner), Corrales, 30 July
1970. Insights into how the Spanish Americans acquired their land are given in
Bureau of Land Management, U.S. Court of Private Land Claims Records (see
chap. 1, n. 50), Report 11, File 11, Reel 34, Frames 35–61.

21. Personal interview with Miguel Griego, 31 July 1970.

22. Bohme, "The Italians in New Mexico," 107–11. For background on the
French influence in Corrales's wine production, see Alary, "Alary Family Growing
Grapes," 5–6.

23. Chilton, Chilton, Arango, Dudley, Neary, and Stelzner, *New Mexico* (see chap. 1, n. 44), 235.

24. Personal interview with Miguel Griego, 22 July 1970.

25. Ibid.

26. Ruth W. Armstrong, "Corrales and the Center of Controversy," *Century: A Southwest Journal of Observation and Opinion* 2 (2 June 1982): 13–16; and Paul Vipperman, "A Touch of Antiquity," *New Mexico Magazine* 34 (September 1956): 24–25, 53.

27. U.S. Department of Commerce, Bureau of the Census, *Census of Population: 1960* (see chap. 6, n. 7), 9; and Woods, "Corrales," 6.

28. Personal interview with Antonio Perea (landowner), Corrales, 26 August 1969.

29. Personal interview with Filiburto Marquez (Sandoval County agricultural agent), Bernalillo, 1 August 1969.

30. U.S. Department of Commerce, Bureau of the Census, *1980 Census of Population,* Number of Inhabitants (see chap. 6, n. 7), 13.

31. "Corrales Hit by Flooding," *Observer* 3 (26 August 1976): A1, A8–A9; Larry Dorman, "Dazed Corrales Residents Bail Out," *Albuquerque Tribune,* 20 August 1976, A-1, A-6; and "Flood Waters Hit Village of Corrales," *Observer* 3 (20 August 1975): 1.

32. Armstrong, "Corrales and the Center of Controversy," 13; Arlene Cinelli, "Corrales' Trek through Incorporation," *New Mexico Independent* 80 (27 February 1976): 27; Robin Frames, "Corrales: Can Charm Survive?" *New Mexico Business Journal* 11 (February 1987): 11; Robin Frames, "Corrales Strives to Preserve Ambience as City Closes In," *New Mexico Business Journal* 10 (April 1986): 51, 53; and Bill Winters, "Battle Brews in Corrales," *Albuquerque Tribune,* 17 February 1978, D-11.

33. Armstrong, "Corrales and the Center of Controversy," 16.

34. Ibid., 14–16; and Susanne Burks, "Judge's Ruling Favors Corrales Development," *Albuquerque Journal,* 2 December 1982, A-1, A-14.

35. U.S. Department of Commerce, Bureau of the Census, *1980 Census of Population,* Number of Inhabitants, 11. For background information on Río Rancho Estates, see Robin Frames, "Rio Rancho's Roaring Growth," *New Mexico Business Journal* 10 (April 1986): 45–50; Karen Groening, "Land Development in New Mexico—Is Legislation Necessary?" *New Mexico Architecture* 13 (January–February 1971): 13–15; Mark Lewis, "Rio Rancho: A Youthful Identity," *New Mexico Business Journal* 12 (July 1988): 17–19; and Sam McIlhaney, "Rio Rancho Emerges From Shadow of Duke City," *New Mexico Magazine* 68 (April 1990): 26–28.

36. Rhonda Hillbery, "Subdivision in Corrales Selling Well," *Albuquerque Journal,* 8 June 1987, 12.

37. Arley Sanchez, "Historic N.M. Homes Exude Warm Charm," *Albuquerque Journal,* 23 April 1983, B-6.

38. U.S. Department of Commerce, Bureau of the Census, *1980 Census of Population,* General Population Characteristics (see chap. 6, n. 7), 59; and *1980 Census of Population and Housing,* New Mexico, PHC80-V-33 (Washington: GPO, 1981), 4.

1. Alvar W. Carlson, "The Río Arriba: A Geographic Appraisal of the Spanish-American Homeland (Upper Río Grande Valley, New Mexico)" (Ph.D. dissertation, University of Minnesota, 1971), 216–29.

2. Leonard, *The Role of the Land Grant in the Social Organization and Social Processes of a Spanish-American Village in New Mexico* (see chap. 6, n. 29), 104–8.

3. Ronald E. Seavoy, *Famine in Peasant Societies* (New York: Greenwood Press, 1986), 2, 10, 12, 13.

4. Carey McWilliams, *North from Mexico: The Spanish Speaking People of the United States* (New York: J. B. Lippincott Company, 1949), 71, 65.

5. Carlson, "Long-Lots in the Río Arriba" (see chap. 2, n. 1), 57.

6. DeBuys, *Enchantment and Exploitation* (see chap. 7, n. 21), 258–59.

7. Ibid., 217–18; and Widdison, "Historical Geography of the Middle Rio Puerco Valley, New Mexico" (see chap. 2, n. 13), 251–52, 265–66, 271–74.

8. Clyde Eastman, Garrey Carruthers, and James A. Leifer, "Contrasting Attitudes toward Land in New Mexico," *New Mexico Business* 24 (March 1971): 3–20; Engstrand, "Land Grant Problems in the Southwest" (see chap. 1, n. 22), 332–33; Knowlton, "Land-Grant Problems among the State's Spanish-Americans" (see chap. 1, n. 47), 3–4; Samora and Simon, *A History of the Mexican-American People* (see chap. 1, n. 3), 135; and John R. Van Ness, "Spanish American vs. Anglo American Land Tenure and the Study of Economic Change in New Mexico," *Social Science Journal* 13 (October 1976): 45–52.

9. DeBuys, "Fractions of Justice" (see chap. 1, n. 70), 92.

10. "Noted City Lawyer, Historian Cites Misconceptions Held in Land Grants," *Albuquerque Journal,* 15 October 1967, A-10. Also see Espinosa, "About New Mexico Land Grants" (see chap. 1, n. 59), 263.

11. Cutter, "The Legacy of the Treaty of Guadalupe Hidalgo" (see chap. 1, n. 69), 305; Ebright, *The Tierra Amarilla Grant* (see chap. 1, n. 59), xii, 28; Jenkins, "Land Tenure History in New Mexico" (see chap. 1, n. 30), 45; Knowlton, "Violence in New Mexico" (see chap. 7, n. 16), 1084; McCarty, *Land Grant Problems in New Mexico* (see chap. 6, n. 43), 22; Ortiz, *Roots of Resistance* (see chap. 6, n. 46), 119; and Westphall, *Mercedes Reales* (see chap. 1, n. 39), 273.

12. Clark S. Knowlton, "Causes of Land Loss among the Spanish Americans in Northern New Mexico," *Rocky Mountain Social Science Journal* 1 (April 1964): 201–11 (quotation, 201).

13. Clark, *Water in New Mexico* (see chap. 1, n. 41), 33; Meyer, *Water in the Hispanic Southwest* (see chap. 2, n. 23), 117–31; and Quintana, "Land Grants and Grazing Grants of New Mexico" (see chap. 1, n. 68).

14. Alvar W. Carlson, "Review of *Mercedes Reales: Hispanic Land Grants of the Upper Rio Grande Region,* by Victor Westphall," *Professional Geographer* 37 (May 1985): 257–58.

15. Morrill, *A Taos Mosaic* (see chap. 5, n. 11), 25.

16. Carlson, "Review of *Pueblo Indian Water Rights*" (see chap. 3, n. 53), 366–67; and DuMars, O'Leary, and Utton, *Pueblo Indian Water Rights* (see chap. 3, n. 50), 116–18.

17. Jenkins, "The Pueblo of Nambe and Its Lands" (see chap. 3, n. 34), 103.

18. D. W. Meinig, *Southwest: Three Peoples in Geographical Change, 1600–1970* (New York: Oxford University Press, 1971), 132.

19. Clark S. Knowlton, "Land Loss as a Cause of Unrest among the Rural

Spanish-American Village Population of Northern New Mexico," *Agriculture and Human Values* 2 (Summer 1985): 25–38 (quotation, 36).

20. "Sheepherder . . . ," *New Mexican* (Santa Fe), 21 April 1987, B-8.

21. McCarty, *Land Grant Problems in New Mexico,* 22.

22. Bureau of the Census, *1980 Census of Population,* General Population Characteristics (see chap. 6, n. 7), 1: 73, 81. Also see Knowlton, "Land Loss as a Cause of Unrest among the Rural Spanish-American Village Population of Northern New Mexico," 33–34.

23. Daniel Gibson, "Tourism by the Numbers," *New Mexico Business Journal* 11 (May 1987): 14–15, 17; Bob Hagan, "What's N.M.'s Largest, Most Lucrative Industry? Tourism," *New Mexico Business Journal* 9 (February 1985): 94–99; C. A. Hundertmark, "A New Blueprint for Tourism, Economic Development?" *New Mexico Business Journal* 10 (February 1986): 10–12; and Paul Logan, "Season Totals Snowball around the State," *Albuquerque Journal,* 7 May 1987, D1, D3.

24. "Fact Sheet: Tourism in New Mexico," New Mexico Economic Development and Tourism Department, Santa Fe. Data are based upon the 1985 *National Travel Survey,* U.S. Travel Data Center, Washington.

25. Gibson, "Tourism by the Numbers," 14.

26. Russell, "When the Work Ends" (see chap. 10, n. 37), B1.

27. Robert V. Kemper, "Tourism in Taos and Patzcuaro: A Comparison of Two Approaches to Regional Development," *Annals of Tourism Research* 6 (January/ March 1979): 91–110.

28. Brown and Ingram, *Water and Poverty in the Southwest* (see chap. 2, n. 40), 84; and Schouten and Osgood, *The Impact of Tourism on Regional Development* (see chap. 6, n. 94), 41–45.

29. Sylvia Rodriguez, "Land, Water, and Ethnic Identity in Taos," *Land, Water, and Culture: New Perspectives on Hispanic Land Grants,* ed. Charles L. Briggs and John R. Van Ness (Albuquerque: University of New Mexico Press, 1987), 313–403.

30. Marylynn Uricchio, "Robert Redford, Moviemaker," *Blade* (Toledo, Ohio), 22 May 1988, F1, F4.

31. Crawford, *Mayordomo* (see chap. 2, n. 46), 44.

32. Simmons and Mays, *People of the Sun* (see chap. 7, n. 1), 57.

33. Louis B. Casagrande, "The Five Nations of Mexico," *Focus* 37 (Spring 1987): 3–9; Chávez, *The Lost Land* (see chap. 7, n. 7), 1–3; and Joel Garreau, *The Nine Nations of North America* (Boston: Houghton Mifflin Company, 1981), 210–11. In regard to Cinco de Mayo celebrations in the Río Arriba, see "Cinco de Mayo Fiestas: Good Times, Large Crowds," *Taos News,* 10 May 1990, A9.

34. Thomas E. Chávez, "Santa Fe's Own: A History of Fiesta," *El Palacio* 91 (Spring 1985): 6–17.

35. For a fascinating account of social change and conditions in the Río Arriba since 1800, see Paul Horgan, *Figures in a Landscape* (New York: Harper and Brothers Publishing, 1931), especially 261, 265–67.

Glossary

acequia. An irrigation ditch. An *acequia madre* is the main or mother ditch from which smaller ditches take water to the individual fields. Can refer also to a community's ditch organization or association.

aguajes. Watering holes found naturally on the land.

alabado. Hymn.

alcalde. Justice of the peace and most prominent local official.

alcaldía. Area assigned to an *alcalde*.

Alianza Federal de Mercedes. A militant organization known as the Federated Alliance of Land Grants. The organization was later renamed the Alianza de los Pueblos Libres (Confederation of Free City-States).

Alianzistas. Members of the Alianza de los Pueblos Libres.

almud. A measure equaling one-twelfth of a *fanega*.

almud de tierra. About half an acre.

alto. A small attic.

arpent. Measurement of 192 feet used in early French-Canadian and French-American settlements.

arroba. A measure of approximately 25 pounds.

arroyo permanente. A permanent creek or stream.

atole. Corn porridge or gruel.

auxiliadoras de la morada. Female auxiliaries that help the male Penitentes (Los Hermanos).

ayuntamiento. Town council.

azotea. The flat roof of a house.

baldíos. Unappropriated or common lands that are also uncultivated.

bando. Decree or proclamation.

barrio. Village or part of a city.

bosque. Wooded area along a river or stream.

bruja. Witch, sorcerer, or practitioner of witchcraft.

bulto. Wooden sculptured carving of a religious subject.

caballería. Tract of land measuring approximately 106 acres for the purposes of planting crops and grazing livestock. Permanently stationed cavalrymen received these tracts as well as building lots in Santa Fe, largely as shares of the spoils system.

caliche. Lime used as a whitewash.

calvario. Calvary. Used also to refer to the large crosses placed on a nearby hill by the Penitentes (Los Hermanos) in their reenactment of Christ's crucifixion.

cambalache. Barter.

Camino Real. Main road or trail from Santa Fe to Mexican cities, including Mexico City.

campanilismo. Community spirit or feeling.

camposanto. Cemetery.

canales. Wooden troughs or gutters around a roof that provide drainage away from adobe house walls.

cañoas. Flumes, usually made of hollowed logs, that carry water across gullies and small canyons.

cañon. A small canyon or gorge, but usually an arroyo.

Carmelites. Female Penitentes (Los Hermanos).

carne adovada. Chunks of pork marinated in red chile.

carnerada. Flock of sheep, normally driven long distances.

carnicería. Carnage or flagellation.

carreta. Cart, usually long and narrow.

carreta de la muerte. Two-wheeled death cart, fashioned after an old Spanish ox-cart, found in a Penitente (Los Hermanos) *morada.*

casa-corral. An enclosed farmyard behind a house where one side of the enclosure is the back wall of the house.

Casa de Dios, La. A Penitente (Los Hermanos) meetinghouse. See *morada.*

casta. Half- or cross-breed.

cédula. Royal decree or order.

ceja. Ridge or summit of mountains and hills, used as a boundary.

cena. Last Supper or supper.

cerquita. A small fence or enclosure around a grave site.

charqui. Buffalo or beef jerky.

chicos. Corn roasted, usually on the cob, in an oven such as the *horno.*

cholla. A spiny cactus.

churro. A degenerate type of sheep from common stock of southern Spain. Many possessed double horns and black wool.

Cinco de Mayo. A fiesta celebrating Mexico's victory over the French invasion, 5 May 1862.

cofradía. Confraternity or brotherhood.

compadrazgo. Godparenthood. The special relationship between a child's parents and the godfather.

conducta. Commercial caravan.

"Conquistadora, La." A fiesta held in Santa Fe that commemorates Diego de Vargas's reconquest of New Mexico in 1692 and the role of a statue of the Virgin Mary.

conquistadores. Spanish soldiers and military officers who participated in the conquest of New Mexico.

cordel. A cord or rope used for measuring distances. Also, a distance of about five steps.

cordilleras. Continuous rows of houses and walls surrounding a *plaza.*

Cortes. Spain's legislative assembly.

criadero de ganado mayor. Tract of land consisting of approximately 1,100 acres used for stock grazing, especially cattle, but also horses. One-fourth the size of a *sitio de ganado mayor.*

criadero de ganado menor. Tract of land consisting of approximately 500 acres used for stock grazing, especially sheep. One-fourth the size of a *sitio de ganado menor.*

Cristo. Christ.

cuadrilla de carros. Supply caravan made up of carts.

cuartilla. A measure equaling about one-fourth of a *fanega.*

curandera. A woman who uses herbs in medicinal practices.

dehesas. Uplands used for communal pastures.

descansos. Resting places in the procession of the fourteen stations en route to Calvary on Good Friday.

Diez y Seis de Septiembre. A fiesta celebrating Mexico's independence day, 16 September.

disciplina. Whip used for flagellation.

diseño. Sketch or map.

dispensa. Storehouse.

don. Mister, the title for a gentleman.

Doña Sebastiana, La. Angel of Death (skeleton figure) who sits in the death cart found in a *morada.*

ejido. Common land in the valleys used by Spanish Americans for grazing milch cows and horses and sometimes keeping their livestock during the winter months.

empresario. A contractor or promoter who was given a land grant when he agreed to organize and settle a colony of families within a frontier region.

encomendero. Person who received an *encomienda,* an assigned territory, in exchange for providing certain services, such as escort duty for the early supply caravans for the colonial government.

encomienda. Territory assigned by the Spanish colonial government to prominent individuals for their use, including the resident natives, who were often required to provide labor and tributes. An assigned territory often took the character of a privately owned land grant whereby both the land and the natives became possessions.

encuentro. Dramatization of the encounter between Christ and his mother before the crucifixion.

escudero. A gentleman who came from a prominent and usually wealthy family whose namesake was highly respected through the generations.

estación. Station.

estancia. A large cattle ranch.

europeo. Person born in Spain.

expediente. The written record of the proceedings or actions taken in the bestowing of a land grant.

Fachwerk. Rammed-earth wall construction used in German houses.

fanega. A measure of 2.6 bushels of seed.

fanega de sembradura. Ground, varying upon local conditions, needed to sow 2.6 bushels of seed.

fanega de tierra. Approximately 3 acres.

fatalismo. Belief that nature has a strong influence over one's destiny.

fatiga. Labor in the annual cleaning of a community's irrigation ditches.

fiesta. Social or religious occasion to honor an event or saint.

Floresta, La. Forest Service.

fogón. Fireplace or hearth.

frijoles. Beans.

fuerte. Small barn or shed.

fundo legal. Four square leagues of land or approximately 17,300 acres. A league (*legua*) was a measure of distance equal in this case to 2.6 miles (see *legua legal*).

gente de razón. Wealthy or prominent educated Spaniards.

Gorras Blancas. Spanish Americans known as White Caps whose purpose was to disrupt Anglo-American settlement and development in New Mexico in the late 1800s and on into the 1920s.

guardia. Guard.

hacienda. Farm or range as well as farmstead or ranch headquarters that include the buildings and corrals. See *casa-corral.*

hermano mayor supremo. The Penitentes' (Los Hermanos) hierarchical leader. Also known as *hermano supremo arzobispal* (archbishop).

Hermanos de Jesús, Los. Penitentes, brothers.

hijo. Son.

hijuela. A deed for landownership. Also, an oral or written list (inventory) of items that are to be included in each heir's share of an estate. Similar to a will.

horno. A beehive-shaped outdoor oven introduced into the Río Arriba by the Spaniards, who adopted it from the Moors.

huerta. Garden.

jacal. A small one- or two-room, flat-roofed house that has walls built by placing small poles upright and filling the cracks with an earthen material.

Jornada del Muerto. Long stretch of desert in New Mexico's lower Río Grande Valley.

joya. Bottomland on an alluvial floodplain that is valued for irrigated agriculture.

latias. Peeled saplings or branches used in the construction of a roof. Placed mostly in a herringbone design.

legua comun. A measure of 3.5 miles used to figure distance traveled.

legua legal. A measure of 2.6 miles used in laying out land units.

leña. Firewood.

lobos. Name given to Spanish Americans (half- or cross-breeds).

llerno. Son-in-law.

machismo. Male or manly strength.

madero. Cross made from beams or rough-sawn timbers.

madressa. An Islamic school.

mal de ojo. The evil eye that allegedly possessed harmful power.

Mano Negra. Spanish Americans belonging to an organization known as the Black Hand, which harassed Anglo Americans in the 1920s and 1930s.

masjid. An Islamic mosque.

mayordomía. A Mexican association that honors a local patron or saint.

mayordomo. Irrigation ditch boss or overseer who is responsible for keeping the community's irrigation system operational and distributing water to property owners who have water rights.

médica. A woman who practices medicine.

merced de agua. Grant or gift to use water; essentially irrigation rights.

merced. Grant or gift of land.

mesteñada. Mustang or wild horse.

misericordia. Sense of misery or forlornness.

molino. Gristmill.

montes. Mountains, also mountain forests or woodlands.

morada. Chapter house or building used by the Penitentes (Los Hermanos), especially during Lent and the Easter Holy Week.

"Moros y Cristianos, Los." A drama that commemorates Spain's conquest of the Moors.

muerte. Death.

oratorio. Chapel inside a *morada,* a Penitente (Los Hermanos) meetinghouse.

padre. Priest.

padrino. Godfather, also godparent.

panocha. A sprouted wheat pudding eaten by the Penitentes (Los Hermanos) on Good Friday.

parciantes. Users of water taken from a community's irrigation system.

partera. Midwife.

partida. Flock of sheep under contract to a renter, *partidario.*

partidario. Person, usually poor and landless, who rented sheep from a large sheepowner on a contract basis. See *partido.*

partido. Written contract for renting sheep from a large sheepowner for a period of three to five years. In return, the sheepman was paid a percentage of the annual production of lambs and fleeces.

pastores la communida. Community herders.

patrón. Boss or protector who is a prominent person in a community.

peninsular. Person born in Spain.

peonía. Tract of land of approximately twenty acres given to a permanently stationed foot soldier who also may have received a house site in Santa Fe.

His tract of land was to be used for planting crops and grazing a few live-stock, providing his family with largely a subsistence livelihood.

pergamino. Translucent parchment made from sheepskins and used for win-dowpanes.

peso de la tierra. Values given to products derived from the land.

piñon. Pine tree, pine-nut.

piones. Shares of irrigation water.

pitero. Flutist.

placita. Small square or yard that is enclosed by the dwellings of an extended family. Also called a *plazuela.*

plaza. Town square that is enclosed and fortified by buildings.

plazuela. See *placita.*

poblador principal. Person who recruited settlers for a community land grant in exchange for a larger share of land.

poblador. Settler who was recruited by a *poblador principal*; person who orig-inated a petition for a community land grant.

político. An influential person, usually a relatively large landowner, in a com-munity where he/she has many relatives.

pommée. Celtic cross.

presa. Dam or dike.

presidio. Garrison or fort housing soldiers.

Procesión de la Sangre de Cristo, La. Procession of the Blood of Christ.

pueblo. Village or town.

puesto. Military outpost.

punche. A variety of tobacco.

ranchería. A cluster of farm dwellings.

ranchero. Small farmer.

ranchito. A two- or three-room adobe farmhouse.

rancho. A small farm.

reales. Currency; also fee for a deed to property.

Recopilación de leyes de los reynos de las Indias. Codified Spanish laws and instructions for establishing colonial settlements.

reducción. Village or mission compound inhabited by Indians who had been rounded up largely to facilitate their conversion to Christianity.

regador. Person who irrigates land.

remedio. Medicinal remedy, usually herbs.

rescates. Fairs for trading items.

retablo. Painting of religious scenes and saints on skin panels.

rezador. Reader of biblical verses during the procession of the fourteen sta-tions en route to Calvary during the reenactment of the crucifixion.

rico. A wealthy person, usually of the landed gentry.

río. River or stream.

ristra. A string of chiles.

sangrías. Lateral or secondary irrigation ditches that carried water to the indi-vidual farmers' fields.

"Santa Espina, La." A song from Spain's province of Catalonia that is used *santo.* Saint.

seigneury. Land grant bestowed by the French colonial government.

Semana Santa, La. Easter Holy Week.

sitio de ganado mayor. Tract of land measuring one square league or approximately 4,340 acres used for stock raising, especially cattle but also horses.

sitio de ganado menor. Tract of land consisting of approximately 1,930 acres used for stock grazing, especially sheep.

solar. Lot or plot of ground used for a house site.

sopaipilla. A fritter eaten with honey.

soterraño. Basement.

Strassendorf. European settlement characterized by a row or line of continuous houses through a valley.

suerte. Tract of cropland or a field.

terron. Sod brick used for building houses.

testimonio. An affidavit or deposition.

tierra amarilla. Beige-yellow dirt that usually contains mica. Used in a plaster for the interior walls of houses.

tierra bayeta. A fawn-colored dirt used in a plaster for interior walls of houses.

tierra blanca. Powdered gypsum rock used for whitewash.

tierra sobrante. Unused or abandoned cropland.

tierra de labor. Cropland without irrigation rights.

tierra en regadizo. Land given with irrigation rights.

tierra en secano. Land given without irrigation rights.

tierras de agostadero. Large land grants bestowed for ranching in Texas. Their surface water was to be used solely for livestock.

tierras de riego. Small land grants bestowed in Texas for the production of crops by using surface water for irrigation.

tierras de temporal. Land grants bestowed in Texas that included no water rights for irrigation.

tierras realengas y baldías. Unappropriated lands that were in the royal domain.

tinieblas. Earthquake in darkness. A Penitente (Los Hermanos) ritual that symbolizes chaos after Christ's death.

torreón. Watchtower, usually round, and placed at a corner or corners of a house compound.

tortahuevo. Eggs in a chile (meatless) sauce eaten by the Penitentes (Los Hermanos) on Good Friday.

tortilla. Flat cake made of cornmeal or wheat flour.

troja. A barn, often with a bin for storing grain. Also a granary or a storehouse.

vara. A measure of about thirty-three inches, usually used in determining the widths of irrigable land parcels or long-lots.

vega. Meadow.

velorio. Wake.

vendidos. Spanish-American landowners who sell their land to non–Spanish Americans, especially Anglo Americans. Betrayers.

yeso. Mixture of powdered gypsum rock and wheat paste.

Via Crucis. Way of the Cross.

vigas. Ceiling beams or rafters in a dwelling.

villa. Town, usually associated with governmental functions.

visita. Small mission or chapel served by a visiting priest.

Index

Page numbers in italic denote illustrations.